ALL GLORY TO ŚRĪ GURU AND GAURĀṄGA

# ŚRĪMAD BHĀGAVATAM

of

KṚṢṆA-DVAIPĀYANA VYĀSA

ऋषिरुवाच

जुष्टं बताद्याखिलसत्त्वराशेः
सांसिद्ध्यमक्ष्णोस्तव दर्शनान्नः ।
यद्दर्शनं जन्मभिरीड्य सद्भि-
राशासते योगिनो रूढयोगाः ॥

*ṛṣir uvāca*
*juṣṭaṁ batādyākhila-sattva-rāśeḥ*
*sāṁsiddhyam akṣṇos tava darśanān naḥ*
*yad-darśanaṁ janmabhir īḍya sadbhir*
*āśāsate yogino rūḍha-yogāḥ*

(p. 152)

## BOOKS by
## His Divine Grace
## A. C. Bhaktivedanta Swami Prabhupāda

Bhagavad-gītā As It Is
Śrīmad-Bhāgavatam, Cantos 1–10 (50 Vols.)
Śrī Caitanya-caritāmṛta (17 Vols.)
Teachings of Lord Caitanya
The Nectar of Devotion
The Nectar of Instruction
Śrī Īśopaniṣad
Easy Journey to Other Planets
Kṛṣṇa Consciousness: The Topmost Yoga System
Kṛṣṇa, the Supreme Personality of Godhead (3 Vols.)
Perfect Questions, Perfect Answers
Dialectical Spiritualism—A Vedic View of Western Philosophy
Teachings of Lord Kapila, the Son of Devahūti
Transcendental Teachings of Prahlād Mahārāja
Kṛṣṇa, the Reservoir of Pleasure
The Science of Self-Realization
Life Comes From Life
The Perfection of Yoga
Beyond Birth and Death
On the Way to Kṛṣṇa
Geetār-gan (Bengali)
Vairagya Vidya (Bengali)
Buddhi Yoga (Bengali)
Bhakti Ratna Boli (Bengali)
Rāja-vidyā: The King of Knowledge
Elevation to Kṛṣṇa Consciousness
Kṛṣṇa Consciousness: The Matchless Gift
Back to Godhead Magazine (Founder)

*A complete catalog is available upon request.*

Bhaktivedanta Book Trust
3764 Watseka Avenue
Los Angeles, California 90034

# ŚRĪMAD BHĀGAVATAM

## Third Canto
"The Status Quo"

## (Part Three—Chapters 17–24)

*With the Original Sanskrit Text,*
*Its Roman Transliteration, Synonyms,*
*Translation and Elaborate Purports*

*by*

His Divine Grace
A.C. Bhaktivedanta Swami Prabhupāda
Founder-*Ācārya* of the International Society for Krishna Consciousness

THE BHAKTIVEDANTA BOOK TRUST
New York · Los Angeles · London · Bombay

Readers interested in the subject matter of this book
are invited by the International Society for Krishna Consciousness
to correspond with its Secretary.

International Society for Krishna Consciousness
3764 Watseka Avenue
Los Angeles, California 90034

First English Printing, 1974: 15,000 copies
Second English Printing, 1978: 20,000 copies
German: 20,000 copies

**TOTAL: 55,000 copies in print**


Printed in the United States of America

*Library of Congress Cataloging in Publication Data (Revised)*

Puranas. Bhāgavatapurāna.
Śrīmad-Bhāgavatam.

Includes bibliographical references and indexes.
CONTENTS: Canto 1. Creation. 3 v.—Canto 2. The cosmic manifestation. 2 v.—Canto 3. The status quo. 4 v.—Canto 4. The creation of the Fourth Order. 4 v.—Canto 5. The creative impetus. 2 v.
1. Chaitanya, 1486-1534. I. Bhaktivedanta Swami, A. C., 1896-1977 II. Title.
BL1135.P7A22 1972 73-169353
ISBN 0-912776-46-3

# Table of Contents

# Preface

We must know the present need of human society. And what is that need? Human society is no longer bounded by geographical limits to particular countries or communities. Human society is broader than in the Middle Ages, and the world tendency is toward one state or one human society. The ideals of spiritual communism, according to *Śrīmad-Bhāgavatam*, are based more or less on the oneness of the entire human society, nay, of the entire energy of living beings. The need is felt by great thinkers to make this a successful ideology. *Śrīmad-Bhāgavatam* will fill this need in human society. It begins, therefore, with the aphorism of Vedānta philosophy *janmādy asya yataḥ* to establish the ideal of a common cause.

Human society, at the present moment, is not in the darkness of oblivion. It has made rapid progress in the field of material comforts, education and economic development throughout the entire world. But there is a pinprick somewhere in the social body at large, and therefore there are large-scale quarrels, even over less important issues. There is need of a clue as to how humanity can become one in peace, friendship and prosperity with a common cause. *Śrīmad-Bhāgavatam* will fill this need, for it is a cultural presentation for the respiritualization of the entire human society.

*Śrīmad-Bhāgavatam* should be introduced also in the schools and colleges, for it is recommended by the great student-devotee Prahlāda Mahārāja in order to change the demoniac face of society.

*kaumāra ācaret prājño*
*dharmān bhāgavatān iha*
*durlabhaṁ mānuṣaṁ janma*
*tad apy adhruvam arthadam*
(*Bhāg.* 7.6.1)

Disparity in human society is due to lack of principles in a godless civilization. There is God, or the Almighty One, from whom everything emanates, by whom everything is maintained and in whom everything is merged to rest. Material science has tried to find the ultimate source of creation very insufficiently, but it is a fact that there is one ultimate source of everything that be. This ultimate source is explained rationally and authoritatively in the beautiful *Bhāgavatam*, or *Śrīmad-Bhāgavatam.*

*Śrīmad-Bhāgavatam* is the transcendental science not only for knowing the ultimate source of everything but also for knowing our relation with Him and our duty toward perfection of the human society on the basis of this perfect knowledge. It is powerful reading matter in the Sanskrit language, and it is now rendered into English elaborately so that simply by a careful reading one will know God perfectly well, so much so that the reader will be sufficiently educated to defend himself from the onslaught of atheists. Over and above this, the reader will be able to convert others to accepting God as a concrete principle.

*Śrīmad-Bhāgavatam* begins with the definition of the ultimate source. It is a bona fide commentary on the *Vedānta-sūtra* by the same author, Śrīla Vyāsadeva, and gradually it develops into nine cantos up to the highest state of God realization. The only qualification one needs to study this great book of transcendental knowledge is to proceed step by step cautiously and not jump forward haphazardly like with an ordinary book. It should be gone through chapter by chapter, one after another. The reading matter is so arranged with its original Sanskrit text, its English transliteration, synonyms, translation and purports so that one is sure to become a God-realized soul at the end of finishing the first nine cantos.

The Tenth Canto is distinct from the first nine cantos because it deals directly with the transcendental activities of the Personality of Godhead Śrī Kṛṣṇa. One will be unable to capture the effects of the Tenth Canto without going through the first nine cantos. The book is complete in twelve cantos, each independent, but it is good for all to read them in small installments one after another.

I must admit my frailties in presenting *Śrīmad-Bhāgavatam*, but still I am hopeful of its good reception by the thinkers and leaders of society on the strength of the following statement of *Śrīmad-Bhāgavatam* (1.5.11):

*tad-vāg-visargo janatāgha-viplavo*
*yasmin prati-ślokam abaddhavaty api*

*nāmāny anantasya yaśo 'ṅkitāni yac*
*chṛṇvanti gāyanti gṛṇanti sādhavaḥ*

"On the other hand, that literature which is full with descriptions of the transcendental glories of the name, fame, form and pastimes of the unlimited Supreme Lord is a transcendental creation meant to bring about a revolution in the impious life of a misdirected civilization. Such transcendental literatures, even though irregularly composed, are heard, sung and accepted by purified men who are thoroughly honest."

*Oṁ tat sat*

A. C. Bhaktivedanta Swami

# Introduction

"This *Bhāgavata Purāṇa* is as brilliant as the sun, and it has arisen just after the departure of Lord Kṛṣṇa to His own abode, accompanied by religion, knowledge, etc. Persons who have lost their vision due to the dense darkness of ignorance in the age of Kali shall get light from this *Purāṇa.*" (*Śrīmad-Bhāgavatam* 1.3.43)

The timeless wisdom of India is expressed in the *Vedas,* ancient Sanskrit texts that touch upon all fields of human knowledge. Originally preserved through oral tradition, the *Vedas* were first put into writing five thousand years ago by Śrīla Vyāsadeva, the "literary incarnation of God." After compiling the *Vedas,* Vyāsadeva set forth their essence in the aphorisms known as *Vedānta-sūtras. Śrīmad-Bhāgavatam* is Vyāsadeva's commentary on his own *Vedānta-sūtras.* It was written in the maturity of his spiritual life under the direction of Nārada Muni, his spiritual master. Referred to as "the ripened fruit of the tree of Vedic literature," *Śrīmad-Bhāgavatam* is the most complete and authoritative exposition of Vedic knowledge.

After compiling the *Bhāgavatam,* Vyāsa impressed the synopsis of it upon his son, the sage Śukadeva Gosvāmī. Śukadeva Gosvāmī subsequently recited the entire *Bhāgavatam* to Mahārāja Parīkṣit in an assembly of learned saints on the bank of the Ganges at Hastināpura (now Delhi). Mahārāja Parīkṣit was the emperor of the world and was a great *rājarṣi* (saintly king). Having received a warning that he would die within a week, he renounced his entire kingdom and retired to the bank of the Ganges to fast until death and receive spiritual enlightenment. The *Bhāgavatam* begins with Emperor Parīkṣit's sober inquiry to Śukadeva Gosvāmī: "You are the spiritual master of great saints and devotees. I am therefore begging you to show the way of perfection for all persons, and especially for one who is about to die. Please let me know what a man should hear, chant, remember and worship, and also what he should not do. Please explain all this to me."

Śukadeva Gosvāmī's answer to this question, and numerous other questions posed by Mahārāja Parīkṣit, concerning everything from the nature of the self to the origin of the universe, held the assembled sages in rapt attention continuously for the seven days leading to the King's death. The sage Sūta Gosvāmī, who was present on the bank of the Ganges when Śukadeva Gosvāmī first recited *Śrīmad-Bhāgavatam*, later repeated the *Bhāgavatam* before a gathering of sages in the forest of Naimiṣāraṇya. Those sages, concerned about the spiritual welfare of the people in general, had gathered to perform a long, continuous chain of sacrifices to counteract the degrading influence of the incipient age of Kali. In response to the sages' request that he speak the essence of Vedic wisdom, Sūta Gosvāmī repeated from memory the entire eighteen thousand verses of *Śrīmad-Bhāgavatam*, as spoken by Śukadeva Gosvāmī to Mahārāja Parīkṣit.

The reader of *Śrīmad-Bhāgavatam* hears Sūta Gosvāmī relate the questions of Mahārāja Parīkṣit and the answers of Śukadeva Gosvāmī. Also, Sūta Gosvāmī sometimes responds directly to questions put by Śaunaka Ṛṣi, the spokesman for the sages gathered at Naimiṣāraṇya. One therefore simultaneously hears two dialogues: one between Mahārāja Parīkṣit and Śukadeva Gosvāmī on the bank of the Ganges, and another at Naimiṣāraṇya between Sūta Gosvāmī and the sages at Naimiṣāraṇya Forest, headed by Śaunaka Ṛṣi. Furthermore, while instructing King Parīkṣit, Śukadeva Gosvāmī often relates historical episodes and gives accounts of lengthy philosophical discussions between such great souls as the saint Maitreya and his disciple Vidura. With this understanding of the history of the *Bhāgavatam*, the reader will easily be able to follow its intermingling of dialogues and events from various sources. Since philosophical wisdom, not chronological order, is most important in the text, one need only be attentive to the subject matter of *Śrīmad-Bhāgavatam* to appreciate fully its profound message.

The translator of this edition compares the *Bhāgavatam* to sugar candy—wherever you taste it, you will find it equally sweet and relishable. Therefore, to taste the sweetness of the *Bhāgavatam*, one may begin by reading any of its volumes. After such an introductory taste, however, the serious reader is best advised to go back to Volume One of the First Canto and then proceed through the *Bhāgavatam*, volume after volume, in its natural order.

This edition of the *Bhāgavatam* is the first complete English translation of this important text with an elaborate commentary, and it is the first widely available to the English-speaking public. It is the product of the scholarly and devotional effort of His Divine Grace A. C. Bhaktivedanta Swami Prabhupāda, the world's most distinguished teacher of Indian religious and philosophical thought. His consummate Sanskrit scholarship and intimate familiarity with Vedic culture and thought as well as the modern way of life combine to reveal to the West a magnificent exposition of this important classic.

Readers will find this work of value for many reasons. For those interested in the classical roots of Indian civilization, it serves as a vast reservoir of detailed information on virtually every one of its aspects. For students of comparative philosophy and religion, the *Bhāgavatam* offers a penetrating view into the meaning of India's profound spiritual heritage. To sociologists and anthropologists, the *Bhāgavatam* reveals the practical workings of a peaceful and scientifically organized Vedic culture, whose institutions were integrated on the basis of a highly developed spiritual world-view. Students of literature will discover the *Bhāgavatam* to be a masterpiece of majestic poetry. For students of psychology, the text provides important perspectives on the nature of consciousness, human behavior and the philosophical study of identity. Finally, to those seeking spiritual insight, the *Bhāgavatam* offers simple and practical guidance for attainment of the highest self-knowledge and realization of the Absolute Truth. The entire multivolume text, presented by the Bhaktivedanta Book Trust, promises to occupy a significant place in the intellectual, cultural and spiritual life of modern man for a long time to come.

—The Publishers

His Divine Grace
A. C. Bhaktivedanta Swami Prabhupāda
*Founder-Ācārya of the International Society for Krishna Consciousness*

PLATE ONE

Being challenged by the Personality of Godhead in the form of a boar, the demon Hiraṇyākṣa became angry and agitated, and he trembled like a challenged cobra. Hissing indignantly, all his senses shaken by wrath, the demon quickly sprang upon the Lord and dealt Him a blow with his powerful mace. But by moving slightly aside, the Lord dodged the violent mace-blow aimed at His breast, just as an accomplished *yogī* would elude death. Lord Boar now exhibited His anger and rushed to meet the demon, who bit his lip in rage, took up his mace again and began to brandish it about. Then with His own mace the Lord struck the enemy on the right side of his brow, but since the demon was expert in fighting, he softened the blow by a maneuver of his own mace. In this way the Lord and the demon Hiraṇyākṣa struck each other with their huge maces, each enraged and seeking his own victory. (*pp. 41–45*)

PLATE TWO

Under the guidance of Lord Viṣṇu, Brahmā brought his intelligence to bear and began to create the universe. From his buttocks he created the demons, who are very fond of sex. Then, to absorb the demons' attention, he created from his mind the twilight, which took the form of a beautiful damsel playing with a ball. From his loveliness Brahmā then created the heavenly dancers and musicians, and from his sloth the ghosts and fiends. Brahmā next cast off his subtle mental body in the form of yawning, and the ghosts took possession of it. Concerned that the work of creation had not proceeded apace, Brahmā stretched his subtle mental body down on the ground full length. When he cast off that body, the hair that dropped from it transformed into snakes, and as the body crawled along with its hands and feet contracted, there sprang from it ferocious serpents with their hoods expanded. (*pp. 105–33*)

PLATE THREE

Commanded by Lord Brahmā to beget children in the worlds, the worshipable Kardama Muni practiced penance on the bank of the River Sarasvatī. By performing devotional service in trance, the sage Kardama propitiated the Personality of Godhead, who is the bestower of all blessings upon those who flee to Him for protection. After ten thousand years, the lotus-eyed Supreme Personality of Godhead became pleased with Kardama and showed him His transcendental form. The sage saw the Lord in His eternal form, effulgent like the sun, wearing a garland of white lotuses and water lilies. The Lord was clad in spotless yellow silk, and His lotus face was fringed with slick dark locks of curly hair. Adorned with a crown and earrings, and holding a conch, disc, mace and water lily, the Lord glanced about in a happy, smiling mood. With a golden streak on His chest, and the famous Kaustubha gem suspended from His neck, He stood in the air with His lotus feet placed on the shoulders of Garuḍa. (*pp. 144–49*)

PLATE FOUR

Seeking to please his beloved wife, the sage Kardama exercised his yogic power and instantly produced an aerial mansion that could travel at his will. It was a wonderful structure, bedecked with all sorts of jewels, adorned with pillars of precious stones, and capable of yielding whatever one desired. Equipped with every form of furniture and wealth, which tended to increase in the course of time, the palace was decorated all around with flags, festoons and artistic work of variegated colors. It was further embellished with wreaths of charming flowers that attracted sweetly humming bumblebees, and with tapestries of linen, silk and various other fabrics. The charming palace had beds, couches, fans and seats, all separately arranged in seven stories. The palace's beauty was enhanced by artistic engravings here and there on the walls, the floor was of emerald, with coral diases, and gold pinnacles crowned its sapphire domes. With the choicest rubies set in its diamond walls, the palace appeared as though possessed of eyes. It was furnished with wonderful canopies, greatly valuable gates of gold, resting chambers, bedrooms and inner and outer yards—all designed with an eye to comfort. All this caused astonishment to Kardama Muni himself. (*pp. 264–70*)

PLATE FIVE

Following the order of Kardama Muni, Devahūti entered Lake Bindu-sarovara. In a house inside the lake she saw one thousand girls, all in the prime of youth and fragrant as lotuses. Seeing Devahūti, the damsels suddenly rose and said, with folded hands, "We are your maidservants." The girls then very respectfully bathed Devahūti with valuable oils and ointments and then gave her fine, new spotless cloth to cover her body. After decorating her with very excellent and valuable jewels, they offered her food containing all good qualities, along with a sweet, health-giving drink called *āsavam.* When Devahūti beheld her own reflection in a mirror, she saw that her body was completely free from all dirt and that she was adorned with a garland and unsullied robes. The maids then very respectfully decorated her with ornaments, including a special necklace with a locket, bangles for her wrists and tinkling anklets of gold. About her hips they tied a golden girdle set with numerous jewels, and on her neck they placed a precious pearl necklace and auspicious substances. Devahūti's face was surrounded by dark curling tresses, and her countenance shone, with beautiful teeth and charming eyebrows. Her eyes, distinguished by lovely moist corners, defeated the beauty of lotus buds. (*pp. 274–79*)

PLATE SIX

Appearing at Kardama Muni's hermitage, Lord Brahmā said, "My dear Kardama, your nine thin-waisted daughters are certainly very chaste, and I am sure they will expand the creation with their descendants. Therefore, today please give away your daughters to these foremost sages, with due regard for the girls' temperaments and likings, and thereby spread your fame all over the universe." Then Brahmā told Devahūti about the incarnation of God presently in her womb: "My dear daughter of Manu, the Supreme Personality of Godhead is now within your womb. He will cut all knots of your ignorance and doubt. Then He will travel all over the world. Your son will be the head of all the perfected souls. He will be approved by the spiritual exemplars, expert in disseminating real knowledge, and among the people He will be celebrated by the name Kapila. As your son, He will increase your fame." After thus speaking to Kardama Muni's wife Devahūti, Lord Brahmā, accompanied by the four Kumāras and Nārada, went back to the highest of the three planetary systems on his swan carrier. (*pp. 319–26*)

PLATE SEVEN

Before taking leave of his wife, Devahūti, and his divine son, Kapila, Kardama Muni said, "My dear son, I wish to accept the order of an itinerant mendicant. Renouncing this family life, I wish to wander about, free from lamentation, thinking always of You in my heart." Lord Kapila answered, "I appear in this world especially to explain the philosophy of Sāṅkhya, which is a highly esteemed process of self-realization. This path of self-realization has now been lost in the course of time, so I have assumed this body of Kapila to introduce and explain this philosophy to human society again. Now, being sanctioned by Me, go as you desire, surrendering all your activities to Me. By using your intellect you should always see Me dwelling within your own heart as the self-effulgent Supersoul. Seeing Me as well within the hearts of all other living entities, you will achieve the state of eternal life, free from all lamentation and fear. I shall also teach My mother the sublime knowledge of Sāṅkhya, which is the door to spiritual life, so that she also can attain perfection and self-realization." Thereupon Kardama Muni, the progenitor of human society, circumambulated his son, Kapila, and with a pacified mind, he at once left for the forest. (*pp. 340–51*)

## CHAPTER SEVENTEEN

# Victory of Hiraṇyākṣa Over All the Directions of the Universe

### TEXT 1

मैत्रेय उवाच

निशम्यात्मभुवा गीतं कारणं शङ्कयोज्झिताः ।
ततः सर्वे न्यवर्तन्त त्रिदिवाय दिवौकसः ॥ १ ॥

*maitreya uvāca*
*niśamyātma-bhuvā gītaṁ*
*kāraṇaṁ śaṅkayojjhitāḥ*
*tataḥ sarve nyavartanta*
*tridivāya divaukasaḥ*

*maitreyaḥ*—the sage Maitreya; *uvāca*—said; *niśamya*—upon hearing; *ātma-bhuvā*—by Brahmā; *gītam*—explanation; *kāraṇam*—the cause; *śaṅkayā*—from fear; *ujjhitāḥ*—freed; *tataḥ*—then; *sarve*—all; *nyavartanta*—returned; *tri-divāya*—to the heavenly planets; *diva-okasaḥ*—the demigods (who inhabit the higher planets).

### TRANSLATION

**Śrī Maitreya said: The demigods, the inhabitants of the higher planets, were freed from all fear upon hearing the cause of the darkness explained by Brahmā, who was born from Viṣṇu. Thus they all returned to their respective planets.**

### PURPORT

The demigods, who are denizens of higher planets, are also very much afraid of incidents such as the universe's becoming dark, and so they consulted Brahmā. This indicates that the quality of fear exists for every living entity in the material world. The four principal activities of material existence are eating, sleeping, fearing and mating. The fear element exists also in the demigods. On every planet, even in the higher planetary systems, including the moon and the sun, as well as on this earth, the same principles of animal life exist. Otherwise, why are the demigods also afraid of the darkness? The difference between the demigods and ordinary human beings is that the demigods approach authority, whereas the inhabitants of this earth defy authority. If people would only approach the authority, then every adverse condition in this universe could be rectified. Arjuna was also disturbed on the Battlefield of Kurukṣetra, but he approached the authority, Kṛṣṇa, and his problem was solved. The conclusive instruction of this incident is that we may be disturbed by some material condition, but if we approach the authority who can actually explain the matter, then our problem is solved. The demigods approached Brahmā for the meaning of the disturbance, and after hearing from him they were satisfied and returned home peacefully.

## TEXT 2

दितिस्तु भर्तुरादेशादपत्यपरिशङ्किनी ।
पूर्णे वर्षशते साध्वी पुत्रौ प्रसुषुवे यमौ ॥ २ ॥

*ditis tu bhartur ādeśād*
*apatya-pariśaṅkinī*
*pūrṇe varṣa-śate sādhvī*
*putrau prasuṣuve yamau*

*ditiḥ*—Diti; *tu*—but; *bhartuḥ*—of her husband; *ādeśāt*—by the order; *apatya*—from her children; *pariśaṅkinī*—being apprehensive of trouble; *pūrṇe*—full; *varṣa-śate*—after one hundred years; *sādhvī*—the virtuous lady; *putrau*—two sons; *prasuṣuve*—begot; *yamau*—twins.

## TRANSLATION

**The virtuous lady Diti had been very apprehensive of trouble to the gods from the children in her womb, and her husband pre-**

**dicted the same. She brought forth twin sons after a full one hundred years of pregnancy.**

## TEXT 3

उत्पाता बहवस्तत्र निपेतुर्जायमानयोः ।
दिवि भुव्यन्तरिक्षे च लोकस्योरुभयावहाः ॥ ३ ॥

*utpātā bahavas tatra*
*nipetur jāyamānayoḥ*
*divi bhuvy antarikṣe ca*
*lokasyoru-bhayāvahāḥ*

*utpātāḥ*—natural disturbances; *bahavaḥ*—many; *tatra*—there; *nipetuḥ*—occurred; *jāyamānayoḥ*—on their birth; *divi*—in the heavenly planets; *bhuvi*—on the earth; *antarikṣe*—in outer space; *ca*—and; *lokasya*—to the world; *uru*—greatly; *bhaya-āvahāḥ*—causing fear.

## TRANSLATION

**On the birth of the two demons there were many natural disturbances, all very fearful and wonderful, in the heavenly planets, the earthly planets and in between them.**

## TEXT 4

सहाचला भुवश्चेलुर्दिशः सर्वाः प्रजज्वलुः ।
सोल्काश्चाशनयः पेतुः केतवश्चार्तिहेतवः ॥ ४ ॥

*sahācalā bhuvaś celur*
*diśaḥ sarvāḥ prajajvaluḥ*
*solkāś cāśanayaḥ petuḥ*
*ketavaś cārti-hetavaḥ*

*saha*—along with; *acalāḥ*—the mountains; *bhuvaḥ*—of the earth; *celuḥ*—shook; *diśaḥ*—directions; *sarvāḥ*—all; *prajajvaluḥ*—blazed like fire; *sa*—with; *ulkāḥ*—meteors; *ca*—and; *aśanayaḥ*—thunderbolts;

*petuḥ*—fell; *ketavaḥ*—comets; *ca*—and; *ārti-hetavaḥ*—the cause of all inauspiciousness.

## TRANSLATION

**There were earthquakes along the mountains on the earth, and it appeared that there was fire everywhere. Many inauspicious planets like Saturn appeared, along with comets, meteors and thunderbolts.**

## PURPORT

When natural disturbances occur on a planet, one should understand that a demon must have taken birth there. In the present age the number of demoniac people is increasing; therefore natural disturbances are also increasing. There is no doubt about this, as we can understand from the statements of the *Bhāgavatam.*

## TEXT 5

ववौ वायुः सुदुःस्पर्शः फूत्कारानीरयन्मुहुः ।
उन्मूलयन्नगपतीन्वात्यानीको रजोध्वजः ॥ ५ ॥

*vavau vāyuḥ suduḥsparśaḥ*
*phūt-kārān īrayan muhuḥ*
*unmūlayan naga-patīn*
*vātyānīko rajo-dhvajaḥ*

*vavau*—blew; *vāyuḥ*—the winds; *su-duḥsparśaḥ*—unpleasant to touch; *phūt-kārān*—hissing sounds; *īrayan*—giving out; *muhuḥ*—again and again; *unmūlayan*—uprooting; *naga-patīn*—gigantic trees; *vātyā*—cyclonic air; *anīkaḥ*—armies; *rajaḥ*—dust; *dhvajaḥ*—ensigns.

## TRANSLATION

**There blew winds which were most uninviting to the touch, hissing again and again and uprooting gigantic trees. They had storms for their armies and clouds of dust for their ensigns.**

## PURPORT

When there are natural disturbances like blowing cyclones, too much heat or snowfall, and uprooting of trees by hurricanes, it is to be understood that the demoniac population is increasing and so the natural disturbance is also taking place. There are many countries on the globe, even at the present moment, where all these disturbances are current. This is true all over the world. There is insufficient sunshine, and there are always clouds in the sky, snowfall and severe cold. These assure that such places are inhabited by demoniac people who are accustomed to all kinds of forbidden, sinful activity.

## TEXT 6

उद्धसत्तडिदम्भोदघटया नष्टभागणे ।
व्योम्नि प्रविष्टतमसा न स्म व्यादृश्यते पदम् ॥ ६ ॥

*uddhasat-taḍid-ambhoda-*
*ghaṭayā naṣṭa-bhāgaṇe*
*vyomni praviṣṭa-tamasā*
*na sma vyādṛśyate padam*

*uddhasat*—laughing loudly; *taḍit*—lightning; *ambhoda*—of clouds; *ghaṭayā*—by masses; *naṣṭa*—lost; *bhā-gaṇe*—the luminaries; *vyomni*—in the sky; *praviṣṭa*—enveloped; *tamasā*—by darkness; *na*—not; *sma vyādṛśyate*—could be seen; *padam*—any place.

## TRANSLATION

**The luminaries in the heavens were screened by masses of clouds, in which lightning sometimes flashed as though laughing. Darkness reigned everywhere, and nothing could be seen.**

## TEXT 7

चुक्रोश विमना वार्धिरुदूर्मिः क्षुभितोदरः ।
सोदपानाश्च सरितश्चुक्षुभुः शुष्कपङ्कजाः ॥ ७ ॥

*cukrośa vimanā vārdhir*
*udūrmiḥ kṣubhitodaraḥ*
*sodapānāś ca saritaś*
*cukṣubhuḥ śuṣka-paṅkajāḥ*

*cukrośa*—wailed aloud; *vimanāḥ*—stricken with sorrow; *vārdhiḥ*—the ocean; *udūrmiḥ*—high waves; *kṣubhita*—agitated; *udaraḥ*—the creatures inside; *sa-udapānāḥ*—with the drinking water of the lakes and the wells; *ca*—and; *saritaḥ*—the rivers; *cukṣubhuḥ*—were agitated; *śuṣka*—withered; *paṅkajāḥ*—lotus flowers.

## TRANSLATION

**The ocean with its high waves wailed aloud as if stricken with sorrow, and there was a commotion among the creatures inhabiting the ocean. The rivers and lakes were also agitated, and lotuses withered.**

## TEXT 8

मुहुः परिधयोऽभूवन् सराह्वोः शशिसूर्ययोः ।
निर्घाता रथनिर्ह्रादा विवरेभ्यः प्रजज्ञिरे ॥ ८ ॥

*muhuḥ paridhayo 'bhūvan*
*sarāhvoḥ śaśi-sūryayoḥ*
*nirghātā ratha-nirhrādā*
*vivarebhyaḥ prajajñire*

*muhuḥ*—again and again; *paridhayaḥ*—misty halos; *abhūvan*—appeared; *sa-rāhvoḥ*—during eclipses; *śaśi*—of the moon; *sūryayoḥ*—of the sun; *nirghātāḥ*—claps of thunder; *ratha-nirhrādāḥ*—sounds like those of rattling chariots; *vivarebhyaḥ*—from the mountain caves; *prajajñire*—were produced.

## TRANSLATION

**Misty halos appeared around the sun and the moon during solar and lunar eclipses again and again. Claps of thunder were heard**

**even without clouds, and sounds like those of rattling chariots emerged from the mountain caves.**

## TEXT 9

अन्तर्ग्रामेषु मुखतो वमन्त्यो वह्निमुल्बणम् ।
सृगालोलूकटङ्कारैः प्रणेदुरशिवं शिवाः ॥ ९ ॥

*antar-grāmeṣu mukhato*
*vamantyo vahnim ulbaṇam*
*sṛgālolūka-ṭaṅkāraiḥ*
*praṇedur aśivaṁ śivāḥ*

*antaḥ*—in the interior; *grāmeṣu*—in the villages; *mukhataḥ*—from their mouths; *vamantyaḥ*—vomiting; *vahnim*—fire; *ulbaṇam*—fearful; *sṛgāla*—jackals; *ulūka*—owls; *ṭaṅkāraiḥ*—with their cries; *praṇeduḥ*—created their respective vibrations; *aśivam*—portentously; *śivāḥ*—the she-jackals.

### TRANSLATION

**In the interior of the villages she-jackals yelled portentously, vomiting strong fire from their mouths, and jackals and owls also joined them with their cries.**

## TEXT 10

सङ्गीतवद्रोदनवदुन्नमय्य शिरोधराम् ।
व्यमुञ्चन् विविधा वाचो ग्रामसिंहास्ततस्ततः ॥१०॥

*saṅgītavad rodanavad*
*unnamayya śirodharām*
*vyamuñcan vividhā vāco*
*grāma-siṁhās tatas tataḥ*

*saṅgīta-vat*—like singing; *rodana-vat*—like wailing; *unnamayya*—raising; *śirodharām*—the neck; *vyamuñcan*—uttered; *vividhāḥ*—various; *vācaḥ*—cries; *grāma-siṁhāḥ*—the dogs; *tataḥ tataḥ*—here and there.

## TRANSLATION

**Raising their necks, dogs cried here and there, now in the manner of singing and now of wailing.**

## TEXT 11

खराश्च कर्कशैः क्षत्तः खुरैर्घ्नन्तो धरातलम् ।
खार्काररभसा मत्ताः पर्यधावन् वरूथशः ॥११॥

*kharāś ca karkaśaiḥ kṣattaḥ*
*khurair ghnanto dharā-talam*
*khārkāra-rabhasā mattāḥ*
*paryadhāvan varūthaśaḥ*

*kharāḥ*—asses; *ca*—and; *karkaśaiḥ*—hard; *kṣattaḥ*—O Vidura; *khuraiḥ*—with their hooves; *ghnantaḥ*—striking; *dharā-talam*—the surface of the earth; *khāḥ-kāra*—braying; *rabhasāḥ*—wildly engaged in; *mattāḥ*—mad; *paryadhāvan*—ran hither and thither; *varūthaśaḥ*—in herds.

## TRANSLATION

**O Vidura, the asses ran hither and thither in herds, striking the earth with their hard hooves and wildly braying.**

## PURPORT

Asses also feel very respectable as a race, and when they run in flocks hither and thither in so-called jollity, it is understood to be a bad sign for human society.

## TEXT 12

रुदन्तो रासभत्रस्ता नीडादुदपतन् खगाः ।
घोषेऽरण्ये च पशवः शकृन्मूत्रमकुर्वत ॥१२॥

*rudanto rāsabha-trastā*
*nīḍād udapatan khagāḥ*

*ghoṣe 'raṇye ca paśavaḥ*
*śakṛn-mūtram akurvata*

*rudantaḥ*—shrieking; *rāsabha*—by the asses; *trastāḥ*—frightened; *nīḍāt*—from the nest; *udapatan*—flew up; *khagāḥ*—birds; *ghoṣe*—in the cowshed; *araṇye*—in the woods; *ca*—and; *paśavaḥ*—the cattle; *śakṛt*—dung; *mūtram*—urine; *akurvata*—passed.

## TRANSLATION

**Frightened by the braying of the asses, birds flew shrieking from their nests, while cattle in the cowsheds as well as in the woods passed dung and urine.**

## TEXT 13

गावोऽत्रसन्नसृग्दोहास्तोयदाः पूयवर्षिणः ।
व्यरुदन्देवलिङ्गानि द्रुमाः पेतुर्विनानिलम् ॥१३॥

*gāvo 'trasann asṛg-dohās*
*toyadāḥ pūya-varṣiṇaḥ*
*vyarudan deva-liṅgāni*
*drumāḥ petur vinānilam*

*gāvaḥ*—the cows; *atrasan*—were frightened; *asṛk*—blood; *dohāḥ*—yielding; *toyadāḥ*—clouds; *pūya*—pus; *varṣiṇaḥ*—raining; *vyarudan*—shed tears; *deva-liṅgāni*—the images of the gods; *drumāḥ*—trees; *petuḥ*—fell down; *vinā*—without; *anilam*—a blast of wind.

## TRANSLATION

**Cows, terrified, yielded blood in place of milk, clouds rained pus, the images of the gods in the temples shed tears, and trees fell down without a blast of wind.**

## TEXT 14

ग्रहान् पुण्यतमानन्ये भगणांश्चापि दीपिताः ।
अतिचेरुर्वक्रगत्या युयुधुश्च परस्परम् ॥१४॥

*grahān puṇyatamān anye*
*bhagaṇāṁś cāpi dīpitāḥ*
*aticerur vakra-gatyā*
*yuyudhuś ca parasparam*

*grahān*—planets; *puṇya-tamān*—most auspicious; *anye*—others (the ominous planets); *bha-gaṇān*—luminaries; *ca*—and; *api*—also; *dīpitāḥ*—illuminating; *aticeruḥ*—overlapped; *vakra-gatyā*—taking retrograde courses; *yuyudhuḥ*—came into conflict; *ca*—and; *paraḥ-param*—with one another.

## TRANSLATION

**Ominous planets such as Mars and Saturn shone brighter and surpassed the auspicious ones such as Mercury, Jupiter and Venus as well as a number of lunar mansions. Taking seemingly retrograde courses, the planets came in conflict with one another.**

## PURPORT

The entire universe is moving under the three modes of material nature. Those living entities who are in goodness are called the pious species—pious lands, pious trees, etc. It is similar with the planets also; many planets are considered pious, and others are considered impious. Saturn and Mars are considered impious. When the pious planets shine very brightly, it is an auspicious sign, but when the inauspicious planets shine very brightly, this is not a very good sign.

## TEXT 15

दृष्ट्वान्यांश्च महोत्पातानतत्तत्त्वविदः प्रजाः ।
ब्रह्मपुत्रानृते भीता मेनिरे विश्वसम्प्लवम् ॥१५॥

*dṛṣṭvānyāṁś ca mahotpātān*
*atat-tattva-vidaḥ prajāḥ*
*brahma-putrān ṛte bhītā*
*menire viśva-samplavam*

*dṛṣṭvā*—having seen; *anyān*—others; *ca*—and; *mahā*—great; *utpātān*—evil omens; *a-tat-tattva-vidaḥ*—not knowing the secret (of the portents); *prajāḥ*—people; *brahma-putrān*—the sons of Brahmā (the four Kumāras); *ṛte*—except; *bhītāḥ*—being fearful; *menire*—thought; *viśva-samplavam*—the dissolution of the universe.

## TRANSLATION

**Marking these and many other omens of evil times, everyone but the four sage-sons of Brahmā, who were aware of the fall of Jaya and Vijaya and of their birth as Diti's sons, was seized with fear. They did not know the secrets of these potents and thought that the dissolution of the universe was at hand.**

## PURPORT

According to *Bhagavad-gītā*, Seventh Chapter, the laws of nature are so stringent that it is impossible for the living entity to surpass their enforcement. It is also explained that only those who are fully surrendered to Kṛṣṇa in Kṛṣṇa consciousness can be saved. We can learn from the description of the *Śrīmad-Bhāgavatam* that it is because of the birth of two great demons that there were so many natural disturbances. It is to be indirectly understood, as previously described, that when there are constant disturbances on the earth, that is an omen that some demoniac people have been born or that the demoniac population has increased. In former days there were only two demons—those born of Diti—yet there were so many disturbances. At the present day, especially in this age of Kali, these disturbances are always visible, which indicates that the demoniac population has certainly increased.

To check the increase of demoniac population, the Vedic civilization enacted so many rules and regulations of social life, the most important of which is the *garbhādhāna* process for begetting good children. In *Bhagavad-gītā* Arjuna informed Kṛṣṇa that if there is unwanted population (*varṇa-saṅkara*), the entire world will appear to be hell. People are very anxious for peace in the world, but there are so many unwanted children born without the benefit of the *garbhādhāna* ceremony, just like the demons born from Diti. Diti was so lusty that she forced her husband to copulate at a time which was inauspicious, and therefore the demons were born to create disturbances. In having sex life to beget children, one should observe the process for begetting nice children; if each and every householder in every family observes the Vedic system, then there are nice children, not demons, and automatically there is peace in the world. If we do not follow regulations in life for social tranquillity, we cannot expect peace. Rather, we will have to undergo the stringent reactions of natural laws.

## TEXT 16

तावादिदैत्यौ सहसा व्यज्यमानात्मपौरुषौ ।
ववृधातेऽश्मसारेण कायेनाद्रिपती इव ॥१६॥

*tāv ādi-daityau sahasā*
*vyajyamānātma-pauruṣau*
*vavṛdhāte 'śma-sāreṇa*
*kāyenādri-patī iva*

*tau*—those two; *ādi-daityau*—demons in the beginning of creation; *sahasā*—quickly; *vyajyamāna*—being manifest; *ātma*—own; *pauruṣau*—prowess; *vavṛdhāte*—grew; *aśma-sāreṇa*—steellike; *kāyena*—with bodily frames; *adri-patī*—two great mountains; *iva*—like.

## TRANSLATION

**These two demons who appeared in ancient times soon began to exhibit uncommon bodily features; they had steellike frames which began to grow just like two great mountains.**

## PURPORT

There are two classes of men in the world; one is called the demon, and the other is called the demigod. The demigods concern themselves with the spiritual upliftment of human society, whereas the demons are concerned with physical and material upliftment. The two demons born of Diti began to make their bodies as strong as iron frames, and they were so tall that they seemed to touch outer space. They were decorated with valuable ornaments, and they thought that this was success in life. Originally it was planned that Jaya and Vijaya, the two doorkeepers of

Vaikuṇṭha, were to take birth in this material world, where, by the curse of the sages, they were to play the part of always being angry with the Supreme Personality of Godhead. As demoniac persons, they became so angry that they were not concerned with the Supreme Personality of Godhead, but simply with physical comforts and physical upliftment.

## TEXT 17

दिवि स्पृशौ हेमकिरीटकोटिभि-
निरुद्धकाष्ठौ स्फुरदङ्गदाभुजौ ।
गां कम्पयन्तौ चरणैः पदे पदे
कट्या सुकाञ्च्यार्कमतीत्य तस्थतुः ॥१७॥

*divi-spṛśau hema-kirīṭa-koṭibhir*
*niruddha-kāṣṭhau sphurad-aṅgadā-bhujau*
*gāṁ kampayantau caraṇaiḥ pade pade*
*kaṭyā sukāñcyārkam atītya tasthatuḥ*

*divi-spṛśau*—touching the sky; *hema*—golden; *kirīṭa*—of their helmets; *koṭibhiḥ*—with the crests; *niruddha*—blocked; *kāṣṭhau*—the directions; *sphurat*—brilliant; *aṅgadā*—bracelets; *bhujau*—on whose arms; *gām*—the earth; *kampayantau*—shaking; *caraṇaiḥ*—with their feet; *pade pade*—at every step; *kaṭyā*—with their waists; *su-kāñcyā*—with beautiful decorated belts; *arkam*—the sun; *atītya*—surpassing; *tasthatuḥ*—they stood.

## TRANSLATION

**Their bodies became so tall that they seemed to kiss the sky with the crests of their gold crowns. They blocked the view of all directions and while walking shook the earth at every step. Their arms were adorned with brilliant bracelets, and they stood as if covering the sun with their waists, which were bound with excellent and beautiful girdles.**

## PURPORT

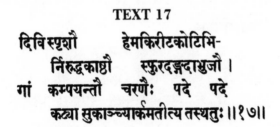

In the demoniac way of civilization, people are interested in getting a body constructed in such a way that when they walk on the street the earth will tremble and when they stand it will appear that they cover the sun and the vision of the four directions. If a race appears strong in body, their country is materially considered to be among the highly advanced nations of the world.

## TEXT 18

प्रजापतिर्नाम तयोरकार्षीद्
यः प्राक् स्वदेहाद्यमयोरजायत ।
तं वै हिरण्यकशिपुं विदुः प्रजा
यं तं हिरण्याक्षमसूत साग्रतः ॥१८॥

*prajāpatir nāma tayor akārṣīd*
*yaḥ prāk sva-dehād yamayor ajāyata*
*taṁ vai hiraṇyakaśipuṁ viduḥ prajā*
*yaṁ taṁ hiraṇyākṣam asūta sāgrataḥ*

*prajāpatiḥ*—Kaśyapa; *nāma*—names; *tayoḥ*—of the two; *akārṣīt*—gave; *yaḥ*—who; *prāk*—first; *sva-dehāt*—from his body; *yamayoḥ*—of the twins; *ajāyata*—was delivered; *tam*—him; *vai*—indeed; *hiraṇyakaśipum*—Hiraṇyakaśipu; *viduḥ*—know; *prajāḥ*—people; *yam*—whom; *tam*—him; *hiraṇyākṣam*—Hiraṇyākṣa; *asūta*—gave birth to; *sā*—she (Diti); *agrataḥ*—first.

## TRANSLATION

**Kaśyapa, Prajāpati, the creator of the living entities, gave his twin sons their names; the one who was born first he named Hiraṇyākṣa, and the one who was first conceived by Diti he named Hiraṇyakaśipu.**

## PURPORT

There is an authoritative Vedic literature called *Piṇḍa-siddhi* in which the scientific understanding of pregnancy is very nicely described. It is stated that when the male secretion enters the menstrual flux in the uterus in two successive drops, the mother develops two embryos in her womb, and she brings forth twins in a reverse order to that in which they were first conceived; the child conceived first is born later, and the one conceived later is brought forth first. The first child conceived in the womb lives behind the second child, so when birth takes place the second child appears first, and the first child appears second. In this case it is understood that Hiraṇyākṣa, the second child conceived, was delivered first, whereas Hiraṇyakaśipu, the child who was behind him, having been conceived first, was born second.

## TEXT 19

चक्रे हिरण्यकशिपुर्दोर्भ्यां ब्रह्मवरेण च ।
वशे सपालाँल्लोकांस्त्रीनकुतोमृत्युरुद्धतः ॥१९॥

*cakre hiraṇyakaśipur*
*dorbhyāṁ brahma-vareṇa ca*
*vaśe sa-pālāl̐ lokāṁs trīn*
*akuto-mṛtyur uddhataḥ*

*cakre*—made; *hiraṇyakaśipuḥ*—Hiraṇyakaśipu; *dorbhyām*—by his two arms; *brahma-vareṇa*—by the benediction of Brahmā; *ca*—and; *vaśe*—under his control; *sa-pālān*—along with their protectors; *lokān*—the worlds; *trīn*—three; *akutaḥ-mṛtyuḥ*—fearing death from no one; *uddhataḥ*—puffed up.

## TRANSLATION

**The elder child, Hiraṇyakaśipu, was unafraid of death from anyone within the three worlds because he received a benediction from Lord Brahmā. He was proud and puffed up due to this benediction and was able to bring all three planetary systems under his control.**

## PURPORT

As will be revealed in later chapters, Hiraṇyakaśipu underwent severe austerity and penance to satisfy Brahmā and thus receive a benediction of immortality. Actually, it is impossible even for Lord Brahmā to give anyone the benediction of becoming immortal, but indirectly Hiraṇyakaśipu received the benediction that no one within this material world would be able to kill him. In other words, because he originally came from the abode of Vaikuṇṭha, he was not to be killed by anyone within this material world. The Lord desired to appear Himself to kill him. One may be very proud of his material advancement in knowledge, but he cannot be immune to the four principles of material existence, namely birth, death, old age and disease. It was the Lord's plan to teach people that even Hiraṇyakaśipu, who was so powerful and strongly built, could not live more than his destined duration of life. One may become as strong and puffed up as Hiraṇyakaśipu and bring under his control all the three worlds, but there is no possibility of continuing life eternally or keeping the conquered booty forever. So many emperors have ascended to power, and they are now lost in oblivion; that is the history of the world.

## TEXT 20

हिरण्याक्षोऽनुजस्तस्य प्रियः प्रीतिकृदन्वहम् ।
गदापाणिर्दिवं यातो युयुत्सुर्मृगयन् रणम् ॥२०॥

*hiraṇyākṣo 'nujas tasya*
*priyaḥ prīti-kṛd anvaham*
*gadā-pāṇir divaṁ yāto*
*yuyutsur mṛgayan raṇam*

*hiraṇyākṣaḥ*—Hiraṇyākṣa; *anujaḥ*—younger brother; *tasya*—his; *priyaḥ*—beloved; *prīti-kṛt*—ready to please; *anu-aham*—every day; *gadā-pāṇiḥ*—with a club in hand; *divam*—to the higher planets; *yātaḥ*—traveled; *yuyutsuḥ*—desirous to fight; *mṛgayan*—seeking; *raṇam*—combat.

## TRANSLATION

**His younger brother, Hiraṇyākṣa, was always ready to satisfy his elder brother by his activities. Hiraṇyākṣa took a club on his shoulder and traveled all over the universe with a fighting spirit just to satisfy Hiraṇyakaśipu.**

## PURPORT

The demoniac spirit is to train all family members to exploit the resources of this universe for personal sense gratification, whereas the godly spirit is to engage everything in the service of the Lord. Hiraṇyakaśipu was himself very powerful, and he made his younger brother, Hiraṇyākṣa, powerful to assist him in fighting with everyone and lording it over material nature as long as possible. If possible, he wanted to rule the universe eternally. These are demonstrations of the spirit of the demoniac living entity.

## TEXT 21

तं वीक्ष्य दुःसहजवं रणत्काञ्चननूपुरम् ।
वैजयन्त्या स्रजा जुष्टमंसन्यस्तमहागदम् ॥२१॥

*taṁ vīkṣya duḥsaha-javaṁ*
*raṇat-kāñcana-nūpuram*
*vaijayantyā srajā juṣṭam*
*aṁsa-nyasta-mahā-gadam*

*tam*—him; *vīkṣya*—having seen; *duḥsaha*—difficult to control; *javam*—temper; *raṇat*—tinkling; *kāñcana*—gold; *nūpuram*—anklets; *vaijayantyā srajā*—with a *vaijayantī* garland; *juṣṭam*—adorned; *aṁsa*—on his shoulder; *nyasta*—rested; *mahā-gadam*—a huge mace.

### TRANSLATION

**Hiraṇyākṣa's temper was difficult to control. He had anklets of gold tinkling about his feet, he was adorned with a gigantic garland, and he rested his huge mace on one of his shoulders.**

## TEXT 22

मनोवीर्यवरोत्सिक्तमसृण्यमकुतोभयम् ।
भीता निलिल्यिरे देवास्तार्क्ष्यत्रस्ता इवाहयः ॥२२॥

*mano-vīrya-varotsiktam*
*asṛṇyam akuto-bhayam*
*bhītā nililyire devās*
*tārkṣya-trastā ivāhayaḥ*

*manaḥ-vīrya*—by mental and bodily strength; *vara*—by the boon; *ut-siktam*—proud; *asṛṇyam*—not able to be checked; *akutaḥ-bhayam*—fearing no one; *bhītāḥ*—frightened; *nililyire*—hid themselves; *devāḥ*—the demigods; *tārkṣya*—Garuḍa; *trastāḥ*—frightened of; *iva*—like; *ahayaḥ*—snakes.

## TRANSLATION

**His mental and bodily strength as well as the boon conferred upon him had made him proud. He feared death at the hands of no one, and there was no checking him. The gods, therefore, were seized with fear at his very sight, and they hid themselves even as snakes hide themselves for fear of Garuḍa.**

## PURPORT

The *asuras* are generally strongly built, as described here, and therefore their mental condition is very sound, and their prowess is also extraordinary. Hiraṇyākṣa and Hiraṇyakaśipu, having received the boon that they would not be killed by any other living entity within this universe, were almost immortal, and thus they were completely fearless.

## TEXT 23

स वै तिरोहितान् दृष्ट्वा महसा स्वेन दैत्यराट् ।
सेन्द्रान्देवगणान् क्षीबानपश्यन् व्यनदद् भृशम् ॥२३॥

*sa vai tirohitān dṛṣṭvā*
*mahasā svena daitya-rāṭ*
*sendrān deva-gaṇān kṣībān*
*apaśyan vyanadad bhṛśam*

*saḥ*—he; *vai*—indeed; *tirohitān*—vanished; *dṛṣṭvā*—having seen; *mahasā*—by might; *svena*—his own; *daitya-rāṭ*—the chief of the Daityas (demons); *sa-indrān*—along with Indra; *deva-gaṇān*—the demigods; *kṣībān*—intoxicated; *apaśyan*—not finding; *vyanadat*—roared; *bhṛśam*—loudly.

## TRANSLATION

**On not finding Indra and the other demigods, who had previously been intoxicated with power, the chief of the Daityas, seeing that they had all vanished before his might, roared loudly.**

## TEXT 24

ततो निवृत्तः क्रीडिष्यन् गम्भीरं भीमनिस्वनम् ।
विजगाहे महासत्त्वो वार्धिं मत्त इव द्विपः ॥२४॥

*tato nivṛttaḥ krīḍiṣyan*
*gambhīraṁ bhīma-nisvanam*
*vijagāhe mahā-sattvo*
*vārdhiṁ matta iva dvipaḥ*

*tataḥ*—then; *nivṛttaḥ*—returned; *krīḍiṣyan*—for the sake of sport; *gambhīram*—deep; *bhīma-nisvanam*—making a terrible sound; *vijagāhe*—dived; *mahā-sattvaḥ*—the mighty being; *vārdhim*—in the ocean; *mattaḥ*—in wrath; *iva*—like; *dvipaḥ*—an elephant.

## TRANSLATION

**After returning from the heavenly kingdom, the mighty demon, who was like an elephant in wrath, for the sake of sport dived into the deep ocean, which was roaring terribly.**

## TEXT 25

तस्मिन् प्रविष्टे वरुणस्य सैनिका
यादोगणाः सन्नधियः ससाध्वसाः ।
अहन्यमाना अपि तस्य वर्चसा
प्रधर्षिता दूरतरं प्रदुद्रुवुः ॥२५॥

*tasmin praviṣṭe varuṇasya sainikā*
*yādo-gaṇāḥ sanna-dhiyaḥ sasādhvasāḥ*
*ahanyamānā api tasya varcasā*
*pradharṣitā dūrataraṁ pradudruvuḥ*

*tasmin praviṣṭe*—when he entered the ocean; *varuṇasya*—of Varuṇa; *sainikāḥ*—the defenders; *yādaḥ-gaṇāḥ*—the aquatic animals; *sanna-dhiyaḥ*—depressed; *sa-sādhvasāḥ*—with fear; *ahanyamānāḥ*—not being hit; *api*—even; *tasya*—his; *varcasā*—by splendor; *pradhar-ṣitāḥ*—stricken; *dūra-taram*—far away; *pradudruvuḥ*—they ran fast.

## TRANSLATION

**On his entering the ocean, the aquatic animals who formed the host of Varuṇa were stricken with fear and ran far away. Thus Hiraṇyākṣa showed his splendor without dealing a blow.**

## PURPORT

Materialistic demons sometimes appear to be very powerful and are seen to establish their supremacy throughout the world. Here also it appears that Hiraṇyākṣa, by his demoniac strength, actually established his supremacy throughout the universe, and the demigods were afraid of his uncommon power. Not only were the demigods in space afraid of the demons Hiraṇyakaśipu and Hiraṇyākṣa, but so also were the aquatic animals within the sea.

## TEXT 26

स वर्षपूगानुदधौ महाबल-
श्चरन्महोर्मीञ्छ्वसनेरितान्मुहुः ।
मौर्व्याभिजघ्ने गदया विभावरी-
मासेदिवांस्तात पुरीं प्रचेतसः ॥२६॥

*sa varṣa-pūgān udadhau mahā-balaś*
*caran mahormīñ chvasaneritān muhuḥ*
*maurvyābhijaghne gadayā vibhāvarīm*
*āsedivāṁs tāta purīṁ pracetasaḥ*

*saḥ*—he; *varṣa-pūgān*—for many years; *udadhau*—in the ocean; *mahā-balaḥ*—mighty; *caran*—moving; *mahā-ūrmīn*—gigantic waves; *śvasana*—by the wind; *īritān*—tossed; *muhuḥ*—again and again; *maur-vyā*—iron; *abhijaghne*—he struck; *gadayā*—with his mace; *vibhāva-*

*rīm*—Vibhāvarī; *āsedivān*—reached; *tāta*—O dear Vidura; *purīm*—the capital; *pracetasaḥ*—of Varuṇa.

## TRANSLATION

**Moving about in the ocean for many, many years, the mighty Hiraṇyākṣa smote the gigantic wind-tossed waves again and again with his iron mace and reached Vibhāvarī, the capital of Varuṇa.**

## PURPORT

Varuṇa is supposed to be the predominating deity of the waters, and his capital, which is known as Vibhāvarī, is within the watery kingdom.

## TEXT 27

तत्रोपलभ्यासुरलोकपालकं
यादोगणानामृषभं प्रचेतसम् ।
स्मयन् प्रलब्धुं प्रणिपत्य नीचव-
ज्जगाद मे देह्यधिराज संयुगम् ॥२७॥

*tatropalabhyāsura-loka-pālakaṁ*
*yādo-gaṇānām ṛṣabhaṁ pracetasam*
*smayan pralabdhuṁ praṇipatya nīcavaj*
*jagāda me dehy adhirāja saṁyugam*

*tatra*—there; *upalabhya*—having reached; *asura-loka*—of the regions where the demons reside; *pālakam*—the guardian; *yādaḥ-gaṇānām*—of the aquatic creatures; *ṛṣabham*—the lord; *pracetasam*—Varuṇa; *smayan*—smiling; *pralabdhum*—to make fun; *praṇipatya*—having bowed down; *nīca-vat*—like a lowborn man; *jagāda*—he said; *me*—to me; *dehi*—give; *adhirāja*—O great lord; *saṁyugam*—battle.

## TRANSLATION

**Vibhāvarī is the home of Varuṇa, lord of the aquatic creatures and guardian of the lower regions of the universe, where the**

**demons generally reside. There Hiraṇyākṣa fell at Varuṇa's feet like a lowborn man, and to make fun of him he said with a smile, "Give me battle, O Supreme Lord!"**

## PURPORT

The demoniac person always challenges others and tries to occupy others' property by force. Here these symptoms are fully displayed by Hiraṇyākṣa, who begged war from a person who had no desire to fight.

## TEXT 28

त्वं लोकपालोऽधिपतिर्बृहच्छ्रवा
वीर्यापहो दुर्मदवीरमानिनाम् ।
विजित्य लोकेऽखिलदैत्यदानवान्
यद्राजसूयेन पुरायजत्प्रभो ॥२८॥

*tvaṁ loka-pālo 'dhipatir bṛhac-chravā*
*vīryāpaho durmada-vīra-māninām*
*vijitya loke 'khila-daitya-dānavān*
*yad rājasūyena purāyajat prabho*

*tvam*—you (Varuṇa); *loka-pālaḥ*—guardian of the planet; *adhipatiḥ*—a ruler; *bṛhat-śravāḥ*—of wide fame; *vīrya*—the power; *apahaḥ*—diminished; *durmada*—of the proud; *vīra-māninām*—thinking themselves very big heroes; *vijitya*—having conquered; *loke*—in the world; *akhila*—all; *daitya*—the demons; *dānavān*—the Dānavas; *yat*—whence; *rāja-sūyena*—with a Rājasūya sacrifice; *purā*—formerly; *ayajat*—worshiped; *prabho*—O lord.

## TRANSLATION

**You are the guardian of an entire sphere and a ruler of wide fame. Having crushed the might of arrogant and conceited warriors and having conquered all the Daityas and Dānavas in the world, you once performed a Rājasūya sacrifice to the Lord.**

## TEXT 29

स एवमुत्सिक्तमदेन विद्विषा
दृढं प्रलब्धो भगवानपां पतिः ।
रोषं समुत्थं शमयन् स्वया धिया
व्यवोचदङ्गोपशमं गता वयम् ॥२९॥

*sa evam utsikta-madena vidviṣā*
*dṛḍhaṁ pralabdho bhagavān apāṁ patiḥ*
*roṣaṁ samutthaṁ śamayan svayā dhiyā*
*vyavocad aṅgopaśamaṁ gatā vayam*

*saḥ*—Varuṇa; *evam*—thus; *utsikta*—puffed up; *madena*—with vanity; *vidviṣā*—by the enemy; *dṛḍham*—deeply; *pralabdhaḥ*—mocked; *bhagavān*—worshipful; *apām*—of the waters; *patiḥ*—the lord; *roṣam*—anger; *samuttham*—sprung up; *śamayan*—controlling; *svayā dhiyā*—by his reason; *vyavocat*—he replied; *aṅga*—O dear one; *upaśamam*—desisting from warfare; *gatāḥ*—gone; *vayam*—we.

## TRANSLATION

**Thus mocked by an enemy whose vanity knew no bounds, the worshipful lord of the waters waxed angry, but by dint of his reason he managed to curb the anger that had sprung up in him, and he replied: O dear one, we have now desisted from warfare, having grown too old for combat.**

## PURPORT

As we see, warmongering materialists always create fighting without reason.

## TEXT 30

पश्यामि नान्यं पुरुषात्पुरातनाद्
यः संयुगे त्वां रणमार्गकोविदम् ।

आराधयिष्यत्यसुरर्षभेहि तं
मनस्विनो यं गृणते भवादृशाः ॥३०॥

*paśyāmi nānyaṁ puruṣāt purātanād*
*yaḥ saṁyuge tvāṁ raṇa-mārga-kovidam*
*ārādhayiṣyaty asurarṣabhehi taṁ*
*manasvino yaṁ gṛṇate bhavādṛśāḥ*

*paśyāmi*—I see; *na*—not; *anyam*—other; *puruṣāt*—than the person; *purātanāt*—most ancient; *yaḥ*—who; *saṁyuge*—in battle; *tvām*—to you; *raṇa-mārga*—in the tactics of war; *kovidam*—very much skilled; *ārādhayiṣyati*—will give satisfaction; *asura-ṛṣabha*—O chief of the *asuras; ihi*—approach; *tam*—Him; *manasvinaḥ*—heroes; *yam*—whom; *gṛṇate*—praise; *bhavādṛśāḥ*—like you.

## TRANSLATION

**You are so skilled in war that I do not see anyone else but the most ancient person, Lord Viṣṇu, who can give satisfaction in battle to you. Therefore, O chief of the asuras, approach Him, whom even heroes like you mention with praise.**

## PURPORT

Aggressive materialistic warriors are actually punished by the Supreme Lord for their policy of unnecessarily disturbing world peace. Therefore Varuṇa advised Hiraṇyākṣa that the right course to satisfy his fighting spirit would be to seek to fight with Viṣṇu.

## TEXT 31

तं वीरमारादभिपद्य विस्मयः
शयिष्यसे वीरशये श्वभिर्वृतः ।
यस्त्वद्विधानामसतां प्रशान्तये
रूपाणि धत्ते सदनुग्रहेच्छया ॥३१॥

*taṁ vīram ārād abhipadya vismayaḥ*
*śayiṣyase vīra-śaye śvabhir vṛtaḥ*

*yas tvad-vidhānām asatāṁ praśāntaye*
*rūpāṇi dhatte sad-anugrahecchayā*

*tam*—Him; *vīram*—the great hero; *ārāt*—quickly; *abhipadya*—on reaching; *vismayaḥ*—rid of pride; *śayiṣyase*—you will lie down; *vīra-śaye*—on the battlefield; *śvabhiḥ*—by dogs; *vṛtaḥ*—surrounded; *yaḥ*—He who; *tvat-vidhānām*—like you; *asatām*—of wicked persons; *praśān-taye*—for the extermination; *rūpāṇi*—forms; *dhatte*—He assumes; *sat*—to the virtuous; *anugraha*—to show His grace; *icchayā*—with a desire.

## TRANSLATION

**Varuṇa continued: On reaching Him you will be rid of your pride at once and will lie down on the field of battle, surrounded by dogs, for eternal sleep. It is in order to exterminate wicked fellows like you and to show His grace to the virtuous that He assumes His various incarnations like Varāha.**

## PURPORT

*Asuras* do not know that their bodies consist of the five elements of material nature and that when they fall they become objects of pastimes for dogs and vultures. Varuṇa advised Hiraṇyākṣa to meet Viṣṇu in His boar incarnation so that his hankering for aggressive war would be satisfied and his powerful body would be vanquished.

*Thus end the Bhaktivedanta purports of the Third Canto, Seventeenth Chapter, of the* Śrīmad-Bhāgavatam, *entitled "Victory of Hiraṇyākṣa Over All the Directions of the Universe."*

CHAPTER EIGHTEEN

# The Battle Between Lord Boar and the Demon Hiraṇyākṣa

## TEXT 1

मैत्रेय उवाच
तदेवमाकर्ण्य जलेशभाषितं
महामनास्तद्विगणय्य दुर्मदः ।
हरेर्विदित्वा गतिमङ्ग नारदाद्
रसातलं निर्विविशे त्वरान्वितः ॥ १ ॥

*maitreya uvāca*
*tad evam ākarṇya jaleśa-bhāṣitaṁ*
*mahā-manās tad vigaṇayya durmadaḥ*
*harer viditvā gatim aṅga nāradād*
*rasātalaṁ nirviviśe tvarānvitaḥ*

*maitreyaḥ*—the great sage Maitreya; *uvāca*—said; *tat*—that; *evam*—thus; *ākarṇya*—hearing; *jala-īśa*—of the controller of water, Varuṇa; *bhāṣitam*—words; *mahā-manāḥ*—proud; *tat*—those words; *vigaṇayya*—having paid little heed to; *durmadaḥ*—vainglorious; *hareḥ*—of the Supreme Personality of Godhead; *viditvā*—having learned; *gatim*—the whereabouts; *aṅga*—O dear Vidura; *nāradāt*—from Nārada; *rasātalam*—to the depths of the ocean; *nirviviśe*—entered; *tvarā-anvitaḥ*—with great speed.

## TRANSLATION

**Maitreya continued: The proud and falsely glorious Daitya paid little heed to the words of Varuṇa. O dear Vidura, he learned from Nārada the whereabouts of the Supreme Personality of Godhead and hurriedly betook himself to the depths of the ocean.**

## PURPORT

Materialistic warmongers are not even afraid to fight with their mightiest enemy, the Personality of Godhead. The demon was very encouraged to learn from Varuṇa that there was one fighter who could actually combat him, and he was very enthusiastic to search out the Supreme Personality of Godhead just to give Him a fight, even though it was predicted by Varuṇa that by fighting with Viṣṇu he would become prey for dogs, jackals and vultures. Since demoniac persons are less intelligent, they dare to fight with Viṣṇu, who is known as Ajita, or one who has never been conquered.

## TEXT 2

ददर्श तत्राभिजितं धराधरं
प्रोन्नीयमानावनिमग्रदंष्ट्रया ।
मुष्णन्तमक्ष्णा स्वरुचोऽरुणश्रिया
जहास चाहो वनगोचरो मृगः ॥ २ ॥

*dadarśa tatrābhijitaṁ dharā-dharaṁ*
*pronnīyamānāvanim agra-daṁṣṭrayā*
*muṣṇantam akṣṇā sva-ruco 'ruṇa-śriyā*
*jahāsa cāho vana-gocaro mṛgaḥ*

*dadarśa*—he saw; *tatra*—there; *abhijitam*—the victorious; *dharā*—the earth; *dharam*—bearing; *pronnīyamāna*—being raised upward; *avanim*—the earth; *agra-daṁṣṭrayā*—by the tip of His tusk; *muṣṇantam*—who was diminishing; *akṣṇā*—with His eyes; *sva-rucaḥ*—Hiraṇyākṣa's own splendor; *aruṇa*—reddish; *śriyā*—radiant; *jahāsa*—he laughed; *ca*—and; *aho*—oh; *vana-gocaraḥ*—amphibious; *mṛgaḥ*—beast.

## TRANSLATION

**He saw there the all-powerful Personality of Godhead in His boar incarnation, bearing the earth upward on the ends of His tusks and robbing him of his splendor with His reddish eyes. The demon laughed: Oh, an amphibious beast!**

## PURPORT

In a previous chapter we have discussed the incarnation of the Supreme Personality of Godhead as Varāha, the boar. While Varāha, with His tusks, engaged in uplifting the submerged earth from the depths of the waters, this great demon Hiraṇyākṣa met Him and challenged Him, calling Him a beast. Demons cannot understand the incarnations of the Lord; they think that His incarnations as a fish or boar or tortoise are big beasts only. They misunderstand the body of the Supreme Personality of Godhead, even in His human form, and they deride His descent. In the Caitanya-sampradāya there is sometimes a demoniac misconception about the descent of Nityānanda Prabhu. Nityānanda Prabhu's body is spiritual, but demoniac persons consider the body of the Supreme Personality to be material, just like ours. *Avajānanti māṁ mūḍhāḥ:* persons who have no intelligence deride the transcendental form of the Lord as material.

## TEXT 3

आहैनमेह्यज्ञ महीं विमुञ्च नो
रसौकसां विश्वसृजेयमर्पिता ।
न स्वस्ति यास्यस्यनया ममेक्षतः
सुराधमासादितसूकराकृते ॥ ३ ॥

*āhainam ehy ajña mahīṁ vimuñca no*
*rasaukasāṁ viśva-sṛjeyam arpitā*
*na svasti yāsyasy anayā mamekṣataḥ*
*surādhamāsādita-sūkarākṛte*

*āha*—Hiraṇyākṣa said; *enam*—to the Lord; *ehi*—come and fight; *ajña*—O fool; *mahīm*—the earth; *vimuñca*—give up; *naḥ*—to us; *rasā-okasām*—of the inhabitants of the lower regions; *viśva-sṛjā*—by the creator of the universe; *iyam*—this earth; *arpitā*—entrusted; *na*—not; *svasti*—well-being; *yāsyasi*—You will go; *anayā*—with this; *mama īkṣataḥ*—while I am seeing; *sura-adhama*—O lowest of the demigods; *āsādita*—having taken; *sūkara-ākṛte*—the form of a boar.

## TRANSLATION

**The demon addressed the Lord: O best of the demigods, dressed in the form of a boar, just hear me. This earth is entrusted to us, the inhabitants of the lower regions, and You cannot take it from my presence and not be hurt by me.**

## PURPORT

Śrīdhara Svāmī, commenting on this verse, states that although the demon wanted to deride the Personality of Godhead in the form of a boar, actually he worshiped Him in several words. For example, he addressed Him as *vana-gocaraḥ*, which means "one who is a resident of the forest," but another meaning of *vana-gocaraḥ* is "one who lies on the water." Viṣṇu lies on the water, so the Supreme Personality of Godhead can be properly addressed in this way. The demon also addressed Him as *mṛgaḥ*, indicating, unintentionally, that the Supreme Personality is sought after by great sages, saintly persons and transcendentalists. He also addressed Him as *ajña*. Śrīdhara Svāmī says that *jña* means "knowledge," and there is no knowledge which is unknown to the Supreme Personality of Godhead. Indirectly, therefore, the demon said that Viṣṇu knows everything. The demon addressed Him as *surādhama*. *Sura* means "the demigods," and *adhama* means "Lord of all there is." He is Lord of all the demigods; therefore He is the best of all demigods, or God. When the demon used the phrase "in my presence," the implied meaning was, "In spite of my presence, You are completely able to take away the earth." *Na svasti yāsyasi:* "Unless You kindly take this earth from our custody, there can be no good fortune for us."

## TEXT 4

त्वं नः सपत्नैरभवाय किं भृतो
यो मायया हन्त्यसुरान् परोक्षजित् ।
त्वां योगमायाबलमल्पपौरुषं
संस्थाप्य मूढ प्रमृजे सुहृच्छुचः ॥ ४ ॥

*tvaṁ naḥ sapatnair abhavāya kiṁ bhṛto*
*yo māyayā hanty asurān parokṣa-jit*

*tvāṁ yogamāyā-balam alpa-pauruṣaṁ*
*saṁsthāpya mūḍha pramṛje suhṛc-chucaḥ*

*tvam*—You; *naḥ*—us; *sapatnaiḥ*—by our enemies; *abhavāya*—for killing; *kim*—is it that; *bhṛtaḥ*—maintained; *yaḥ*—He who; *māyayā*—by deception; *hanti*—kills; *asurān*—the demons; *parokṣa-jit*—who conquered by remaining invisible; *tvām*—You; *yogamāyā-balam*—whose strength is bewildering power; *alpa-pauruṣam*—whose power is meager; *saṁsthāpya*—after killing; *mūḍha*—fool; *pramṛje*—I shall wipe out; *suhṛt-śucaḥ*—the grief of my kinsmen.

## TRANSLATION

**You rascal, You have been nourished by our enemies to kill us, and You have killed some demons by remaining invisible. O fool, Your power is only mystic, so today I shall enliven my kinsmen by killing You.**

## PURPORT

The demon used the word *abhavāya,* which means "for killing." Śrīdhara Svāmī comments that this "killing" means liberating, or, in other words, killing the process of continued birth and death. The Lord kills the process of birth and death and keeps Himself invisible. The activities of the Lord's internal potency are inconceivable, but by a slight exhibition of this potency, the Lord, by His grace, can deliver one from nescience. *Śucaḥ* means "miseries"; the miseries of material existence can be extinguished by the Lord by His potential energy of internal *yogamāyā.* In the *Upaniṣads* (*Śvetāśvatara Up.* 6.8) it is stated, *parāsya śaktir vividhaiva śrūyate.* The Lord is invisible to the eyes of the common man, but His energies act in various ways. When demons are in adversity, they think that God is hiding Himself and is working by His mystic potency. They think that if they can find God they can kill Him just by seeing Him. Hiraṇyākṣa thought that way, and he challenged the Lord: "You have done tremendous harm to our community, taking the part of the demigods, and You have killed our kinsmen in so many ways, always keeping Yourself hidden. Now I see You face to face, and I am not going to let You go. I shall kill You and save my kinsmen from Your mystic misdeeds."

Not only are demons always anxious to kill God with words and philosophy, but they think that if one is materially powerful he can kill God with materially fatal weapons. Demons like Kaṁsa, Rāvaṇa and Hiraṇyakaśipu thought themselves powerful enough to kill even God. Demons cannot understand that God, by His multifarious potencies, can work so wonderfully that He can be present everywhere and still remain in His eternal abode, Goloka Vṛndāvana.

## TEXT 5

त्वयि संस्थिते गदया शीर्णशीर्ष-
ण्यस्मद्भुजच्युतया ये च तुभ्यम् ।
बलिं हरन्त्यृषयो ये च देवाः
स्वयं सर्वे न भविष्यन्त्यमूलाः ॥ ५ ॥

*tvayi saṁsthite gadayā śīrṇa-śīrṣaṇy*
*asmad-bhuja-cyutayā ye ca tubhyam*
*baliṁ haranty ṛṣayo ye ca devāḥ*
*svayaṁ sarve na bhaviṣyanty amūlāḥ*

*tvayi*—when You; *saṁsthite*—are killed; *gadayā*—by the mace; *śīrṇa*—smashed; *śīrṣaṇi*—skull; *asmat-bhuja*—from my hand; *cyutayā*—released; *ye*—those who; *ca*—and; *tubhyam*—to You; *balim*—presentations; *haranti*—offer; *ṛṣayaḥ*—sages; *ye*—those who; *ca*—and; *devāḥ*—demigods; *svayam*—automatically; *sarve*—all; *na*—not; *bhaviṣyanti*—will exist; *amūlāḥ*—without roots.

## TRANSLATION

**The demon continued: When You fall dead with Your skull smashed by the mace hurled by my arms, the demigods and sages who offer You oblations and sacrifice in devotional service will also automatically cease to exist, like trees without roots.**

## PURPORT

Demons are very much disturbed when devotees worship the Lord in the prescribed ways recommended in the scriptures. In the Vedic scriptures, the neophyte devotees are advised to engage in nine kinds of devotional service, such as to hear and chant the holy name of God, to remember Him always, to chant on beads Hare Kṛṣṇa, Hare Kṛṣṇa, Kṛṣṇa Kṛṣṇa, Hare Hare/ Hare Rāma, Hare Rāma, Rāma Rāma, Hare Hare, to worship the Lord in the form of His Deity incarnation in the temples, and to engage in various activities of Kṛṣṇa consciousness to increase the number of godly persons for perfect peace in the world. Demons do not like such activity. They are always envious of God and His devotees. Their propaganda not to worship in the temple or church but simply to make material advancement for satisfaction of the senses is always current. The demon Hiraṇyākṣa, upon seeing the Lord face to face, wanted to make a permanent solution by killing the Personality of Godhead with his powerful mace. The example of an uprooted tree mentioned here by the demon is very significant. Devotees accept that God is the root of everything. Their example is that just as the stomach is the source of energy of all the limbs of the body, God is the original source of all energy manifested in the material and spiritual worlds; therefore, as supplying food to the stomach is the process to satisfy all the limbs of the body, Kṛṣṇa consciousness, or developing love of Kṛṣṇa, is the sublime method for satisfying the source of all happiness. The demon wants to uproot this source because if the root, God, were to be checked, the activities of the Lord and the devotees would automatically stop. The demon would be very much satisfied by such a situation in society. Demons are always anxious to have a godless society for their sense gratification. According to Śrīdhara Svāmī, this verse means that when the demon would be deprived of his mace by the Supreme Personality of Godhead, not only the neophyte devotees but also the ancient sagacious devotees of the Lord would be very much satisfied.

## TEXT 6

स तुद्यमानोऽरिदुरुक्ततोमरै-
र्दंष्ट्राग्रगां गामुपलक्ष्य भीताम् ।
तोदं मृषन्निरगादम्बुमध्याद्
ग्राहाहतः सकरेणुर्यथेभः ॥ ६ ॥

*sa tudyamāno 'ri-durukta-tomarair*
*daṁṣṭrāgra-gāṁ gām upalakṣya bhītām*
*todaṁ mṛṣan niragād ambu-madhyād*
*grāhāhataḥ sa-kareṇur yathebhaḥ*

*saḥ*—He; *tudyamānaḥ*—being pained; *ari*—of the enemy; *durukta*—by the abusive words; *tomaraiḥ*—by the weapons; *daṁṣṭra-agra*—on the ends of His tusks; *gām*—situated; *gām*—the earth; *upalakṣya*—seeing; *bhītām*—frightened; *todam*—the pain; *mṛṣan*—bearing; *niragāt*—He came out; *ambu-madhyāt*—from the midst of the water; *grāha*—by a crocodile; *āhataḥ*—attacked; *sa-kareṇuḥ*—along with a she-elephant; *yathā*—as; *ibhaḥ*—an elephant.

## TRANSLATION

**Although the Lord was pained by the shaftlike abusive words of the demon, He bore the pain. But seeing that the earth on the ends of His tusks was frightened, He rose out of the water just as an elephant emerges with its female companion when assailed by an alligator.**

## PURPORT

The Māyāvādī philosopher cannot understand that the Lord has feelings. The Lord is satisfied if someone offers Him a nice prayer, and similarly, if someone decries His existence or calls Him by ill names, God is dissatisfied. The Supreme Personality of Godhead is decried by the Māyāvādī philosophers, who are almost demons. They say that God has no head, no form, no existence and no legs, hands or other bodily limbs. In other words, they say that He is dead or lame. All these misconceptions of the Supreme Lord are a source of dissatisfaction to Him; He is never pleased with such atheistic descriptions. In this case, although the Lord felt sorrow from the piercing words of the demon, He delivered the earth for the satisfaction of the demigods, who are ever His devotees. The conclusion is that God is as sentient as we are. He is satisfied by our prayers and dissatisfied by our harsh words against Him. In order to give protection to His devotee, He is always ready to tolerate insulting words from the atheists.

## TEXT 7

तं निःसरन्तं सलिलादनुद्रुतो
हिरण्यकेशो द्विरदं यथा झषः ।
करालदंष्ट्रोऽशनिनिस्वनोऽब्रवीद्
गतह्रियां किं त्वसतां विगर्हितम् ॥ ७ ॥

*taṁ niḥsarantaṁ salilād anudruto*
*hiraṇya-keśo dviradaṁ yathā jhaṣaḥ*
*karāla-daṁṣṭro 'śani-nisvano 'bravīd*
*gata-hriyāṁ kiṁ tv asatāṁ vigarhitam*

*tam*—Him; *niḥsarantam*—coming out; *salilāt*—from the water; *anudrutaḥ*—chased; *hiraṇya-keśaḥ*—having golden hair; *dviradam*—an elephant; *yathā*—as; *jhaṣaḥ*—a crocodile; *karāla-daṁṣṭraḥ*—having fearful teeth; *aśani-nisvanaḥ*—roaring like thunder; *abravīt*—he said; *gata-hriyām*—for those who are shameless; *kim*—what; *tu*—indeed; *asatām*—for the wretches; *vigarhitam*—reproachable.

## TRANSLATION

**The demon, who had golden hair on his head and fearful tusks, gave chase to the Lord while He was rising from the water, even as an alligator would chase an elephant. Roaring like thunder, he said: Are You not ashamed of running away before a challenging adversary? There is nothing reproachable for shameless creatures!**

## PURPORT

When the Lord was coming out of the water, taking the earth in His arms to deliver it, the demon derided Him with insulting words, but the Lord did not care because He was very conscious of His duty. For a dutiful man there is nothing to fear. Similarly, those who are powerful have no fear of derision or unkind words from an enemy. The Lord had nothing to fear from anyone, yet He was merciful to His enemy by neglecting him. Although apparently He fled from the challenge, it was just to protect the earth from calamity that He tolerated Hiraṇyākṣa's deriding words.

## TEXT 8

स गामुदस्तात्सलिलस्य गोचरे
विन्यस्य तस्यामदधात्स्वसत्त्वम् ।
अभिष्टुतो विश्वसृजा प्रसूनै-
रापूर्यमाणो विबुधैः पश्यतोऽरेः ॥ ८ ॥

*sa gām udastāt salilasya gocare*
*vinyasya tasyām adadhāt sva-sattvam*
*abhiṣṭuto viśva-sṛjā prasūnair*
*āpūryamāṇo vibudhaiḥ paśyato 'reḥ*

*saḥ*—the Lord; *gām*—the earth; *udastāt*—on the surface; *salilasya*—of the water; *gocare*—within His sight; *vinyasya*—having placed; *tasyām*—to the earth; *adadhāt*—He invested; *sva*—His own; *sattvam*—existence; *abhiṣṭutaḥ*—praised; *viśva-sṛjā*—by Brahmā (the creator of the universe); *prasūnaiḥ*—by flowers; *āpūryamāṇaḥ*—becoming satisfied; *vibudhaiḥ*—by the demigods; *paśyataḥ*—while looking on; *areḥ*—the enemy.

## TRANSLATION

**The Lord placed the earth within His sight on the surface of the water and transferred to her His own energy in the form of the ability to float on the water. While the enemy stood looking on, Brahmā, the creator of the universe, extolled the Lord, and the other demigods rained flowers on Him.**

## PURPORT

Those who are demons cannot understand how the Supreme Personality of Godhead floated the earth on water, but to devotees of the Lord this is not a very wonderful act. Not only the earth but many, many millions of planets are floating in the air, and this floating power is endowed upon them by the Lord; there is no other possible explanation. The materialists can explain that the planets are floating by the law of gravitation, but the law of gravitation works under the control or direction of the Supreme Lord. That is the version of *Bhagavad-gītā*, which confirms, by the Lord's statement, that behind the material laws or nature's laws and behind the growth, maintenance, production and evolution of all the planetary systems—behind everything—is the Lord's direction. The Lord's activities could be appreciated only by the demigods, headed by Brahmā, and therefore when they saw the uncommon prowess of the Lord in keeping the earth on the surface of the water, they showered flowers on Him in appreciation of His transcendental activity.

## TEXT 9

परानुषक्तं तपनीयोपकल्पं
महागदं काञ्चनचित्रदंशम् ।
मर्माण्यभीक्ष्णं प्रतुदन्तं दुरुक्तैः
प्रचण्डमन्युः प्रहसंस्तं बभाषे ॥ ९ ॥

*parānuṣaktaṁ tapanīyopakalpaṁ*
*mahā-gadaṁ kāñcana-citra-daṁśam*
*marmāṇy abhīkṣṇaṁ pratudantaṁ duruktaiḥ*
*pracaṇḍa-manyuḥ prahasaṁs taṁ babhāṣe*

*parā*—from behind; *anuṣaktam*—who followed very closely; *tapanīya-upakalpam*—who had a considerable amount of gold ornaments; *mahā-gadam*—with a great mace; *kāñcana*—golden; *citra*—beautiful; *daṁśam*—armor; *marmāṇi*—the core of the heart; *abhīkṣṇam*—constantly; *pratudantam*—piercing; *duruktaiḥ*—by abusive words; *pracaṇḍa*—terrible; *manyuḥ*—anger; *prahasan*—laughing; *tam*—to him; *babhāṣe*—He said.

## TRANSLATION

**The demon, who had a wealth of ornaments, bangles and beautiful golden armor on his body, chased the Lord from behind with a great mace. The Lord tolerated his piercing ill words, but in order to reply to him, He expressed His terrible anger.**

## PURPORT

The Lord could have chastised the demon immediately while the demon was deriding the Lord with ill words, but the Lord tolerated him to please the demigods and to show that they should not be afraid of demons while discharging their duties. Therefore His toleration was displayed mainly to drive away the fears of the demigods, who should know that the Lord is always present to protect them. The demon's derision of the Lord was just like the barking of dogs; the Lord did not care about it, since He was doing His own work in delivering the earth from the midst of the water. Materialistic demons always possess large amounts of gold in various shapes, and they think that a large amount of gold, physical strength and popularity can save them from the wrath of the Supreme Personality of Godhead.

## TEXT 10

श्रीभगवानुवाच
सत्यं वयं भो वनगोचरा मृगा
युष्मद्विधान्मृगये ग्रामसिंहान् ।
न मृत्युपाशैः प्रतिमुक्तस्य वीरा
विकत्थनं तव गृह्णन्त्यभद्र ॥१०॥

*śrī-bhagavān uvāca*
*satyaṁ vayaṁ bho vana-gocarā mṛgā*
*yuṣmad-vidhān mṛgaye grāma-siṁhān*
*na mṛtyu-pāśaiḥ pratimuktasya vīrā*
*vikatthanaṁ tava gṛhṇanty abhadra*

*śrī-bhagavān uvāca*—the Supreme Personality of Godhead said; *satyam*—indeed; *vayam*—We; *bhoḥ*—O; *vana-gocarāḥ*—dwelling in the forest; *mṛgāḥ*—creatures; *yuṣmat-vidhān*—like you; *mṛgaye*—I am searching to kill; *grāma-siṁhān*—dogs; *na*—not; *mṛtyu-pāśaiḥ*—by the bonds of death; *pratimuktasya*—of one who is bound; *vīrāḥ*—the heroes; *vikatthanam*—loose talk; *tava*—your; *gṛhṇanti*—take notice of; *abhadra*—O mischievous one.

## TRANSLATION

**The Personality of Godhead said: Indeed, We are creatures of the jungle, and We are searching after hunting dogs like you. One who is freed from the entanglement of death has no fear from the loose talk in which you are indulging, for you are bound up by the laws of death.**

## PURPORT

Demons and atheistic persons can go on insulting the Supreme Personality of Godhead, but they forget that they are subjected to the laws of birth and death. They think that simply by decrying the existence of the Supreme Lord or defying His stringent laws of nature, one can be freed from the clutches of birth and death. In *Bhagavad-gītā* it is said that simply by understanding the transcendental nature of God one can go back home, back to Godhead. But demons and atheistic persons do not try to understand the nature of the Supreme Lord; therefore they remain in the entanglement of birth and death.

## TEXT 11

एते वयं न्यासहरा रसौकसां
गतह्रियो गदया द्रावितास्ते ।
तिष्ठामहेऽथापि कथञ्चिदाजौ
स्थेयं क्व यामो बलिनोत्पाद्य वैरम् ॥११॥

*ete vayaṁ nyāsa-harā rasaukasāṁ*
*gata-hriyo gadayā drāvitās te*
*tiṣṭhāmahe 'thāpi kathañcid ājau*
*stheyaṁ kva yāmo balinotpādya vairam*

*ete*—Ourselves; *vayam*—We; *nyāsa*—of the charge; *harāḥ*—thieves; *rasā-okasām*—of the inhabitants of Rasātala; *gata-hriyaḥ*—shameless; *gadayā*—by the mace; *drāvitāḥ*—chased; *te*—your; *tiṣṭhāmahe*—We shall stay; *atha api*—nevertheless; *kathañcit*—somehow; *ājau*—on the battlefield; *stheyam*—We must stay; *kva*—where; *yāmaḥ*—can We go;

*balinā*—with a powerful enemy; *utpādya*—having created; *vairam*—enmity.

## TRANSLATION

**Certainly We have stolen the charge of the inhabitants of Rasātala and have lost all shame. Although bitten by your powerful mace, I shall stay here in the water for some time because, having created enmity with a powerful enemy, I now have no place to go.**

## PURPORT

The demon should have known that God cannot be driven out of any place, for He is all-pervading. Demons think of their possessions as their property, but actually everything belongs to the Supreme Personality of Godhead, who can take anything at any time He likes.

## TEXT 12

त्वं पद्रथानां किल यूथपाधिपो
घटस्व नोऽस्वस्तय आश्वनूहः ।
संस्थाप्य चास्मान् प्रमृजाश्रु स्वकानां
यः स्वां प्रतिज्ञां नातिपिपर्त्यसभ्यः ॥१२॥

*tvaṁ pad-rathānāṁ kila yūthapādhipo*
*ghaṭasva no 'svastaya āśv anūhaḥ*
*saṁsthāpya cāsmān pramṛjāśru svakānāṁ*
*yaḥ svāṁ pratijñāṁ nātipiparty asabhyaḥ*

*tvam*—you; *pad-rathānām*—of foot soldiers; *kila*—indeed; *yūtha-pa*—of the leaders; *adhipaḥ*—the commander; *ghaṭasva*—take steps; *naḥ*—Our; *asvastaye*—for defeat; *āśu*—promptly; *anūhaḥ*—without consideration; *saṁsthāpya*—having killed; *ca*—and; *asmān*—Us; *pramṛja*—wipe away; *aśru*—tears; *svakānām*—of your kith and kin; *yaḥ*—he who; *svām*—his own; *pratijñām*—promised word; *na*—not; *atipiparti*—fulfills; *asabhyaḥ*—not fit to sit in an assembly.

## TRANSLATION

**You are supposed to be the commander of many foot soldiers, and now you may take prompt steps to overthrow Us. Give up all your foolish talk and wipe out the cares of your kith and kin by slaying Us. One may be proud, yet he does not deserve a seat in an assembly if he fails to fulfill his promised word.**

## PURPORT

A demon may be a great soldier and commander of a large number of infantry, but in the presence of the Supreme Personality of Godhead he is powerless and is destined to die. The Lord, therefore, challenged the demon not to go away, but to fulfill his promised word to kill Him.

## TEXT 13

मैत्रेय उवाच

सोऽधिक्षिप्तो भगवता प्रलब्धश्च रुषा भृशम् ।
आजहारोल्बणं क्रोधं क्रीड्यमानोऽहिराडिव ॥१३॥

*maitreya uvāca*
*so 'dhikṣipto bhagavatā*
*pralabdhaś ca ruṣā bhṛśam*
*ājahārolbaṇaṁ krodhaṁ*
*krīḍyamāno 'hi-rāḍ iva*

*maitreyaḥ*—the great sage Maitreya; *uvāca*—said; *saḥ*—the demon; *adhikṣiptaḥ*—having been insulted; *bhagavatā*—by the Personality of Godhead; *pralabdhaḥ*—ridiculed; *ca*—and; *ruṣā*—angry; *bhṛśam*—greatly; *ājahāra*—collected; *ulbaṇam*—great; *krodham*—anger; *krīḍyamānaḥ*—being played with; *ahi-rāṭ*—a great cobra; *iva*—like.

## TRANSLATION

**Śrī Maitreya said: The demon, being thus challenged by the Personality of Godhead, became angry and agitated, and he trembled in anger like a challenged cobra.**

## PURPORT

A cobra is very fierce before ordinary persons, but before an enchanter who can play with him, he is a plaything. Similarly, a demon may be very powerful in his own domain, but before the Lord he is insignificant. The demon Rāvaṇa was a fierce figure before the demigods, but when he was before Lord Rāmacandra he trembled and prayed to his deity, Lord Śiva, but to no avail.

## TEXT 14

सृजन्नमर्षितः श्वासान्मन्युप्रचलितेन्द्रियः ।
आसाद्य तरसा दैत्यो गदयान्यहनद्धरिम् ॥१४॥

*sṛjann amarṣitaḥ śvāsān*
*manyu-pracalitendriyaḥ*
*āsādya tarasā daityo*
*gadayā nyahanad dharim*

*sṛjan*—giving out; *amarṣitaḥ*—being angry; *śvāsān*—breaths; *manyu*—by wrath; *pracalita*—agitated; *indriyaḥ*—whose senses; *āsādya*—attacking; *tarasā*—quickly; *daityaḥ*—the demon; *gadayā*—with his mace; *nyahanat*—struck; *harim*—Lord Hari.

## TRANSLATION

**Hissing indignantly, all his senses shaken by wrath, the demon quickly sprang upon the Lord and dealt Him a blow with his powerful mace.**

## TEXT 15

भगवांस्तु गदावेगं विसृष्टं रिपुणोरसि ।
अवञ्चयत्तिरश्चीनो योगारूढ इवान्तकम् ॥१५॥

*bhagavāṁs tu gadā-vegaṁ*
*visṛṣṭaṁ ripuṇorasi*
*avañcayat tiraścīno*
*yogārūḍha ivāntakam*

*bhagavān*—the Lord; *tu*—however; *gadā-vegam*—the blow of the mace; *visṛṣṭam*—thrown; *ripuṇā*—by the enemy; *urasi*—at His breast; *avañcayat*—dodged; *tiraścīnaḥ*—aside; *yoga-ārūḍhaḥ*—an accomplished *yogī; iva*—like; *antakam*—death.

## TRANSLATION

**The Lord, however, by moving slightly aside, dodged the violent mace-blow aimed at His breast by the enemy, just as an accomplished yogī would elude death.**

## PURPORT

The example is given herein that the perfect *yogī* can overcome a deathblow although it is offered by the laws of nature. It is useless for a demon to beat the transcendental body of the Lord with a powerful mace, for no one can surpass His prowess. Those who are advanced transcendentalists are freed from the laws of nature, and even a deathblow cannot act on them. Superficially it may be seen that a *yogī* is attacked by a deathblow, but by the grace of the Lord he can overcome many such attacks for the service of the Lord. As the Lord exists by His own independent prowess, by the grace of the Lord the devotees also exist for His service.

## TEXT 16

पुनर्गदां स्वामादाय भ्रामयन्तमभीक्ष्णशः ।
अभ्यधावद्धरिः क्रुद्धः संरम्भाद्दष्टदच्छदम् ॥१६॥

*punar gadāṁ svām ādāya*
*bhrāmayantam abhīkṣṇaśaḥ*
*abhyadhāvad dhariḥ kruddhaḥ*
*saṁrambhād daṣṭa-dacchadam*

*punaḥ*—again; *gadām*—mace; *svām*—his; *ādāya*—having taken; *bhrāmayantam*—brandishing; *abhīkṣṇaśaḥ*—repeatedly; *abhyadhāvat*—rushed to meet; *hariḥ*—the Personality of Godhead; *kruddhaḥ*—angry; *saṁrambhāt*—in rage; *daṣṭa*—bitten; *dacchadam*—his lip.

## TRANSLATION

**The Personality of Godhead now exhibited His anger and rushed to meet the demon, who bit his lip in rage, took up his mace again and began to repeatedly brandish it about.**

## TEXT 17

ततश्च गदयारातिं दक्षिणस्यां भ्रुवि प्रभुः ।
आजघ्ने स तु तां सौम्य गदया कोविदोऽहनत् ॥१७॥

*tataś ca gadayārātiṁ*
*dakṣiṇasyāṁ bhruvi prabhuḥ*
*ājaghne sa tu tāṁ saumya*
*gadayā kovido 'hanat*

*tataḥ*—then; *ca*—and; *gadayā*—with His mace; *arātim*—the enemy; *dakṣiṇasyām*—on the right; *bhruvi*—on the brow; *prabhuḥ*—the Lord; *ājaghne*—struck; *saḥ*—the Lord; *tu*—but; *tām*—the mace; *saumya*—O gentle Vidura; *gadayā*—with his mace; *kovidaḥ*—expert; *ahanat*—he saved himself.

## TRANSLATION

**Then with His mace the Lord struck the enemy on the right of his brow, but since the demon was expert in fighting, O gentle Vidura, he protected himself by a maneuver of his own mace.**

## TEXT 18

एवं गदाभ्यां गुर्वीभ्यां हर्यक्षो हरिरेव च ।
जिगीषया सुसंरब्धावन्योन्यमभिजघ्नतुः ॥१८॥

*evaṁ gadābhyāṁ gurvībhyāṁ*
*haryakṣo harir eva ca*
*jigīṣayā susaṁrabdhāv*
*anyonyam abhijaghnatuḥ*

*evam*—in this way; *gadābhyām*—with their maces; *gurvībhyām*—huge; *haryakṣaḥ*—the demon Haryakṣa (Hiraṇyākṣa); *hariḥ*—Lord

Hari; *eva*—certainly; *ca*—and; *jigīṣayā*—with a desire for victory; *susaṁrabdhau*—enraged; *anyonyam*—each other; *abhijaghnatuḥ*—they struck.

## TRANSLATION

**In this way, the demon Haryakṣa and the Lord, the Personality of Godhead, struck each other with their huge maces, each enraged and seeking his own victory.**

## PURPORT

Haryakṣa is another name for Hiraṇyākṣa, the demon.

## TEXT 19

तयोः स्पृधोस्तिग्मगदाहताङ्गयोः
क्षतास्रवघ्राणविवृद्धमन्य्वोः ।
विचित्रमार्गांश्चरतोर्जिगीषया
व्यभादिलायामिव शुष्मिणोर्मृधः ॥१९॥

*tayoḥ spṛdhos tigma-gadāhatāṅgayoḥ*
*kṣatāsrava-ghrāṇa-vivṛddha-manyvoḥ*
*vicitra-mārgāṁś carator jigīṣayā*
*vyabhād ilāyām iva śuṣmiṇor mṛdhaḥ*

*tayoḥ*—them; *spṛdhoḥ*—the two combatants; *tigma*—pointed; *gadā*—by the maces; *āhata*—injured; *aṅgayoḥ*—their bodies; *kṣata-āsrava*—blood coming out from the injuries; *ghrāṇa*—smell; *vivṛddha*—increased; *manyvoḥ*—anger; *vicitra*—of various kinds; *mārgān*—maneuvers; *caratoḥ*—performing; *jigīṣayā*—with a desire to win; *vyabhāt*—it looked like; *ilāyām*—for the sake of a cow (or the earth); *iva*—like; *śuṣmiṇoḥ*—of two bulls; *mṛdhaḥ*—an encounter.

## TRANSLATION

**There was keen rivalry between the two combatants; both had sustained injuries on their bodies from the blows of each other's pointed maces, and each grew more and more enraged at the smell of blood on his person. In their eagerness to win, they performed**

**maneuvers of various kinds, and their contest looked like an encounter between two forceful bulls for the sake of a cow.**

## PURPORT

Here the earth planet is called *ilā.* This earth was formerly known as Ilāvṛta-varṣa, and when Mahārāja Parīkṣit ruled the earth it was called Bhārata-varṣa. Actually, Bhārata-varṣa is the name for the entire planet, but gradually Bhārata-varṣa has come to mean India. As India has recently been divided into Pakistan and Hindustan, similarly the earth was formerly called Ilāvṛta-varṣa, but gradually as time passed it was divided by national boundaries.

## TEXT 20

दैत्यस्य यज्ञावयवस्य माया-
गृहीतवाराहतनोर्महात्मनः ।
कौरव्य मह्यां द्विषतोर्विमर्दनं
दिदृक्षुरागादृषिभिर्वृतः स्वराट् ॥२०॥

*daityasya yajñāvayavasya māyā-*
*gṛhīta-vārāha-tanor mahātmanaḥ*
*kauravya mahyāṁ dviṣator vimardanaṁ*
*didṛkṣur āgād ṛṣibhir vṛtaḥ svarāṭ*

*daityasya*—of the demon; *yajña-avayavasya*—of the Personality of Godhead (of whose body *yajña* is a part); *māyā*—through His potency; *gṛhīta*—was assumed; *vārāha*—of a boar; *tanoḥ*—whose form; *mahā-ātmanaḥ*—of the Supreme Lord; *kauravya*—O Vidura (descendant of Kuru); *mahyām*—for the sake of the world; *dviṣatoḥ*—of the two enemies; *vimardanam*—the fight; *didṛkṣuḥ*—desirous to see; *āgāt*—came; *ṛṣibhiḥ*—by the sages; *vṛtaḥ*—accompanied; *svarāṭ*—Brahmā.

## TRANSLATION

**O descendant of Kuru, Brahmā, the most independent demigod of the universe, accompanied by his followers, came to see the terrible fight for the sake of the world between the demon and the Personality of Godhead, who appeared in the form of a boar.**

## PURPORT

The fight between the Lord, the Supreme Personality of Godhead, and the demon is compared to a fight between bulls for the sake of a cow. The earth planet is also called *go*, or cow. As bulls fight between themselves to ascertain who will have union with a cow, there is always a constant fight between the demons and the Supreme Lord or His representative for supremacy over the earth. Here the Lord is significantly described as *yajñāvayava.* One should not consider the Lord to have the body of an ordinary boar. He can assume any form, and He possesses all such forms eternally. It is from Him that all other forms have emanated. This boar form is not to be considered the form of an ordinary hog; His body is actually full of *yajña,* or worshipful offerings. *Yajña* (sacrifices) are offered to Viṣṇu. *Yajña* means the body of Viṣṇu. His body is not material; therefore He should not be taken to be an ordinary boar.

Brahmā is described in this verse as *svarāṭ.* Actually, full independence is exclusive to the Lord Himself, but as part and parcel of the Supreme Lord, every living entity has a minute quantity of independence. Each and every one of the living entities within this universe has this minute independence, but Brahmā, being the chief of all living entities, has a greater potential of independence than any other. He is the representative of Kṛṣṇa, the Supreme Personality of Godhead, and has been assigned to preside over universal affairs. All other demigods work for him; therefore he is described here as *svarāṭ.* He is always accompanied by great sages and transcendentalists, all of whom came to see the bullfight between the demon and the Lord.

## TEXT 21

आसन्नशौण्डीरमपेतसाध्वसं
कृतप्रतीकारमहार्यविक्रमम् ।
विलक्ष्य दैत्यं भगवान् सहस्रणी-
र्जगाद नारायणमादिसूकरम् ॥२१॥

*āsanna-śauṇḍīram apeta-sādhvasaṁ*
*kṛta-pratīkāram ahārya-vikramam*

*vilakṣya daityaṁ bhagavān sahasra-ṇīr*
*jagāda nārāyaṇam ādi-sūkaram*

*āsanna*—attained; *śauṇḍīram*—power; *apeta*—devoid of; *sādhvasam*—fear; *kṛta*—making; *pratīkāram*—opposition; *ahārya*—unopposable; *vikramam*—having power; *vilakṣya*—having seen; *daityam*—the demon; *bhagavān*—the worshipful Brahmā; *sahasra-nīḥ*—the leader of thousands of sages; *jagāda*—addressed; *nārāyaṇam*—Lord Nārāyaṇa; *ādi*—the original; *sūkaram*—having the form of a boar.

## TRANSLATION

**After arriving at the place of combat, Brahmā, the leader of thousands of sages and transcendentalists, saw the demon, who had attained such unprecedented power that no one could fight with him. Brahmā then addressed Nārāyaṇa, who was assuming the form of a boar for the first time.**

## TEXTS 22–23

ब्रह्मोवाच
एष ते देव देवानामङ्घ्रिमूलमुपेयुषाम् ।
विप्राणां सौरभेयीणां भूतानामप्यनागसाम् ॥२२॥
आगस्कृद्भयकृद्दुष्कृदस्मद्राद्धवरोऽसुरः ।
अन्वेषन्नप्रतिरथो लोकानटति कण्टकः ॥२३॥

*brahmovāca*
*eṣa te deva devānām*
*aṅghri-mūlam upeyuṣām*
*viprāṇāṁ saurabheyīṇāṁ*
*bhūtānām apy anāgasām*

*āgas-kṛd bhaya-kṛd duṣkṛd*
*asmad-rāddha-varo 'suraḥ*
*anveṣann apratiratho*
*lokān aṭati kaṇṭakaḥ*

*brahmā uvāca*—Lord Brahmā said; *eṣaḥ*—this demon; *te*—Your; *deva*—O Lord; *devānām*—to the demigods; *aṅghri-mūlam*—Your feet; *upeyuṣām*—to those having obtained; *viprāṇām*—to the *brāhmaṇas; saurabheyīṇām*—to the cows; *bhūtānām*—to ordinary living entities; *api*—also; *anāgasām*—innocent; *āgaḥ-kṛt*—an offender; *bhaya-kṛt*—a source of fear; *duṣkṛt*—wrongdoer; *asmat*—from me; *rāddha-varaḥ*—having attained a boon; *asuraḥ*—a demon; *anveṣan*—searching; *apratirathaḥ*—having no proper combatant; *lokān*—all over the universe; *aṭati*—he wanders; *kaṇṭakaḥ*—being a pinprick for everyone.

## TRANSLATION

**Lord Brahmā said: My dear Lord, this demon has proved to be a constant pinprick to the demigods, the brāhmaṇas, the cows and innocent persons who are spotless and always dependent upon worshiping Your lotus feet. He has become a source of fear by unnecessarily harassing them. Since he has attained a boon from me, he has become a demon, always searching for a proper combatant, wandering all over the universe for this infamous purpose.**

## PURPORT

There are two classes of living entities; one is called *sura*, or the demigods, and the other is called *asura*, or the demons. Demons are generally fond of worshiping the demigods, and there are evidences that by such worship they get extensive power for their sense gratification. This later proves to be a cause of trouble to the *brāhmaṇas*, demigods and other innocent living entities. Demons habitually find fault with the demigods, *brāhmaṇas* and innocent, to whom they are a constant source of fear. The way of the demon is to take power from the demigods and then tease the demigods themselves. There is an instance of a great devotee of Lord Śiva who obtained a boon from Lord Śiva that the head of whomever he touched with his hand would come off its trunk. As soon as the boon was offered to him, the demon wanted to touch the very head of Lord Śiva. That is their way. The devotees of the Supreme Personality of Godhead do not, however, ask any favor for sense gratification. Even if they are offered liberation, they refuse it. They are happy simply engaging in the transcendental loving service of the Lord.

## TEXT 24

मैनं मायाविनं दृप्तं निरङ्कुशमसत्तमम् ।
आक्रीड बालवद्देव यथाशीविषमुत्थितम् ॥२४॥

*mainaṁ māyāvinaṁ dṛptaṁ*
*niraṅkuśam asattamam*
*ākrīḍa bālavad deva*
*yathāśīviṣam utthitam*

*mā*—do not; *enam*—him; *māyā-vinam*—skilled in conjuring tricks; *dṛptam*—arrogant; *niraṅkuśam*—self-sufficient; *asat-tamam*—most wicked; *ākrīḍa*—play with; *bāla-vat*—like a child; *deva*—O Lord; *yathā*—as; *āśīviṣam*—a serpent; *utthitam*—aroused.

## TRANSLATION

**Lord Brahmā continued: My dear Lord, there is no need to play with this serpentine demon, who is always very skilled in conjuring tricks and is arrogant, self-sufficient and most wicked.**

## PURPORT

No one is unhappy when a serpent is killed. It is a practice among village boys to catch a serpent by the tail and play with it for some time and then kill it. Similarly, the Lord could have killed the demon at once, but He played with him in the same way as a child plays with a snake before killing it. Brahmā requested, however, that since the demon was more wicked and undesirable than a serpent, there was no need to play with him. It was his wish that he be killed at once, without delay.

## TEXT 25

न यावदेष वर्धेत स्वां वेलां प्राप्य दारुणः ।
स्वां देव मायामास्थाय तावज्जह्यघमच्युत ॥२५॥

*na yāvad eṣa vardheta*
*svāṁ velāṁ prāpya dāruṇaḥ*

*svāṁ deva māyām āsthāya*
*tāvaj jahy agham acyuta*

*na yāvat*—before; *esaḥ*—this demon; *vardheta*—may increase; *svām*—his own; *velām*—demoniac hour; *prāpya*—having reached; *dāruṇaḥ*—formidable; *svām*—Your own; *deva*—O Lord; *māyām*—internal potency; *āsthāya*—using; *tāvat*—at once; *jahi*—kill; *agham*—the sinful one; *acyuta*—O infallible one.

### TRANSLATION

**Brahmā continued: My dear Lord, You are infallible. Please kill this sinful demon before the demoniac hour arrives and he presents another formidable approach favorable to him. You can kill him by Your internal potency without doubt.**

### TEXT 26

एषा घोरतमा सन्ध्या लोकच्छम्बट्करी प्रभो ।
उपसर्पति सर्वात्मन् सुराणां जयमावह ॥२६॥

*eṣā ghoratamā sandhyā*
*loka-cchambaṭ-karī prabho*
*upasarpati sarvātman*
*surāṇāṁ jayam āvaha*

*eṣā*—this; *ghora-tamā*—darkest; *sandhyā*—evening time; *loka*—the world; *chambaṭ-karī*—destroying; *prabho*—O Lord; *upasarpati*—is approaching; *sarva-ātman*—O Soul of all souls; *surāṇām*—to the demigods; *jayam*—victory; *āvaha*—bring.

### TRANSLATION

**My Lord, the darkest evening, which covers the world, is fast approaching. Since You are the Soul of all souls, kindly kill him and win victory for the demigods.**

## TEXT 27

अधुनैषोऽभिजिन्नाम योगो मौहूर्तिको ह्यगात् ।
शिवाय नस्त्वं सुहृदामाशु निस्तर दुस्तरम् ॥२७॥

*adhunaiṣo 'bhijin nāma*
*yogo mauhūrtiko hy agāt*
*śivāya nas tvaṁ suhṛdām*
*āśu nistara dustaram*

*adhunā*—now; *eṣaḥ*—this; *abhijit nāma*—called *abhijit; yogaḥ*—auspicious; *mauhūrtikaḥ*—moment; *hi*—indeed; *agāt*—has almost passed; *śivāya*—for the welfare; *naḥ*—of us; *tvam*—You; *suhṛdām*—of Your friends; *āśu*—quickly; *nistara*—dispose of; *dustaram*—the formidable foe.

## TRANSLATION

**The auspicious period known as abhijit, which is most opportune for victory, commenced at midday and has all but passed; therefore, in the interest of Your friends, please dispose of this formidable foe quickly.**

## TEXT 28

दिष्ट्या त्वां विहितं मृत्युमयमासादितः स्वयम् ।
विक्रम्यैनं मृधे हत्वा लोकानाधेहि शर्मणि ॥२८॥

*diṣṭyā tvāṁ vihitaṁ mṛtyum*
*ayam āsāditaḥ svayam*
*vikramyainaṁ mṛdhe hatvā*
*lokān ādhehi śarmaṇi*

*diṣṭyā*—by fortune; *tvām*—to You; *vihitam*—ordained; *mṛtyum*—death; *ayam*—this demon; *āsāditaḥ*—has come; *svayam*—of his own accord; *vikramya*—exhibiting Your prowess; *enam*—him; *mṛdhe*—in the duel; *hatvā*—killing; *lokān*—the worlds; *ādhehi*—establish; *śarmaṇi*—in peace.

## TRANSLATION

**This demon, luckily for us, has come of his own accord to You, his death ordained by You; therefore, exhibiting Your ways, kill him in the duel and establish the worlds in peace.**

*Thus end the Bhaktivedanta purports of the Third Canto, Eighteenth Chapter, of the* Śrīmad-Bhāgavatam, *entitled "The Battle Between Lord Boar and the Demon Hiraṇyākṣa."*

## CHAPTER NINETEEN

# The Killing of the Demon Hiraṇyākṣa

### TEXT 1

मैत्रेय उवाच
अवधार्य विरिञ्चस्य निर्व्यलीकामृतं वचः ।
प्रहस्य प्रेमगर्भेण तदपाङ्गेन सोऽग्रहीत् ॥ १ ॥

*maitreya uvāca*
*avadhārya viriñcasya*
*nirvyalīkāmṛtaṁ vacaḥ*
*prahasya prema-garbheṇa*
*tad apāṅgena so 'grahīt*

*maitreyaḥ uvāca*—Maitreya said; *avadhārya*—after hearing; *viriñcasya*—of Lord Brahmā; *nirvyalīka*—free from all sinful purposes; *amṛtam*—nectarean; *vacaḥ*—words; *prahasya*—heartily laughing; *prema-garbheṇa*—laden with love; *tat*—those words; *apāṅgena*—with a glance; *saḥ*—the Supreme Personality of Godhead; *agrahīt*—accepted.

### TRANSLATION

**Śrī Maitreya said: After hearing the words of Brahmā, the creator, which were free from all sinful purposes and as sweet as nectar, the Lord heartily laughed and accepted his prayer with a glance laden with love.**

### PURPORT

The word *nirvyalīka* is very significant. The prayers of the demigods or devotees of the Lord are free from all sinful purposes, but the prayers of demons are always filled with sinful purposes. The demon Hiraṇyākṣa became powerful by deriving a boon from Brahmā, and after attaining that boon he created a disturbance because of his sinful intentions. The prayers of Brahmā and other demigods are not to be compared to the prayers of the demons. Their purpose is to please the Supreme Lord; therefore the Lord smiled and accepted the prayer to kill the demon. Demons, who are never interested in praising the Supreme Personality of Godhead because they have no information of Him, go to the demigods, and in *Bhagavad-gītā* this is condemned. Persons who go to the demigods and pray for advancement in sinful activities are considered to be bereft of all intelligence. Demons have lost all intelligence because they do not know what is actually their self-interest. Even if they have information of the Supreme Personality of Godhead, they decline to approach Him; it is not possible for them to get their desired boons from the Supreme Lord because their purposes are always sinful. It is said that the dacoits in Bengal used to worship the goddess Kālī for fulfillment of their sinful desires to plunder others' property, but they never went to a Viṣṇu temple because they might have been unsuccessful in praying to Viṣṇu. Therefore the prayers of the demigods or the devotees of the Supreme Personality of Godhead are always untinged by sinful purposes.

## TEXT 2

ततः सपत्नं मुखतश्चरन्तमकुतोभयम् ।
जघानोत्पत्य गदया हनावसुरमक्षजः ॥ २ ॥

*tataḥ sapatnaṁ mukhataś*
*carantam akuto-bhayam*
*jaghānotpatya gadayā*
*hanāv asuram akṣajaḥ*

*tataḥ*—then; *sapatnam*—enemy; *mukhataḥ*—in front of Him; *carantam*—stalking; *akutaḥ-bhayam*—fearlessly; *jaghāna*—struck; *utpatya*—after springing up; *gadayā*—with His mace; *hanau*—at the chin; *asuram*—the demon; *akṣa-jaḥ*—the Lord, who was born from the nostril of Brahmā.

## TRANSLATION

**The Lord, who had appeared from the nostril of Brahmā, sprang and aimed His mace at the chin of His enemy, the Hiraṇyākṣa demon, who was stalking fearlessly before Him.**

### TEXT 3

सा हता तेन गदया विहता भगवत्करात् ।
विघूर्णितापतद्रेजे तदद्भुतमिवाभवत् ॥ ३ ॥

*sā hatā tena gadayā*
*vihatā bhagavat-karāt*
*vighūrṇitāpatad reje*
*tad adbhutam ivābhavat*

*sā*—that mace; *hatā*—struck; *tena*—by Hiraṇyākṣa; *gadayā*—with his mace; *vihatā*—slipped; *bhagavat*—of the Supreme Personality of Godhead; *karāt*—from the hand; *vighūrṇitā*—whirling; *apatat*—fell down; *reje*—was shining; *tat*—that; *adbhutam*—miraculous; *iva*—indeed; *abhavat*—was.

### TRANSLATION

**Struck by the demon's mace, however, the Lord's mace slipped from His hand and looked splendid as it fell down whirling. This was miraculous, for the mace was blazing wonderfully.**

### TEXT 4

स तदा लब्धतीर्थोऽपि न बबाधे निरायुधम् ।
मानयन् स मृधे धर्मं विष्वक्सेनं प्रकोपयन् ॥ ४ ॥

*sa tadā labdha-tīrtho 'pi*
*na babādhe nirāyudham*
*mānayan sa mṛdhe dharmaṁ*
*viṣvaksenaṁ prakopayan*

*saḥ*—that Hiraṇyākṣa; *tadā*—then; *labdha-tīrthaḥ*—having gained an excellent opportunity; *api*—although; *na*—not; *babādhe*—attacked; *nirāyudham*—having no weapon; *mānayan*—respecting; *saḥ*—Hiraṇyākṣa; *mṛdhe*—in battle; *dharmam*—the code of combat; *viṣvaksenam*—the Supreme Personality of Godhead; *prakopayan*—making angry.

## TRANSLATION

**Even though the demon had an excellent opportunity to strike his unarmed foe without obstruction, he respected the law of single combat, thereby kindling the fury of the Supreme Lord.**

## TEXT 5

गदायामपविद्धायां हाहाकारे विनिर्गते ।
मानयामास तद्धर्मं सुनाभं चास्मरद्विभुः ॥ ५ ॥

*gadāyām apaviddhāyāṁ*
*hāhā-kāre vinirgate*
*mānayām āsa tad-dharmaṁ*
*sunābhaṁ cāsmarad vibhuḥ*

*gadāyām*—as His mace; *apaviddhāyām*—fell; *hāhā-kāre*—a cry of alarm; *vinirgate*—arose; *mānayām āsa*—acknowledged; *tat*—of Hiraṇyākṣa; *dharmam*—righteousness; *sunābham*—the Sudarśana *cakra;* *ca*—and; *asmarat*—remembered; *vibhuḥ*—the Supreme Personality of Godhead.

## TRANSLATION

**As the Lord's mace fell to the ground and a cry of alarm arose from the witnessing crowd of gods and ṛṣis, the Personality of Godhead acknowledged the demon's love of righteousness and therefore invoked His Sudarśana discus.**

## TEXT 6

तं व्यग्रचक्रं दितिपुत्राधमेन
स्वपार्षदमुख्येन विषज्जमानम् ।
चित्रा वाचोऽतद्विदां खेचराणां
तत्र स्मासन् स्वस्ति तेऽमुं जहीति ॥ ६ ॥

*taṁ vyagra-cakraṁ diti-putrādhamena*
*sva-pārṣada-mukhyena viṣajjamānam*

*citrā vāco 'tad-vidāṁ khe-carāṇāṁ*
*tatra smāsan svasti te 'muṁ jahīti*

*tam*—unto the Personality of Godhead; *vyagra*—revolving; *cakram*—whose discus; *diti-putra*—son of Diti; *adhamena*—vile; *sva-pārṣada*—of His associates; *mukhyena*—with the chief; *viṣajjamānam*—playing; *citrāḥ*—various; *vācaḥ*—expressions; *a-tat-vidām*—of those who did not know; *khe-carāṇām*—flying in the sky; *tatra*—there; *sma āsan*—occurred; *svasti*—fortune; *te*—unto You; *amum*—him; *jahi*—please kill; *iti*—thus.

## TRANSLATION

**As the discus began to revolve in the Lord's hands and the Lord contended at close quarters with the chief of His Vaikuṇṭha attendants, who had been born as Hiraṇyākṣa, a vile son of Diti, there issued from every direction strange expressions uttered by those who were witnessing from airplanes. They had no knowledge of the Lord's reality, and they cried, "May victory attend You! Pray dispatch him. Play no more with him."**

## TEXT 7

स तं निशाम्यात्तरथाङ्गमग्रतो
व्यवस्थितं पद्मपलाशलोचनम् ।
विलोक्य चामर्षपरिप्लुतेन्द्रियो
रुषा स्वदन्तच्छदमादशच्छ्वसन् ॥ ७ ॥

*sa taṁ niśāmyātta-rathāṅgam agrato*
*vyavasthitaṁ padma-palāśa-locanam*
*vilokya cāmarṣa-pariplutendriyo*
*ruṣā sva-danta-cchadam ādaśac chvasan*

*saḥ*—that demon; *tam*—the Supreme Personality of Godhead; *niśāmya*—after seeing; *ātta-rathāṅgam*—armed with the Sudarśana disc; *agrataḥ*—before him; *vyavasthitam*—standing in position; *padma*—lotus flower; *palāśa*—petals; *locanam*—eyes; *vilokya*—after seeing; *ca*—and; *amarṣa*—by indignation; *paripluta*—overpowered; *indriyaḥ*—his senses; *ruṣā*—with great resentment; *sva-danta-chadam*—his own lip; *ādaśat*—bit; *śvasan*—hissing.

## TRANSLATION

**When the demon saw the Personality of Godhead, who had eyes just like lotus petals, standing in position before him, armed with His Sudarśana discus, his senses were overpowered by indignation. He began to hiss like a serpent, and he bit his lip in great resentment.**

## TEXT 8

करालदंष्ट्रश्चक्षुर्भ्यां सञ्चक्षाणो दहन्निव ।
अभिप्लुत्य स्वगदया हतोऽसीत्याहनद्धरिम् ॥ ८ ॥

*karāla-daṁṣṭraś cakṣurbhyāṁ*
*sañcakṣāṇo dahann iva*
*abhiplutya sva-gadayā*
*hato 'sīty āhanad dharim*

*karāla*—fearful; *daṁṣṭraḥ*—having tusks; *cakṣurbhyām*—with both eyes; *sañcakṣāṇaḥ*—staring; *dahan*—burning; *iva*—as if; *abhiplutya*—attacking; *sva-gadayā*—with his own club; *hataḥ*—slain; *asi*—You are; *iti*—thus; *āhanat*—struck; *harim*—at Hari.

## TRANSLATION

**The demon, who had fearful tusks, stared at the Personality of Godhead as though to burn Him. Springing into the air, he aimed his mace at the Lord, exclaiming at the same time, "You are slain!"**

## TEXT 9

पदा सव्येन तां साधो भगवान् यज्ञसूकरः ।
लीलया मिषतः शत्रोः प्राहरद्वातरंहसम् ॥ ९ ॥

*padā savyena tāṁ sādho*
*bhagavān yajña-sūkaraḥ*
*līlayā miṣataḥ śatroḥ*
*prāharad vāta-raṁhasam*

*padā*—with His foot; *savyena*—left; *tām*—that mace; *sādho*—O Vidura; *bhagavān*—the Supreme Personality of Godhead; *yajña-sūkaraḥ*—in His boar form, the enjoyer of all sacrifices; *līlayā*—playfully; *miṣataḥ*—looking on; *śatroḥ*—of His enemy (Hiraṇyākṣa); *prāharat*—knocked down; *vāta-raṁhasam*—having the force of a tempest.

## TRANSLATION

**O saintly Vidura, while His enemy looked on, the Lord in His boar form, the enjoyer of all sacrificial offerings, playfully knocked down the mace with His left foot, even as it came upon Him with the force of a tempest.**

## TEXT 10

आह चायुधमाधत्स्व घटस्व त्वं जिगीषसि ।
इत्युक्तः स तदा भूयस्ताडयन् व्यनदद् भृशम् ॥१०॥

*āha cāyudham ādhatsva*
*ghaṭasva tvaṁ jigīṣasi*
*ity uktaḥ sa tadā bhūyas*
*tāḍayan vyanadad bhṛśam*

*āha*—He said; *ca*—and; *āyudham*—weapon; *ādhatsva*—take up; *ghaṭasva*—try; *tvam*—you; *jigīṣasi*—are eager to conquer; *iti*—thus; *uktaḥ*—challenged; *saḥ*—Hiraṇyākṣa; *tadā*—at that time; *bhūyaḥ*—again; *tāḍayan*—striking at; *vyanadat*—roared; *bhṛśam*—loudly.

## TRANSLATION

**The Lord then said: "Take up your weapon and try again, eager as you are to conquer Me." Challenged in these words, the demon aimed his mace at the Lord and once more loudly roared.**

## TEXT 11

तां स आपततीं वीक्ष्य भगवान् समवस्थितः ।
जग्राह लीलया प्राप्तां गरुत्मानिव पन्नगीम् ॥११॥

*tāṁ sa āpatatīṁ vīkṣya*
*bhagavān samavasthitaḥ*
*jagrāha līlayā prāptāṁ*
*garutmān iva pannagīm*

*tām*—that mace; *saḥ*—He; *āpatatīm*—flying toward; *vīkṣya*—after seeing; *bhagavān*—the Supreme Personality of Godhead; *samavasthitaḥ*—stood firmly; *jagrāha*—caught; *līlayā*—easily; *prāptām*—entered into His presence; *garutmān*—Garuḍa; *iva*—as; *pannagīm*—a serpent.

## TRANSLATION

**When the Lord saw the mace flying toward Him, He stood firmly where He was and caught it with the same ease as Garuḍa, the king of birds, would seize a serpent.**

## TEXT 12

स्वपौरुषे प्रतिहते हतमानो महासुरः ।
नैच्छद्गदां दीयमानां हरिणा विगतप्रभः ॥१२॥

*sva-pauruṣe pratihate*
*hata-māno mahāsuraḥ*
*naicchad gadāṁ dīyamānāṁ*
*hariṇā vigata-prabhaḥ*

*sva-pauruṣe*—his valor; *pratihate*—frustrated; *hata*—destroyed; *mānaḥ*—pride; *mahā-asuraḥ*—the great demon; *na aicchat*—desired not (to take); *gadām*—the mace; *dīyamānām*—being offered; *hariṇā*—by Hari; *vigata-prabhaḥ*—reduced in splendor.

## TRANSLATION

**His valor thus frustrated, the great demon felt humiliated and was put out of countenance. He was reluctant to take back the mace when it was offered by the Personality of Godhead.**

### TEXT 13

जग्राह त्रिशिखं शूलं ज्वलज्ज्वलनलोलुपम् ।
यज्ञाय धृतरूपाय विप्रायाभिचरन् यथा ॥१३॥

*jagrāha tri-śikhaṁ śūlaṁ*
*jvalaj-jvalana-lolupam*
*yajñāya dhṛta-rūpāya*
*viprāyābhicaran yathā*

*jagrāha*—took up; *tri-śikham*—three-pointed; *śūlam*—trident; *jvalat*—flaming; *jvalana*—fire; *lolupam*—rapacious; *yajñāya*—at the enjoyer of all sacrifices; *dhṛta-rūpāya*—in the form of Varāha; *viprāya*—unto a *brāhmaṇa; abhicaran*—acting malevolently; *yathā*—as.

### TRANSLATION

**He now took a trident which was as rapacious as a flaming fire and hurled it against the Lord, the enjoyer of all sacrifices, even as one would use penance for a malevolent purpose against a holy brāhmaṇa.**

### TEXT 14

तदोजसा दैत्यमहाभटार्पितं
चकासदन्तःख उदीर्णदीधिति ।
चक्रेण चिच्छेद निशातनेमिना
हरिर्यथा तार्क्ष्यपतत्रमुज्झितम् ॥१४॥

*tad ojasā daitya-mahā-bhaṭārpitaṁ*
*cakāsad antaḥ-kha udīrṇa-dīdhiti*
*cakreṇa ciccheda niśāta-neminā*
*harir yathā tārkṣya-patatram ujjhitam*

*tat*—that trident; *ojasā*—with all his strength; *daitya*—among the demons; *mahā-bhaṭa*—by the mighty fighter; *arpitam*—hurled; *cakāsat*—shining; *antaḥ-khe*—in the middle of the sky; *udīrṇa*—increased; *dīdhiti*—illumination; *cakreṇa*—by the Sudarśana disc; *ciccheda*—He cut to pieces; *niśāta*—sharpened; *neminā*—rim; *hariḥ*—

Indra; *yathā*—as; *tārkṣya*—of Garuḍa; *patatram*—the wing; *ujjhitam*—abandoned.

## TRANSLATION

**Hurled by the mighty demon with all his strength, the flying trident shone brightly in the sky. The Personality of Godhead, however, tore it to pieces with His discus Sudarśana, which had a sharp-edged rim, even as Indra cut off a wing of Garuḍa.**

## PURPORT

The context of the reference given herein regarding Garuḍa and Indra is this. Once upon a time, Garuḍa, the carrier of the Lord, snatched away a nectar pot from the hands of the demigods in heaven in order to liberate his mother, Vinatā, from the clutches of his stepmother, Kadrū, the mother of the serpents. On learning of this, Indra, the King of heaven, hurled his thunderbolt against Garuḍa. With a view to respect the infallibility of Indra's weapon, Garuḍa, though otherwise invincible, being the Lord's own mount, dropped one of his wings, which was shattered to pieces by the thunderbolt. The inhabitants of higher planets are so sensible that even in the process of fighting they observe the preliminary rules and regulations of gentleness. In this case, Garuḍa wanted to show respect for Indra; since he knew that Indra's weapon must destroy something, he offered his wing.

## TEXT 15

वृक्णे स्वशूले बहुधारिणा हरेः
प्रत्येत्य विस्तीर्णमुरो विभूतिमत् ।
प्रवृद्धरोषः स कठोरमुष्टिना
नदन् प्रहृत्यान्तरधीयतासुरः ॥१५॥

*vṛkṇe sva-śūle bahudhāriṇā hareḥ*
*pratyetya vistīrṇam uro vibhūtimat*
*pravṛddha-roṣaḥ sa kaṭhora-muṣṭinā*
*nadan prahṛtyāntaradhīyatāsuraḥ*

*vṛkṇe*—when cut; *sva-śūle*—his trident; *bahudhā*—to many pieces; *ariṇā*—by the Sudarśana *cakra; hareḥ*—of the Supreme Personality of Godhead; *pratyetya*—after advancing toward; *vistīrṇam*—broad; *uraḥ*—chest; *vibhūti-mat*—the abode of the goddess of fortune; *pravṛddha*—having been increased; *roṣaḥ*—anger; *saḥ*—Hiraṇyākṣa; *kaṭhora*—hard; *muṣṭinā*—with his fist; *nadan*—roaring; *prahṛtya*—after striking; *antaradhīyata*—disappeared; *asuraḥ*—the demon.

## TRANSLATION

**The demon was enraged when his trident was cut to pieces by the discus of the Personality of Godhead. He therefore advanced toward the Lord and, roaring aloud, struck his hard fist against the Lord's broad chest, which bore the mark of Śrīvatsa. Then he went out of sight.**

## PURPORT

Śrīvatsa is a curl of white hair on the chest of the Lord which is a special sign of His being the Supreme Personality of Godhead. In Vaikuṇṭhaloka or in Goloka Vṛndāvana, the inhabitants are exactly of the same form as the Personality of Godhead, but by this Śrīvatsa mark on the chest of the Lord He is distinguished from all others.

## TEXT 16

तेनेत्थमाहतः क्षत्तर्भगवानादिसूकरः ।
नाकम्पत मनाक् क्वापि स्रजा हत इव द्विपः ॥१६॥

*tenettham āhataḥ kṣattar*
*bhagavān ādi-sūkaraḥ*
*nākampata manāk kvāpi*
*srajā hata iva dvipaḥ*

*tena*—by Hiraṇyākṣa; *ittham*—thus; *āhataḥ*—struck; *kṣattaḥ*—O Vidura; *bhagavān*—the Supreme Personality of Godhead; *ādi-sūkaraḥ*—the first boar; *na akampata*—did not feel quaking; *manāk*—even slightly; *kva api*—anywhere; *srajā*—by a garland of flowers; *hataḥ*—struck; *iva*—as; *dvipaḥ*—an elephant.

## TRANSLATION

**Hit in this manner by the demon, O Vidura, the Lord, who had appeared as the first boar, did not feel the least quaking in any part of His body, any more than an elephant would when struck with a wreath of flowers.**

## PURPORT

As previously explained, the demon was originally a servitor of the Lord in Vaikuṇṭha, but somehow or other he fell as a demon. His fight with the Supreme Lord was meant for his liberation. The Lord enjoyed the striking on His transcendental body, just like a fully grown-up father fighting with his child. Sometimes a father takes pleasure in having a mock fight with his small child, and similarly the Lord felt Hiraṇyākṣa's striking on His body to be like flowers offered for worship. In other words, the Lord desired to fight in order to enjoy His transcendental bliss; therefore He enjoyed the attack.

## TEXT 17

अथोरुधासृजन्मायां योगमायेश्वरे हरौ ।
यां विलोक्य प्रजास्त्रस्ता मेनिरेऽस्योपसंयमम् ॥१७॥

*athorudhāsṛjan māyāṁ*
*yoga-māyeśvare harau*
*yāṁ vilokya prajās trastā*
*menire 'syopasaṁyamam*

*atha*—then; *urudhā*—in many ways; *asṛjat*—he cast; *māyām*—conjuring tricks; *yoga-māyā-īśvare*—the Lord of *yogamāyā; harau*—at Hari; *yām*—which; *vilokya*—after seeing; *prajāḥ*—the people; *trastāḥ*—fearful; *menire*—thought; *asya*—of this universe; *upasaṁyamam*—the dissolution.

## TRANSLATION

**The demon, however, employed many conjuring tricks against the Personality of Godhead, who is the Lord of yogamāyā. At the sight of this the people were filled with alarm and thought that the dissolution of the universe was near.**

## PURPORT

The fighting enjoyment of the Supreme Lord with His devotee, who had been converted into a demon, appeared severe enough to bring about the dissolution of the universe. This is the greatness of the Supreme Personality of Godhead; even the wavering of His little finger appears to be a great and very dangerous movement in the eyes of the inhabitants of the universe.

## TEXT 18

प्रववुर्वायवश्चण्डास्तमः पांसवमैरयन्।
दिग्भ्यो निपेतुर्ग्रावाणः क्षेपणैः प्रहिता इव ॥१८॥

*pravavur vāyavaś caṇḍās*
*tamaḥ pāṁsavam airayan*
*digbhyo nipetur grāvāṇaḥ*
*kṣepaṇaiḥ prahitā iva*

*pravavuḥ*—were blowing; *vāyavaḥ*—winds; *caṇḍāḥ*—fierce; *tamaḥ*—darkness; *pāṁsavam*—caused by dust; *airayan*—were spreading; *digbhyaḥ*—from every direction; *nipetuḥ*—came down; *grāvāṇaḥ*—stones; *kṣepaṇaiḥ*—by machine guns; *prahitāḥ*—thrown; *iva*—as if.

## TRANSLATION

**Fierce winds began to blow from all directions, spreading darkness occasioned by dust and hail storms; stones came in volleys from every corner, as if thrown by machine guns.**

## TEXT 19

द्यौर्नष्टभगणाभ्रौघैः सविद्युत्स्तनयित्नुभिः।
वर्षद्भिः पूयकेशासृग्विण्मूत्रास्थीनि चासकृत्॥१९॥

*dyaur naṣṭa-bhagaṇābhraughaiḥ*
*sa-vidyut-stanayitnubhiḥ*
*varṣadbhiḥ pūya-keśāsṛg-*
*viṇ-mūtrāsthīni cāsakṛt*

*dyauḥ*—the sky; *naṣṭa*—having disappeared; *bha-gaṇa*—luminaries; *abhra*—of clouds; *oghaiḥ*—by masses; *sa*—accompanied by; *vidyut*—lightning; *stanayitnubhiḥ*—and thunder; *varṣadbhiḥ*—raining; *pūya*—pus; *keśa*—hair; *asṛk*—blood; *viṭ*—stool; *mūtra*—urine; *asthīni*—bones; *ca*—and; *asakṛt*—again and again.

## TRANSLATION

**The luminaries in outer space disappeared due to the sky's being overcast with masses of clouds, which were accompanied by lightning and thunder. The sky rained pus, hair, blood, stool, urine and bones.**

## TEXT 20

गिरयः प्रत्यदृश्यन्त नानायुधमुचोऽनघ ।
दिग्वाससो यातुधान्यः शूलिन्यो मुक्तमूर्धजाः ॥२०॥

*girayaḥ pratyadṛśyanta*
*nānāyudha-muco 'nagha*
*dig-vāsaso yātudhānyaḥ*
*śūlinyo mukta-mūrdhajāḥ*

*girayaḥ*—mountains; *pratyadṛśyanta*—appeared; *nānā*—various; *āyudha*—weapons; *mucaḥ*—discharging; *anagha*—O sinless Vidura; *dik-vāsasaḥ*—naked; *yātudhānyaḥ*—demonesses; *śūlinyaḥ*—armed with tridents; *mukta*—hanging loose; *mūrdhajāḥ*—hair.

## TRANSLATION

**O sinless Vidura, mountains discharged weapons of various kinds, and naked demonesses armed with tridents appeared with their hair hanging loose.**

## TEXT 21

बहुभिर्यक्षरक्षोभिः पत्त्यश्वरथकुञ्जरैः ।
आततायिभिरुत्सृष्टा हिंस्रा वाचोऽतिवैशसाः ॥२१॥

*bahubhir yakṣa-rakṣobhiḥ*
*patty-aśva-ratha-kuñjaraiḥ*
*ātatāyibhir utsṛṣṭā*
*hiṁsrā vāco 'tivaiśasāḥ*

*bahubhiḥ*—by many; *yakṣa-rakṣobhiḥ*—Yakṣas and Rākṣasas; *patti*—marching on foot; *aśva*—on horses; *ratha*—on chariots; *kuñjaraiḥ*—or on elephants; *ātatāyibhiḥ*—ruffians; *utsṛṣṭāḥ*—were uttered; *hiṁsrāḥ*—cruel; *vācaḥ*—words; *ati-vaiśasāḥ*—murderous.

## TRANSLATION

**Cruel and savage slogans were uttered by hosts of ruffian Yakṣas and Rākṣasas, who all either marched on foot or rode on horses, elephants or chariots.**

## TEXT 22

प्रादुष्कृतानां मायानामासुरीणां विनाशयत् ।
सुदर्शनास्त्रं भगवान् प्रायुङ्क्त दयितं त्रिपात् ॥२२॥

*prāduṣkṛtānāṁ māyānām*
*āsurīṇāṁ vināśayat*
*sudarśanāstraṁ bhagavān*
*prāyuṅkta dayitaṁ tri-pāt*

*prāduṣkṛtānām*—displayed; *māyānām*—the magical forces; *āsurīṇām*—displayed by the demon; *vināśayat*—desiring to destroy; *sudarśana-astram*—the Sudarśana weapon; *bhagavān*—the Supreme Personality of Godhead; *prāyuṅkta*—threw; *dayitam*—beloved; *tri-pāt*—the enjoyer of all sacrifices.

## TRANSLATION

**The Lord, the personal enjoyer of all sacrifices, now discharged His beloved Sudarśana, which was capable of dispersing the magical forces displayed by the demon.**

## PURPORT

Even famous *yogīs* and demons can sometimes enact very magical feats by their mystic power, but in the presence of the Sudarśana *cakra*, when it is let loose by the Lord, all such magical jugglery is dispersed. The instance of the quarrel between Durvāsā Muni and Mahārāja Ambarīṣa is a practical example in this matter. Durvāsā Muni wanted to display many magical wonders, but when the Sudarśana *cakra* appeared, Durvāsā himself was afraid and fled to various planets for his personal protection. The Lord is described here as *tri-pāt*, which means that He is the enjoyer of three kinds of sacrifices. In *Bhagavad-gītā* the Lord confirms that He is the beneficiary and enjoyer of all sacrifices, penances and austerities. The Lord is the enjoyer of three kinds of *yajña*. As further described in *Bhagavad-gītā*, there are sacrifices of goods, sacrifices of meditation and sacrifices of philosophical speculation. Those on the paths of *jñāna*, *yoga* and *karma* all have to come in the end to the Supreme Lord because *vāsudevaḥ sarvam iti*—the Supreme Lord is the ultimate enjoyer of everything. That is the perfection of all sacrifice.

## TEXT 23

तदा दितेः समभवत्सहसा हृदि वेपथुः ।
स्मरन्त्या भर्तुरादेशं स्तनाच्चासृक् प्रसुस्रुवे ॥२३॥

*tadā diteḥ samabhavat*
*sahasā hṛdi vepathuḥ*
*smarantyā bhartur ādeśaṁ*
*stanāc cāsṛk prasusruve*

*tadā*—at that moment; *diteḥ*—of Diti; *samabhavat*—occurred; *sahasā*—suddenly; *hṛdi*—in the heart; *vepathuḥ*—a shudder; *smarantyāḥ*—recalling; *bhartuḥ*—of her husband, Kaśyapa; *ādeśam*—the words; *stanāt*—from her breast; *ca*—and; *asṛk*—blood; *prasusruve*—flowed.

## TRANSLATION

**At that very moment, a shudder suddenly ran through the heart of Diti, the mother of Hiraṇyākṣa. She recalled the words of her husband, Kaśyapa, and blood flowed from her breasts.**

## PURPORT

At Hiraṇyākṣa's last moment, his mother, Diti, remembered what her husband had said. Although her sons would be demons, they would have the advantage of being killed by the Personality of Godhead Himself. She remembered this incident by the grace of the Lord, and her breasts flowed blood instead of milk. In many instances we find that when a mother is moved by affection for her sons, milk flows from her breasts. In the case of the demon's mother, the blood could not transform into milk, but it flowed down her breasts as it was. Blood transforms into milk. To drink milk is auspicious, but to drink blood is inauspicious, although they are one and the same thing. This formula is applicable in the case of cow's milk also.

## TEXT 24

विनष्टासु स्वमायासु भूयश्चाव्रज्य केशवम् ।
रुषोपगूहमानोऽमुं ददृशेऽवस्थितं बहिः ॥२४॥

*vinaṣṭāsu sva-māyāsu*
*bhūyaś cāvrajya keśavam*
*ruṣopagūhamāno 'muṁ*
*dadṛśe 'vasthitaṁ bahiḥ*

*vinaṣṭāsu*—when dispelled; *sva-māyāsu*—his magic forces; *bhūyaḥ*—again; *ca*—and; *āvrajya*—after coming into the presence; *keśavam*—the Supreme Personality of Godhead; *ruṣā*—full of rage; *upagūhamānaḥ*—embracing; *amum*—the Lord; *dadṛśe*—saw; *avasthitam*—standing; *bahiḥ*—outside.

## TRANSLATION

**When the demon saw his magic forces dispelled, he once again came into the presence of the Personality of Godhead, Keśava, and, full of rage, tried to embrace Him within his arms to crush Him. But to his great amazement he found the Lord standing outside the circle of his arms.**

## PURPORT

In this verse the Lord is addressed as Keśava because He killed the demon Keśī in the beginning of creation. Keśava is also a name of Kṛṣṇa.

Kṛṣṇa is the origin of all incarnations, and it is confirmed in *Brahma-saṁhitā* that Govinda, the Supreme Personality of Godhead, the cause of all causes, exists simultaneously in His different incarnations and expansions. The demon's attempt to measure the Supreme Personality of Godhead is significant. The demon wanted to embrace Him with his arms, thinking that with his limited arms he could capture the Absolute by material power. He did not know that God is the greatest of the great and the smallest of the small. No one can capture the Supreme Lord or bring Him under his control. But the demoniac person always attempts to measure the length and breadth of the Supreme Lord. By His inconceivable potency the Lord can become the universal form, as explained in *Bhagavad-gītā*, and at the same time He can remain within the box of His devotees as their worshipable Deity. There are many devotees who keep a statue of the Lord in a small box and carry it with them everywhere; every morning they worship the Lord in the box. The Supreme Lord, Keśava, or the Personality of Godhead, Kṛṣṇa, is not bound by any measurement of our calculation. He can remain with His devotee in any suitable form, yet He is unapproachable by any amount of demoniac activities.

## TEXT 25

**तं मुष्टिभिर्विनिघ्नन्तं वज्रसारैरधोक्षजः ।**
**करेण कर्णमूलेऽहन् यथा त्वाष्ट्रं मरुत्पतिः ॥२५॥**

*taṁ muṣṭibhir vinighnantaṁ*
*vajra-sārair adhokṣajaḥ*
*kareṇa karṇa-mūle 'han*
*yathā tvāṣṭraṁ marut-patiḥ*

*tam*—Hiraṇyākṣa; *muṣṭibhiḥ*—with his fists; *vinighnantam*—striking; *vajra-sāraiḥ*—as hard as a thunderbolt; *adhokṣajaḥ*—Lord Adhokṣaja; *kareṇa*—with the hand; *karṇa-mūle*—at the root of the ear; *ahan*—struck; *yathā*—as; *tvāṣṭram*—the demon Vṛtra (son of Tvaṣṭā); *marut-patiḥ*—Indra (lord of the Maruts).

## TRANSLATION

**The demon now began to strike the Lord with his hard fists, but Lord Adhokṣaja slapped him in the root of the ear, even as Indra, the lord of the Maruts, hit the demon Vṛtra.**

## PURPORT

The Lord is explained here to be *adhokṣaja,* beyond the reach of all material calculation. *Akṣaja* means "the measurement of our senses," and *adhokṣaja* means "that which is beyond the measurement of our senses."

## TEXT 26

स आहतो विश्वजिता ह्यवज्ञया
परिभ्रमद्गात्र उदस्तलोचनः ।
विशीर्णबाह्वङ्घ्रिशिरोरुहोऽपतद्
यथा नगेन्द्रो लुलितो नभस्वता ॥२६॥

*sa āhato viśva-jitā hy avajñayā*
*paribhramad-gātra udasta-locanaḥ*
*viśīrṇa-bāhv-aṅghri-śiroruho 'patad*
*yathā nagendro lulito nabhasvatā*

*saḥ*—he; *āhataḥ*—having been struck; *viśva-jitā*—by the Supreme Personality of Godhead; *hi*—though; *avajñayā*—indifferently; *paribhramat*—wheeling; *gātraḥ*—body; *udasta*—bulged out; *locanaḥ*—eyes; *viśīrṇa*—broken; *bāhu*—arms; *aṅghri*—legs; *śiraḥ-ruhaḥ*—hair; *apatat*—fell down; *yathā*—like; *naga-indraḥ*—a gigantic tree; *lulitaḥ*—uprooted; *nabhasvatā*—by the wind.

## TRANSLATION

**Though struck indifferently by the Lord, the conqueror of all, the demon's body began to wheel. His eyeballs bulged out of their sockets. His arms and legs broken and the hair on his head scattered, he fell down dead, like a gigantic tree uprooted by the wind.**

## PURPORT

It does not take even a moment for the Lord to kill any powerful demon, including Hiraṇyākṣa. The Lord could have killed him long before, but He allowed the demon to display the full extent of his magical feats. One may know that by magical feats, by scientific advancement of knowledge or by material power one cannot become the equal of the

Supreme Personality of Godhead. His one signal is sufficient to destroy all our attempts. His inconceivable power, as displayed here, is so strong that the demon, despite all his demoniac maneuvers, was killed by the Lord when the Lord desired, simply by one slap.

## TEXT 27

क्षितौ शयानं तमकुण्ठवर्चसं
करालदंष्ट्रं परिदष्टदच्छदम् ।
अजादयो वीक्ष्य शशंसुरागता
अहो इमां को नु लभेत संस्थितिम् ॥२७॥

*kṣitau śayānaṁ tam akuṇṭha-varcasaṁ*
*karāla-daṁṣṭraṁ paridaṣṭa-dacchadam*
*ajādayo vīkṣya śaśaṁsur āgatā*
*aho imaṁ ko nu labheta saṁsthitim*

*kṣitau*—on the ground; *śayānam*—lying; *tam*—Hiraṇyākṣa; *akuṇṭha*—unfaded; *varcasam*—glow; *karāla*—fearful; *daṁṣṭram*—teeth; *paridaṣṭa*—bitten; *dat-chadam*—lip; *aja-ādayaḥ*—Brahmā and others; *vīkṣya*—having seen; *śaśaṁsuḥ*—admiringly said; *āgatāḥ*—arrived; *aho*—oh; *imam*—this; *kaḥ*—who; *nu*—indeed; *labheta*—could meet; *saṁsthitim*—death.

## TRANSLATION

**Aja [Brahmā] and others arrived on the spot to see the fearfully tusked demon lying on the ground, biting his lip. The glow of his face was yet unfaded, and Brahmā admiringly said: Oh, who could meet such blessed death?**

## PURPORT

Although the demon was dead, his bodily luster was unfaded. This is very peculiar because when a man or animal is dead, the body immediately becomes pale, the luster gradually fades, and decomposition takes place. But here, although Hiraṇyākṣa lay dead, his bodily luster was unfaded because the Lord, the Supreme Spirit, was touching his body. One's bodily luster remains fresh only as long as the spirit soul is present. Although the demon's soul had departed his body, the Supreme Spirit touched the body, and therefore his bodily luster did not fade. The individual soul is different from the Supreme Personality of Godhead. One who sees the Supreme Personality of Godhead when he quits his body is certainly very fortunate, and therefore personalities like Brahmā and the other demigods eulogized the death of the demon.

## TEXT 28

यं योगिनो योगसमाधिना रहो
ध्यायन्ति लिङ्गादसतो मुमुक्षया ।
तस्यैष दैत्यऋषभः पदाहतो
मुखं प्रपश्यंस्तनुमुत्ससर्ज ह ॥२८॥

*yaṁ yogino yoga-samādhinā raho*
*dhyāyanti liṅgād asato mumukṣayā*
*tasyaiṣa daitya-ṛṣabhaḥ padāhato*
*mukhaṁ prapaśyaṁs tanum utsasarja ha*

*yam*—whom; *yoginaḥ*—the *yogīs; yoga-samādhinā*—in mystic trance; *rahaḥ*—in seclusion; *dhyāyanti*—meditate upon; *liṅgāt*—from the body; *asataḥ*—unreal; *mumukṣayā*—seeking freedom; *tasya*—of Him; *eṣaḥ*—this; *daitya*—son of Diti; *ṛṣabhaḥ*—the crest jewel; *padā*—by a foot; *āhataḥ*—struck; *mukham*—countenance; *prapaśyan*—while gazing on; *tanum*—the body; *utsasarja*—he cast off; *ha*—indeed.

## TRANSLATION

**Brahmā continued: He was struck by a forefoot of the Lord, whom yogīs, seeking freedom from their unreal material bodies, meditate upon in seclusion in mystic trance. While gazing on His countenance, this crest jewel of Diti's sons has cast off his mortal coil.**

## PURPORT

The process of *yoga* is very clearly described in this verse of *Śrīmad-Bhāgavatam.* It is said here that the ultimate end of the *yogīs* and mystics who perform meditation is to get rid of this material body. Therefore they meditate in secluded places to attain yogic trance. *Yoga* has to be performed in a secluded place, not in public or in a demonstration on stage, as nowadays practiced by many so-called *yogīs*. Real *yoga* aims at ridding one of the material body. *Yoga* practice is not intended to keep the body fit and young. Such advertisements of so-called *yoga* are not approved by any standard method. Particularly mentioned in this verse is the word *yam*, or "unto whom," indicating that meditation should be targeted on the Personality of Godhead. Even if one concentrates his mind on the boar form of the Lord, that is also *yoga*. As confirmed in *Bhagavad-gītā*, one who concentrates his mind constantly in meditation upon the Personality of Godhead in one of His many varieties of forms is the first-class *yogī*, and he can very easily attain trance simply by meditating upon the form of the Lord. If one is able to continue such meditation on the Lord's form at the time of one's death, one is liberated from this mortal body and is transferred to the kingdom of God. This opportunity was given to the demon by the Lord, and therefore Brahmā and other demigods were astonished. In other words, the perfection of *yoga* practice can be attained by a demon also if he is simply kicked by the Lord.

## TEXT 29

एतौ तौ पार्षदावस्य शापाद्यातावसद्गतिम् ।
पुनः कतिपयैः स्थानं प्रपत्स्येते ह जन्मभिः ॥२९॥

*etau tau pārṣadāv asya*
*śāpād yātāv asad-gatim*
*punaḥ katipayaiḥ sthānaṁ*
*prapatsyete ha janmabhiḥ*

*etau*—these two; *tau*—both; *pārṣadau*—personal assistants; *asya*—of the Personality of Godhead; *śāpāt*—because of being cursed; *yātau*—have gone; *asat-gatim*—to take birth in a demoniac family; *punaḥ*—again; *katipayaiḥ*—a few; *sthānam*—own place; *prapatsyete*—will get back; *ha*—indeed; *janmabhiḥ*—after births.

## TRANSLATION

**These two personal assistants of the Supreme Lord, having been cursed, have been destined to take birth in demoniac families. After a few such births, they will return to their own positions.**

## TEXT 30

देवा ऊचुः

नमो नमस्तेऽखिलयज्ञतन्तवे
स्थितौ गृहीतामलसत्त्वमूर्तये ।
दिष्ट्या हतोऽयं जगतामरुन्तुद-
स्त्वत्पादभक्त्या वयमीश निर्वृताः ॥३०॥

*devā ūcuḥ*
*namo namas te 'khila-yajña-tantave*
*sthitau gṛhītāmala-sattva-mūrtaye*
*diṣṭyā hato 'yaṁ jagatām aruntudas*
*tvat-pāda-bhaktyā vayam īśa nirvṛtāḥ*

*devāḥ*—the demigods; *ūcuḥ*—said; *namaḥ*—obeisances; *namaḥ*—obeisances; *te*—unto You; *akhila-yajña-tantave*—the enjoyer of all sacrifices; *sthitau*—for the purpose of maintaining; *gṛhīta*—assumed; *amala*—pure; *sattva*—goodness; *mūrtaye*—form; *diṣṭyā*—fortunately; *hataḥ*—slain; *ayam*—this; *jagatām*—to the worlds; *aruntudaḥ*—causing torment; *tvat-pāda*—to Your feet; *bhaktyā*—with devotion; *vayam*—we; *īśa*—O Lord; *nirvṛtāḥ*—have attained happiness.

## TRANSLATION

**The demigods addressed the Lord: All obeisances unto You! You are the enjoyer of all sacrifices, and You have assumed the form of a boar, in pure goodness, for the purpose of maintaining the world. Fortunately for us, this demon, who was a torment to the worlds, has been slain by You, and we too, O Lord, are now at ease, in devotion to Your lotus feet.**

## PURPORT

The material world consists of three modes—goodness, passion and ignorance—but the spiritual world is pure goodness. It is said here that the form of the Lord is pure goodness, which means that it is not material. In the material world there is no pure goodness. In the *Bhāgavatam* the stage of pure goodness is called *sattvaṁ viśuddham. Viśuddham* means "pure." In pure goodness there is no contamination by the two inferior qualities, namely passion and ignorance. The form of the boar, therefore, in which the Lord appeared, is nothing of the material world. There are many other forms of the Lord, but none of them belong to the material qualities. Such forms are nondifferent from the Viṣṇu form, and Viṣṇu is the enjoyer of all sacrifices.

The sacrifices which are recommended in the *Vedas* are meant to please the Supreme Personality of Godhead. In ignorance only, people try to satisfy many other agents, but the real purpose of life is to satisfy the Supreme Lord, Viṣṇu. All sacrifices are meant to please the Supreme Lord. The living entities who know this perfectly well are called demigods, godly or almost God. Since the living entity is part and parcel of the Supreme Lord, it is his duty to serve the Lord and please Him. The demigods are all attached to the Personality of Godhead, and for their pleasure the demon, who was a source of trouble to the world, was killed. Purified life is meant to please the Lord, and all sacrifices performed in purified life are called Kṛṣṇa consciousness. This Kṛṣṇa consciousness is developed by devotional service, as clearly mentioned here.

## TEXT 31

मैत्रेय उवाच

एवं हिरण्याक्षमसह्यविक्रमं
स सादयित्वा हरिरादिसूकरः ।
जगाम लोकं स्वमखण्डितोत्सवं
समीडितः पुष्करविष्टरादिभिः ॥३१॥

*maitreya uvāca*
*evaṁ hiraṇyākṣam asahya-vikramaṁ*
*sa sādayitvā harir ādi-sūkaraḥ*

*jagāma lokaṁ svam akhaṇḍitotsavaṁ*
*samīḍitaḥ puṣkara-viṣṭarādibhiḥ*

*maitreyaḥ uvāca*—Śrī Maitreya said; *evam*—thus; *hiraṇyākṣam*—Hiraṇyākṣa; *asahya-vikramam*—very powerful; *saḥ*—the Lord; *sādayitvā*—after killing; *hariḥ*—the Supreme Personality of Godhead; *ādi-sūkaraḥ*—the origin of the boar species; *jagāma*—returned; *lokam*—to His abode; *svam*—own; *akhaṇḍita*—uninterrupted; *utsavam*—festival; *samīḍitaḥ*—being praised; *puṣkara-viṣṭara*—lotus seat (by Lord Brahmā, whose seat is a lotus); *ādibhiḥ*—and the others.

## TRANSLATION

**Śrī Maitreya continued: After thus killing the most formidable demon Hiraṇyākṣa, the Supreme Lord Hari, the origin of the boar species, returned to His own abode, where there is always an uninterrupted festival. The Lord was praised by all the demigods, headed by Brahmā.**

## PURPORT

The Lord is spoken of herewith as the origin of the boar species. As stated in the *Vedānta-sūtra* (1.1.2), the Absolute Truth is the origin of everything. Therefore it is to be understood that all 8,400,000 species of bodily forms originate from the Lord, who is always *ādi*, or the beginning. In *Bhagavad-gītā* Arjuna addresses the Lord as *ādyam*, or the original. Similarly, in the *Brahma-saṁhitā* the Lord is addressed as *ādi-puruṣam*, the original person. Indeed, in *Bhagavad-gītā* (10.8) the Lord Himself declares, *mattaḥ sarvaṁ pravartate:* "From Me everything proceeds."

In this situation the Lord assumed the shape of a boar to kill the demon Hiraṇyākṣa and pick up the earth from the Garbha Ocean. Thus He became *ādi-sūkara*, the original boar. In the material world a boar or pig is considered most abominable, but the *ādi-sūkara*, the Supreme Personality of Godhead, was not treated as an ordinary boar. Even Lord Brahmā and the other demigods praised the Lord's form as a boar.

This verse confirms the statement in *Bhagavad-gītā* that the Lord appears as He is from His transcendental abode for the sake of killing the miscreants and saving the devotees. By killing the demon Hiraṇyākṣa He fulfilled His promise to kill the demons and always protect the demigods headed by Brahmā. The statement that the Lord returned to His own abode indicates that He has His own particular transcendental residence. Since He is full of all energies, He is all-pervasive in spite of His residing in Goloka Vṛndāvana, just as the sun, although situated in a particular place within the universe, is present by its sunshine throughout the universe.

Although the Lord has His particular abode in which to reside, He is all-pervasive. The impersonalists accept one aspect of the Lord's features, the all-pervasive aspect, but they cannot understand His localized situation in His transcendental abode, where He always engages in fully transcendental pastimes. Especially mentioned in this verse is the word *akhaṇḍitotsavam. Utsava* means "pleasure." Whenever some function takes place to express happiness, it is called *utsava. Utsava*, the expression of complete happiness, is always present in the Vaikuṇṭhalokas, the abode of the Lord, who is worshipable even by demigods like Brahmā, to say nothing of other, less important entities such as human beings.

The Lord descends from His abode to this world, and therefore He is called *avatāra*, which means "one who descends." Sometimes *avatāra* is understood to refer to an incarnation who assumes a material form of flesh and bone, but actually *avatāra* refers to one who descends from higher regions. The Lord's abode is situated far above this material sky, and He descends from that higher position; thus He is called *avatāra.*

## TEXT 32

मया यथानूक्तमवादि ते हरेः
कृतावतारस्य सुमित्र चेष्टितम् ।
यथा हिरण्याक्ष उदारविक्रमो
महामृधे क्रीडनवन्निराकृतः ॥३२॥

*mayā yathānūktam avādi te hareḥ*
*kṛtāvatārasya sumitra ceṣṭitam*
*yathā hiraṇyākṣa udāra-vikramo*
*mahā-mṛdhe krīḍanavan nirākṛtaḥ*

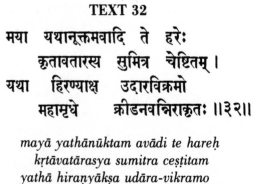

*mayā*—by me; *yathā*—as; *anūktam*—told; *avādi*—was explained; *te*—to you; *hareḥ*—of the Supreme Personality of Godhead; *kṛta-avatārasya*—who assumed the incarnation; *sumitra*—O dear Vidura; *ceṣṭitam*—the activities; *yathā*—as; *hiraṇyākṣaḥ*—Hiraṇyākṣa; *udāra*—very extensive; *vikramaḥ*—prowess; *mahā-mṛdhe*—in a great fight; *krīḍana-vat*—like a plaything; *nirākṛtaḥ*—was killed.

## TRANSLATION

**Maitreya continued: My dear Vidura, I have explained to you the Personality of Godhead's coming down as the first boar incarnation and killing in a great fight a demon of unprecedented prowess as if he were just a plaything. This has been narrated by me as I heard it from my predecessor spiritual master.**

## PURPORT

Here the sage Maitreya admits that he explained the incident of the killing of Hiraṇyākṣa by the Supreme Personality of Godhead as a straight narration; he did not manufacture anything or add interpretation, but explained whatever he had heard from his spiritual master. Thus he accepted as bona fide the system of *paramparā*, or receiving the transcendental message in disciplic succession. Unless received by this bona fide process of hearing from a spiritual master, the statement of an *ācārya* or preceptor cannot be valid.

It is also stated here that although the demon Hiraṇyākṣa was unlimited in prowess, he was just like a doll for the Lord. A child breaks so many dolls without real endeavor. Similarly, although a demon may be very powerful and extraordinary in the eyes of an ordinary man in the material world, to the Lord, killing such a demon is no difficulty. He can kill millions of demons as simply as a child plays with dolls and breaks them.

## TEXT 33

सूत उवाच

इति कौषारवाख्यातामाश्रुत्य भगवत्कथाम् ।
क्षत्तानन्दं परं लेभे महाभागवतो द्विज ॥३३॥

*sūta uvāca*
*iti kauṣāravākhyātām*
*āśrutya bhagavat-kathām*
*kṣattānandaṁ paraṁ lebhe*
*mahā-bhāgavato dvija*

*sūtaḥ*—Sūta Gosvāmī; *uvāca*—said; *iti*—thus; *kauṣārava*—from Maitreya (son of Kuṣāru); *ākhyātām*—told; *āśrutya*—having heard; *bhagavat-kathām*—the narration about the Lord; *kṣattā*—Vidura; *ānandam*—bliss; *param*—transcendental; *lebhe*—achieved; *mahā-bhāgavataḥ*—the great devotee; *dvija*—O *brāhmaṇa* (Śaunaka).

## TRANSLATION

**Śrī Sūta Gosvāmī continued: My dear brāhmaṇa, Kṣattā [Vidura] the great devotee of the Lord achieved transcendental bliss by hearing the narration of the pastimes of the Supreme Personality of Godhead from the authoritative source of the sage Kauṣārava [Maitreya], and he was very pleased.**

## PURPORT

If anyone wants to derive transcendental pleasure by hearing the pastimes of the Lord, he must hear from the authoritative source, as explained here. Maitreya heard the narration from his bona fide spiritual master, and Vidura also heard from Maitreya. One becomes an authority simply by presenting whatever he has heard from his spiritual master, and one who does not accept a bona fide spiritual master cannot be an authority. This is clearly explained here. If one wants to have transcendental pleasure, he must find a person with authority. It is also stated in the *Bhāgavatam* that simply by hearing from an authoritative source, with the ear and the heart, one can relish the pastimes of the Lord, otherwise it is not possible. Sanātana Gosvāmī, therefore, has especially warned that one should not hear anything about the personality of the Lord from the lips of a nondevotee. Nondevotees are considered to be like serpents; as milk is poisoned by a serpent's touch, so, although the narration of the pastimes of the Lord is as pure as milk, when administered by serpentlike nondevotees it becomes poisonous. Not only does it have no effect in transcendental pleasure, but it is dangerous also. Lord Caitanya Mahāprabhu has warned that no description of the pastimes of the Lord should be heard from the Māyāvāda, or impersonalist, school. He has clearly said, *māyāvādi-bhāṣya śunile haya sarva nāśa:* if anyone hears the Māyāvādīs' interpretation of the pastimes of the Lord, or their interpretation of *Bhagavad-gītā, Śrīmad-Bhāgavatam* or any other Vedic literature, then he is doomed. Once one is associated with impersonalists, he can never understand the personal feature of the Lord and His transcendental pastimes.

Sūta Gosvāmī was speaking to the sages headed by Śaunaka, and therefore he addressed them in this verse as *dvija,* twice-born. The sages assembled in Naimiṣāraṇya hearing *Śrīmad-Bhāgavatam* from Sūta Gosvāmī were all *brāhmaṇas,* but to acquire the qualifications of a *brāhmaṇa* is not everything. Merely to be twice-born is not perfection. Perfection is attained when one hears the pastimes and activities of the Lord from a bona fide source.

## TEXT 34

अन्येषां पुण्यश्लोकानामुद्दामयशसां सताम् ।
उपश्रुत्य भवेन्मोदः श्रीवत्साङ्कस्य किं पुनः ॥३४॥

*anyeṣāṁ puṇya-ślokānām*
*uddāma-yaśasāṁ satām*
*upaśrutya bhaven modaḥ*
*śrīvatsāṅkasya kiṁ punaḥ*

*anyeṣām*—of others; *puṇya-ślokānām*—of pious reputation; *uddāma-yaśasām*—whose fame is spread everywhere; *satām*—of the devotees; *upaśrutya*—by hearing; *bhavet*—may arise; *modaḥ*—pleasure; *śrīvatsa-aṅkasya*—of the Lord, who bears the mark Śrīvatsa; *kim punaḥ*—what to speak of.

## TRANSLATION

**What to speak of hearing the pastimes of the Lord, whose chest is marked with Śrīvatsa, people may take transcendental pleasure**

**even in hearing of the works and deeds of the devotees, whose fame is immortal.**

## PURPORT

*Bhāgavatam* literally means the pastimes of the Lord and the Lord's devotees. For example, there are pastimes of Lord Kṛṣṇa and narrations of devotees like Prahlāda, Dhruva and Mahārāja Ambarīṣa. Both pastimes pertain to the Supreme Personality of Godhead because the devotees' pastimes are in relation with Him. The *Mahābhārata*, for example, the history of the Pāṇḍavas and their activities, is sacred because the Pāṇḍavas had a direct relationship with the Supreme Personality of Godhead.

## TEXT 35

यो गजेन्द्रं झषग्रस्तं ध्यायन्तं चरणाम्बुजम् ।
क्रोशन्तीनां करेणूनां कृच्छ्रतोऽमोचयद् द्रुतम् ॥३५॥

*yo gajendraṁ jhaṣa-grastaṁ*
*dhyāyantaṁ caraṇāmbujam*
*krośantīnāṁ kareṇūnāṁ*
*kṛcchrato 'mocayad drutam*

*yaḥ*—He who; *gaja-indram*—the king of elephants; *jhaṣa*—an alligator; *grastam*—attacked by; *dhyāyantam*—meditating upon; *caraṇa*—feet; *ambujam*—lotus; *krośantīnām*—while crying; *kareṇūnām*—the female elephants; *kṛcchrataḥ*—from danger; *amocayat*—delivered; *drutam*—quickly.

## TRANSLATION

**The Personality of Godhead delivered the king of the elephants, who was attacked by an alligator and who meditated upon the lotus feet of the Lord. At that time the female elephants who accompanied him were crying, and the Lord saved them from the impending danger.**

## PURPORT

The example of the elephant in danger who was saved by the Supreme Lord is especially cited here because even if one is an animal he can approach the Personality of Godhead in devotional service, whereas even a demigod cannot approach the Supreme Person unless he is a devotee.

## TEXT 36

तं सुखाराध्यमृजुभिरनन्यशरणैर्नृभिः ।
कृतज्ञः को न सेवेत दुराराध्यमसाधुभिः ॥३६॥

*taṁ sukhārādhyam ṛjubhir*
*ananya-śaraṇair nṛbhiḥ*
*kṛtajñaḥ ko na seveta*
*durārādhyam asādhubhiḥ*

*tam*—unto Him; *sukha*—easily; *ārādhyam*—worshiped; *ṛjubhiḥ*—by the unpretentious; *ananya*—no other; *śaraṇaiḥ*—who take shelter; *nṛbhiḥ*—by men; *kṛta-jñaḥ*—grateful soul; *kaḥ*—what; *na*—not; *seveta*—would render service; *durārādhyam*—impossible to be worshiped; *asādhubhiḥ*—by the nondevotees.

## TRANSLATION

**What grateful soul is there who would not render his loving service to such a great master as the Personality of Godhead? The Lord can be easily pleased by spotless devotees who resort exclusively to Him for protection, though the unrighteous man finds it difficult to propitiate Him.**

## PURPORT

Every living entity, especially persons in the human race, must feel grateful for the benedictions offered by the grace of the Supreme Lord. Anyone, therefore, with a simple heart of gratefulness must be Kṛṣṇa conscious and offer devotional service to the Lord. Those who are actually thieves and rogues do not recognize or acknowledge the benedictions offered to them by the Supreme Lord, and they cannot render Him devotional service. Ungrateful persons are those who do not understand how much benefit they are deriving by the arrangement of the Lord. They enjoy the sunshine and moonshine, and they get water free of charge, yet they do not feel grateful, but simply go on enjoying these gifts of the Lord. Therefore, they must be called thieves and rogues.

## TEXT 37

यो वै हिरण्याक्षवधं महाद्भुतं
विक्रीडितं कारणसूकरात्मनः ।
शृणोति गायत्यनुमोदतेऽञ्जसा
विमुच्यते ब्रह्मवधादपि द्विजाः ॥३७॥

*yo vai hiraṇyākṣa-vadhaṁ mahādbhutaṁ*
*vikrīḍitaṁ kāraṇa-sūkarātmanaḥ*
*śṛṇoti gāyaty anumodate 'ñjasā*
*vimucyate brahma-vadhād api dvijāḥ*

*yaḥ*—he who; *vai*—indeed; *hiraṇyākṣa-vadham*—of the killing of Hiraṇyākṣa; *mahā-adbhutam*—most wonderful; *vikrīḍitam*—pastime; *kāraṇa*—for reasons like raising the earth from the ocean; *sūkara*—appearing in the form of a boar; *ātmanaḥ*—of the Supreme Personality of Godhead; *śṛṇoti*—hears; *gāyati*—chants; *anumodate*—takes pleasure; *añjasā*—at once; *vimucyate*—becomes freed; *brahma-vadhāt*—from the sin of killing a *brāhmaṇa; api*—even; *dvijāḥ*—O *brāhmaṇas.*

## TRANSLATION

**O brāhmaṇas, anyone who hears, chants, or takes pleasure in the wonderful narration of the killing of the Hiraṇyākṣa demon by the Lord, who appeared as the first boar in order to deliver the world, is at once relieved of the results of sinful activities, even the killing of a brāhmaṇa.**

## PURPORT

Since the Personality of Godhead is in the absolute position, there is no difference between His pastimes and His personality. Anyone who hears about the pastimes of the Lord associates with the Lord directly, and one who associates directly with the Lord is certainly freed from all sinful activities, even to the extent of the killing of a *brāhmaṇa*, which is considered the most sinful activity in the material world. One should be very eager to hear about the activities of the Lord from the bona fide source, the pure devotee. If one simply gives aural reception to the narration and accepts the glories of the Lord, then he is qualified. The impersonalist philosophers cannot understand the activities of the Lord. They think that all His activities are *māyā;* therefore they are called Māyāvādīs. Since everything to them is *māyā*, these narrations are not for them. Some impersonalists are reluctant to hear *Śrīmad-Bhāgavatam*, although many of them are now taking an interest in it just for monetary gain. Actually, however, they have no faith. On the contrary, they describe it in their own way. We should not hear, therefore, from the Māyāvādīs. We have to hear from Sūta Gosvāmī or Maitreya, who actually present the narrations as they are, and only then can we relish the pastimes of the Lord; otherwise the effects on the neophyte audience will be poisonous.

## TEXT 38

एतन्महापुण्यमलं पवित्रं
धन्यं यशस्यं पदमायुराशिषाम् ।
प्राणेन्द्रियाणां युधि शौर्यवर्धनं
नारायणोऽन्ते गतिरङ्ग शृण्वताम् ॥३८॥

*etan mahā-puṇyam alaṁ pavitraṁ*
*dhanyaṁ yaśasyaṁ padam āyur-āśiṣām*
*prāṇendriyāṇāṁ yudhi śaurya-vardhanaṁ*
*nārāyaṇo 'nte gatir aṅga śṛṇvatām*

*etat*—this narrative; *mahā-puṇyam*—conferring great merit; *alam*—very; *pavitram*—sacred; *dhanyam*—conferring wealth; *yaśasyam*—bearing fame; *padam*—the receptacle; *āyuḥ*—of longevity; *āśiṣām*—of the objects of one's desire; *prāṇa*—of the vital organs; *indriyāṇām*—of the organs of action; *yudhi*—on the field of battle; *śaurya*—the strength; *vardhanam*—increasing; *nārāyaṇaḥ*—Lord Nārāyaṇa; *ante*—at the end of life; *gatiḥ*—shelter; *aṅga*—O dear Śaunaka; *śṛṇvatām*—of those who listen.

## TRANSLATION

**This most sacred narrative confers extraordinary merit, wealth, fame, longevity, and all the objects of one's desire. On the field of battle it promotes the strength of one's vital organs and organs of action. One who listens to it at the last moment of his life is transferred to the supreme abode of the Lord, O dear Śaunaka.**

## PURPORT

Devotees are generally attracted by the narratives of the pastimes of the Lord, and even though they do not prosecute austerities or meditation, this very process of *hearing* attentively about the pastimes of the Lord will endow them with innumerable benefits, such as wealth, fame, longevity and other desirable aims of life. If one continues to hear *Śrīmad-Bhāgavatam,* which is full of narratives of the pastimes of the Lord, at the end of this life, one is sure to be transferred to the eternal, transcendental abode of the Lord. Thus hearers are benefited both ultimately and for as long as they are in the material world. That is the supreme, sublime result of engaging in devotional service. The beginning of devotional service is to spare some time and listen to *Śrīmad-Bhāgavatam* from the right source. Lord Caitanya Mahāprabhu also recommended five items of devotional service, namely to serve the devotees of the Lord, to chant Hare Kṛṣṇa, to hear *Śrīmad-Bhāgavatam,* to worship the Deity of the Lord and to live in a place of pilgrimage. Just performing these five activities can deliver one from the miserable condition of material life.

*Thus end the Bhaktivedanta purports of the Third Canto, Nineteenth Chapter, of the* Śrīmad-Bhāgavatam, *entitled "The Killing of the Demon Hiraṇyākṣa."*

CHAPTER TWENTY

# Conversation Between Maitreya and Vidura

## TEXT 1

शौनक उवाच
महीं प्रतिष्ठामध्यस्य सौते स्वायम्भुवो मनुः ।
कान्यन्वतिष्ठद् द्वाराणि मार्गायावरजन्मनाम् ॥ १ ॥

*śaunaka uvāca*
*mahīṁ pratiṣṭhām adhyasya*
*saute svāyambhuvo manuḥ*
*kāny anvatiṣṭhad dvārāṇi*
*mārgāyāvara-janmanām*

*śaunakaḥ*—Śaunaka; *uvāca*—said; *mahīm*—the earth; *pratiṣṭhām*—situated; *adhyasya*—having secured; *saute*—O Sūta Gosvāmī; *svāyambhuvaḥ*—Svāyambhuva; *manuḥ*—Manu; *kāni*—what; *anvatiṣṭhat*—performed; *dvārāṇi*—ways; *mārgāya*—to get out; *avara*—later; *janmanām*—of those to be born.

## TRANSLATION

**Śrī Śaunaka inquired: O Sūta Gosvāmī, after the earth was again situated in its orbit, what did Svāyambhuva Manu do to show the path of liberation to persons who were to take birth later on?**

## PURPORT

The appearance of the Lord as the first boar incarnation occurred during the time of Svāyambhuva Manu, whereas the present age is in the period of Vaivasvata Manu. Each Manu's period lasts seventy-two times the cycle of four ages, and one cycle of ages equals 4,320,000 solar years. Thus 4,320,000 X 72 solar years is the reign of one Manu. In each

Manu's period there are many changes in many ways, and there are fourteen Manus within one day of Brahmā. It is understood here that Manu creates scriptural regulations for the salvation of the conditioned souls, who come to the material world for material enjoyment. The Lord is so kind that any soul who wants to enjoy in this material world is given full facility for enjoyment, and at the same time he is shown the path of salvation. Śaunaka Ṛṣi, therefore, inquired from Sūta Gosvāmī: "What did Svāyambhuva Manu do after the reinstatement of the earth in its orbital situation?"

## TEXT 2

क्षत्ता महाभागवतः कृष्णस्यैकान्तिकः सुहृत् ।
यस्तत्याजाग्रजं कृष्णे सापत्यमघवानिति ॥ २ ॥

*kṣattā mahā-bhāgavataḥ*
*kṛṣṇasyaikāntikaḥ suhṛt*
*yas tatyājāgrajaṁ kṛṣṇe*
*sāpatyam aghavān iti*

*kṣattā*—Vidura; *mahā-bhāgavataḥ*—a great devotee of the Lord; *kṛṣṇasya*—of Lord Kṛṣṇa; *ekāntikaḥ*—unalloyed devotee; *suhṛt*—intimate friend; *yaḥ*—he who; *tatyāja*—abandoned; *agra-jam*—his elder brother (King Dhṛtarāṣṭra); *kṛṣṇe*—toward Kṛṣṇa; *sa-apatyam*—along with his one hundred sons; *agha-vān*—offender; *iti*—thus.

## TRANSLATION

**Śaunaka Ṛṣi inquired about Vidura, who was a great devotee and friend of Lord Kṛṣṇa and who gave up the company of his elder brother because the latter, along with his sons, played tricks against the desires of the Lord.**

## PURPORT

The incident referred to here is that Vidura left the protection of his elder brother Dhṛtarāṣṭra, went traveling everywhere to sacred places and met Maitreya at Hardwar. Śaunaka Ṛṣi here inquires about the topics of the conversation between Maitreya Ṛṣi and Vidura. Vidura's qualification was that he was not only a friend of the Lord but also a great devotee. When Kṛṣṇa tried to stop the war and mitigate the misunderstanding between the cousin-brothers, they refused to accept His counsel; therefore Kṣattā, or Vidura, was unsatisfied with them, and he left the palace. As a devotee, Vidura showed by example that anywhere that Kṛṣṇa is not honored is a place unfit for human habitation. A devotee may be tolerant regarding his own interests, but he should not be tolerant when there is misbehavior toward the Lord or the Lord's devotee. Here the word *aghavān* is very significant, for it indicates that the Kauravas, Dhṛtarāṣṭra's sons, lost the war because of being sinful in disobeying the instructions of Kṛṣṇa.

## TEXT 3

द्वैपायनादनवरो महित्वे तस्य देहजः ।
सर्वात्मना श्रितः कृष्णं तत्परांश्चाप्यनुव्रतः ॥ ३ ॥

*dvaipāyanād anavaro*
*mahitve tasya dehajaḥ*
*sarvātmanā śritaḥ kṛṣṇaṁ*
*tat-parāṁś cāpy anuvrataḥ*

*dvaipāyanāt*—from Vyāsadeva; *anavaraḥ*—in no way inferior; *mahitve*—in greatness; *tasya*—his (Vyāsa's); *deha-jaḥ*—born of his body; *sarva-ātmanā*—with all his heart; *śritaḥ*—took shelter; *kṛṣṇam*—Lord Kṛṣṇa; *tat-parān*—those devoted to Him; *ca*—and; *api*—also; *anuvrataḥ*—followed.

## TRANSLATION

**Vidura was born from the body of Vedavyāsa and was not less than he. Thus he accepted the lotus feet of Kṛṣṇa wholeheartedly and was attached to His devotees.**

## PURPORT

The history of Vidura is that he was born of a *śūdra* mother, but his seminal father was Vyāsadeva; thus he was not less than Vyāsadeva in any respect. Since he was born of a great father, who was supposed to be an incarnation of Nārāyaṇa and who composed all the Vedic literatures, Vidura was also a great personality. He accepted Kṛṣṇa as his worshipable Lord and followed His instructions wholeheartedly.

## TEXT 4

किमन्वपृच्छन्मैत्रेयं विरजास्तीर्थसेवया ।
उपगम्य कुशावर्त आसीनं तत्त्ववित्तमम् ॥ ४ ॥

*kim anvapṛcchan maitreyaṁ*
*virajās tīrtha-sevayā*
*upagamya kuśāvarta*
*āsīnaṁ tattva-vittamam*

*kim*—what; *anvapṛcchat*—inquired; *maitreyam*—from the sage Maitreya; *virajāḥ*—Vidura, who was without material contamination; *tīrtha-sevayā*—by visiting sacred places; *upagamya*—having met; *kuśāvarte*—at Kuśāvarta (Haridvāra, or Hardwar); *āsīnam*—who was abiding; *tattva-vit-tamam*—the foremost knower of the science of spiritual life.

## TRANSLATION

**Vidura was purified of all passion by wandering in sacred places, and at last he reached Hardwar, where he met the great sage who knew the science of spiritual life, and he inquired from him. Śaunaka Ṛṣi therefore asked: What more did Vidura inquire from Maitreya?**

## PURPORT

Here the words *virajās tīrtha-sevayā* refer to Vidura, who was completely cleansed of all contamination by traveling to places of pilgrimage. In India there are hundreds of sacred places of pilgrimage, of which Prayāga, Hardwar, Vṛndāvana and Rāmeśvaram are considered principal. After leaving his home, which was full of politics and diplomacy, Vidura wanted to purify himself by traveling to all the sacred places, which are so situated that anyone who goes there automatically becomes purified. This is especially true in Vṛndāvana; any person may go there, and even if he is sinful he will at once contact an atmosphere of spiritual life and will automatically chant the names of Kṛṣṇa and Rādhā. That we have actually seen and experienced. It is recommended in the *śāstras* that after retiring from active life and accepting the *vānaprastha* (retired) order, one should travel everywhere to places of pilgrimage in order to purify himself. Vidura completely discharged this duty, and at last he reached Kuśāvarta, or Hardwar, where the sage Maitreya was sitting.

Another significant point is that one must go to sacred places not only to take bath there but to search out great sages like Maitreya and take instructions from them. If one does not do so, his traveling to places of pilgrimage is simply a waste of time. Narottama dāsa Ṭhākura, a great *ācārya* of the Vaiṣṇava sect, has, for the present, forbidden us to go to such places of pilgrimage because in this age, the times having so changed, a sincere person may have a different impression on seeing the behavior of the present residents of the pilgrimage sites. He has recommended that instead of taking the trouble to travel to such places, one should concentrate his mind on Govinda, and that will help him. Of course, to concentrate one's mind on Govinda in any place is a path meant for those who are the most spiritually advanced; it is not for ordinary persons. Ordinary persons may still derive benefit from traveling to holy places like Prayāga, Mathurā, Vṛndāvana and Hardwar.

It is recommended in this verse that one find a person who knows the science of God, or a *tattva-vit. Tattva-vit* means "one who knows the Absolute Truth." There are many pseudotranscendentalists, even at places of pilgrimage. Such men are always present, and one has to be intelligent enough to find the actual person to be consulted; then one's attempt to progress by traveling to different holy places will be successful. One has to be freed from all contamination, and at the same time he has to find a person who knows the science of Kṛṣṇa. Kṛṣṇa helps a sincere person; as stated in the *Caitanya-caritāmṛta, guru-kṛṣṇa-prasāde:* by the mercy of the spiritual master and Kṛṣṇa, one attains the path of salvation, devotional service. If one sincerely searches for spiritual salvation, then Kṛṣṇa, being situated in everyone's heart, gives him the intelligence to find a suitable spiritual master. By the grace of a spiritual master like Maitreya, one gets the proper instruction and advances in his spiritual life.

## TEXT 5

तयोः संवदतोः सूत प्रवृत्ता ह्यमलाः कथाः ।
आपो गाङ्गा इवाघघ्नीर्हरेः पादाम्बुजाश्रयाः ॥ ५ ॥

*tayoḥ saṁvadatoḥ sūta*
*pravṛttā hy amalāḥ kathāḥ*
*āpo gāṅgā ivāgha-ghnīr*
*hareḥ pādāmbujāśrayāḥ*

*tayoḥ*—while the two (Maitreya and Vidura); *saṁvadatoḥ*—were conversing; *sūta*—O Sūta; *pravṛttāḥ*—arose; *hi*—certainly; *amalāḥ*—spotless; *kathāḥ*—narrations; *āpaḥ*—waters; *gāṅgāḥ*—of the River Ganges; *iva*—like; *agha-ghnīḥ*—vanquishing all sins; *hareḥ*—of the Lord; *pāda-ambuja*—the lotus feet; *āśrayāḥ*—taking shelter.

## TRANSLATION

**Śaunaka inquired about the conversation between Vidura and Maitreya: There must have been many narrations of the spotless pastimes of the Lord. The hearing of such narrations is exactly like bathing in the water of the Ganges, for it can free one from all sinful reactions.**

## PURPORT

The water of the Ganges is purified because it pours forth from the lotus feet of the Lord. Similarly, *Bhagavad-gītā* is as good as the water of the Ganges because it is spoken from the mouth of the Supreme Lord. So it is with any topic on the pastimes of the Lord or the characteristics of His transcendental activities. The Lord is absolute; there is no difference between His words, His perspiration or His pastimes. The water of the Ganges, the narrations of His pastimes and the words spoken by Him are all on the absolute platform, and thus taking shelter of any one of them is equally good. Śrīla Rūpa Gosvāmī has enunciated that anything in relationship with Kṛṣṇa is on the transcendental platform. If we can dovetail all our activities in relationship with Kṛṣṇa, then we do not stand on the material platform, but always on the spiritual platform.

## TEXT 6

ता नः कीर्तय भद्रं ते कीर्तन्योदारकर्मणः ।
रसज्ञः को नु तृप्येत हरिलीलामृतं पिबन् ॥ ६ ॥

*tā naḥ kīrtaya bhadraṁ te*
*kīrtanyodāra-karmaṇaḥ*
*rasajñaḥ ko nu tṛpyeta*
*hari-līlāmṛtaṁ piban*

*tāḥ*—those talks; *naḥ*—to us; *kīrtaya*—narrate; *bhadram te*—may all good come unto you; *kīrtanya*—should be chanted; *udāra*—liberal; *karmaṇaḥ*—activities; *rasa-jñaḥ*—a devotee who can appreciate mellow tastes; *kaḥ*—who; *nu*—indeed; *tṛpyeta*—would feel satisfied; *hari-līlā-amṛtam*—the nectar of the pastimes of the Lord; *piban*—drinking.

### TRANSLATION

**O Sūta Gosvāmī, all good fortune to you! Please narrate the activities of the Lord, which are all magnanimous and worth glorifying. What sort of devotee can be satiated by hearing the nectarean pastimes of the Lord?**

### PURPORT

The narration of the pastimes of the Lord, which are always enacted on the transcendental platform, should be received with all respect by devotees. Those who are actually on the transcendental platform are never satiated by hearing the continuous narration of the pastimes of the Lord. For example, if any self-realized soul reads from *Bhagavad-gītā*, he will never feel satiated. The narrations of *Bhagavad-gītā* and *Śrīmad-Bhāgavatam* may be read thousands and thousands of times, and still, without fail, new aspects of the subject matter will be relished by the devotee.

## TEXT 7

एवमुग्रश्रवाः पृष्ट ऋषिभिर्नैमिषायनैः ।
भगवत्यर्पिताध्यात्मस्तानाह श्रूयतामिति ॥ ७ ॥

*evam ugraśravāḥ pṛṣṭa*
*ṛṣibhir naimiṣāyanaiḥ*
*bhagavaty arpitādhyātmas*
*tān āha śrūyatām iti*

*evam*—thus; *ugraśravāḥ*—Sūta Gosvāmī; *pṛṣṭaḥ*—being asked; *ṛṣibhiḥ*—by the sages; *naimiṣa-ayanaiḥ*—who were assembled in the forest of Naimiṣa; *bhagavati*—unto the Lord; *arpita*—dedicated; *adhyātmaḥ*—his mind; *tān*—to them; *āha*—said; *śrūyatām*—just hear; *iti*—thus.

## TRANSLATION

**On being asked to speak by the great sages of Naimiṣāraṇya, the son of Romaharṣaṇa, Sūta Gosvāmī, whose mind was absorbed in the transcendental pastimes of the Lord, said: Please hear what I shall now speak.**

## TEXT 8

सूत उवाच
हरेर्धृतक्रोडतनोः स्वमायया
निशम्य गोरुद्धरणं रसातलात् ।
लीलां हिरण्याक्षमवज्ञया हतं
सञ्जातहर्षो मुनिमाह भारतः ॥ ८ ॥

*sūta uvāca*
*harer dhṛta-kroḍa-tanoḥ sva-māyayā*
*niśamya gor uddharaṇaṁ rasātalāt*
*līlāṁ hiraṇyākṣam avajñayā hataṁ*
*sañjāta-harṣo munim āha bhārataḥ*

*sūtaḥ uvāca*—Sūta said; *hareḥ*—of the Lord; *dhṛta*—who had assumed; *kroḍa*—of a boar; *tanoḥ*—body; *sva-māyayā*—by His divine potency; *niśamya*—having heard; *goḥ*—of the earth; *uddharaṇam*—uplifting; *rasātalāt*—from the bottom of the ocean; *līlām*—sport; *hiraṇyākṣam*—the demon Hiraṇyākṣa; *avajñayā*—neglectfully;

*hatam*—killed; *sañjāta-harṣaḥ*—being overjoyed; *munim*—to the sage (Maitreya); *āha*—said; *bhārataḥ*—Vidura.

## TRANSLATION

**Sūta Gosvāmī continued: Vidura, the descendant of Bharata, was delighted to hear the story of the Lord, who, having assumed by His own divine potency the form of a boar, had enacted the sport of lifting the earth from the bottom of the ocean and indifferently killing the demon Hiraṇyākṣa. Vidura then spoke to the sage as follows.**

## PURPORT

It is stated here that the Lord assumed the form of a boar by His own potency. His form is not actually the form of a conditioned soul. A conditioned soul is forced to accept a particular type of body by the higher authority of material laws, but here it is clearly said that the Lord was not forced to accept the form of a boar by the external power. In *Bhagavad-gītā* the same fact is confirmed; when the Lord descends to this earth, He assumes a form by His own internal potency. The form of the Lord, therefore, can never consist of material energy. The Māyāvāda version that when Brahman assumes a form the form is accepted from *māyā* is not acceptable, because although *māyā* is superior to the conditioned soul, she is not superior to the Supreme Personality of Godhead; she is under the control of the Supreme Godhead, as confirmed in *Bhagavad-gītā*. *Māyā* is under His superintendence; *māyā* cannot overcome the Lord. The Māyāvāda idea that the living entity is the Supreme Absolute Truth but has become covered by *māyā* is invalid, because *māyā* cannot be so great that it can cover the Supreme. The covering capacity can be employed on the part and parcel of Brahman, not on the Supreme Brahman.

## TEXT 9

विदुर उवाच

प्रजापतिपतिः सृष्ट्वा प्रजासर्गे प्रजापतीन् ।
किमारभत मे ब्रह्मन् प्रब्रूह्यव्यक्तमार्गवित् ॥ ९ ॥

*vidura uvāca*
*prajāpati-patiḥ sṛṣṭvā*
*prajā-sarge prajāpatīn*
*kim ārabhata me brahman*
*prabrūhy avyakta-mārga-vit*

*viduraḥ uvāca*—Vidura said; *prajāpati-patiḥ*—Lord Brahmā; *sṛṣṭvā*—after creating; *prajā-sarge*—for the purpose of creating living beings; *prajāpatīn*—the Prajāpatis; *kim*—what; *ārabhata*—started; *me*—to me; *brahman*—O holy sage; *prabrūhi*—tell; *avyakta-mārga-vit*—knower of that which we do not know.

## TRANSLATION

**Vidura said: Since you know of matters inconceivable to us, tell me, O holy sage, what did Brahmā do to create living beings after evolving the Prajāpatis, the progenitors of living beings?**

## PURPORT

Significant here is the word *avyakta-mārga-vit,* "one who knows that which is beyond our perception." To know matters beyond one's perception, one has to learn from a superior authority in the line of disciplic succession. Just to know who is our father is beyond our perception. For that, the mother is the authority. Similarly, we have to understand everything beyond our perception from the authority who actually knows. The first *avyakta-mārga-vit,* or authority, is Brahmā, and the next authority in disciplic succession is Nārada. Maitreya Ṛṣi belongs to that disciplic succession, so he also is *avyakta-mārga-vit.* Anyone in the bona fide line of disciplic succession is *avyakta-mārga-vit,* a personality who knows that which is beyond ordinary perception.

## TEXT 10

ये मरीच्यादयो विप्रा यस्तु स्वायम्भुवो मनुः ।
ते वै ब्रह्मण आदेशात्कथमेतदभावयन् ॥१०॥

*ye marīcy-ādayo viprā*
*yas tu svāyambhuvo manuḥ*
*te vai brahmaṇa ādeśāt*
*katham etad abhāvayan*

*ye*—those; *marīci-ādayaḥ*—great sages headed by Marīci; *viprāḥ*—*brāhmaṇas; yaḥ*—who; *tu*—indeed; *svāyambhuvaḥ manuḥ*—and Svāyambhuva Manu; *te*—they; *vai*—indeed; *brahmaṇaḥ*—of Lord Brahmā; *ādeśāt*—by the order; *katham*—how; *etat*—this universe; *abhāvayan*—evolved.

## TRANSLATION

**Vidura inquired: How did the Prajāpatis [such progenitors of living entities as Marīci and Svāyambhuva Manu] create according to the instruction of Brahmā, and how did they evolve this manifested universe?**

## TEXT 11

सद्वितीयाः किमसृजन् स्वतन्त्रा उत कर्मसु ।
आहोस्वित्संहताः सर्व इदं स्म समकल्पयन् ॥११॥

*sa-dvitīyāḥ kim asṛjan*
*svatantrā uta karmasu*
*āho svit saṁhatāḥ sarva*
*idaṁ sma samakalpayan*

*sa-dvitīyāḥ*—with their wives; *kim*—whether; *asṛjan*—created; *svatantrāḥ*—remaining independent; *uta*—or; *karmasu*—in their actions; *āho svit*—or else; *saṁhatāḥ*—jointly; *sarve*—all the Prajāpatis; *idam*—this; *sma samakalpayan*—produced.

## TRANSLATION

**Did they evolve the creation in conjunction with their respective wives, did they remain independent in their action, or did they all jointly produce it?**

## TEXT 12

मैत्रेय उवाच
दैवेन दुर्वितर्क्येण परेणानिमिषेण च ।
जातक्षोभाद्भगवतो महानासीद् गुणत्रयात् ॥१२॥

*maitreya uvāca*
*daivena durvitarkyeṇa*
*pareṇānimiṣeṇa ca*
*jāta-kṣobhād bhagavato*
*mahān āsīd guṇa-trayāt*

*maitreyaḥ uvāca*—Maitreya said; *daivena*—by superior management known as destiny; *durvitarkyeṇa*—beyond empiric speculation; *pareṇa*—by Mahā-Viṣṇu; *animiṣeṇa*—by the potency of eternal time; *ca*—and; *jāta-kṣobhāt*—the equilibrium was agitated; *bhagavataḥ*—of the Personality of Godhead; *mahān*—the total material elements (the *mahat-tattva*); *āsīt*—were produced; *guṇa-trayāt*—from the three modes of nature.

## TRANSLATION

**Maitreya said: When the equilibrium of the combination of the three modes of nature was agitated by the unseen activity of the living entity, by Mahā-Viṣṇu and by the force of time, the total material elements were produced.**

## PURPORT

The cause of the material creation is described here very lucidly. The first cause is *daiva*, or the destiny of the conditioned soul. The material creation exists for the conditioned soul who wanted to become a false lord for sense enjoyment. One cannot trace out the history of when the conditioned soul first desired to lord it over material nature, but in Vedic literature we always find that the material creation is meant for the sense enjoyment of the conditioned soul. There is a nice verse which says that the sum and substance of the conditioned soul's sense enjoyment is that as soon as he forgets his primary duty, to render service to the Lord, he creates an atmosphere of sense enjoyment, which is called *māyā;* that is the cause of material creation.

Another word used here is *durvitarkyeṇa*. No one can argue about when and how the conditioned soul became desirous of sense enjoyment, but the cause is there. Material nature is an atmosphere meant only for the sense enjoyment of the conditioned soul, and it is created by the Personality of Godhead. It is mentioned here that in the beginning of the creation the material nature, or *prakṛti*, is agitated by the Personality of Godhead, Viṣṇu. There are three Viṣṇus mentioned. One is Mahā-Viṣṇu, another is Garbhodakaśāyī Viṣṇu, and the third is Kṣīrodakaśāyī Viṣṇu. The First Canto of *Śrīmad-Bhāgavatam* discusses all these three Viṣṇus, and here also it is confirmed that Viṣṇu is the cause of creation. From *Bhagavad-gītā* also we learn that *prakṛti* begins to work and is still working under Kṛṣṇa's, or Viṣṇu's, glance of superintendence, but the Supreme Personality of Godhead is unchangeable. One should not mistakenly think that because the creation emanates from the Supreme Personality of Godhead, He has therefore transformed into this material cosmic manifestation. He exists in His personal form always, but the cosmic manifestation takes place by His inconceivable potency. The workings of that energy are difficult to comprehend, but it is understood from Vedic literature that the conditioned soul creates his own destiny and is offered a particular body by the laws of nature under the superintendence of the Supreme Personality of Godhead, who always accompanies him as Paramātmā.

## TEXT 13

रजःप्रधानान्महतस्त्रिलिङ्गो दैवचोदितात् ।
जातः ससर्ज भूतादिर्वियदादीनि पञ्चशः ॥१३॥

*rajaḥ-pradhānān mahatas*
*tri-liṅgo daiva-coditāt*
*jātaḥ sasarja bhūtādir*
*viyad-ādīni pañcaśaḥ*

*rajaḥ-pradhānāt*—in which the element of *rajas*, or passion, predominates; *mahataḥ*—from the *mahat-tattva; tri-liṅgaḥ*—of three kinds; *daiva-coditāt*—impelled by superior authority; *jātaḥ*—was born; *sasarja*—evolved; *bhūta-ādiḥ*—the false ego (origin of the material elements); *viyat*—the ether; *ādīni*—beginning with; *pañcaśaḥ*—in groups of five.

## TRANSLATION

**As impelled by the destiny of the jīva, the false ego, which is of three kinds, evolved from the mahat-tattva, in which the element of rajas predominates. From the ego, in turn, evolved many groups of five principles.**

## PURPORT

The primordial matter, or *prakṛti,* material nature, consisting of three modes, generates four groups of five. The first group is called elementary and consists of earth, water, fire, air and ether. The second group of five is called *tan-mātra,* referring to the subtle elements (sense objects): sound, touch, form, taste and smell. The third group is the five sense organs for acquiring knowledge: eyes, ears, nose, tongue and skin. The fourth group is the five working senses: speech, hands, feet, anus and genitals. Some say that there are five groups of five. One group is the sense objects, one is the five elements, one is the five sense organs for acquiring knowledge, another is the senses for working, and the fifth group is the five deities who control these divisions.

## TEXT 14

तानि चैकैकशः स्रष्टुमसमर्थानि भौतिकम् ।
संहत्य दैवयोगेन हैममण्डमवासृजन् ॥१४॥

*tāni caikaikaśaḥ sraṣṭum*
*asamarthāni bhautikam*
*saṁhatya daiva-yogena*
*haimam aṇḍam avāsṛjan*

*tāni*—those elements; *ca*—and; *eka-ekaśaḥ*—separately; *sraṣṭum*—to produce; *asamarthāni*—unable; *bhautikam*—the material universe; *saṁhatya*—having combined; *daiva-yogena*—with the energy of the Supreme Lord; *haimam*—shining like gold; *aṇḍam*—globe; *avāsṛjan*—produced.

## TRANSLATION

**Separately unable to produce the material universe, they combined with the help of the energy of the Supreme Lord and were able to produce a shining egg.**

## TEXT 15

सोऽशयिष्टाब्धिसलिले आण्डकोशो निरात्मकः ।
साग्रं वै वर्षसाहस्रमन्ववात्सीत्तमीश्वरः ॥१५॥

*so 'śayiṣṭābdhi-salile*
*āṇḍakośo nirātmakaḥ*
*sāgraṁ vai varṣa-sāhasram*
*anvavātsīt tam īśvaraḥ*

*saḥ*—it; *aśayiṣṭa*—lay; *abdhi-salile*—on the waters of the Causal Ocean; *āṇḍa-kośaḥ*—egg; *nirātmakaḥ*—in an unconscious state; *sa-agram*—a little more than; *vai*—in fact; *varṣa-sāhasram*—a thousand years; *anvavātsīt*—became situated; *tam*—in the egg; *īśvaraḥ*—the Lord.

## TRANSLATION

**For over one thousand years the shiny egg lay on the waters of the Causal Ocean in the lifeless state. Then the Lord entered it as Garbhodakaśāyī Viṣṇu.**

## PURPORT

From this verse it appears that all the universes are floating in the Causal Ocean.

## TEXT 16

तस्य नाभेरभूत्पद्मं सहस्रार्कोरुदीधिति ।
सर्वजीवनिकायौको यत्र स्वयमभूत्स्वराट् ॥१६॥

*tasya nābher abhūt padmaṁ*
*sahasrārkoru-dīdhiti*

*sarva-jīvanikāyauko*
*yatra svayam abhūt svarāṭ*

*tasya*—of the Lord; *nābheḥ*—from the navel; *abhūt*—sprouted up; *padmam*—a lotus; *sahasra-arka*—a thousand suns; *uru*—more; *dīdhiti*—with dazzling splendor; *sarva*—all; *jīva-nikāya*—resting place of conditioned souls; *okaḥ*—place; *yatra*—where; *svayam*—himself; *abhūt*—emanated; *sva-rāṭ*—the omnipotent (Lord Brahmā).

## TRANSLATION

**From the navel of the Personality of Godhead Garbhodakaśāyī Viṣṇu sprouted a lotus flower effulgent like a thousand blazing suns. This lotus flower is the reservoir of all conditioned souls, and the first living entity who came out of the lotus flower was the omnipotent Brahmā.**

## PURPORT

It appears from this verse that the conditioned souls who rested within the body of the Personality of Godhead after the dissolution of the last creation came out in the sum total form of the lotus. This is called *hiraṇyagarbha.* The first living entity to come out was Lord Brahmā, who is independently able to create the rest of the manifested universe. The lotus is described here as effulgent as the glare of a thousand suns. This indicates that the living entities, as parts and parcels of the Supreme Lord, are also of the same quality, since the Lord also diffuses His bodily glare, known as *brahmajyoti.* The description of Vaikuṇṭhaloka, as stated in *Bhagavad-gītā* and other Vedic literatures, is confirmed herewith. In Vaikuṇṭha, the spiritual sky, there is no need of sunshine, moonshine, electricity or fire. Every planet there is self-effulgent like the sun.

## TEXT 17

**सोऽनुविष्टो भगवता यः शेते सलिलाशये ।**
**लोकसंस्थां यथापूर्वं निर्ममे संस्थया स्वया ॥१७॥**

*so 'nuviṣṭo bhagavatā*
*yaḥ śete salilāśaye*

*loka-saṁsthāṁ yathā pūrvaṁ*
*nirmame saṁsthayā svayā*

*saḥ*—Lord Brahmā; *anuviṣṭaḥ*—was entered; *bhagavatā*—by the Lord; *yaḥ*—who; *śete*—sleeps; *salila-āśaye*—on the Garbhodaka Ocean; *loka-saṁsthām*—the universe; *yathā pūrvam*—as previously; *nirmame*—created; *saṁsthayā*—by intelligence; *svayā*—his own.

## TRANSLATION

**When that Supreme Personality of Godhead who is lying on the Garbhodaka Ocean entered the heart of Brahmā, Brahmā brought his intelligence to bear, and with the intelligence invoked he began to create the universe as it was before.**

## PURPORT

At a certain time, the Personality of Godhead, Kāraṇodakaśāyī Viṣṇu, lies in the Kāraṇa Ocean and produces many thousands of universes from His breathing; then He enters again into each and every universe as Garbhodakaśāyī Viṣṇu and fills up half of each universe with His own perspiration. The other half of the universe remains vacant, and that vacant region is called outer space. Then the lotus flower sprouts from His abdomen and produces the first living creature, Brahmā. Then again, as Kṣīrodakaśāyī Viṣṇu, the Lord enters into the heart of every living entity, including Brahmā. This is confirmed in *Bhagavad-gītā*, Fifteenth Chapter. The Lord says, "I am seated in everyone's heart, and by Me are remembrance and forgetfulness made possible." As the witness of the activities of the individual entities, the Lord gives each one remembrance and intelligence to act according to his desire at the time he was annihilated in his last birth in the last millennium. This intelligence is invoked according to one's own capacity, or by the law of *karma.*

Brahmā was the first living entity, and he was empowered by the Supreme Lord to act in charge of the mode of passion; therefore, he was given the required intelligence, which is so powerful and extensive that he is almost independent of the control of the Supreme Personality of Godhead. Just as a highly posted manager is almost as independent as the owner of a firm, Brahmā is described here as independent because, as the Lord's representative to control the universe, he is almost as powerful and independent as the Supreme Personality of Godhead. The Lord, as the Supersoul within Brahmā, gave him the intelligence to create. The creative power, therefore, of every living entity is not his own; it is by the grace of the Lord that one can create. There are many scientists and great workers in this material world who have wonderful creative force, but they act and create only according to the direction of the Supreme Lord. A scientist may create many wonderful inventions by the direction of the Lord, but it is not possible for him to overcome the stringent laws of material nature by his intelligence, nor is it possible to acquire such intelligence from the Lord, for the Lord's supremacy would then be hampered. It is stated in this verse that Brahmā created the universe as it was before. This means that he created everything by the same name and form as in the previous cosmic manifestation.

## TEXT 18

ससर्ज च्छाययाविद्यां पञ्चपर्वाणमग्रतः ।
तामिस्रमन्धतामिस्रं तमो मोहो महातमः ॥१८॥

*sasarja cchāyayāvidyāṁ*
*pañca-parvāṇam agrataḥ*
*tāmisram andha-tāmisraṁ*
*tamo moho mahā-tamaḥ*

*sasarja*—created; *chāyayā*—with his shadow; *avidyām*—ignorance; *pañca-parvāṇam*—five varieties; *agrataḥ*—first of all; *tāmisram*—*tāmisra; andha-tāmisram*—*andha-tāmisra; tamaḥ*—*tamas; mohaḥ*—*moha; mahā-tamaḥ*—*mahā-tamas*, or *mahā-moha.*

## TRANSLATION

**First of all, Brahmā created from his shadow the coverings of ignorance of the conditioned souls. They are five in number and are called tāmisra, andha-tāmisra, tamas, moha and mahā-moha.**

## PURPORT

The conditioned souls, or living entities who come to the material world to enjoy sense gratification, are covered in the beginning by five different conditions. The first condition is a covering of *tāmisra,* or anger. Constitutionally, each and every living entity has minute independence; it is misuse of that minute independence for the conditioned soul to think that he can also enjoy like the Supreme Lord or to think, "Why shall I not be a free enjoyer like the Supreme Lord?" This forgetfulness of his constitutional position is due to anger or envy. The living entity, being eternally a part-and-parcel servitor of the Supreme Lord, can never, by constitution, be an equal enjoyer with the Lord. When he forgets this, however, and tries to be one with Him, his condition is called *tāmisra.* Even in the field of spiritual realization, this *tāmisra* mentality of the living entity is hard to overcome. In trying to get out of the entanglement of material life, there are many who want to be one with the Supreme. Even in their transcendental activities, this lower-grade mentality of *tāmisra* continues.

*Andha-tāmisra* involves considering death to be the ultimate end. The atheists generally think that the body is the self and that everything is therefore ended with the end of the body. Thus they want to enjoy material life as far as possible during the existence of the body. Their theory is: "As long as you live, you should live prosperously. Never mind whether you commit all kinds of so-called sins. You must eat sumptuously. Beg, borrow and steal, and if you think that by stealing and borrowing you are being entangled in sinful activities for which you will have to pay, then just forget that misconception because after death everything is finished. No one is responsible for anything he does during his life." This atheistic conception of life is killing human civilization, for it is without knowledge of the continuation of eternal life.

This *andha-tāmisra* ignorance is due to *tamas.* The condition of not knowing anything about the spirit soul is called *tamas.* This material world is also generally called *tamas* because ninety-nine percent of its living entities are ignorant of their identity as soul. Almost everyone is thinking that he is this body; he has no information of the spirit soul. Guided by this misconception, one always thinks, "This is my body, and anything in relationship with this body is mine." For such misguided living entities, sex life is the background of material existence. Actually, the conditioned souls, in ignorance in this material world, are simply guided by sex life, and as soon as they get the opportunity for sex life, they become attached to so-called home, motherland, children, wealth and opulence. As these attachments increase, *moha*, or the illusion of the bodily concept of life, also increases. Thus the idea that "I am this body, and everything belonging to this body is mine" also increases, and as the whole world is put into *moha*, sectarian societies, families and nationalities are created, and they fight with one another. *Mahā-moha* means to be mad after material enjoyment. Especially in this age of Kali, everyone is overwhelmed by the madness to accumulate paraphernalia for material enjoyment. These definitions are very nicely given in *Viṣṇu Purāṇa*, wherein it is said:

*tamo 'viveko mohaḥ syād*
*antaḥ-karaṇa-vibhramaḥ*
*mahā-mohas tu vijñeyo*
*grāmya-bhoga-sukhaiṣaṇā*

*maraṇaṁ hy andha-tāmisraṁ*
*tāmisraṁ krodha ucyate*
*avidyā pañca-parvaiṣā*
*prādurbhūtā mahātmanaḥ*

## TEXT 19

**विससर्जात्मनः कायं नाभिनन्दंस्तमोमयम् ।**
**जगृहुर्यक्षरक्षांसि रात्रिं क्षुत्तृट्समुद्भवाम् ॥१९॥**

*visasarjātmanaḥ kāyaṁ*
*nābhinandaṁs tamomayam*
*jagṛhur yakṣa-rakṣāṁsi*
*rātriṁ kṣut-tṛṭ-samudbhavām*

*visasarja*—threw off; *ātmanaḥ*—his own; *kāyam*—body; *na*—not; *abhinandan*—being pleased; *tamaḥ-mayam*—made of ignorance; *jagṛhuḥ*—took possession; *yakṣa-rakṣāṁsi*—the Yakṣas and Rākṣasas; *rātrim*—night; *kṣut*—hunger; *tṛṭ*—thirst; *samudbhavām*—the source.

## TRANSLATION

**Out of disgust, Brahmā threw off the body of ignorance, and taking this opportunity, Yakṣas and Rākṣasas sprang for possession of the body, which continued to exist in the form of night. Night is the source of hunger and thirst.**

## TEXT 20

क्षुत्तृड्भ्यामुपसृष्टास्ते तं जग्धुमभिदुद्रुवुः ।
मा रक्षतैनं जक्षध्वमित्यूचुः क्षुत्तृडर्दिताः ॥२०॥

*kṣut-tṛḍbhyām upasṛṣṭās te*
*taṁ jagdhum abhidudruvuḥ*
*mā rakṣatainaṁ jakṣadhvam*
*ity ūcuḥ kṣut-tṛḍ-arditāḥ*

*kṣut-tṛḍbhyām*—by hunger and thirst; *upasṛṣṭāḥ*—were overcome; *te*—the demons (Yakṣas and Rākṣasas); *tam*—Lord Brahmā; *jagdhum*—to eat; *abhidudruvuḥ*—ran toward; *mā*—do not; *rakṣata*—spare; *enam*—him; *jakṣadhvam*—eat; *iti*—thus; *ūcuḥ*—said; *kṣut-tṛṭ-arditāḥ*—afflicted by hunger and thirst.

## TRANSLATION

**Overpowered by hunger and thirst, they ran to devour Brahmā from all sides and cried, "Spare him not! Eat him up!"**

## PURPORT

The representatives of the Yakṣas and Rākṣasas still exist in some countries of the world. It is understood that such uncivilized men take pleasure in killing their own grandfathers and holding a "love feast" by roasting the bodies.

## TEXT 21

देवस्तानाह संविग्नो मा मां जक्षत रक्षत ।
अहो मे यक्षरक्षांसि प्रजा यूयं बभूविथ ॥२१॥

*devas tān āha saṁvigno*
*mā māṁ jakṣata rakṣata*
*aho me yakṣa-rakṣāṁsi*
*prajā yūyaṁ babhūvitha*

*devaḥ*—Lord Brahmā; *tān*—to them; *āha*—said; *saṁvignaḥ*—being anxious; *mā*—do not; *mām*—me; *jakṣata*—eat; *rakṣata*—protect; *aho*—oh; *me*—my; *yakṣa-rakṣāṁsi*—O Yakṣas and Rākṣasas; *prajāḥ*—sons; *yūyam*—you; *babhūvitha*—were born.

## TRANSLATION

**Brahmā, the head of the demigods, full of anxiety, asked them, "Do not eat me, but protect me. You are born from me and have become my sons. Therefore you are Yakṣas and Rākṣasas."**

## PURPORT

The demons who were born from the body of Brahmā were called Yakṣas and Rākṣasas because some of them cried that Brahmā should be eaten and the others cried that he should not be protected. The ones who said that he should be eaten were called Yakṣas, and the ones who said that he should not be protected became Rākṣasas, man-eaters. The two, Yakṣas and Rākṣasas, are the original creation by Brahmā and are represented even until today in the uncivilized men who are scattered all over the universe. They are born of the mode of ignorance, and therefore, because of their behavior, they are called Rākṣasas, or man-eaters.

## TEXT 22

देवताः प्रभया या या दीव्यन् प्रमुखतोऽसृजत् ।
ते अहार्षुर्देवयन्तो विसृष्टां तां प्रभामहः ॥२२॥

*devatāḥ prabhayā yā yā*
*dīvyan pramukhato 'sṛjat*
*te ahārṣur devayanto*
*visṛṣṭāṁ tāṁ prabhām ahaḥ*

*devatāḥ*—the demigods; *prabhayā*—with the glory of light; *yāḥ yāḥ*—those who; *dīvyan*—shining; *pramukhataḥ*—chiefly; *asṛjat*—created; *te*—they; *ahārṣuḥ*—took possession of; *devayantaḥ*—being active; *visṛṣṭām*—separated; *tām*—that; *prabhām*—effulgent form; *ahaḥ*—daytime.

## TRANSLATION

**He then created the chief demigods, who were shining with the glory of goodness. He dropped before them the effulgent form of daytime, and the demigods sportingly took possession of it.**

## PURPORT

Demons were born from the creation of night, and the demigods were born from the creation of day. In other words, demons like the Yakṣas and Rākṣasas are born of the quality of ignorance, and demigods are born of the quality of goodness.

## TEXT 23

देवोऽदेवाञ्जघनतः सृजति स्मातिलोलुपान् ।
त एनं लोलुपतया मैथुनायाभिपेदिरे ॥२३॥

*devo 'devāñ jaghanataḥ*
*sṛjati smātilolupān*
*ta enaṁ lolupatayā*
*maithunāyābhipedire*

*devaḥ*—Lord Brahmā; *adevān*—demons; *jaghanataḥ*—from his buttocks; *sṛjati sma*—gave birth; *ati-lolupān*—excessively fond of sex; *te*—they; *enam*—Lord Brahmā; *lolupatayā*—with lust; *maithunāya*—for copulation; *abhipedire*—approached.

## TRANSLATION

**Lord Brahmā then gave birth to the demons from his buttocks, and they were very fond of sex. Because they were too lustful, they approached him for copulation.**

## PURPORT

Sex life is the background of material existence. Here also it is repeated that demons are very fond of sex life. The more one is free from the desires for sex, the more he is promoted to the level of the demigods; the more one is inclined to enjoy sex, the more he is degraded to the level of demoniac life.

## TEXT 24

ततो हसन् स भगवानसुरैर्निरपत्रपैः ।
अन्वीयमानस्तरसा क्रुद्धो भीतः परापतत् ॥२४॥

*tato hasan sa bhagavān*
*asurair nirapatrapaiḥ*
*anvīyamānas tarasā*
*kruddho bhītaḥ parāpatat*

*tataḥ*—then; *hasan*—laughing; *saḥ bhagavān*—the worshipful Lord Brahmā; *asuraiḥ*—by the demons; *nirapatrapaiḥ*—shameless; *anvīyamānaḥ*—being followed; *tarasā*—in great haste; *kruddhaḥ*—angry; *bhītaḥ*—being afraid; *parāpatat*—ran away.

## TRANSLATION

**The worshipful Brahmā first laughed at their stupidity, but finding the shameless asuras close upon him, he grew indignant and ran in great haste out of fear.**

## PURPORT

Sexually inclined demons have no respect even for their father, and the best policy for a saintly father like Brahmā is to leave such demoniac sons.

## TEXT 25

स उपव्रज्य वरदं प्रपन्नार्तिहरं हरिम् ।
अनुग्रहाय भक्तानामनुरूपात्मदर्शनम् ॥२५॥

*sa upavrajya varadaṁ*
*prapannārti-haraṁ harim*
*anugrahāya bhaktānām*
*anurūpātma-darśanam*

*saḥ*—Lord Brahmā; *upavrajya*—approaching; *vara-dam*—the bestower of all boons; *prapanna*—of those taking shelter at His lotus feet; *ārti*—distress; *haram*—who dispels; *harim*—Lord Śrī Hari; *anugrahāya*—for showing mercy; *bhaktānām*—to His devotees; *anurūpa*—in suitable forms; *ātma-darśanam*—who manifests Himself.

## TRANSLATION

**He approached the Personality of Godhead, who bestows all boons and who dispels the agony of His devotees and of those who take shelter of His lotus feet. He manifests His innumerable transcendental forms for the satisfaction of His devotees.**

## PURPORT

Here the words *bhaktānām anurūpātma-darśanam* mean that the Personality of Godhead manifests His multiforms according to the desires of the devotees. For example, Hanumānjī (Vajrāṅgajī) wanted to see the form of the Lord as the Personality of Godhead Rāmacandra, whereas other Vaiṣṇavas want to see the form of Rādhā-Kṛṣṇa, and still other devotees want to see the Lord in the form of Lakṣmī-Nārāyaṇa. The Māyāvādī philosophers think that although all these forms are assumed by the Lord just as the devotees desire to see Him, actually He is impersonal. From *Brahma-saṁhitā*, however, we can understand that this is not so, for the Lord has multiforms. It is said in the *Brahma-saṁhitā, advaitam acyutam.* The Lord does not appear before the devotee because of the devotee's imagination. *Brahma-saṁhitā* further explains that the Lord has innumerable forms: *rāmādi-mūrtiṣu kalā-niyamena tiṣṭhan.* He exists in millions and millions of forms. There are 8,400,000 species of living entities, but the incarnations of the Supreme Lord are innumerable. In the *Bhāgavatam* it is stated that as the waves in the sea cannot be counted but appear and disappear continually, the incarnations and forms of the Lord are innumerable. A devotee is attached to a particular form, and it is that form which he worships. We have just described the first appearance of the boar within this universe. There are innumerable universes, and somewhere or other the boar form is now existing. All the forms of the Lord are eternal. It is the devotee's inclination to worship a particular form, and he engages in devotional service to that form. In a verse in the *Rāmāyaṇa*, Hanumān, the great devotee of Rāma, said, "I know that there is no difference between the Sītā-Rāma and Lakṣmī-Nārāyaṇa forms of the Supreme Personality of Godhead, but nevertheless, the form of Rāma and Sītā has absorbed my affection and love. Therefore I want to see the Lord in the forms of Rāma and Sītā." Similarly, the Gauḍīya Vaiṣṇava loves the forms of Rādhā and Kṛṣṇa, and Kṛṣṇa and Rukmiṇī at Dvārakā. The words *bhaktānām anurūpātma-darśanam* mean that the Lord is always pleased to favor the devotee in the particular form in which the devotee wants to worship and render service unto Him. In this verse it is stated that Brahmā approached Hari, the Supreme Personality of Godhead. This form of the Lord is Kṣīrodakaśāyī Viṣṇu. Whenever there is some trouble and Brahmā has to approach the Lord, he can approach Kṣīrodakaśāyī Viṣṇu, and it is the grace of the Lord that whenever Brahmā approaches about disturbances in the universe, the Lord gives him relief in so many ways.

## TEXT 26

पाहि मां परमात्मंस्ते प्रेषणेनासृजं प्रजाः ।
ता इमा यभितुं पापा उपाक्रामन्ति मां प्रभो ॥२६॥

*pāhi māṁ paramātmaṁs te*
*preṣaṇenāsṛjaṁ prajāḥ*
*tā imā yabhituṁ pāpā*
*upākrāmanti māṁ prabho*

*pāhi*—protect; *mām*—me; *parama-ātman*—O Supreme Lord; *te*—Your; *preṣaṇena*—by order; *asṛjam*—I created; *prajāḥ*—living beings; *tāḥ imāḥ*—those very persons; *yabhitum*—to have sex; *pāpāḥ*—sinful beings; *upākrāmanti*—are approaching; *mām*—me; *prabho*—O Lord.

## TRANSLATION

**Lord Brahmā, approaching the Lord, addressed Him thus: My Lord, please protect me from these sinful demons, who were created by me under Your order. They are infuriated by an appetite for sex and have come to attack me.**

## PURPORT

It appears here that the homosexual appetite of males for each other is created in this episode of the creation of the demons by Brahmā. In other words, the homosexual appetite of a man for another man is demoniac and is not for any sane male in the ordinary course of life.

## TEXT 27

त्वमेकः किल लोकानां क्लिष्टानां क्लेशनाशनः ।
त्वमेकः क्लेशदस्तेषामनासन्नपदां तव ॥२७॥

*tvam ekaḥ kila lokānāṁ*
*kliṣṭānāṁ kleśa-nāśanaḥ*
*tvam ekaḥ kleśadas teṣām*
*anāsanna-padāṁ tava*

*tvam*—You; *ekaḥ*—alone; *kila*—indeed; *lokānām*—of the people; *kliṣṭānām*—afflicted with miseries; *kleśa*—the distresses; *nāśanaḥ*—relieving; *tvam ekaḥ*—You alone; *kleśa-daḥ*—inflicting distress; *teṣām*—on those; *anāsanna*—not taken shelter; *padām*—feet; *tava*—Your.

## TRANSLATION

**My Lord, You are the only one capable of ending the affliction of the distressed and inflicting agony on those who never resort to Your feet.**

## PURPORT

The words *kleśadas teṣām anāsanna-padāṁ tava* indicate that the Lord has two concerns. The first is to give protection to persons who take shelter of His lotus feet, and the second is to give trouble to those who are always demoniac and who are inimical toward the Lord. *Māyā's* function is to give afflictions to the nondevotees. Here Brahmā said, "You are the protector of the surrendered souls; therefore I surrender unto Your lotus feet. Please give me protection from these demons."

## TEXT 28

सोऽवधार्यास्य कार्पण्यं विविक्ताध्यात्मदर्शनः ।
विमुञ्चात्मतनुं घोरामित्युक्तो विमुमोच ह ॥२८॥

*so 'vadhāryāsya kārpaṇyaṁ*
*viviktādhyātma-darśanaḥ*
*vimuñcātma-tanuṁ ghorām*
*ity ukto vimumoca ha*

*saḥ*—the Supreme Lord, Hari; *avadhārya*—perceiving; *asya*—of Lord Brahmā; *kārpaṇyam*—the distress; *vivikta*—without a doubt; *adhyātma*—minds of others; *darśanaḥ*—one who can see; *vimuñca*—cast off; *ātma-tanum*—your body; *ghorām*—impure; *iti uktaḥ*—thus commanded; *vimumoca ha*—Lord Brahmā threw it off.

## TRANSLATION

**The Lord, who can distinctly see the minds of others, perceived Brahmā's distress and said to him: "Cast off this impure body of yours." Thus commanded by the Lord, Brahmā cast off his body.**

## PURPORT

The Lord is described here by the word *viviktādhyātma-darśanaḥ*. If anyone can completely perceive another's distress without doubt, it is the Lord Himself. If someone is in distress and wants to get relief from his friend, sometimes it so happens that his friend does not appreciate the volume of distress he is suffering. But for the Supreme Lord it is not difficult. The Supreme Lord, as Paramātmā, is sitting within the heart of every living entity, and He directly perceives the exact causes of distress. In *Bhagavad-gītā* the Lord says, *sarvasya cāhaṁ hṛdi sanniviṣṭaḥ:* "I am sitting in everyone's heart, and because of Me one's remembrance and forgetfulness occur." Thus whenever one fully surrenders unto the Supreme Lord, one finds that He is sitting within one's heart. He can give us direction how to get out of dangers or how to approach Him in devotional service. The Lord, however, asked Brahmā to give up his present body because it had created the demoniac principle. According to Śrīdhara Svāmī, Brahmā's constant dropping of his body does not refer to his actually giving up his body. Rather, he suggests that Brahmā gave up a particular mentality. Mind is the subtle body of the living entity. We may sometimes be absorbed in some thought which is sinful, but if we give up the sinful thought, it may be said that we give up the body. Brahmā's mind was not in correct order when he created the demons. It must have been full of passion because the entire creation was passionate; therefore such passionate sons were born. It follows that any father and mother should also be careful while begetting children. The mental condition of a child depends upon the mental status of his parents at the time he is conceived. According to the Vedic system, therefore, the *garbhādhāna-saṁskāra*, or the ceremony for giving birth to a child, is observed. Before begetting a child, one has to sanctify his perplexed mind. When the parents engage their minds in the lotus feet of the Lord and in such a state the child is born, naturally good devotee children come; when the society is full of such good population, there is no trouble from demoniac mentalities.

## TEXT 29

तां क्वणच्चरणाम्भोजां मदविह्वललोचनाम् ।
काञ्चीकलापविलसद्दुकूलच्छन्नरोधसम् ॥२९॥

*tāṁ kvaṇac-caraṇāmbhojāṁ*
*mada-vihvala-locanām*
*kāñcī-kalāpa-vilasad-*
*dukūla-cchanna-rodhasam*

*tām*—that body; *kvaṇat*—tinkling with ankle bells; *caraṇa-ambhojām*—with lotus feet; *mada*—intoxication; *vihvala*—overwhelmed; *locanām*—with eyes; *kāñcī-kalāpa*—with a girdle made of golden ornaments; *vilasat*—shining; *dukūla*—by fine cloth; *channa*—covered; *rodhasam*—having hips.

## TRANSLATION

**The body given up by Brahmā took the form of the evening twilight, when the day and night meet, a time which kindles passion. The asuras, who are passionate by nature, dominated as they are by the element of rajas, took it for a damsel, whose lotus feet resounded with the tinkling of anklets, whose eyes were wide with intoxication and whose hips were covered by fine cloth, over which shone a girdle.**

## PURPORT

As early morning is the period for spiritual cultivation, the beginning of evening is the period for passion. Demoniac men are generally very fond of sex enjoyment; therefore they very much appreciate the approach of evening. The demons took the approach of the evening twilight to be a beautiful woman, and they began to adore her in various ways. They imagined the twilight to be a very beautiful woman with tinkling bangles on her feet, a girdle on her hips, and beautiful breasts, and for their sexual satisfaction they imagined the appearance of this beautiful girl before them.

## TEXT 30

अन्योन्यश्लेषयोत्तुङ्गनिरन्तरपयोधराम् ।
सुनासां सुद्विजां स्निग्धहासलीलावलोकनाम् ॥३०॥

*anyonya-śleṣayottuṅga-*
*nirantara-payodharām*
*sunāsāṁ sudvijāṁ snigdha-*
*hāsa-līlāvalokanām*

*anyonya*—to each other; *śleṣayā*—because of clinging; *uttuṅga*—raised; *nirantara*—without intervening space; *payaḥ-dharām*—breasts; *su-nāsām*—shapely nose; *su-dvijām*—beautiful teeth; *snigdha*—lovely; *hāsa*—smile; *līlā-avalokanām*—sportful glance.

## TRANSLATION

**Her breasts projected upward because of their clinging to each other, and they were too contiguous to admit any intervening**

**space. She had a shapely nose and beautiful teeth; a lovely smile played on her lips, and she cast a sportful glance at the asuras.**

## TEXT 31

गूहन्तीं व्रीडयात्मानं नीलालकवरूथिनीम्।
उपलभ्यासुरा धर्म सर्वे सम्मुमुहुः स्त्रियम् ॥३१॥

*gūhantīṁ vrīḍayātmānaṁ*
*nīlālaka-varūthinīm*
*upalabhyāsurā dharma*
*sarve sammumuhuḥ striyam*

*gūhantīm*—hiding; *vrīḍayā*—out of shyness; *ātmānam*—herself; *nīla*—dark; *alaka*—hair; *varūthinīm*—a bunch; *upalabhya*—upon imagining; *asurāḥ*—the demons; *dharma*—O Vidura; *sarve*—all; *sammumuhuḥ*—were captivated; *striyam*—woman.

## TRANSLATION

**Adorned with dark tresses, she hid herself, as it were, out of shyness. Upon seeing that girl, the asuras were all infatuated with an appetite for sex.**

## PURPORT

The difference between demons and demigods is that a beautiful woman very easily attracts the minds of demons, but she cannot attract the mind of a godly person. A godly person is full of knowledge, and a demoniac person is full of ignorance. Just as a child is attracted by a beautiful doll, similarly a demon, who is less intelligent and full of ignorance, is attracted by material beauty and an appetite for sex. The godly person knows that this nicely dressed and ornamented attraction of high breasts, high hips, beautiful nose and fair complexion is *māyā*. All the beauty a woman can display is only a combination of flesh and blood. Śrī Śaṅkarācārya has advised all persons not to be attracted by the interaction of flesh and blood; they should be attracted by the real beauty in spiritual life. The real beauty is Kṛṣṇa and Rādhā. One who is attracted by the beauty of Rādhā and Kṛṣṇa cannot be attracted by the false beauty of this material world. That is the difference between a demon and a godly person or devotee.

## TEXT 32

अहो रूपमहो धैर्यमहो अस्या नवं वयः ।
मध्ये कामयमानानामकामेव विसर्पति ॥३२॥

*aho rūpam aho dhairyam*
*aho asyā navaṁ vayaḥ*
*madhye kāmayamānānām*
*akāmeva visarpati*

*aho*—oh; *rūpam*—what beauty; *aho*—oh; *dhairyam*—what self-control; *aho*—oh; *asyāḥ*—her; *navam*—budding; *vayaḥ*—youth; *madhye*—in the midst; *kāmayamānānām*—of those passionately longing for; *akāmā*—free from passion; *iva*—like; *visarpati*—walking with us.

## TRANSLATION

**The demons praised her: Oh, what a beauty! What rare self-control! What a budding youth! In the midst of us all, who are passionately longing for her, she is moving about like one absolutely free from passion.**

## TEXT 33

वितर्कयन्तो बहुधा तां सन्ध्यां प्रमदाकृतिम् ।
अभिसम्भाव्य विश्रम्भात्पर्यपृच्छन् कुमेधसः ॥३३॥

*vitarkayanto bahudhā*
*tāṁ sandhyāṁ pramadākṛtim*
*abhisambhāvya viśrambhāt*
*paryapṛcchan kumedhasaḥ*

*vitarkayantaḥ*—indulging in speculations; *bahudhā*—various kinds; *tām*—her; *sandhyām*—the evening twilight; *pramadā*—a young woman; *ākṛtim*—in the form of; *abhisambhāvya*—treating with great respect; *viśrambhāt*—fondly; *paryapṛcchan*—questioned; *ku-medhasaḥ*—wicked-minded.

## TRANSLATION

**Indulging in various speculations about the evening twilight, which appeared to them endowed with the form of a young woman, the wicked-minded asuras treated her with respect and fondly spoke to her as follows.**

## TEXT 34

कासि कस्यासि रम्भोरु को वार्थस्तेऽत्र भामिनि।
रूपद्रविणपण्येन दुर्भगान्नो विबाधसे ॥३४॥

*kāsi kasyāsi rambhoru*
*ko vārthas te 'tra bhāmini*
*rūpa-draviṇa-paṇyena*
*durbhagān no vibādhase*

*kā*—who; *asi*—are you; *kasya*—belonging to whom; *asi*—are you; *rambhoru*—O pretty one; *kaḥ*—what; *vā*—or; *arthaḥ*—object; *te*—your; *atra*—here; *bhāmini*—O passionate lady; *rūpa*—beauty; *draviṇa*—priceless; *paṇyena*—with the commodity; *durbhagān*—unfortunate; *naḥ*—us; *vibādhase*—you tantalize.

## TRANSLATION

**Who are you, O pretty girl? Whose wife or daughter are you, and what can be the object of your appearing before us? Why do you tantalize us, unfortunate as we are, with the priceless commodity of your beauty?**

## PURPORT

The mentality of the demons in being enamored by the false beauty of this material world is expressed herein. The demoniac can pay any price for the skin beauty of this material world. They work very hard all day and night, but the purpose of their hard work is to enjoy sex life. Sometimes they misrepresent themselves as *karma-yogīs*, not knowing the meaning of the word *yoga. Yoga* means to link up with the Supreme Personality of Godhead, or to act in Kṛṣṇa consciousness. A person who works very hard, no matter in what occupation, and who offers the result of the work to the service of the Supreme Personality of Godhead, Kṛṣṇa, is called a *karma-yogī.*

## TEXT 35

**या वा काचित्त्वमबले दिष्ट्या सन्दर्शनं तव ।**
**उत्सुनोषीक्षमाणानां कन्दुकक्रीडया मनः ॥३५॥**

*yā vā kācit tvam abale*
*diṣṭyā sandarśanaṁ tava*
*utsunoṣīkṣamāṇānāṁ*
*kanduka-krīḍayā manaḥ*

*yā*—whosoever; *vā*—or; *kācit*—anyone; *tvam*—you; *abale*—O beautiful girl; *diṣṭyā*—by fortune; *sandarśanam*—seeing; *tava*—of you; *utsunoṣi*—you agitate; *īkṣamāṇānām*—of the onlookers; *kanduka*—with a ball; *krīḍayā*—by play; *manaḥ*—the mind.

## TRANSLATION

**Whosoever you may be, O beautiful girl, we are fortunate in being able to see you. While playing with a ball, you have agitated the minds of all onlookers.**

## PURPORT

Demons arrange many kinds of performances to see the glaring beauty of a beautiful woman. Here it is stated that they saw the girl playing with a ball. Sometimes the demoniac arrange for so-called sports, like tennis, with the opposite sex. The purpose of such sporting is to see the bodily construction of the beautiful girl and enjoy a subtle sex mentality. This demoniac sex mentality of material enjoyment is sometimes encouraged by so-called *yogīs* who encourage the public to enjoy sex life in different varieties and at the same time advertise that if one meditates on a certain manufactured *mantra* one can become God within six months. The public wants to be cheated, and Kṛṣṇa therefore creates such cheaters to misrepresent and delude. These so-called *yogīs* are actually enjoyers of the world garbed as *yogīs*. *Bhagavad-gītā*, however, recommends that if one wants to enjoy life, then it cannot be with these gross senses. A patient is advised by the experienced physician to refrain from ordinary enjoyment while in the diseased condition. A diseased person cannot enjoy anything; he has to restrain his enjoyment in order to get rid of the disease. Similarly, our material condition is a diseased condition. If one wants to enjoy real sense enjoyment, then one must get free of the entanglement of material existence. In spiritual life we can enjoy sense enjoyment which has no end. The difference between material and spiritual enjoyment is that material enjoyment is limited. Even if a man engages in material sex enjoyment, he cannot enjoy it for long. But when the sex enjoyment is given up, then one can enter spiritual life, which is unending. In the *Bhāgavatam* (5.5.1) it is stated that *brahma-saukhya*, spiritual happiness, is *ananta*, unending. Foolish creatures are enamored by the beauty of matter and think that the enjoyment it offers is real, but actually that is not real enjoyment.

## TEXT 36

नैकत्र ते जयति शालिनि पादपद्मं
घ्नन्त्या मुहुः करतलेन पतत्पतङ्गम् ।
मध्यं विषीदति बृहत्स्तनभारभीतं
शान्तेव दृष्टिरमला सुशिखासमूहः ॥३६॥

*naikatra te jayati śālini pāda-padmaṁ*
*ghnantyā muhuḥ kara-talena patat-pataṅgam*
*madhyaṁ viṣīdati bṛhat-stana-bhāra-bhītaṁ*
*śānteva dṛṣṭir amalā suśikhā-samūhaḥ*

*na*—not; *ekatra*—in one place; *te*—your; *jayati*—stay; *śālini*—O beautiful woman; *pāda-padmam*—lotus feet; *ghnantyāḥ*—striking; *muhuḥ*—again and again; *kara-talena*—by the palm of the hand; *patat*—bouncing; *pataṅgam*—the ball; *madhyam*—waist; *viṣīdati*—

gets fatigued; *bṛhat*—full grown; *stana*—of your breasts; *bhāra*—by the weight; *bhītam*—oppressed; *śāntā iva*—as if fatigued; *dṛṣṭiḥ*—vision; *amalā*—clear; *su*—beautiful; *śikhā*—your hair; *samūhaḥ*—bunch.

## TRANSLATION

**O beautiful woman, when you strike the bouncing ball against the ground with your hand again and again, your lotus feet do not stay in one place. Oppressed by the weight of your full-grown breasts, your waist becomes fatigued, and your clear vision grows dull, as it were. Pray braid your comely hair.**

## PURPORT

The demons observed beautiful gestures in the woman's every step. Here they praise her full-grown breasts, her scattered hair and her movements in stepping forward and backward while playing with the ball. In every step they enjoy her womanly beauty, and while they enjoy her beauty their minds become agitated by sex desire. As moths at night surround a fire and are killed, so the demons become victims of the movements of the ball-like breasts of a beautiful woman. The scattered hair of a beautiful woman also afflicts the heart of a lusty demon.

## TEXT 37

इति सायन्तनीं सन्ध्यामसुराः प्रमदायतीम् ।
प्रलोभयन्तीं जगृहुर्मत्वा मूढधियः स्त्रियम् ॥३७॥

*iti sāyantanīṁ sandhyām*
*asurāḥ pramadāyatīm*
*pralobhayantīṁ jagṛhur*
*matvā mūḍha-dhiyaḥ striyam*

*iti*—in this way; *sāyantanīm*—the evening; *sandhyām*—twilight; *asurāḥ*—the demons; *pramadāyatīm*—behaving like a wanton woman; *pralobhayantīm*—alluring; *jagṛhuḥ*—seized; *matvā*—thinking to be; *mūḍha-dhiyaḥ*—unintelligent; *striyam*—a woman.

## TRANSLATION

**The asuras, clouded in their understanding, took the evening twilight to be a beautiful woman showing herself in her alluring form, and they seized her.**

## PURPORT

The *asuras* are described here as *mūḍha-dhiyaḥ*, meaning that they are captivated by ignorance, just like the ass. The demons were captivated by the false, glaring beauty of this material form, and thus they embraced her.

## TEXT 38

प्रहस्य भावगम्भीरं जिघ्रन्त्यात्मानमात्मना ।
कान्त्या ससर्ज भगवान् गन्धर्वाप्सरसां गणान् ॥३८॥

*prahasya bhāva-gambhīraṁ*
*jighrantyātmānam ātmanā*
*kāntyā sasarja bhagavān*
*gandharvāpsarasāṁ gaṇān*

*prahasya*—smiling; *bhāva-gambhīram*—with a deep purpose; *jighrantyā*—understanding; *ātmānam*—himself; *ātmanā*—by himself; *kāntyā*—by his loveliness; *sasarja*—created; *bhagavān*—the worshipful Lord Brahmā; *gandharva*—the celestial musicians; *apsarasām*—and of the heavenly dancing girls; *gaṇān*—the hosts of.

## TRANSLATION

**With a laugh full of deep significance, the worshipful Brahmā then evolved by his own loveliness, which seemed to enjoy itself by itself, the hosts of Gandharvas and Apsarās.**

## PURPORT

The musicians in the upper planetary systems are called Gandharvas, and the dancing girls are called Apsarās. After being attacked by the demons and evolving a form of a beautiful woman in the twilight, Brahmā next created Gandharvas and Apsarās. Music and dancing employed in sense gratification are to be accepted as demoniac, but the same music and dancing, when employed in glorifying the Supreme Lord as *kīrtana*, are transcendental, and they bring about a life completely fit for spiritual enjoyment.

## TEXT 39

विससर्ज तनुं तां वै ज्योत्स्नां कान्तिमतीं प्रियाम् ।
त एव चाददुः प्रीत्या विश्वावसुपुरोगमाः ॥३९॥

*visasarja tanuṁ tāṁ vai*
*jyotsnāṁ kāntimatīṁ priyām*
*ta eva cādaduḥ prītyā*
*viśvāvasu-purogamāḥ*

*visasarja*—gave up; *tanum*—form; *tām*—that; *vai*—in fact; *jyotsnām*—moonlight; *kānti-matīm*—shining; *priyām*—beloved; *te*—the Gandharvas; *eva*—certainly; *ca*—and; *ādaduḥ*—took possession; *prītyā*—gladly; *viśvāvasu-puraḥ-gamāḥ*—headed by Viśvāvasu.

### TRANSLATION

**After that, Brahmā gave up that shining and beloved form of moonlight. Viśvāvasu and other Gandharvas gladly took possession of it.**

## TEXT 40

सृष्ट्वा भूतपिशाचांश्च भगवानात्मतन्द्रिणा ।
दिग्वाससो मुक्तकेशान् वीक्ष्य चामीलयद् दृशौ ॥४०॥

*sṛṣṭvā bhūta-piśācāṁś ca*
*bhagavān ātma-tandriṇā*
*dig-vāsaso mukta-keśān*
*vīkṣya cāmīlayad dṛśau*

*sṛṣṭvā*—having created; *bhūta*—ghosts; *piśācān*—fiends; *ca*—and; *bhagavān*—Lord Brahmā; *ātma*—his; *tandriṇā*—from laziness; *dik-vāsasaḥ*—naked; *mukta*—disheveled; *keśān*—hair; *vīkṣya*—seeing; *ca*—and; *amīlayat*—closed; *dṛśau*—two eyes.

## TRANSLATION

**The glorious Brahmā next evolved from his sloth the ghosts and fiends, but he closed his eyes when he saw them stand naked with their hair scattered.**

## PURPORT

Ghosts and mischievous hobgoblins are also the creation of Brahmā; they are not false. All of them are meant for putting the conditioned soul into various miseries. They are understood to be the creation of Brahmā under the direction of the Supreme Lord.

## TEXT 41

जगृहुस्तद्विसृष्टां तां जृम्भणाख्यां तनुं प्रभोः ।
निद्रामिन्द्रियविक्लेदो यया भूतेषु दृश्यते ।
येनोच्छिष्टान्धर्षयन्ति तमुन्मादं प्रचक्षते ॥४१॥

*jagṛhus tad-visṛṣṭāṁ tāṁ*
*jṛmbhaṇākhyāṁ tanuṁ prabhoḥ*
*nidrām indriya-vikledo*
*yayā bhūteṣu dṛśyate*
*yenocchiṣṭān dharṣayanti*
*tam unmādaṁ pracakṣate*

*jagṛhuḥ*—took possession; *tat-visṛṣṭām*—thrown off by him; *tām*—that; *jṛmbhaṇa-ākhyām*—known as yawning; *tanum*—the body; *prabhoḥ*—of Lord Brahmā; *nidrām*—sleep; *indriya-vikledaḥ*—drooling; *yayā*—by which; *bhūteṣu*—among the living beings; *dṛśyate*—is observed; *yena*—by which; *ucchiṣṭān*—smeared with stool and urine; *dharṣayanti*—bewilder; *tam*—that; *unmādam*—madness; *pracakṣate*—is spoken of.

### TRANSLATION

**The ghosts and hobgoblins took possession of the body thrown off in the form of yawning by Brahmā, the creator of the living entities. This is also known as the sleep which causes drooling. The hobgoblins and ghosts attack men who are impure, and their attack is spoken of as insanity.**

### PURPORT

The disease of insanity or being haunted by ghosts takes place in an unclean state of existence. Here it is clearly stated that when a man is fast asleep and saliva flows from his mouth and he remains unclean, ghosts then take advantage of his unclean state and haunt his body. In other words, those who drool while sleeping are considered unclean and are subject to be haunted by ghosts or to go insane.

### TEXT 42

ऊर्जस्वन्तं मन्यमान आत्मानं भगवानजः ।
साध्यान् गणान् पितृगणान् परोक्षेणासृजत्प्रभुः ॥४२॥

*ūrjasvantaṁ manyamāna*
*ātmānaṁ bhagavān ajaḥ*
*sādhyān gaṇān pitṛ-gaṇān*
*parokṣeṇāsṛjat prabhuḥ*

*ūrjaḥ-vantam*—full of energy; *manyamānaḥ*—recognizing; *ātmānam*—himself; *bhagavān*—the most worshipful; *ajaḥ*—Brahmā; *sādhyān*—the demigods; *gaṇān*—hosts; *pitṛ-gaṇān*—and the Pitās; *parokṣeṇa*—from his invisible form; *asṛjat*—created; *prabhuḥ*—the lord of beings.

### TRANSLATION

**Recognizing himself to be full of desire and energy, the worshipful Brahmā, the creator of the living entities, evolved from his own invisible form, from his navel, the hosts of Sādhyas and Pitās.**

## PURPORT

The Sādhyas and Pitās are invisible forms of departed souls, and they are also created by Brahmā.

## TEXT 43

त आत्मसर्गं तं कायं पितरः प्रतिपेदिरे ।
साध्येभ्यश्च पितृभ्यश्च कवयो यद्वितन्वते ॥४३॥

*ta ātma-sargaṁ taṁ kāyaṁ*
*pitaraḥ pratipedire*
*sādhyebhyaś ca pitṛbhyaś ca*
*kavayo yad vitanvate*

*te*—they; *ātma-sargam*—source of their existence; *tam*—that; *kāyam*—body; *pitaraḥ*—the Pitās; *pratipedire*—accepted; *sādhyebhyaḥ*—to the Sādhyas; *ca*—and; *pitṛbhyaḥ*—to the Pitās; *ca*—also; *kavayaḥ*—those well versed in rituals; *yat*—through which; *vitanvate*—offer oblations.

## TRANSLATION

**The Pitās themselves took possession of the invisible body, the source of their existence. It is through the medium of this invisible body that those well versed in the rituals offer oblations to the Sādhyas and Pitās [in the form of their departed ancestors] on the occasion of śrāddha.**

## PURPORT

*Śrāddha* is a ritualistic performance observed by the followers of the *Vedas.* There is a yearly occasion of fifteen days when ritualistic religionists follow the principle of offering oblations to departed souls. Thus those fathers and ancestors who, by freaks of nature, might not have a gross body for material enjoyment can again gain such bodies due to the offering of *śrāddha* oblations by their descendants. The performance of *śrāddha,* or offering oblations with *prasāda,* is still current in India, especially at Gayā, where oblations are offered at the lotus feet of

Viṣṇu in a celebrated temple. Because the Lord is thus pleased with the devotional service of the descendants, by His grace He liberates the condemned souls of forefathers who do not have gross bodies, and He favors them to again receive a gross body for development of spiritual advancement.

Unfortunately, by the influence of *māyā*, the conditioned soul employs the body he gets for sense gratification, forgetting that such an occupation may lead him to return to an invisible body. The devotee of the Lord, or one who is in Kṛṣṇa consciousness, however, does not need to perform such ritualistic ceremonies as *śrāddha* because he is always pleasing the Supreme Lord; therefore his fathers and ancestors who might have been in difficulty are automatically relieved. The vivid example is Prahlāda Mahārāja. Prahlāda Mahārāja requested Lord Nṛsiṁhadeva to deliver his sinful father, who had so many times offended the lotus feet of the Lord. The Lord replied that in a family where a Vaiṣṇava like Prahlāda is born, not only his father but his father's father and their fathers—up to the fourteenth father back—are all automatically delivered. The conclusion, therefore, is that Kṛṣṇa consciousness is the sum total of all good work for the family, for society and for all living entities. In the *Caitanya-caritāmṛta* the author says that a person fully conversant with Kṛṣṇa consciousness does not perform any rituals because he knows that simply by serving Kṛṣṇa in full Kṛṣṇa consciousness, all rituals are automatically performed.

## TEXT 44

सिद्धान्विद्याधरांश्चैव तिरोधानेन सोऽसृजत् ।
तेभ्योऽददात्तमात्मानमन्तर्धानाख्यमद्भुतम् ॥४४॥

*siddhān vidyādharāṁś caiva*
*tirodhānena so 'sṛjat*
*tebhyo 'dadāt tam ātmānam*
*antardhānākhyam adbhutam*

*siddhān*—the Siddhas; *vidyādharān*—Vidyādharas; *ca eva*—and also; *tirodhānena*—by the faculty of remaining hidden from vision; *saḥ*—Lord Brahmā; *asṛjat*—created; *tebhyaḥ*—to them; *adadāt*—gave;

*tam ātmānam*—that form of his; *antardhāna-ākhyam*—known as the Antardhāna; *adbhutam*—wonderful.

### TRANSLATION

**Then Lord Brahmā, by his ability to be hidden from vision, created the Siddhas and Vidyādharas and gave them that wonderful form of his known as the Antardhāna.**

### PURPORT

*Antardhāna* means that these living creatures can be perceived to be present, but they cannot be seen by vision.

### TEXT 45

स किन्नरान् किम्पुरुषान् प्रत्यात्म्येनासृजत्प्रभुः ।
मानयन्नात्मनात्मानमात्माभासं विलोकयन् ॥४५॥

*sa kinnarān kimpuruṣān*
*pratyātmyenāsṛjat prabhuḥ*
*mānayann ātmanātmānam*
*ātmābhāsaṁ vilokayan*

*saḥ*—Lord Brahmā; *kinnarān*—the Kinnaras; *kimpuruṣān*—the Kimpuruṣas; *pratyātmyena*—from his reflection (in water); *asṛjat*—created; *prabhuḥ*—the lord of the living beings (Brahmā); *mānayan*—admiring; *ātmanā ātmānam*—himself by himself; *ātma-ābhāsam*—his reflection; *vilokayan*—seeing.

### TRANSLATION

**One day, Brahmā, the creator of the living entities, beheld his own reflection in the water, and admiring himself, he evolved Kimpuruṣas as well as Kinnaras out of that reflection.**

### TEXT 46

ते तु तज्जगृहू रूपं त्यक्तं यत्परमेष्ठिना ।
मिथुनीभूय गायन्तस्तमेवोषसि कर्मभिः ॥४६॥

*te tu taj jagṛhū rūpaṁ*
*tyaktaṁ yat parameṣṭhinā*
*mithunī-bhūya gāyantas*
*tam evoṣasi karmabhiḥ*

*te*—they (the Kinnaras and Kimpuruṣas); *tu*—but; *tat*—that; *jagṛhuḥ*—took possession of; *rūpam*—that shadowy form; *tyaktam*—given up; *yat*—which; *parameṣṭhinā*—by Brahmā; *mithunī-bhūya*—coming together with their spouses; *gāyantaḥ*—praise in song; *tam*—him; *eva*—only; *uṣasi*—at daybreak; *karmabhiḥ*—with his exploits.

## TRANSLATION

**The Kimpuruṣas and Kinnaras took possession of that shadowy form left by Brahmā. That is why they and their spouses sing his praises by recounting his exploits at every daybreak.**

## PURPORT

The time early in the morning, one and a half hours before sunrise, is called *brāhma-muhūrta.* During this *brāhma-muhūrta*, spiritual activities are recommended. Spiritual activities performed early in the morning have a greater effect than in any other part of the day.

## TEXT 47

देहेन वै भोगवता शयानो बहुचिन्तया ।
सर्गेऽनुपचिते क्रोधादुत्ससर्ज ह तद्वपुः ॥४७॥

*dehena vai bhogavatā*
*śayāno bahu-cintayā*
*sarge 'nupacite krodhād*
*utsasarja ha tad vapuḥ*

*dehena*—with his body; *vai*—indeed; *bhogavatā*—stretching out full length; *śayānaḥ*—lying fully stretched; *bahu*—great; *cintayā*—with concern; *sarge*—the creation; *anupacite*—not proceeded; *krodhāt*—out of anger; *utsasarja*—gave up; *ha*—in fact; *tat*—that; *vapuḥ*—body.

## TRANSLATION

**Once Brahmā lay down with his body stretched at full length. He was very concerned that the work of creation had not proceeded apace, and in a sullen mood he gave up that body too.**

## TEXT 48

येऽहीयन्तामुतः केशा अहयस्तेऽङ्ग जज्ञिरे ।
सर्पाः प्रसर्पतः क्रूरा नागा भोगोरुकन्धराः ॥४८॥

*ye 'hīyantāmutaḥ keśā*
*ahayas te 'ṅga jajñire*
*sarpāḥ prasarpataḥ krūrā*
*nāgā bhogoru-kandharāḥ*

*ye*—which; *ahīyanta*—dropped out; *amutaḥ*—from that; *keśāḥ*—hairs; *ahayaḥ*—snakes; *te*—they; *aṅga*—O dear Vidura; *jajñire*—took birth as; *sarpāḥ*—snakes; *prasarpataḥ*—from the crawling body; *krūrāḥ*—envious; *nāgāḥ*—cobras; *bhoga*—with hoods; *uru*—big; *kandharāḥ*—whose necks.

## TRANSLATION

**O dear Vidura, the hair that dropped from that body transformed into snakes, and even while the body crawled along with its hands and feet contracted, there sprang from it ferocious serpents and Nāgas with their hoods expanded.**

## TEXT 49

स आत्मानं मन्यमानः कृतकृत्यमिवात्मभूः ।
तदा मनून् ससर्जान्ते मनसा लोकभावनान् ॥४९॥

*sa ātmānaṁ manyamānaḥ*
*kṛta-kṛtyam ivātmabhūḥ*
*tadā manūn sasarjānte*
*manasā loka-bhāvanān*

*saḥ*—Lord Brahmā; *ātmānam*—himself; *manyamānaḥ*—considering; *kṛta-kṛtyam*—had accomplished the object of life; *iva*—as if; *ātma-bhūḥ*—born from the Supreme; *tadā*—then; *manūn*—the Manus; *sasarja*—created; *ante*—at the end; *manasā*—from his mind; *loka*—of the world; *bhāvanān*—promoting the welfare.

### TRANSLATION

**One day Brahmā, the self-born, the first living creature, felt as if the object of his life had been accomplished. At that time he evolved from his mind the Manus, who promote the welfare activities of the universe.**

### TEXT 50

तेभ्यः सोऽसृजत्स्वीयं पुरं पुरुषमात्मवान् ।
तान् दृष्ट्वा ये पुरा सृष्टाः प्रशशंसुः प्रजापतिम् ॥५०॥

*tebhyaḥ so 'sṛjat svīyaṁ*
*puraṁ puruṣam ātmavān*
*tān dṛṣṭvā ye purā sṛṣṭāḥ*
*praśaśaṁsuḥ prajāpatim*

*tebhyaḥ*—to them; *saḥ*—Lord Brahmā; *asṛjat*—gave; *svīyam*—his own; *puram*—body; *puruṣam*—human; *ātma-vān*—self-possessed; *tān*—them; *dṛṣṭvā*—on seeing; *ye*—those who; *purā*—earlier; *sṛṣṭāḥ*—were created (the demigods, Gandharvas, etc., who were created earlier); *praśaśaṁsuḥ*—applauded; *prajāpatim*—Brahmā (the lord of created beings).

### TRANSLATION

**The self-possessed creator gave them his own human form. On seeing the Manus, those who had been created earlier—the demigods, the Gandharvas and so on—applauded Brahmā, the lord of the universe.**

### TEXT 51

अहो एतज्जगत्स्रष्टः सुकृतं बत ते कृतम् ।
प्रतिष्ठिताः क्रिया यस्मिन् साकमन्नमदामहे ॥५१॥

*aho etaj jagat-sraṣṭaḥ*
*sukṛtaṁ bata te kṛtam*
*pratiṣṭhitāḥ kriyā yasmin*
*sākam annam adāma he*

*aho*—oh; *etat*—this; *jagat-sraṣṭaḥ*—O creator of the universe; *su-kṛtam*—well done; *bata*—indeed; *te*—by you; *kṛtam*—produced; *pratiṣṭhitāḥ*—established soundly; *kriyāḥ*—all ritualistic performances; *yasmin*—in which; *sākam*—along with this; *annam*—the sacrificial oblations; *adāma*—we shall share; *he*—O.

## TRANSLATION

**They prayed: O creator of the universe, we are glad; what you have produced is well done. Since ritualistic acts have now been established soundly in this human form, we shall all share the sacrificial oblations.**

## PURPORT

The importance of sacrifice is also mentioned in *Bhagavad-gītā*, Third Chapter, verse 10. The Lord confirms there that in the beginning of creation Brahmā created the Manus, along with the ritualistic sacrificial method, and blessed them: "Continue these sacrificial rites, and you will be gradually elevated to your proper position of self-realization and will also enjoy material happiness." All the living entities created by Brahmā are conditioned souls and are inclined to lord it over material nature. The purpose of sacrificial rituals is to revive, gradually, the spiritual realization of the living entities. That is the beginning of life within this universe. These sacrificial rituals, however, are intended to please the Supreme Lord. Unless one pleases the Supreme Lord, or unless one is Kṛṣṇa conscious, one cannot be happy either in material enjoyment or in spiritual realization.

## TEXT 52

तपसा विद्यया युक्तो योगेन सुसमाधिना ।
ऋषीनृषिर्हृषीकेशः ससर्जाभिमताः प्रजाः ॥५२॥

*tapasā vidyayā yukto*
*yogena susamādhinā*
*ṛṣīn ṛṣir hṛṣīkeśaḥ*
*sasarjābhimatāḥ prajāḥ*

*tapasā*—by penance; *vidyayā*—by worship; *yuktaḥ*—being engaged; *yogena*—by concentration of the mind in devotion; *su-samādhinā*—by nice meditation; *ṛṣīn*—the sages; *ṛṣiḥ*—the first seer (Brahmā); *hṛṣīkeśaḥ*—the controller of his senses; *sasarja*—created; *abhimatāḥ*—beloved; *prajāḥ*—sons.

## TRANSLATION

**Having equipped himself with austere penance, adoration, mental concentration and absorption in devotion, accompanied by dispassion, and having controlled his senses, Brahmā, the self-born living creature, evolved great sages as his beloved sons.**

## PURPORT

The ritualistic performances of sacrifice are meant for material economic development; in other words, they are meant to keep the body in good condition for cultivation of spiritual knowledge. But for actual attainment of spiritual knowledge, other qualifications are needed. What is essential is *vidyā,* or worship of the Supreme Lord. Sometimes the word *yoga* is used to refer to the gymnastic performances of different bodily postures which help mental concentration. Generally, the different bodily postures in the *yoga* system are accepted by less intelligent men to be the end of *yoga,* but actually they are meant to concentrate the mind upon the Supersoul. After creating persons for economic development, Brahmā created sages who would set the example for spiritual realization.

## TEXT 53

तेभ्यश्चैकैकशः स्वस्य देहस्यांशमदादजः ।
यत्तत्समाधियोगर्द्धितपोविद्याविरक्तिमत् ॥५३॥

*tebhyaś caikaikaśaḥ svasya*
*dehasyāṁśam adād ajaḥ*

*yat tat samādhi-yogarddhi-*
*tapo-vidyā-viraktimat*

*tebhyaḥ*—to them; *ca*—and; *ekaikaśaḥ*—each one; *svasya*—of his own; *dehasya*—body; *aṁśam*—part; *adāt*—gave; *ajaḥ*—the unborn Brahmā; *yat*—which; *tat*—that; *samādhi*—deep meditation; *yoga*—concentration of the mind; *ṛddhi*—supernatural power; *tapaḥ*—austerity; *vidyā*—knowledge; *virakti*—renunciation; *mat*—possessing.

## TRANSLATION

**To each one of these sons the unborn creator of the universe gave a part of his own body, which was characterized by deep meditation, mental concentration, supernatural power, austerity, adoration and renunciation.**

## PURPORT

The word *viraktimat* in this verse means "possessed of the qualification of renunciation." Spiritual realization cannot be attained by materialistic persons. For those who are addicted to sense enjoyment, spiritual realization is not possible. In *Bhagavad-gītā* it is stated that those who are too attached to seeking material possessions and material enjoyment cannot reach *yoga-samādhi*, absorption in Kṛṣṇa consciousness. Propaganda that one can enjoy this life materially and at the same time spiritually advance is simply bogus. The principles of renunciation are four: (1) to avoid illicit sex life, (2) to avoid meat-eating, (3) to avoid intoxication and (4) to avoid gambling. These four principles are called *tapasya*, or austerity. To absorb the mind in the Supreme in Kṛṣṇa consciousness is the process of spiritual realization.

*Thus end the Bhaktivedanta purports of the Third Canto, Twentieth Chapter, of the* Śrīmad-Bhāgavatam, *entitled "Conversation Between Maitreya and Vidura."*

## CHAPTER TWENTY-ONE

# Conversation Between Manu and Kardama

### TEXT 1

विदुर उवाच
स्वायम्भुवस्य च मनोर्वंशः परमसम्मतः ।
कथ्यतां भगवन् यत्र मैथुनेनैधिरे प्रजाः ॥ १ ॥

*vidura uvāca*
*svāyambhuvasya ca manor*
*vaṁśaḥ parama-sammataḥ*
*kathyatāṁ bhagavan yatra*
*maithunenaidhire prajāḥ*

*viduraḥ uvāca*—Vidura said; *svāyambhuvasya*—of Svāyambhuva; *ca*—and; *manoḥ*—of Manu; *vaṁśaḥ*—the dynasty; *parama*—most; *sammataḥ*—esteemed; *kathyatām*—kindly describe; *bhagavan*—O worshipful sage; *yatra*—in which; *maithunena*—through sexual intercourse; *edhire*—multiplied; *prajāḥ*—the progeny.

### TRANSLATION

**Vidura said: The line of Svāyambhuva Manu was most esteemed. O worshipful sage, I beg you—give me an account of this race, whose progeny multiplied through sexual intercourse.**

### PURPORT

Regulated sex life to generate good population is worth accepting. Actually, Vidura was not interested in hearing the history of persons who merely engaged in sex life, but he was interested in the progeny of Svāyambhuva Manu because in that dynasty, good devotee kings appeared who protected their subjects very carefully with spiritual knowledge. By hearing the history of their activities, therefore, one becomes more enlightened. An important word used in this connection is *parama-sammataḥ*, which indicates that the progeny created by Svāyambhuva Manu and his sons was approved of by great authorities. In other words, sex life for creating exemplary population is acceptable to all sages and authorities of Vedic scripture.

## TEXT 2

प्रियव्रतोत्तानपादौ सुतौ स्वायम्भुवस्य वै ।
यथाधर्मं जुगुपतुः सप्तद्वीपवतीं महीम् ॥ २ ॥

*priyavratottānapādau*
*sutau svāyambhuvasya vai*
*yathā-dharmaṁ jugupatuḥ*
*sapta-dvīpavatīṁ mahīm*

*priyavrata*—Mahārāja Priyavrata; *uttānapādau*—and Mahārāja Uttānapāda; *sutau*—the two sons; *svāyambhuvasya*—of Svāyambhuva Manu; *vai*—indeed; *yathā*—according to; *dharmam*—religious principles; *jugupatuḥ*—ruled; *sapta-dvīpa-vatīm*—consisting of seven islands; *mahīm*—the world.

## TRANSLATION

**The two great sons of Svāyambhuva Manu—Priyavrata and Uttānapāda—ruled the world, consisting of seven islands, just according to religious principles.**

## PURPORT

*Śrīmad-Bhāgavatam* is also a history of the great rulers of different parts of the universe. In this verse the names of Priyavrata and Uttānapāda, sons of Svāyambhuva, are mentioned. They ruled this earth, which is divided into seven islands. These seven islands are still current, as Asia, Europe, Africa, America, Australia and the North and South Poles. There is no chronological history of all the Indian kings in *Śrīmad-Bhāgavatam*, but the deeds of the most important kings, such as Priyavrata and Uttānapāda, and many others, like Lord Rāmacandra and

Mahārāja Yudhiṣṭhira, are recorded because the activities of such pious kings are worth hearing; people may benefit by studying their histories.

## TEXT 3

तस्य वै दुहिता ब्रह्मन्देवहूतीति विश्रुता ।
पत्नी प्रजापतेरुक्ता कर्दमस्य त्वयानघ ॥ ३ ॥

*tasya vai duhitā brahman*
*devahūtīti viśrutā*
*patnī prajāpater uktā*
*kardamasya tvayānagha*

*tasya*—of that Manu; *vai*—indeed; *duhitā*—the daughter; *brahman*—O holy *brāhmaṇa; devahūti*—named Devahūti; *iti*—thus; *viśrutā*—was known; *patnī*—wife; *prajāpateḥ*—of the lord of created beings; *uktā*—has been spoken of; *kardamasya*—of Kardama Muni; *tvayā*—by you; *anagha*—O sinless one.

## TRANSLATION

**O holy brāhmaṇa, O sinless one, you have spoken of his daughter, known by the name Devahūti, as the wife of the sage Kardama, the lord of created beings.**

## PURPORT

Here we are speaking of Svāyambhuva Manu, but in *Bhagavad-gītā* we hear about Vaivasvata Manu. The present age belongs to the Vaivasvata Manu. Svāyambhuva Manu was previously ruling, and his history begins from the Varāha age, or the millennium when the Lord appeared as the boar. There are fourteen Manus in one day of the life of Brahmā, and in the life of each Manu there are particular incidents. The Vaivasvata Manu of *Bhagavad-gītā* is different from Svāyambhuva Manu.

## TEXT 4

तस्यां स वै महायोगी युक्तायां योगलक्षणैः ।
ससर्ज कतिधा वीर्यं तन्मे शुश्रूषवे वद ॥ ४ ॥

*tasyāṁ sa vai mahā-yogī*
*yuktāyāṁ yoga-lakṣaṇaiḥ*
*sasarja katidhā vīryaṁ*
*tan me śuśrūṣave vada*

*tasyām*—in her; *saḥ*—Kardama Muni; *vai*—in fact; *mahā-yogī*—great mystic *yogī; yuktāyām*—endowed; *yoga-lakṣaṇaiḥ*—with the eightfold symptoms of yogic perfection; *sasarja*—propagated; *katidhā*—how many times; *vīryam*—offspring; *tat*—that narration; *me*—to me; *śuśrūṣave*—who am eager to hear; *vada*—tell.

## TRANSLATION

**How many offspring did that great yogī beget through the princess, who was endowed with eightfold perfection in the yoga principles? Oh, pray tell me this, for I am eager to hear it.**

## PURPORT

Here Vidura inquired about Kardama Muni and his wife, Devahūti, and about their children. It is described here that Devahūti was very much advanced in the performance of eightfold *yoga*. The eight divisions of *yoga* performance are described as (1) control of the senses, (2) strict following of the rules and regulations, (3) practice of the different sitting postures, (4) control of the breath, (5) withdrawing the senses from sense objects, (6) concentration of the mind, (7) meditation and (8) self-realization. After self-realization there are eight further perfectional stages, which are called *yoga-siddhis*. The husband and wife, Kardama and Devahūti, were advanced in *yoga* practice; the husband was a *mahā-yogī*, great mystic, and the wife was a *yoga-lakṣaṇa*, or one advanced in *yoga*. They united and produced children. Formerly, after making their lives perfect, great sages and saintly persons used to beget children, otherwise they strictly observed the rules and regulations of celibacy. *Brahmacarya* (following the rules and regulations of celibacy) is required for perfection of self-realization and mystic power. There is no recommendation in the Vedic scriptures that one can go on enjoying material sense gratification at one's whims, as one likes, and at the same time become a great meditator by paying a rascal some money.

## TEXT 5

रुचिर्यो भगवान् ब्रह्मन्दक्षो वा ब्रह्मणः सुतः ।
यथा ससर्ज भूतानि लब्ध्वा भार्यां च मानवीम् ॥ ५ ॥

*rucir yo bhagavān brahman*
*dakṣo vā brahmaṇaḥ sutaḥ*
*yathā sasarja bhūtāni*
*labdhvā bhāryāṁ ca mānavīm*

*ruciḥ*—Ruci; *yaḥ*—who; *bhagavān*—worshipful; *brahman*—O holy sage; *dakṣaḥ*—Dakṣa; *vā*—and; *brahmaṇaḥ*—of Lord Brahmā; *sutaḥ*—the son; *yathā*—in what way; *sasarja*—generated; *bhūtāni*—offspring; *labdhvā*—after securing; *bhāryām*—as their wives; *ca*—and; *mānavīm*—the daughters of Svāyambhuva Manu.

### TRANSLATION

**O holy sage, tell me how the worshipful Ruci and Dakṣa, the son of Brahmā, generated children after securing as their wives the other two daughters of Svāyambhuva Manu.**

### PURPORT

All the great personalities who increased the population in the beginning of the creation are called Prajāpatis. Brahmā is also known as Prajāpati, as were some of his later sons. Svāyambhuva Manu is also known as Prajāpati, as is Dakṣa, another son of Brahmā. Svāyambhuva had two daughters, Ākūti and Prasūti. The Prajāpati Ruci married Ākūti, and Dakṣa married Prasūti. These couples and their children produced immense numbers of children to populate the entire universe. Vidura's inquiry was, "How did they beget the population in the beginning?"

## TEXT 6

मैत्रेय उवाच

प्रजाः सृजेति भगवान् कर्दमो ब्रह्मणोदितः ।
सरस्वत्यां तपस्तेपे सहस्राणां समा दश ॥ ६ ॥

*maitreya uvāca*
*prajāḥ sṛjeti bhagavān*
*kardamo brahmaṇoditaḥ*
*sarasvatyāṁ tapas tepe*
*sahasrāṇāṁ samā daśa*

*maitreyaḥ uvāca*—the great sage Maitreya said; *prajāḥ*—children; *sṛja*—beget; *iti*—thus; *bhagavān*—the worshipful; *kardamaḥ*—Kardama Muni; *brahmaṇā*—by Lord Brahmā; *uditaḥ*—commanded; *sarasvatyām*—on the bank of the River Sarasvatī; *tapaḥ*—penance; *tepe*—practiced; *sahasrāṇām*—of thousands; *samāḥ*—years; *daśa*—ten.

## TRANSLATION

**The great sage Maitreya replied: Commanded by Lord Brahmā to beget children in the worlds, the worshipful Kardama Muni practiced penance on the bank of the River Sarasvatī for a period of ten thousand years.**

## PURPORT

It is understood herein that Kardama Muni meditated in *yoga* for ten thousand years before attaining perfection. Similarly, we have information that Vālmīki Muni also practiced *yoga* meditation for sixty thousand years before attaining perfection. Therefore, *yoga* practice can be successfully performed by persons who have a very long duration of life, such as one hundred thousand years; in that way it is possible to have perfection in *yoga*. Otherwise, there is no possibility of attaining the real perfection. Following the regulations, controlling the senses and practicing the different sitting postures are merely the preliminary practices. We do not know how people can be captivated by the bogus *yoga* system in which it is stated that simply by meditating fifteen minutes daily one can attain the perfection of becoming one with God. This age (Kali-yuga) is the age of bluffing and quarrel. Actually there is no possibility of attaining *yoga* perfection by such paltry proposals. The Vedic literature, for emphasis, clearly states three times that in this age of Kali—*kalau nāsty eva nāsty eva nāsty eva*—there is no other alternative, no other alternative, no other alternative than *harer nāma*, chanting the holy name of the Lord.

## TEXT 7

ततः समाधियुक्तेन क्रियायोगेन कर्दमः ।
सम्प्रपेदे हरिं भक्त्या प्रपन्नवरदाशुषम् ॥ ७ ॥

*tataḥ samādhi-yuktena*
*kriyā-yogena kardamaḥ*
*samprapede hariṁ bhaktyā*
*prapanna-varadāśuṣam*

*tataḥ*—then, in that penance; *samādhi-yuktena*—in trance; *kriyā-yogena*—by *bhakti-yoga* worship; *kardamaḥ*—the sage Kardama; *samprapede*—served; *harim*—the Personality of Godhead; *bhaktyā*—in devotional service; *prapanna*—to the surrendered souls; *vara-dāśuṣam*—the bestower of all blessings.

## TRANSLATION

**During that period of penance, the sage Kardama, by worship through devotional service in trance, propitiated the Personality of Godhead, who is the quick bestower of all blessings upon those who flee to Him for protection.**

## PURPORT

The significance of meditation is described here. Kardama Muni practiced mystic *yoga* meditation for ten thousand years just to please the Supreme Personality of Godhead, Hari. Therefore, whether one practices *yoga* or speculates and does research to find God, one's efforts must be mixed with the process of devotion. Without devotion, nothing can be perfect. The target of perfection and realization is the Supreme Personality of Godhead. In the Sixth Chapter of *Bhagavad-gītā* it is clearly said that one who constantly engages in Kṛṣṇa consciousness is the topmost *yogī.* The Personality of Godhead, Hari, also fulfills the desires of His surrendered devotee. One has to surrender unto the lotus feet of the Personality of Godhead, Hari, or Kṛṣṇa, in order to achieve real success. Devotional service, or engagement in Kṛṣṇa consciousness, is the direct method, and all other methods, although recommended, are indirect. In this age of Kali the direct method is especially more feasible than the indirect because people are short-living, their intelligence is poor, and they are poverty-stricken and embarrassed by so many miserable disturbances. Lord Caitanya, therefore, has given the greatest boon: in this age one simply has to chant the holy name of God to attain perfection in spiritual life.

The words *samprapede harim* mean that in various ways Kardama Muni satisfied the Supreme Personality of Godhead, Hari, by his devotional service. Devotional service is also expressed by the word *kriyā-yogena.* Kardama Muni not only meditated but also engaged in devotional service; to attain perfection in *yoga* practice or meditation, one must act in devotional service by hearing, chanting, remembering, etc. Remembering is meditation also. But who is to be remembered? One should remember the Supreme Personality of Godhead. Not only must one remember the Supreme Person; one must hear about the activities of the Lord and chant His glories. This information is in the authoritative scriptures. After engaging himself for ten thousand years in performing different types of devotional service, Kardama Muni attained the perfection of meditation, but that is not possible in this age of Kali, wherein it is very difficult to live for as much as one hundred years. At the present moment, who will be successful in the rigid performance of the many *yoga* rules and regulations? Moreover, perfection is attained only by those who are surrendered souls. Where there is no mention of the Personality of Godhead, where is there surrender? And where there is no meditation upon the Personality of Godhead, where is the *yoga* practice? Unfortunately, people in this age, especially persons who are of a demoniac nature, want to be cheated. Thus the Supreme Personality of Godhead sends great cheaters who mislead them in the name of *yoga* and render their lives useless and doomed. In *Bhagavad-gītā,* therefore, it is clearly stated, in the Sixteenth Chapter, verse 17, that rascals of self-made authority, being puffed up by illegally collected money, perform *yoga* without following the authoritative books. They are very proud of the money they have plundered from innocent persons who wanted to be cheated.

## TEXT 8

तावत्प्रसन्नो भगवान् पुष्कराक्षः कृते युगे ।
दर्शयामास तं क्षत्तः शाब्दं ब्रह्म दधद्वपुः ॥ ८ ॥

*tāvat prasanno bhagavān*
*puṣkarākṣaḥ kṛte yuge*
*darśayām āsa taṁ kṣattaḥ*
*śābdaṁ brahma dadhad vapuḥ*

*tāvat*—then; *prasannaḥ*—being pleased; *bhagavān*—the Supreme Personality of Godhead; *puṣkara-akṣaḥ*—lotus-eyed; *kṛte yuge*—in the Satya-yuga; *darśayām āsa*—showed; *tam*—to that Kardama Muni; *kṣattaḥ*—O Vidura; *śābdam*—which is to be understood only through the *Vedas; brahma*—the Absolute Truth; *dadhat*—exhibiting; *vapuḥ*—His transcendental body.

## TRANSLATION

**Then, in the Satya-yuga, the lotus-eyed Supreme Personality of Godhead, being pleased, showed Himself to that Kardama Muni and displayed His transcendental form, which can be understood only through the Vedas.**

## PURPORT

Here two points are very significant. The first is that Kardama Muni attained success by *yoga* practice in the beginning of Satya-yuga, when people used to live for one hundred thousand years. Kardama Muni attained success, and the Lord, being pleased with him, showed him His form, which is not imaginary. Sometimes the impersonalists recommend that one can arbitrarily concentrate one's mind on some form he imagines or which pleases him. But here it is very clearly said that the form which the Lord showed to Kardama Muni by His divine grace is described in the Vedic literature. *Śābdaṁ brahma:* the forms of the Lord are clearly indicated in the Vedic literature. Kardama Muni did not discover any imaginary form of God, as alleged by rascals; he actually saw the eternal, blissful and transcendental form of the Lord.

## TEXT 9

स तं विरजमर्काभं सितपद्मोत्पलस्रजम् ।
स्निग्धनीलालकव्रातवक्त्राब्जं विरजोऽम्बरम् ॥९॥

*sa taṁ virajam arkābhaṁ*
*sita-padmotpala-srajam*

*snigdha-nīlālaka-vrāta-*
*vaktrābjaṁ virajo 'mbaram*

*saḥ*—that Kardama Muni; *tam*—Him; *virajam*—without contamination; *arka-ābham*—effulgent like the sun; *sita*—white; *padma*—lotuses; *utpala*—water lilies; *srajam*—garland; *snigdha*—slick; *nīla*—blackish-blue; *alaka*—of locks of hair; *vrāta*—an abundance; *vaktra*—face; *abjam*—lotuslike; *virajaḥ*—spotless; *ambaram*—clothing.

## TRANSLATION

**Kardama Muni saw the Supreme Personality of Godhead, who is free from material contamination, in His eternal form, effulgent like the sun, wearing a garland of white lotuses and water lilies. The Lord was clad in spotless yellow silk, and His lotus face was fringed with slick dark locks of curly hair.**

## TEXT 10

किरीटिनं कुण्डलिनं शङ्खचक्रगदाधरम् ।
श्वेतोत्पलक्रीडनकं मनःस्पर्शस्मितेक्षणम् ॥१०॥

*kirīṭinaṁ kuṇḍalinaṁ*
*śaṅkha-cakra-gadā-dharam*
*śvetotpala-krīḍanakaṁ*
*manaḥ-sparśa-smitekṣaṇam*

*kirīṭinam*—adorned with a crown; *kuṇḍalinam*—wearing earrings; *śaṅkha*—conch; *cakra*—disc; *gadā*—mace; *dharam*—holding; *śveta*—white; *utpala*—lily; *krīḍanakam*—plaything; *manaḥ*—heart; *sparśa*—touching; *smita*—smiling; *īkṣaṇam*—and glancing.

## TRANSLATION

**Adorned with a crown and earrings, He held His characteristic conch, disc and mace in three of His hands and a white lily in the fourth. He glanced about in a happy, smiling mood whose sight captivates the hearts of all devotees.**

## TEXT 11

विन्यस्तचरणाम्भोजमंसदेशे गरुत्मतः ।
दृष्ट्वा खेऽवस्थितं वक्षःश्रियं कौस्तुभकन्धरम् ॥११॥

*vinyasta-caraṇāmbhojam*
*aṁsa-deśe garutmataḥ*
*dṛṣṭvā khe 'vasthitaṁ vakṣaḥ-*
*śriyaṁ kaustubha-kandharam*

*vinyasta*—having been placed; *caraṇa-ambhojam*—lotus feet; *aṁsa-deśe*—on the shoulders; *garutmataḥ*—of Garuḍa; *dṛṣṭvā*—having seen; *khe*—in the air; *avasthitam*—standing; *vakṣaḥ*—on His chest; *śriyam*—auspicious mark; *kaustubha*—the Kaustubha gem; *kandharam*—neck.

## TRANSLATION

**A golden streak on His chest, the famous Kaustubha gem suspended from His neck, He stood in the air with His lotus feet placed on the shoulders of Garuḍa.**

## PURPORT

The descriptions in verses 9–11 of the Lord in His transcendental, eternal form are understood to be descriptions from the authoritative Vedic version. These descriptions are certainly not the imagination of Kardama Muni. The decorations of the Lord are beyond material conception, as admitted even by impersonalists like Śaṅkarācārya: Nārāyaṇa, the Supreme Personality of Godhead, has nothing to do with the material creation. The varieties of the transcendental Lord—His body, His form, His dress, His instruction, His words—are not manufactured by the material energy, but are all confirmed in the Vedic literature. By performance of *yoga* Kardama Muni actually saw the Supreme Lord as He is. There was no point in seeing an imagined form of God after practicing *yoga* for ten thousand years. The perfection of *yoga*, therefore, does not terminate in voidness or impersonalism; on the contrary, the perfection of *yoga* is attained when one actually sees the Personality of Godhead in His eternal form. The process of Kṛṣṇa consciousness is to deliver the form of Kṛṣṇa directly. The form of Kṛṣṇa is described in the authoritative Vedic literature *Brahma-saṁhitā:* His abode is made of *cintāmaṇi* stone, and the Lord plays there as a cowherd boy and is served by many thousands of *gopīs.* These descriptions are authoritative, and a Kṛṣṇa conscious person takes them directly, acts on them, preaches them and practices devotional service as enjoined in the authoritative scriptures.

## TEXT 12

जातहर्षोऽपतन्मूर्ध्ना क्षितौ लब्धमनोरथः ।
गीर्भिस्त्वभ्यगृणात्प्रीतिस्वभावात्मा कृताञ्जलिः ॥१२॥

*jāta-harṣo 'patan mūrdhnā*
*kṣitau labdha-manorathaḥ*
*gīrbhis tv abhyagṛṇāt prīti-*
*svabhāvātmā kṛtāñjaliḥ*

*jāta-harṣaḥ*—naturally jubilant; *apatat*—he fell down; *mūrdhnā*—with his head; *kṣitau*—on the ground; *labdha*—having been achieved; *manaḥ-rathaḥ*—his desire; *gīrbhiḥ*—with prayers; *tu*—and; *abhyagṛṇāt*—he satisfied; *prīti-svabhāva-ātmā*—whose heart is by nature always full of love; *kṛta-añjaliḥ*—with folded hands.

## TRANSLATION

**When Kardama Muni actually realized the Supreme Personality of Godhead in person, he was greatly satisfied because his transcendental desire was fulfilled. He fell on the ground with his head bowed to offer obeisances unto the lotus feet of the Lord. His heart naturally full of love of God, with folded hands he satisfied the Lord with prayers.**

## PURPORT

The realization of the personal form of the Lord is the highest perfectional stage of *yoga.* In the Sixth Chapter of *Bhagavad-gītā,* where *yoga* practice is described, this realization of the personal form of the Lord is called the perfection of *yoga.* After practicing the sitting postures and other regulative principles of the system, one finally reaches the stage of *samādhi*—absorption in the Supreme. In the *samādhi* stage one can see the Supreme Personality of Godhead in His partial form as Paramātmā, or as He is. *Samādhi* is described in authoritative *yoga* scriptures, such as the *Patañjali-sūtras*, to be a transcendental pleasure. The *yoga* system described in the books of Patañjali is authoritative, and the modern so-called *yogīs* who have manufactured their own ways, not consulting the authorities, are simply ludicrous. The Patañjali *yoga* system is called *aṣṭāṅga-yoga*. Sometimes impersonalists pollute the Patañjali *yoga* system because they are monists. Patañjali describes that the soul is transcendentally pleased when he meets the Supersoul and sees Him. If the existence of the Supersoul and the individual is admitted, then the impersonalist theory of monism is nullified. Therefore some impersonalists and void philosophers twist the Patañjali system in their own way and pollute the whole *yoga* process.

According to Patañjali, when one becomes free from all material desires he attains his real, transcendental situation, and realization of that stage is called spiritual power. In material activities a person engages in the modes of material nature. The aspirations of such people are (1) to be religious, (2) to be economically enriched, (3) to be able to gratify the senses and, at last, (4) to become one with the Supreme. According to the monists, when a *yogī* becomes one with the Supreme and loses his individual existence, he attains the highest stage, called *kaivalya*. But actually, the stage of realization of the Personality of Godhead is *kaivalya*. The oneness of understanding that the Supreme Lord is fully spiritual and that in full spiritual realization one can understand what He is—the Supreme Personality of Godhead—is called *kaivalya*, or, in the language of Patañjali, realization of spiritual power. His proposal is that when one is freed from material desires and fixed in spiritual realization of the self and the Superself, that is called *cit-śakti*. In full spiritual realization there is a perception of spiritual happiness, and that happiness is described in *Bhagavad-gītā* as the supreme happiness, which is beyond the material senses. Trance is described to be of two kinds, *samprajñāta* and *asamprajñāta*, or mental speculation and self-realization. In *samādhi* or *asamprajñāta* one can realize, by his spiritual senses, the spiritual form of the Lord. That is the ultimate goal of spiritual realization.

According to Patañjali, when one is fixed in constant realization of the supreme form of the Lord, one has attained the perfectional stage, as attained by Kardama Muni. Unless one attains this stage of perfection—beyond the perfection of the preliminaries of the *yoga* system—there is no ultimate realization. There are eight perfections in the *aṣṭāṅga-yoga* system. One who has attained them can become lighter than the lightest and greater than the greatest, and he can achieve whatever he likes. But even achieving such material success in *yoga* is not the perfection or the ultimate goal. The ultimate goal is described here: Kardama Muni saw the Supreme Personality of Godhead in His eternal form. Devotional service begins with the relationship of the individual soul and the Supreme Soul, or Kṛṣṇa and Kṛṣṇa's devotees, and when one attains it there is no question of falling down. If, through the *yoga* system, one wants to attain the stage of seeing the Supreme Personality of Godhead face to face, but is attracted instead to attainment of some material power, then he is detoured from proceeding further. Material enjoyment, as encouraged by bogus *yogīs*, has nothing to do with the transcendental realization of spiritual happiness. Real devotees of *bhakti-yoga* accept only the material necessities of life absolutely needed to maintain the body and soul together; they refrain completely from all exaggerated material sense gratification. They are prepared to undergo all kinds of tribulation, provided they can make progress in the realization of the Personality of Godhead.

## TEXT 13

ऋषिरुवाच
जुष्टं बताद्याखिलसत्त्वराशेः
सांसिद्ध्यमक्ष्णोस्तव दर्शनान्नः ।
यद्दर्शनं जन्मभिरीड्य सद्भि-
राशासते योगिनो रूढयोगाः ॥१३॥

*ṛṣir uvāca*
*juṣṭaṁ batādyākhila-sattva-rāśeḥ*
*sāṁsiddhyam akṣṇos tava darśanān naḥ*
*yad-darśanaṁ janmabhir īḍya sadbhir*
*āśāsate yogino rūḍha-yogāḥ*

*ṛṣiḥ uvāca*—the great sage said; *juṣṭam*—is attained; *bata*—ah; *adya*—now; *akhila*—all; *sattva*—of goodness; *rāśeḥ*—who are the reservoir; *sāṁsiddhyam*—the complete success; *akṣṇoḥ*—of the two eyes; *tava*—of You; *darśanāt*—from the sight; *naḥ*—by us; *yat*—of whom; *darśanam*—sight; *janmabhiḥ*—through births; *īḍya*—O worshipable Lord; *sadbhiḥ*—gradually elevated in position; *āśāsate*—aspire; *yoginaḥ*—*yogīs; rūḍha-yogāḥ*—having obtained perfection in *yoga.*

## TRANSLATION

**The great sage Kardama said: O supreme worshipful Lord, my power of sight is now fulfilled, having attained the greatest perfection of the sight of You, who are the reservoir of all existences. Through many successive births of deep meditation, advanced yogīs aspire to see Your transcendental form.**

## PURPORT

The Supreme Personality of Godhead is described here as the reservoir of all goodness and all pleasure. Unless one is situated in the mode of goodness, there is no real pleasure. When, therefore, one's body, mind and activities are situated in the service of the Lord, one is on the highest perfectional stage of goodness. Kardama Muni says, "Your Lordship is the reservoir of all that can be understood by the nomenclature of goodness, and by experiencing You face to face, eye to eye, the perfection of sight has now been attained." These statements are the pure devotional situation; for a devotee, the perfection of the senses is to engage in the service of the Lord. The sense of sight, when engaged in seeing the beauty of the Lord, is perfected; the power to hear, when engaged in hearing the glories of the Lord, is perfected; the power to taste, when one enjoys by eating *prasāda*, is perfected. When all the senses engage in relationship with the Personality of Godhead, one's perfection is technically called *bhakti-yoga*, which entails detaching the senses from material indulgence and attaching them to the service of the Lord. When one is freed from all designated conditional life and fully engages in the service of the Lord, one's service is called *bhakti-yoga.* Kardama Muni admits that seeing the Lord personally in *bhakti-yoga* is the perfection of sight. The exalted perfection of seeing the Lord is not exaggerated by Kardama Muni. He gives evidence that those who are actually elevated in *yoga* aspire in life after life to see this form of the Personality of Godhead. He was not a fictitious *yogī.* Those who are actually on the advanced path aspire only to see the eternal form of the Lord.

## TEXT 14

ये मायया ते हतमेधसस्त्वत्-
पादारविन्दं भवसिन्धुपोतम् ।
उपासते कामलवाय तेषां
रासीश कामान्निरयेऽपि ये स्युः ॥१४॥

*ye māyayā te hata-medhasas tvat-*
*pādāravindaṁ bhava-sindhu-potam*
*upāsate kāma-lavāya teṣāṁ*
*rāsīśa kāmān niraye 'pi ye syuḥ*

*ye*—those persons; *māyayā*—by the deluding energy; *te*—of You; *hata*—has been lost; *medhasaḥ*—whose intelligence; *tvat*—Your; *pāda-aravindam*—lotus feet; *bhava*—of mundane existence; *sindhu*—the ocean; *potam*—the boat for crossing; *upāsate*—worship; *kāma-lavāya*—for obtaining trivial pleasures; *teṣām*—their; *rāsi*—You bestow; *īśa*—O Lord; *kāmān*—desires; *niraye*—in hell; *api*—even; *ye*—which desires; *syuḥ*—can be available.

## TRANSLATION

**Your lotus feet are the true vessel to take one across the ocean of mundane nescience. Only persons deprived of their intelligence by the spell of the deluding energy will worship those feet with a view to attain the trivial and momentary pleasures of the senses, which even persons rotting in hell can attain. However, O my Lord, You are so kind that You bestow mercy even upon them.**

## PURPORT

As stated in *Bhagavad-gītā,* Seventh Chapter, there are two kinds of devotees—those who desire material pleasures and those who desire nothing but service to the Lord. Material pleasures can be attained even by hogs and dogs, whose condition of life is hellish. The hog also eats, sleeps and enjoys sex life to the full extent, and it is also very satisfied with such hellish enjoyment of material existence. Modern *yogīs* advise that because one has senses, one must enjoy to the fullest extent like cats and dogs, yet one can go on and practice *yoga*. This is condemned here by Kardama Muni; he says that such material pleasures are available for cats and dogs in a hellish condition. The Lord is so kind that if so-called *yogīs* are satisfied by hellish pleasures, He can give them facilities to attain all the material pleasures they desire, but they cannot attain the perfectional stage attained by Kardama Muni.

Hellish and demoniac persons do not actually know what is the ultimate attainment in perfection, and therefore they think that sense gratification is the highest goal of life. They advise that one can satisfy the senses and at the same time, by reciting some *mantra* and by some practice, can cheaply aspire for perfection. Such persons are described here as *hata-medhasaḥ*, which means "those whose brains are spoiled." They aspire for material enjoyment by perfection of *yoga* or meditation. In *Bhagavad-gītā* it is stated by the Lord that the intelligence of those who worship the demigods has been spoiled. Similarly, here too it is stated by Kardama Muni that one who aspires after material enjoyment by practice of *yoga* has spoiled his brain substance and is fool number one. Actually, the intelligent practitioner of *yoga* should aspire for nothing else but to cross over the ocean of nescience by worshiping the Personality of Godhead and to see the lotus feet of the Lord. The Lord is so kind, however, that even today persons whose brain substance is spoiled are given the benediction to become cats, dogs or hogs and enjoy material happiness from sex life and sense gratification. The Lord confirms this benediction in *Bhagavad-gītā:* "Whatever a person aspires to receive from Me, I offer him as he desires."

## TEXT 15

तथा स चाहं परिवोढुकामः
समानशीलां गृहमेधधेनुम् ।
उपेयिवान्मूलमशेषमूलं
दुराशयः कामदुघाङ्घ्रिपस्य ॥१५॥

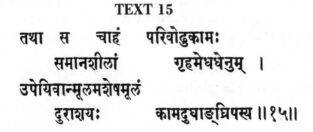

*tathā sa cāhaṁ parivoḍhu-kāmaḥ*
*samāna-śīlāṁ gṛhamedha-dhenum*
*upeyivān mūlam aśeṣa-mūlaṁ*
*durāśayaḥ kāma-dughāṅghripasya*

*tathā*—similarly; *saḥ*—myself; *ca*—also; *aham*—I; *parivoḍhu-kāmaḥ*—desiring to marry; *samāna-śīlām*—a girl of like disposition; *gṛha-medha*—in married life; *dhenum*—a cow of plenty; *upeyivān*—have approached; *mūlam*—the root (lotus feet); *aśeṣa*—of everything; *mūlam*—the source; *durāśayaḥ*—with lustful desire; *kāma-dugha*—yielding all desires; *aṅghripasya*—(of You) who are the tree.

## TRANSLATION

**Therefore, desiring to marry a girl of like disposition who may prove to be a veritable cow of plenty in my married life, to satisfy my lustful desire I too have sought the shelter of Your lotus feet, which are the source of everything, for You are like a desire tree.**

## PURPORT

In spite of his condemning persons who approach the Lord for material advantages, Kardama Muni expressed his material inability and desire before the Lord by saying, "Although I know that nothing material should be asked from You, I nevertheless desire to marry a girl of like disposition." The phrase "like disposition" is very significant. Formerly, boys and girls of similar dispositions were married; the similar natures of the boy and girl were united in order to make them happy. Not more than twenty-five years ago, and perhaps it is still current, parents in India used to consult the horoscope of the boy and girl to see whether there would be factual union in their psychological conditions. These considerations are very important. Nowadays marriage takes place without such consultation, and therefore, soon after the marriage, there is divorce and separation. Formerly husband and wife used to live together peacefully throughout their whole lives, but nowadays it is a very difficult task.

Kardama Muni wanted to have a wife of like disposition because a wife is necessary to assist in spiritual and material advancement. It is said that a wife yields the fulfillment of all desires in religion, economic development and sense gratification. If one has a nice wife, he is to be considered a most fortunate man. In astrology, a man is considered fortunate who has great wealth, very good sons or a very good wife. Of these three, one who has a very good wife is considered the most fortunate. Before marrying, one should select a wife of like disposition and not be enamored by so-called beauty or other attractive features for sense gratification. In the *Bhāgavatam*, Twelfth Canto, it is said that in the Kali-yuga marriage will be based on the consideration of sex life; as soon as there is deficiency in sex life, the question of divorce will arise.

Kardama Muni could have asked his benediction from Umā, for it is recommended in the scriptures that if anyone wants a good wife, he should worship Umā. But he preferred to worship the Supreme Personality of Godhead because it is recommended in the *Bhāgavatam* that everyone, whether he is full of desires, has no desire or desires liberation, should worship the Supreme Lord. Of these three classes of men, one tries to be happy by fulfillment of material desires, another wants to be happy by becoming one with the Supreme, and another, the perfect man, is a devotee. He does not want anything in return from the Personality of Godhead; he only wants to render transcendental loving service. In any case, everyone should worship the Supreme Personality of Godhead, for He will fulfill everyone's desire. The advantage of worshiping the Supreme Person is that even if one has desires for material enjoyment, if he worships Kṛṣṇa he will gradually become a pure devotee and have no more material hankering.

## TEXT 16

प्रजापतेस्ते वचसाधीश तन्त्या
लोकः किलायं कामहतोऽनुबद्धः ।
अहं च लोकानुगतो वहामि
बलिं च शुक्लानिमिषाय तुभ्यम् ॥१६॥

*prajāpates te vacasādhīśa tantyā*
*lokaḥ kilāyaṁ kāma-hato 'nubaddhaḥ*

*ahaṁ ca lokānugato vahāmi*
*baliṁ ca śuklānimiṣāya tubhyam*

*prajāpateḥ*—who are the master of all living entities; *te*—of You; *vacasā*—under the direction; *adhīśa*—O my Lord; *tantyā*—by a rope; *lokaḥ*—conditioned souls; *kila*—indeed; *ayam*—these; *kāma-hataḥ*—conquered by lusty desires; *anubaddhaḥ*—are bound; *aham*—I; *ca*—and; *loka-anugataḥ*—following the conditioned souls; *vahāmi*—offer; *balim*—oblations; *ca*—and; *śukla*—O embodiment of religion; *animiṣāya*—existing as eternal time; *tubhyam*—to You.

## TRANSLATION

**O my Lord, You are the master and leader of all living entities. Under Your direction, all conditioned souls, as if bound by rope, are constantly engaged in satisfying their desires. Following them, O embodiment of religion, I also bear oblations for You, who are eternal time.**

## PURPORT

In the *Kaṭha Upaniṣad* it is stated that the Supreme Lord is the leader of all living entities. He is their sustainer and the awarder of all their necessities and desires. No living entity is independent; all are dependent on the mercy of the Supreme Lord. Therefore the Vedic instruction is that one should enjoy life under the direction of the supreme leader, the Personality of Godhead. Vedic literatures like *Īśopaniṣad* direct that since everything belongs to the Supreme Personality of Godhead, one should not encroach upon another's property, but should enjoy one's individual allotment. The best program for every living entity is to take direction from the Supreme Lord and enjoy material or spiritual life.

A question may be raised: Since Kardama Muni was advanced in spiritual life, why then did he not ask the Lord for liberation? Why did he want to enjoy material life in spite of his personally seeing and experiencing the Supreme Lord? The answer is that not everyone is competent to be liberated from material bondage. It is everyone's duty, therefore, to enjoy according to his present position, but under the direction of the Lord or the *Vedas*. The *Vedas* are considered to be the direct words of the Lord. The Lord gives us the opportunity to enjoy material life as we want, and at the same time He gives directions for the modes and processes of abiding by the *Vedas* so that gradually one may be elevated to liberation from material bondage. The conditioned souls who have come to the material world to fulfill their desires to lord it over material nature are bound by the laws of nature. The best course is to abide by the Vedic rules; that will help one to be gradually elevated to liberation.

Kardama Muni addresses the Lord as *śukla*, which means "the leader of religion." One who is pious should follow the rules of religion, for such rules are prescribed by the Lord Himself. No one can manufacture or concoct a religion; "religion" refers to the injunctions or laws of the Lord. In *Bhagavad-gītā* the Lord says that religion means to surrender unto Him. Therefore one should follow the Vedic regulations and surrender unto the Supreme Lord because that is the ultimate goal of perfection in human life. One should live a life of piety, follow the religious rules and regulations, marry and live peacefully for elevation to the higher status of spiritual realization.

## TEXT 17

लोकांश्च लोकानुगतान् पशूंश्च
हित्वा श्रितास्ते चरणातपत्रम् ।
परस्परं त्वद्गुणवादसीधु-
पीयूषनिर्यापितदेहधर्माः ॥१७॥

*lokāṁś ca lokānugatān paśūṁś ca*
*hitvā śritās te caraṇātapatram*
*parasparaṁ tvad-guṇa-vāda-sīdhu-*
*pīyūṣa-niryāpita-deha-dharmāḥ*

*lokān*—worldly affairs; *ca*—and; *loka-anugatān*—the followers of worldly affairs; *paśūn*—beastly; *ca*—and; *hitvā*—having given up; *śritāḥ*—taken shelter; *te*—Your; *caraṇa*—of lotus feet; *ātapatram*—the umbrella; *parasparam*—with one another; *tvat*—Your; *guṇa*—of qualities; *vāda*—by discussion; *sīdhu*—intoxicating; *pīyūṣa*—by the nectar; *niryāpita*—extinguished; *deha-dharmāḥ*—the primary necessities of the body.

## TRANSLATION

**However, persons who have given up stereotyped worldly affairs and the beastly followers of these affairs, and who have taken shelter of the umbrella of Your lotus feet by drinking the intoxicating nectar of Your qualities and activities in discussions with one another, can be freed from the primary necessities of the material body.**

## PURPORT

After describing the necessity of married life, Kardama Muni asserts that marriage and other social affairs are stereotyped regulations for persons who are addicted to material sense enjoyment. The principles of animal life—eating, sleeping, mating and defending—are actually necessities of the body, but those who engage in transcendental Kṛṣṇa consciousness, giving up all the stereotyped activities of this material world, are freed from social conventions. Conditioned souls are under the spell of material energy, or eternal time—past, present and future—but as soon as one engages in Kṛṣṇa consciousness, he transcends the limits of past and present and becomes situated in the eternal activities of the soul. One has to act in terms of the Vedic injunctions in order to enjoy material life, but those who have taken to the devotional service of the Lord are not afraid of the regulations of this material world. Such devotees do not care for the conventions of material activities; they boldly take to that shelter which is like an umbrella against the sun of repeated birth and death.

Constant transmigration of the soul from one body to another is the cause of suffering in material existence. This conditional life in material existence is called *saṁsāra.* One may perform good work and take his birth in a very nice material condition, but the process under which birth and death take place is like a terrible fire. Śrī Viśvanātha Cakravartī Ṭhākura, in his prayer to the spiritual master, has described this. *Saṁsāra,* or the repetition of birth and death, is compared to a forest fire. A forest fire takes place automatically, without anyone's endeavor, by the friction of dried wood, and no fire department or sympathetic person can extinguish it. The raging forest fire can be extinguished only when there is a constant downpour of water from a cloud. The cloud is compared to the mercy of the spiritual master. By the grace of the spiritual master the cloud of the mercy of the Personality of Godhead is brought in, and then only, when the rains of Kṛṣṇa consciousness fall, can the fire of material existence be extinguished. This is also explained here. In order to find freedom from the stereotyped conditional life of material existence, one has to take shelter of the lotus feet of the Lord, not in the manner in which the impersonalists indulge, but in devotional service, chanting and hearing of the activities of the Lord. Only then can one be freed from the actions and reactions of material existence. It is recommended here that one should give up the conditional life of this material world and the association of so-called civilized human beings who are simply following, in a polished way, the same stereotyped principles of eating, sleeping, defending and mating. Chanting and hearing of the glories of the Lord is described here as *tvad-guṇa-vāda-sīdhu*. Only by drinking the nectar of chanting and hearing the pastimes of the Lord can one forget the intoxication of material existence.

## TEXT 18

न तेऽजराक्षभ्रमिरायुरेषां
त्रयोदशारं त्रिशतं षष्टिपर्व ।
षण्नेम्यनन्तच्छदि यत्त्रिणाभि
करालस्रोतो जगदाच्छिद्य धावत् ॥१८॥

*na te 'jarākṣa-bhramir āyur eṣāṁ*
*trayodaśāraṁ tri-śataṁ ṣaṣṭi-parva*
*ṣaṇ-nemy ananta-cchadi yat tri-ṇābhi*
*karāla-sroto jagad ācchidya dhāvat*

*na*—not; *te*—Your; *ajara*—of imperishable Brahman; *akṣa*—on the axle; *bhramiḥ*—rotating; *āyuḥ*—span of life; *eṣām*—of the devotees; *trayodaśa*—thirteen; *aram*—spokes; *tri-śatam*—three hundred; *ṣaṣṭi*—sixty; *parva*—functions; *ṣaṭ*—six; *nemi*—rims; *ananta*—innumerable; *chadi*—leaves; *yat*—which; *tri*—three; *nābhi*—naves; *karāla-srotaḥ*—with tremendous velocity; *jagat*—the universe; *ācchidya*—cutting short; *dhāvat*—running.

## TRANSLATION

**Your wheel, which has three naves, rotates around the axis of the imperishable Brahman. It has thirteen spokes, 360 joints, six rims and numberless leaves carved upon it. Though its revolution cuts short the life-span of the entire creation, this wheel of tremendous velocity cannot touch the life-span of the devotees of the Lord.**

## PURPORT

The time factor cannot affect the span of life of the devotees. In *Bhagavad-gītā* it is stated that a little execution of devotional service saves one from the greatest danger. The greatest danger is transmigration of the soul from one body to another, and only devotional service to the Lord can stop this process. It is stated in the Vedic literatures, *hariṁ vinā na sṛtiṁ taranti:* without the mercy of the Lord, one cannot stop the cycle of birth and death. In *Bhagavad-gītā* it is stated that only by understanding the transcendental nature of the Lord and His activities, His appearance and disappearance, can one stop the cycle of death and go back to Him. The time factor is divided into many fractions of moments, hours, months, years, periods, seasons, etc. All the divisions in this verse are determined according to the astronomical calculations of Vedic literature. There are six seasons, called *ṛtus,* and there is the period of four months called *cāturmāsya.* Three periods of four months complete one year. According to Vedic astronomical calculations, there are thirteen months. The thirteenth month is called *adhi-māsa* or *mala-māsa* and is added every third year. The time factor, however, cannot touch the life-span of the devotees. In another verse it is stated that when the sun rises and sets it takes away the life of all living entities, but it cannot take away the life of those who are engaged in devotional service. Time is compared here to a big wheel which has 360 joints, six rims in the shape of seasons, and numberless leaves in the shape of moments. It rotates on the eternal existence, Brahman.

## TEXT 19

एकः स्वयं सञ्जगतः सिसृक्षया-
द्वितीययात्मन्नधियोगमायया ।

सृजस्यदः पासि पुनर्ग्रसिष्यसे
यथोर्णनाभिर्भगवन् स्वशक्तिभिः ॥१९॥

*ekaḥ svayaṁ sañ jagataḥ sisṛkṣayā-*
*dvitīyayātmann adhi-yogamāyayā*
*sṛjasy adaḥ pāsi punar grasiṣyase*
*yathorṇa-nābhir bhagavan sva-śaktibhiḥ*

*ekaḥ*—one; *svayam*—Yourself; *san*—being; *jagataḥ*—the universes; *sisṛkṣayā*—with a desire to create; *advitīyayā*—without a second; *ātman*—in Yourself; *adhi*—controlling; *yoga-māyayā*—by *yogamāyā; sṛjasi*—You create; *adaḥ*—those universes; *pāsi*—You maintain; *punaḥ*—again; *grasiṣyase*—You will wind up; *yathā*—like; *ūrṇa-nābhiḥ*—a spider; *bhagavan*—O Lord; *sva-śaktibhiḥ*—by its own energy.

## TRANSLATION

**My dear Lord, You alone create the universes. O Personality of Godhead, desiring to create these universes, You create them, maintain them and again wind them up by Your own energies, which are under the control of Your second energy, called yogamāyā, just as a spider creates a cobweb by its own energy and again winds it up.**

## PURPORT

In this verse two important words nullify the impersonalist theory that everything is God. Here Kardama says, "O Personality of Godhead, You are alone, but You have various energies." The example of the spider is very significant also. The spider is an individual living entity, and by its energy it creates a cobweb and plays on it, and whenever it likes it winds up the cobweb, thus ending the play. When the cobweb is manufactured by the saliva of the spider, the spider does not become impersonal. Similarly, the creation and manifestation of the material or spiritual energy does not render the creator impersonal. Here the very prayer suggests that God is sentient and can hear the prayers and fulfill the desires of the devotee. Therefore, He is *sac-cid-ānanda-vigraha*, the form of bliss, knowledge and eternity.

## TEXT 20

नैतद्बताधीश पदं तवेप्सितं
यन्मायया नस्तनुषे भूतसूक्ष्मम् ।
अनुग्रहायास्त्वपि यर्हि मायया
लसत्तुलस्या भगवान् विलक्षितः ॥२०॥

*naitad batādhīśa padaṁ tavepsitaṁ*
*yan māyayā nas tanuṣe bhūta-sūkṣmam*
*anugrahāyāstv api yarhi māyayā*
*lasat-tulasyā bhagavān vilakṣitaḥ*

*na*—not; *etat*—this; *bata*—indeed; *adhīśa*—O Lord; *padam*—material world; *tava*—Your; *īpsitam*—desire; *yat*—which; *māyayā*—by Your external energy; *naḥ*—for us; *tanuṣe*—You manifest; *bhūta-sūkṣmam*—the elements, gross and subtle; *anugrahāya*—for bestowing mercy; *astu*—let it be; *api*—also; *yarhi*—when; *māyayā*—through Your causeless mercy; *lasat*—splendid; *tulasyā*—with a wreath of *tulasī* leaves; *bhagavān*—the Supreme Personality of Godhead; *vilakṣitaḥ*—is perceived.

## TRANSLATION

**My dear Lord, although it is not Your desire, You manifest this creation of gross and subtle elements just for our sensual satisfaction. Let Your causeless mercy be upon us, for You have appeared before us in Your eternal form, adorned with a splendid wreath of tulasī leaves.**

## PURPORT

It is clearly stated here that the material world is not created by the personal will of the Supreme Lord; it is created by His external energy because the living entities want to enjoy it. This material world is not created for those who do not want to enjoy sense gratification, who constantly remain in transcendental loving service and who are eternally Kṛṣṇa conscious. For them, the spiritual world is eternally existing, and they enjoy there. Elsewhere in the *Śrīmad-Bhāgavatam* it is stated that for those who have taken shelter of the lotus feet of the Supreme Personality of Godhead, this material world is useless; because this material world is full of danger at every step, it is not meant for the devotees but for living entities who want to lord it over the material energy at their own risk. Kṛṣṇa is so kind that He allows the sense-enjoying living entities a separate world created by Him to enjoy as they like, yet at the same time He appears in His personal form. The Lord unwillingly creates this material world, but He descends in His personal form or sends one of His reliable sons or a servant or a reliable author like Vyāsadeva to give instruction. He Himself also instructs in His speeches of *Bhagavad-gītā.* This propaganda work goes on side by side with the creation to convince the misguided living entities who are rotting in this material world to come back to Him and surrender unto Him. Therefore the last instruction of *Bhagavad-gītā* is this: "Give up all your manufactured engagements in the material world and just surrender unto Me. I shall protect you from all sinful reactions."

## TEXT 21

तं त्वानुभूत्योपरतक्रियार्थं
स्वमायया वर्तितलोकतन्त्रम् ।
नमाम्यभीक्ष्णं नमनीयपाद-
सरोजमल्पीयसि कामवर्षम् ॥२१॥

*taṁ tvānubhūtyoparata-kriyārthaṁ*
*sva-māyayā vartita-loka-tantram*
*namāmy abhīkṣṇaṁ namanīya-pāda-*
*sarojam alpīyasi kāma-varṣam*

*tam*—that; *tvā*—You; *anubhūtyā*—by realizing; *uparata*—disregarded; *kriyā*—enjoyment of fruitive activities; *artham*—in order that; *sva-māyayā*—by Your own energy; *vartita*—brought about; *loka-tantram*—the material worlds; *namāmi*—I offer obeisances; *abhīkṣṇam*—continuously; *namanīya*—worshipable; *pāda-sarojam*—lotus feet; *alpīyasi*—on the insignificant; *kāma*—desires; *varṣam*—showering.

## TRANSLATION

**I continuously offer my respectful obeisances unto Your lotus feet, of which it is worthy to take shelter, because You shower all benedictions on the insignificant. To give all living entities detachment from fruitive activity by realizing You, You have expanded these material worlds by Your own energy.**

## PURPORT

Everyone, therefore, whether he desires material enjoyment, liberation or the transcendental loving service of the Lord, should engage himself, offering obeisances unto the Supreme Lord, because the Lord can award everyone his desired benediction. In *Bhagavad-gītā* the Lord affirms, *ye yathā māṁ prapadyante:* anyone who desires to be a successful enjoyer in this material world is awarded that benediction by the Lord, anyone who wants to be liberated from the entanglement of this material world is given liberation by the Lord, and anyone who desires to constantly engage in His service in full Kṛṣṇa consciousness is awarded that benediction by the Lord. For material enjoyment He has prescribed so many ritualistic sacrificial performances in the *Vedas*, and thus people may take advantage of those instructions and enjoy material life in higher planets or in a noble aristocratic family. These processes are mentioned in the *Vedas*, and one can take advantage of them. It is similar with those who want to be liberated from this material world.

Unless one is disgusted with the enjoyment of this material world, he cannot aspire for liberation. Liberation is for one who is disgusted with material enjoyment. *Vedānta-sūtra* says, therefore, *athāto brahma-jijñāsā:* those who have given up the attempt to be happy in this material world can inquire about the Absolute Truth. For those who want to know the Absolute Truth, the *Vedānta-sūtra* is available, as is *Śrīmad-Bhāgavatam*, the actual explanation of *Vedānta-sūtra*. Since *Bhagavad-gītā* is also *Vedānta-sūtra*, by understanding *Śrīmad-Bhāgavatam*, *Vedānta-sūtra* or *Bhagavad-gītā* one can obtain real knowledge. When one obtains real knowledge, he becomes theoretically one with the Supreme, and when he actually begins the service of Brahman, or Kṛṣṇa consciousness, he is not only liberated but situated in his spiritual life. Similarly, for those who want to lord it over material nature, there are so many departments of material enjoyment; material knowledge and material science are available, and the Lord provides for persons who want to enjoy them. The conclusion is that one should worship the Supreme Personality of Godhead for any benediction. The word *kāma-varṣam* is very significant, for it indicates that He satisfies the desires of anyone who approaches Him. But one who sincerely loves Kṛṣṇa and yet wants material enjoyment is in perplexity. Kṛṣṇa, being very kind toward him, gives him an opportunity to engage in the transcendental loving service of the Lord, and so he gradually forgets the hallucination.

## TEXT 22

ऋषिरुवाच
इत्यव्यलीकं प्रणुतोऽब्जनाभ-
स्तमाबभाषे वचसामृतेन ।
सुपर्णपक्षोपरि रोचमानः
प्रेमस्मितोद्वीक्षणविभ्रमद्भ्रूः ॥२२॥

*ṛṣir uvāca*
*ity avyalīkaṁ praṇuto 'bja-nābhas*
*tam ābabhāṣe vacasāmṛtena*
*suparṇa-pakṣopari rocamānaḥ*
*prema-smitodvīkṣaṇa-vibhramad-bhrūḥ*

*ṛṣiḥ uvāca*—the great sage Maitreya said; *iti*—thus; *avyalīkam*—sincerely; *praṇutaḥ*—having been praised; *abja-nābhaḥ*—Lord Viṣṇu; *tam*—to Kardama Muni; *ābabhāṣe*—replied; *vacasā*—with words; *amṛtena*—as sweet as nectar; *suparṇa*—of Garuḍa; *pakṣa*—the shoulders; *upari*—upon; *rocamānaḥ*—shining; *prema*—of affection; *smita*—with a smile; *udvīkṣaṇa*—looking; *vibhramat*—gracefully moving; *bhrūḥ*—eyebrows.

## TRANSLATION

**Maitreya resumed: Sincerely extolled in these words, Lord Viṣṇu, shining very beautifully on the shoulders of Garuḍa, replied with words as sweet as nectar. His eyebrows moved gracefully as He looked at the sage with a smile full of affection.**

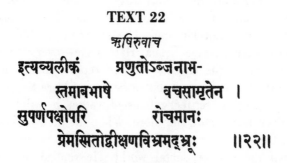

## PURPORT

The word *vacasāmṛtena* is significant. Whenever the Lord speaks, He speaks from the transcendental world. He does not speak from the material world. Since He is transcendental, His speech is also transcendental, as is His activity; everything in relation to Him is transcendental. The word *amṛta* refers to one who does not meet with death. The words and activities of the Lord are deathless; therefore they are not manufactured of this material world. The sound of this material world and that of the spiritual world are completely different. The sound of the spiritual world is nectarean and eternal, whereas the sound of the material world is hackneyed and subject to end. The sound of the holy name—Hare Kṛṣṇa, Hare Kṛṣṇa, Kṛṣṇa Kṛṣṇa, Hare Hare—everlastingly increases the enthusiasm of the chanter. If one repeats monotonous material words, he will feel exhausted, but if he chants Hare Kṛṣṇa twenty-four hours a day, he will never feel exhausted; rather, he will feel encouraged to continue chanting more and more. When the Lord replied to the sage Kardama, the word *vacasāmṛtena* is specifically mentioned, since He spoke from the transcendental world. He replied in transcendental words, and when He spoke His eyebrows moved with great affection. When a devotee praises the glories of the Lord, the Lord is very satisfied, and He bestows His transcendental benediction upon the devotee without reservation because He is always causelessly merciful toward His devotee.

## TEXT 23

श्रीभगवानुवाच
विदित्वा तव चैत्यं मे पुरैव समयोजि तत् ।
यदर्थमात्मनियमैस्त्वयैवाहं समर्चितः ॥२३॥

*śrī-bhagavān uvāca*
*viditvā tava caityaṁ me*
*puraiva samayoji tat*
*yad-artham ātma-niyamais*
*tvayaivāhaṁ samarcitaḥ*

*śrī-bhagavān uvāca*—the Supreme Lord said; *viditvā*—understanding; *tava*—your; *caityam*—mental condition; *me*—by Me; *purā*—

previously; *eva*—certainly; *samayoji*—was arranged; *tat*—that; *yat-artham*—for the sake of which; *ātma*—of the mind and senses; *niyamaiḥ*—by discipline; *tvayā*—by you; *eva*—only; *aham*—I; *samar-citaḥ*—have been worshiped.

## TRANSLATION

**The Supreme Lord said: Having come to know what was in your mind, I have already arranged for that for which you have worshiped Me well through your mental and sensory discipline.**

## PURPORT

The Supreme Personality of Godhead in His Paramātmā feature is situated in everyone's heart. He knows, therefore, the past, present and future of every individual person as well as his desires, activities and everything about him. It is stated in *Bhagavad-gītā* that He is seated in the heart as a witness. The Personality of Godhead knew the heart's desire of Kardama Muni, and He had already arranged for the fulfillment of his desires. He never disappoints a sincere devotee, regardless of what he wants, but He never allows anything which will be detrimental to the individual's devotional service.

## TEXT 24

न वै जातु मृषैव स्यात्प्रजाध्यक्ष मदर्हणम् ।
भवद्विधेष्वतितरां मयि संगृभितात्मनाम् ॥२४॥

*na vai jātu mṛṣaiva syāt*
*prajādhyakṣa mad-arhaṇam*
*bhavad-vidheṣu atitarāṁ*
*mayi saṅgṛbhitātmanām*

*na*—not; *vai*—indeed; *jātu*—ever; *mṛṣā*—useless; *eva*—only; *syāt*—it may be; *prajā*—of the living entities; *adhyakṣa*—O leader; *mat-arhaṇam*—worship of Me; *bhavat-vidheṣu*—unto persons like you; *atitarām*—entirely; *mayi*—on Me; *saṅgṛbhita*—are fixed; *ātmanām*—of those whose minds.

## TRANSLATION

**The Lord continued: My dear ṛṣi, O leader of the living entities, for those who serve Me in devotion by worshiping Me, especially persons like you who have given up everything unto Me, there is never any question of frustration.**

## PURPORT

Even if he has some desires, one engaged in the service of the Lord is never frustrated. Those engaged in His service are called *sakāma* and *akāma.* Those who approach the Supreme Personality of Godhead with desires for material enjoyment are called *sakāma,* and those devotees who have no material desires for sense gratification but serve the Supreme Lord out of spontaneous love for Him are called *akāma. Sakāma* devotees are divided into four classes—those in distress, those in need of money, the inquisitive and the wise. Someone worships the Supreme Lord because of bodily or mental distress, someone else worships the Supreme Lord because he is in need of money, someone else worships the Lord out of inquisitiveness to know Him as He is, and someone wants to know the Lord as a philosopher can know Him, by the research work of his wisdom. There is no frustration for any of these four classes of men; each is endowed with the desired result of his worship.

## TEXT 25

प्रजापतिसुतः सम्राण्मनुर्विख्यातमङ्गलः ।
ब्रह्मावर्तं योऽधिवसन् शास्ति सप्तार्णवां महीम् ॥२५॥

*prajāpati-sutaḥ samrāṇ*
*manur vikhyāta-maṅgalaḥ*
*brahmāvartaṁ yo 'dhivasan*
*śāsti saptārṇavāṁ mahīm*

*prajāpati-sutaḥ*—the son of Lord Brahmā; *samrāṭ*—the Emperor; *manuḥ*—Svāyambhuva Manu; *vikhyāta*—well known; *maṅgalaḥ*—whose righteous acts; *brahmāvartam*—Brahmāvarta; *yaḥ*—he who; *adhivasan*—living in; *śāsti*—rules; *sapta*—seven; *arṇavām*—oceans; *mahīm*—the earth.

## TRANSLATION

**The Emperor Svāyambhuva Manu, the son of Lord Brahmā, who is well known for his righteous acts, has his seat in Brahmāvarta and rules over the earth with its seven oceans.**

## PURPORT

Sometimes it is stated that Brahmāvarta is a part of Kurukṣetra or that Kurukṣetra itself is situated in Brahmāvarta, because the demigods are recommended to perform spiritual ritualistic performances in Kurukṣetra. But in others' opinion, Brahmāvarta is a place in Brahmaloka, where Svāyambhuva ruled. There are many places on the surface of this earth which are also known in the higher planetary systems; we have places on this planet like Vṛndāvana, Dvārakā and Mathurā, but they are also eternally situated in Kṛṣṇaloka. There are many similar names on the surface of the earth, and it may be that in the Boar age Svāyambhuva Manu ruled this planet, as stated here. The word *maṅgalaḥ* is significant. *Maṅgala* means one who is elevated in every respect in the opulences of religious performances, ruling power, cleanliness and all other good qualities. *Vikhyāta* means "celebrated." Svāyambhuva Manu was celebrated for all good qualities and opulences.

## TEXT 26

स चेह विप्र राजर्षिर्महिष्या शतरूपया ।
आयास्यति दिदृक्षुस्त्वां परश्वो धर्मकोविदः ॥२६॥

*sa ceha vipra rājarṣir*
*mahiṣyā śatarūpayā*
*āyāsyati didṛkṣus tvāṁ*
*paraśvo dharma-kovidaḥ*

*saḥ*—Svāyambhuva Manu; *ca*—and; *iha*—here; *vipra*—O holy *brāhmaṇa; rāja-ṛṣiḥ*—the saintly king; *mahiṣyā*—along with his queen; *śatarūpayā*—called Śatarūpā; *āyāsyati*—will come; *didṛkṣuḥ*—desiring to see; *tvām*—you; *paraśvaḥ*—the day after tomorrow; *dharma*—in religious activities; *kovidaḥ*—expert.

### TRANSLATION

**The day after tomorrow, O brāhmaṇa, that celebrated emperor, who is expert in religious activities, will come here with his queen, Śatarūpā, wishing to see you.**

### TEXT 27

आत्मजामसितापाङ्गीं वयःशीलगुणान्विताम् ।
मृगयन्तीं पतिं दास्यत्यनुरूपाय ते प्रभो ॥२७॥

*ātmajām asitāpāṅgīṁ*
*vayaḥ-śīla-guṇānvitām*
*mṛgayantīṁ patiṁ dāsyaty*
*anurūpāya te prabho*

*ātma-jām*—his own daughter; *asita*—black; *apāṅgīm*—eyes; *vayaḥ*—grown-up age; *śīla*—with character; *guṇa*—with good qualities; *anvitām*—endowed; *mṛgayantīm*—searching for; *patim*—a husband; *dāsyati*—he will give; *anurūpāya*—who are suitable; *te*—unto you; *prabho*—My dear sir.

### TRANSLATION

**He has a grown-up daughter whose eyes are black. She is ready for marriage, and she has good character and all good qualities. She is also searching for a good husband. My dear sir, her parents will come to see you, who are exactly suitable for her, just to deliver their daughter as your wife.**

### PURPORT

The selection of a good husband for a good girl was always entrusted to the parents. Here it is clearly stated that Manu and his wife were coming to see Kardama Muni to offer their daughter because the daughter was well qualified and the parents were searching out a similarly qualified man. This is the duty of parents. Girls are never thrown into the public street to search out their husband, for when girls are grown up and are searching after a boy, they forget to consider whether the boy they select is actually sutiable for them. Out of the urge of sex desire, a girl may accept anyone, but if the husband is chosen by the parents, they can consider who is to be selected and who is not. According to the Vedic system, therefore, the girl is given over to a suitable boy by the parents; she is never allowed to select her own husband independently.

## TEXT 28

समाहितं ते हृदयं यत्रेमान् परिवत्सरान् ।
सा त्वां ब्रह्मन्नृपवधूः काममाशु भजिष्यति ॥२८॥

*samāhitaṁ te hṛdayaṁ*
*yatremān parivatsarān*
*sā tvāṁ brahman nṛpa-vadhūḥ*
*kāmam āśu bhajiṣyati*

*samāhitam*—has been fixed; *te*—your; *hṛdayam*—heart; *yatra*—on whom; *imān*—for all these; *parivatsarān*—years; *sā*—she; *tvām*—you; *brahman*—O *brāhmaṇa; nṛpa-vadhūḥ*—the princess; *kāmam*—as you desire; *āśu*—very soon; *bhajiṣyati*—will serve.

## TRANSLATION

**That princess, O holy sage, will be just the type you have been thinking of in your heart for all these long years. She will soon be yours and will serve you to your heart's content.**

## PURPORT

The Lord awards all benedictions according to the heart's desire of a devotee, so the Lord informed Kardama Muni, "The girl who is coming to be married with you is a princess, the daughter of Emperor Svāyambhuva, and so just suitable for your purpose." Only by God's grace can one get a nice wife just as he desires. Similarly, it is only by God's grace that a girl gets a husband suitable to her heart. Thus it is said that if we pray to the Supreme Lord in every transaction of our material existence, everything will be done very nicely and just suitable to our heart's desire. In other words, in all circumstances we must take shelter of the Supreme Personality of Godhead and depend completely on His decision. Man proposes, God disposes. The fulfillment of desires, therefore, should be entrusted to the Supreme Personality of Godhead; that is the nicest solution. Kardama Muni desired only a wife, but because he was a devotee of the Lord, the Lord selected a wife for him who was the Emperor's daughter, a princess. Thus Kardama Muni got a wife beyond his expectation. If we depend on the choice of the Supreme Personality of Godhead, we will receive benedictions in greater opulence than we desire.

It is also significantly noted here that Kardama Muni was a *brāhmaṇa*, whereas Emperor Svāyambhuva was a *kṣatriya.* Therefore, intercaste marriage was current even in those days. The system was that a *brāhmaṇa* could marry the daughter of a *kṣatriya*, but a *kṣatriya* could not marry the daughter of a *brāhmaṇa.* We have evidences from the history of the Vedic age that Śukrācārya offered his daughter to Mahārāja Yayāti, but the King had to refuse to marry the daughter of a *brāhmaṇa;* only with the special permission of the *brāhmaṇa* could they marry. Intercaste marriage, therefore, was not prohibited in the olden days, many millions of years ago, but there was a regular system of social behavior.

## TEXT 29

या त आत्मभृतं वीर्यं नवधा प्रसविष्यति ।
वीर्ये त्वदीये ऋषय आधास्यन्त्यञ्जसात्मनः ॥२९॥

*yā ta ātma-bhṛtaṁ vīryaṁ*
*navadhā prasaviṣyati*
*vīrye tvadīye ṛṣaya*
*ādhāsyanty añjasātmanaḥ*

*yā*—she; *te*—by you; *ātma-bhṛtam*—sown in her; *vīryam*—the seed; *nava-dhā*—nine daughters; *prasaviṣyati*—will bring forth; *vīrye tvadīye*—in the daughters begotten by you; *ṛṣayaḥ*—the sages; *ādhāsyanti*—will beget; *añjasā*—in total; *ātmanaḥ*—children.

## TRANSLATION

**She will bring forth nine daughters from the seed sown in her by you, and through the daughters you beget, the sages will duly beget children.**

## TEXT 30

त्वं च सम्यगनुष्ठाय निदेशं म उशत्तमः ।
मयि तीर्थीकृताशेषक्रियार्थो मां प्रपत्स्यसे ॥३०॥

*tvaṁ ca samyag anuṣṭhāya*
*nideśaṁ ma uśattamaḥ*
*mayi tīrthī-kṛtāśeṣa-*
*kriyārtho māṁ prapatsyase*

*tvam*—you; *ca*—and; *samyak*—properly; *anuṣṭhāya*—having carried out; *nideśam*—command; *me*—My; *uśattamaḥ*—completely cleansed; *mayi*—unto Me; *tīrthī-kṛta*—having resigned; *aśeṣa*—all; *kriyā*—of actions; *arthaḥ*—the fruits; *mām*—to Me; *prapatsyase*—you will attain.

## TRANSLATION

**With your heart cleansed by properly carrying out My command, resigning to Me the fruits of all your acts, you will finally attain to Me.**

## PURPORT

Here the words *tīrthī-kṛtāśeṣa-kriyārthaḥ* are significant. *Tīrtha* means a sanctified place where charity is given. People used to go to places of pilgrimage and give munificently in charity. This system is still current. Therefore the Lord said, "In order to sanctify your activities and the results of your actions, you will offer everything unto Me." This is also confirmed in *Bhagavad-gītā:* "Whatever you do, whatever you eat, whatever you sacrifice, the result should be given to Me only." In another place in *Bhagavad-gītā* the Lord said, "I am the enjoyer of all sacrifices, all penances and everything done for the welfare of mankind or society." All activities, therefore, whether for the welfare of family, society, country or humanity at large, must be performed in Kṛṣṇa consciousness. That is the instruction given by the Lord to Kardama Muni. Mahārāja Yudhiṣṭhira welcomed Nārada Muni: "Wherever you are present, that place becomes sanctified because the Lord Himself is always seated in your heart." Similarly, if we act in Kṛṣṇa consciousness under the direction of the Lord and His representative, then everything is sanctified. This is the indication given to Kardama Muni, who acted on it and therefore received the most excellent wife and child, as will be disclosed in later verses.

## TEXT 31

**कृत्वा दयां च जीवेषु दत्त्वा चाभयमात्मवान् ।**
**मय्यात्मानं सह जगद् द्रक्ष्यस्यात्मनि चापि माम् ॥३१॥**

*kṛtvā dayāṁ ca jīveṣu*
*dattvā cābhayam ātmavān*
*mayy ātmānaṁ saha jagad*
*drakṣyasy ātmani cāpi mām*

*kṛtvā*—having shown; *dayām*—compassion; *ca*—and; *jīveṣu*—toward living beings; *dattvā*—having given; *ca*—and; *abhayam*—assurance of safety; *ātma-vān*—self-realized; *mayi*—in Me; *ātmānam*—yourself; *saha jagat*—along with the universe; *drakṣyasi*—you will perceive; *ātmani*—in yourself; *ca*—and; *api*—also; *mām*—Me.

## TRANSLATION

**Showing compassion to all living entities, you will attain self-realization. Giving assurance of safety to all, you will perceive your own self as well as all the universes in Me, and Myself in you.**

## PURPORT

The simple process of self-realization for every living entity is described here. The first principle to be understood is that this world is a product of the supreme will. There is an identity of this world with the Supreme Lord. This identity is accepted in a misconceived way by the impersonalists; they say that the Supreme Absolute Truth, transforming Himself into the universe, loses His separate existence. Thus they accept the world and everything in it to be the Lord. That is pantheism, wherein everything is considered to be the Lord. This is the view of the impersonalist. But those who are personal devotees of the Lord take everything to be the property of the Supreme Lord. Everything, whatever we see, is the manifestation of the Supreme Lord; therefore, everything should be engaged in the service of the Lord. This is oneness. The difference between the impersonalist and the personalist is that the impersonalist does not accept the separate existence of the Lord, but the personalist accepts the Lord; he understands that although He distributes Himself in so many ways, He has His separate personal existence. This is described in *Bhagavad-gītā:* "I am spread all over the universe in My impersonal form. Everything is resting on Me, but I am not present." There is a nice example regarding the sun and the sunshine. The sun, by its sunshine, is spread all over the universe, and all the planets rest on the sunshine. But all the planets are different from the sun planet; one cannot say that because the planets are resting on the sunshine, these planets are also the sun. Similarly, the impersonal or pantheistic view that everything is God is not a very intelligent proposal. The real position, as explained by the Lord Himself, is that although nothing can exist without Him, it is not a fact that everything *is* Him. He is different from everything. So here also the Lord says: "You will see everything in the world to be nondifferent from Me." This means that everything should be considered a product of the Lord's energy, and therefore everything should be employed in the service of the Lord. One's energy should be utilized for one's self-interest. That is the perfection of the energy.

This energy can be utilized for real self-interest if one is compassionate. A person in Kṛṣṇa consciousness, a devotee of the Lord, is always compassionate. He is not satisfied that only he himself is a devotee, but he tries to distribute the knowledge of devotional service to everyone. There are many devotees of the Lord who faced many risks in distributing the devotional service of the Lord to people in general. That should be done.

It is also said that a person who goes to the temple of the Lord and worships with great devotion, but who does not show sympathy to people in general or show respect to other devotees, is considered to be a third-class devotee. The second-class devotee is he who is merciful and compassionate to the fallen soul. The second-class devotee is always cognizant of his position as an eternal servant of the Lord; he therefore makes friendships with devotees of the Lord, acts compassionately toward the general public in teaching them devotional service, and refuses to cooperate or associate with nondevotees. As long as one is not compassionate to people in general in his devotional service to the Lord, he is a third-class devotee. The first-class devotee gives assurance to every living being that there is no fear of this material existence: "Let us live in Kṛṣṇa consciousness and conquer the nescience of material existence."

It is indicated here that Kardama Muni was directed by the Lord to be very compassionate and liberal in his householder life and to give assurance to the people in his renounced life. A *sannyāsī*, one in the renounced order of life, is meant to give enlightenment to the people. He should travel, going from home to home to enlighten. The householder, by the spell of *māyā*, becomes absorbed in family affairs and forgets his relationship with Kṛṣṇa. If he dies in forgetfulness, like the cats and dogs, then his life is spoiled. It is the duty of a *sannyāsī*, therefore, to go and awaken the forgetful souls with enlightenment of their eternal relationship with the Lord and to engage them in devotional service. The devotee should show mercy to the fallen souls and also give them the assurance of fearlessness. As soon as one becomes a devotee of the Lord, he is convinced that he is protected by the Lord. Fear itself is afraid of the Lord; therefore, what has he to do with fearfulness?

To award fearlessness to the common man is the greatest act of charity. A *sannyāsī*, or one who is in the renounced order of life, should wander from door to door, from village to village, from town to town and from country to country, all over the world as far as he is able to travel, and enlighten the householders about Kṛṣṇa consciousness. A person who is a householder but is initiated by a *sannyāsī* has the duty to spread Kṛṣṇa consciousness at home; as far as possible, he should call his friends and neighbors to his house and hold classes in Kṛṣṇa consciousness. Holding a class means chanting the holy name of Kṛṣṇa and speaking from *Bhagavad-gītā* or *Śrīmad-Bhāgavatam*. There are immense literatures for spreading Kṛṣṇa consciousness, and it is the duty of each and every householder to learn about Kṛṣṇa from his *sannyāsī* spiritual master. There is a division of labor in the Lord's service. The householder's duty is to earn money because a *sannyāsī* is not supposed to earn money but is completely dependent on the householder. The householder should earn money by business or by profession and spend at least fifty percent of his income to spread Kṛṣṇa consciousness; twenty-five percent he can spend for his family, and twenty-five percent he should save to meet emergencies. This example was shown by Rūpa Gosvāmī, so devotees should follow it.

Actually, to be one with the Supreme Lord means to be one with the interest of the Lord. Becoming one with the Supreme Lord does not imply becoming as great as the Supreme Lord. It is impossible. The part is never equal to the whole. The living entity is always a minute part. Therefore his oneness with the Lord is that he is interested in the one interest of the Lord. The Lord wants every living entity to always think about Him, to be His devotee and always worship Him. This is clearly stated in *Bhagavad-gītā: man-manā bhava mad-bhaktaḥ.* Kṛṣṇa wants everyone always to think of Him. Everyone should always offer obeisances to Kṛṣṇa. This is the will of the Supreme Lord, and devotees should try to fulfill His desire. Since the Lord is unlimited, His desire is also unlimited. There is no stoppage, and therefore the service of the devotee is also unlimited. In the transcendental world there is unlimited competition between the Lord and the servitor. The Lord wants to fulfill His desires unlimitedly, and the devotee also serves Him to fulfill His unlimited desires. There is an unlimited oneness of interest between the Lord and His devotee.

## TEXT 32

सहाहं स्वांशकलया त्वद्वीर्येण महामुने ।
तव क्षेत्रे देवहूत्यां प्रणेष्ये तत्त्वसंहिताम् ॥३२॥

*sahāhaṁ svāṁśa-kalayā*
*tvad-vīryeṇa mahā-mune*
*tava kṣetre devahūtyāṁ*
*praṇeṣye tattva-saṁhitām*

*saha*—with; *aham*—I; *sva-aṁśa-kalayā*—My own plenary portion; *tvat-vīryeṇa*—by your semen; *mahā-mune*—O great sage; *tava kṣetre*—in your wife; *devahūtyām*—in Devahūti; *praṇeṣye*—I shall instruct; *tattva*—of the ultimate principles; *saṁhitām*—the doctrine.

## TRANSLATION

**O great sage, I shall manifest My own plenary portion through your wife, Devahūti, along with your nine daughters, and I shall instruct her in the system of philosophy that deals with the ultimate principles or categories.**

## PURPORT

Herein the word *svāṁśa-kalayā* indicates that the Lord would appear as the son of Devahūti and Kardama Muni as Kapiladeva, the first propounder of the Sāṅkhya philosophy, which is mentioned here as *tattva-saṁhitā.* The Lord foretold to Kardama Muni that He would appear in His incarnation Kapiladeva and would propagate the philosophy of Sāṅkhya. Sāṅkhya philosophy is very well known in the world as propagated by another Kapiladeva, but that Sāṅkhya philosophy is different from the Sāṅkhya which was propounded by the Lord Himself. There are two kinds of Sāṅkhya philosophy: one is godless Sāṅkhya philosophy, and the other is godly Sāṅkhya philosophy. The Sāṅkhya propagated by Kapiladeva, son of Devahūti, is godly philosophy.

There are different manifestations of the Lord. He is one, but He has become many. He divides Himself into two different expansions, one called *kalā* and the other *vibhinnāṁśa.* Ordinary living entities are called *vibhinnāṁśa* expansions, and the unlimited expansions of *viṣṇu-tattva,* such as Vāmana, Govinda, Nārāyaṇa, Pradyumna, Vāsudeva and Ananta, are called *svāṁśa-kalā. Svāṁśa* refers to a direct expansion, and *kalā* denotes an expansion from the expansion of the original Lord. Baladeva is an expansion of Kṛṣṇa, and from Baladeva the next expansion is Saṅkarṣaṇa; thus Saṅkarṣaṇa is *kalā,* but Baladeva is *svāṁśa.* There is no difference, however, among Them. This is very nicely explained in the *Brahma-saṁhitā* (5.46): *dīpārcir eva hi daśāntaram abhyupetya.* With one candle one may light a second candle, with the second a third and then a fourth, and in this way one can light up thousands of candles, and no candle is inferior to another in distributing light. Every candle has the full potential candlepower, but there is still the distinction that one candle is the first, another the second, another the third and another the fourth. Similarly, there is no difference between the immediate expansion of the Lord and His secondary expansion. The Lord's names are considered in exactly the same way; since the Lord is absolute, His name, His form, His pastimes, His paraphernalia and His quality all have the same potency. In the absolute world, the name Kṛṣṇa is the transcendental sound representation of the Lord. There is no potential difference between His quality, name, form, etc. If we chant the name of the Lord, Hare Kṛṣṇa, that has as much potency as the Lord Himself. There is no potential difference between the form of the Lord whom we worship and the form of the Lord in the temple. One should not think that one is worshiping a doll or statue of the Lord, even if others consider it to be a statue. Because there is not potential difference, one gets the same result by worshiping the statue of the Lord or the Lord Himself. This is the science of Kṛṣṇa consciousness.

## TEXT 33

मैत्रेय उवाच
एवं तमनुभाष्याथ भगवान् प्रत्यगक्षजः ।
जगाम बिन्दुसरसः सरस्वत्या परिश्रितात् ॥३३॥

*maitreya uvāca*
*evaṁ tam anubhāṣyātha*
*bhagavān pratyag-akṣajaḥ*
*jagāma bindusarasaḥ*
*sarasvatyā pariśritāt*

*maitreyaḥ uvāca*—the great sage Maitreya said; *evam*—thus; *tam*—to him; *anubhāṣya*—having spoken; *atha*—then; *bhagavān*—the Lord; *pratyak*—directly; *akṣa*—by senses; *jaḥ*—who is perceived; *jagāma*—went away; *bindu-sarasaḥ*—from Lake Bindu-sarovara; *sarasvatyā*—by the River Sarasvatī; *pariśritāt*—encircled.

## TRANSLATION

**Maitreya went on: Thus having spoken to Kardama Muni, the Lord, who reveals Himself only when the senses are in Kṛṣṇa consciousness, departed from that lake called Bindu-sarovara, which was encircled by the River Sarasvatī.**

## PURPORT

One word in this verse is very significant. The Lord is stated here to be *pratyag-akṣaja.* He is imperceptible to material senses, but still He can be seen. This appears to be contradictory. We have material senses, but how can we see the Supreme Lord? He is called *adhokṣaja,* which means that He cannot be seen by the material senses. *Akṣaja* means "knowledge perceived by material senses." Because the Lord is not an object that can be understood by speculation with our material senses, He is also called *ajita;* He will conquer, but no one can conquer Him. What does it mean, then, that still He can be seen? It is explained that no one can hear the transcendental name of Kṛṣṇa, no one can understand His transcendental form, and no one can assimilate His transcendental pastimes. It is not possible. Then how is it possible that He can be seen and understood? When one is trained in devotional service and renders service unto Him, gradually one's senses are purified of material contamination. When one's senses are thus purified, then one can see, one can understand, one can hear and so on. The purification of the material senses and perception of the transcendental form, name and quality of Kṛṣṇa are combined together in one word, *pratyag-akṣaja,* which is used here.

## TEXT 34

निरीक्षतस्तस्य ययावशेष-
सिद्धेश्वराभिष्टुतसिद्धमार्गः ।
आकर्णयन् पत्ररथेन्द्रपक्षै-
रुच्चारितं स्तोममुदीर्णसाम ॥३४॥

*nirīkṣatas tasya yayāv aśeṣa-*
*siddheśvarābhiṣṭuta-siddha-mārgaḥ*
*ākarṇayan patra-rathendra-pakṣair*
*uccāritaṁ stomam udīrṇa-sāma*

*nirīkṣataḥ tasya*—while he was looking on; *yayau*—He left; *aśeṣa*—all; *siddha-īśvara*—by liberated souls; *abhiṣṭuta*—is praised; *siddha-mārgaḥ*—the way to the spiritual world; *ākarṇayan*—hearing; *patra-ratha-indra*—of Garuḍa (king of birds); *pakṣaiḥ*—by the wings; *uccāritam*—vibrated; *stomam*—hymns; *udīrṇa-sāma*—forming the *Sāma Veda.*

## TRANSLATION

**While the sage stood looking on, the Lord left by the pathway leading to Vaikuṇṭha, a path extolled by all great liberated souls.**

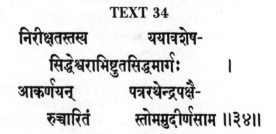

**The sage stood listening as the hymns forming the basis of the Sāma Veda were vibrated by the flapping wings of the Lord's carrier, Garuḍa.**

## PURPORT

In the Vedic literature it is stated that the two wings of the transcendental bird Garuḍa, who carries the Lord everywhere, are two divisions of the *Sāma Veda* known as *bṛhat* and *rathāntara.* Garuḍa works as the carrier of the Lord; therefore he is considered the transcendental prince of all carriers. With his two wings Garuḍa began to vibrate the *Sāma Veda,* which is chanted by great sages to pacify the Lord. The Lord is worshiped by Brahmā, by Lord Śiva, by Garuḍa and other demigods with selected poems, and great sages worship Him with the hymns of Vedic literatures, such as the *Upaniṣads* and *Sāma Veda.* These *Sāma Veda* utterances are automatically heard by the devotee when another great devotee of the Lord, Garuḍa, flaps his wings.

It is clearly stated here that the sage Kardama began to look to the path by which the Lord was being carried to Vaikuṇṭha. It is thus confirmed that the Lord descends from His abode, Vaikuṇṭha, in the spiritual sky, and is carried by Garuḍa. The path which leads to Vaikuṇṭha is not worshiped by the ordinary class of transcendentalists. Only those who are already liberated from material bondage can become devotees of the Lord. Those who are not liberated from material bondage cannot understand transcendental devotional service. In *Bhagavad-gītā* it is clearly stated, *yatatām api siddhānām.* There are many persons who are trying to attain perfection by striving for liberation from material bondage, and those who are actually liberated are called *brahma-bhūta* or *siddha.* Only the *siddhas,* or persons liberated from material bondage, can become devotees. This is also confirmed in *Bhagavad-gītā:* anyone who is engaged in Kṛṣṇa consciousness, or devotional service, is already liberated from the influence of the modes of material nature. Here it is also confirmed that the path of devotional service is worshiped by liberated persons, not the conditioned souls. The conditioned soul cannot understand the devotional service of the Lord. Kardama Muni was a liberated soul who saw the Supreme Lord in person, face to face. There was no doubt that he was liberated, and thus he could see Garuḍa carrying the

Lord on the way to Vaikuṇṭha and hear the flapping of his wings vibrating the sound of Hare Kṛṣṇa, the essence of the *Sāma Veda.*

## TEXT 35

**अथ सम्प्रस्थिते शुक्ले कर्दमो भगवानृषिः ।**
**आस्ते स्म बिन्दुसरसि तं कालं प्रतिपालयन् ॥३५॥**

*atha samprasthite śukle*
*kardamo bhagavān ṛṣiḥ*
*āste sma bindusarasi*
*taṁ kālaṁ pratipālayan*

*atha*—then; *samprasthite śukle*—when the Lord had gone; *kardamaḥ*—Kardama Muni; *bhagavān*—the greatly powerful; *ṛṣiḥ*—sage; *āste sma*—stayed; *bindu-sarasi*—on the bank of Lake Bindu-sarovara; *tam*—that; *kālam*—time; *pratipālayan*—awaiting.

## TRANSLATION

**Then, after the departure of the Lord, the worshipful sage Kardama stayed on the bank of Bindu-sarovara, awaiting the time of which the Lord had spoken.**

## TEXT 36

**मनुः स्यन्दनमास्थाय शातकौम्भपरिच्छदम् ।**
**आरोप्य स्वां दुहितरं सभार्यः पर्यटन्महीम् ॥३६॥**

*manuḥ syandanam āsthāya*
*śātakaumbha-paricchadam*
*āropya svāṁ duhitaraṁ*
*sa-bhāryaḥ paryaṭan mahīm*

*manuḥ*—Svāyambhuva Manu; *syandanam*—the chariot; *āsthāya*—having mounted; *śātakaumbha*—made of gold; *paricchadam*—the outer cover; *āropya*—putting on; *svām*—his own; *duhitaram*—daughter; *sa-bhāryaḥ*—along with his wife; *paryaṭan*—traveling all over; *mahīm*—the globe.

### TRANSLATION

**Svāyambhuva Manu, with his wife, mounted his chariot, which was decorated with golden ornaments. Placing his daughter on it with them, he began traveling all over the earth.**

### PURPORT

The Emperor Manu, as the great ruler of the world, could have engaged an agent to find a suitable husband for his daughter, but because he loved her just as a father should, he himself left his state on a golden chariot, with only his wife, to find her a suitable husband.

### TEXT 37

तस्मिन् सुधन्वन्नहनि भगवान् यत्समादिशत् ।
उपायादाश्रमपदं मुनेः शान्तव्रतस्य तत् ॥३७॥

*tasmin sudhanvann ahani*
*bhagavān yat samādiśat*
*upāyād āśrama-padaṁ*
*muneḥ śānta-vratasya tat*

*tasmin*—on that; *su-dhanvan*—O great bowman Vidura; *ahani*—on the day; *bhagavān*—the Lord; *yat*—which; *samādiśat*—foretold; *upāyāt*—he reached; *āśrama-padam*—the holy hermitage; *muneḥ*—of the sage; *śānta*—completed; *vratasya*—whose vows of austerity; *tat*—that.

### TRANSLATION

**O Vidura, they reached the hermitage of the sage, who had just completed his vows of austerity on the very day foretold by the Lord.**

### TEXTS 38–39

यस्मिन् भगवतो नेत्रान्न्यपतन्नश्रुबिन्दवः ।
कृपया सम्परीतस्य प्रपन्नेऽर्पितया भृशम् ॥३८॥

तद्वै बिन्दुसरो नाम सरस्वत्या परिप्लुतम् ।
पुण्यं शिवामृतजलं महर्षिगणसेवितम् ॥३९॥

*yasmin bhagavato netrān*
*nyapatann aśru-bindavaḥ*
*kṛpayā samparītasya*
*prapanne 'rpitayā bhṛśam*

*tad vai bindusaro nāma*
*sarasvatyā pariplutam*
*puṇyaṁ śivāmṛta-jalaṁ*
*maharṣi-gaṇa-sevitam*

*yasmin*—in which; *bhagavataḥ*—of the Lord; *netrāt*—from the eye; *nyapatan*—fell down; *aśru-bindavaḥ*—teardrops; *kṛpayā*—by compassion; *samparītasya*—who was overwhelmed; *prapanne*—on the surrendered soul (Kardama); *arpitayā*—placed upon; *bhṛśam*—extremely; *tat*—that; *vai*—indeed; *bindu-saraḥ*—lake of tears; *nāma*—called; *sarasvatyā*—by the River Sarasvatī; *pariplutam*—overflowed; *puṇyam*—holy; *śiva*—auspicious; *amṛta*—nectar; *jalam*—water; *mahā-ṛṣi*—of great sages; *gaṇa*—by hosts; *sevitam*—served.

## TRANSLATION

**The holy Lake Bindu-sarovara, flooded by the waters of the River Sarasvatī, was resorted to by hosts of eminent sages. Its holy water was not only auspicious but as sweet as nectar. It was called Bindu-sarovara because drops of tears had fallen there from the eyes of the Lord, who was overwhelmed by extreme compassion for the sage who had sought His protection.**

## PURPORT

Kardama underwent austerities to gain the causeless mercy of the Lord, and when the Lord arrived there He was so compassionate that in pleasure He shed tears, which became Bindu-sarovara. Bindu-sarovara, therefore, is worshiped by great sages and learned scholars because, according to the philosophy of the Absolute Truth, the Lord and the tears from His eyes are not different. Just as drops of perspiration which fell from the toe of the Lord became the sacred Ganges, so teardrops from the transcendental eyes of the Lord became Bindu-sarovara. Both are transcendental entities and are worshiped by great sages and scholars. The water of Bindu-sarovara is described here as *śivāmṛta-jala. Śiva* means "curing." Anyone who drinks the water of Bindu-sarovara is cured of all material diseases; similarly, anyone who takes his bath in the Ganges also is relieved of all material diseases. These claims are accepted by great scholars and authorities and are still being acted upon even in this fallen age of Kali.

## TEXT 40

पुण्यद्रुमलताजालैः कूजत्पुण्यमृगद्विजैः ।
सर्वर्तुफलपुष्पाढ्यं वनराजिश्रियान्वितम् ॥४०॥

*puṇya-druma-latā-jālaiḥ*
*kūjat-puṇya-mṛga-dvijaiḥ*
*sarvartu-phala-puṣpāḍhyaṁ*
*vana-rāji-śriyānvitam*

*puṇya*—pious; *druma*—of trees; *latā*—of creepers; *jālaiḥ*—with clusters; *kūjat*—uttering cries; *puṇya*—pious; *mṛga*—animals; *dvijaiḥ*—with birds; *sarva*—in all; *ṛtu*—seasons; *phala*—in fruits; *puṣpa*—in flowers; *āḍhyam*—rich; *vana-rāji*—of groves of trees; *śriyā*—by the beauty; *anvitam*—adorned.

## TRANSLATION

**The shore of the lake was surrounded by clusters of pious trees and creepers, rich in fruits and flowers of all seasons, that afforded shelter to pious animals and birds, which uttered various cries. It was adorned by the beauty of groves of forest trees.**

## PURPORT

It is stated here that Bindu-sarovara was surrounded by pious trees and birds. As there are different classes of men in human society, some pious and virtuous and some impious and sinful, so also among trees and birds there are the pious and the impious. Trees which do not bear nice fruit or flowers are considered impious, and birds which are very nasty, such as crows, are considered impious. In the land surrounding Bindu-sarovara there was not a single impious bird or tree. Every tree bore fruits and flowers, and every bird sang the glories of the Lord—Hare Kṛṣṇa, Hare Kṛṣṇa, Kṛṣṇa Kṛṣṇa, Hare Hare/ Hare Rāma, Hare Rāma, Rāma Rāma, Hare Hare.

## TEXT 41

मत्तद्विजगणैर्घुष्टं मत्तभ्रमरविभ्रमम् ।
मत्तबर्हिनटाटोपमाह्वयन्मत्तकोकिलम् ॥४१॥

*matta-dvija-gaṇair ghuṣṭaṁ*
*matta-bhramara-vibhramam*
*matta-barhi-naṭāṭopam*
*āhvayan-matta-kokilam*

*matta*—overjoyed; *dvija*—of birds; *gaṇaiḥ*—by flocks; *ghuṣṭam*—resounded; *matta*—intoxicated; *bhramara*—of bees; *vibhramam*—wandering; *matta*—maddened; *barhi*—of peacocks; *naṭa*—of dancers; *āṭopam*—pride; *āhvayat*—calling one another; *matta*—merry; *kokilam*—cuckoos.

## TRANSLATION

**The area resounded with the notes of overjoyed birds. Intoxicated bees wandered there, intoxicated peacocks proudly danced, and merry cuckoos called one another.**

## PURPORT

The beauty of the pleasant sounds heard in the area surrounding Lake Bindu-sarovara is described here. After drinking honey, the black bees became maddened, and they hummed in intoxication. Merry peacocks danced just like actors and actresses, and merry cuckoos called their mates very nicely.

## TEXTS 42–43

कदम्बचम्पकाशोककरञ्जबकुलासनैः ।
कुन्दमन्दारकुटजैश्चूतपोतैरलङ्कृतम् ॥४२॥
कारण्डवैः प्लवैर्हंसैः कुररैर्जलकुक्कुटैः ।
सारसैश्चक्रवाकैश्च चकोरैर्वल्गु कूजितम् ॥४३॥

*kadamba-campakāśoka-*
*karañja-bakulāsanaiḥ*
*kunda-mandāra-kuṭajaiś*
*cūta-potair alaṅkṛtam*

*kāraṇḍavaiḥ plavair haṁsaiḥ*
*kurarair jala-kukkuṭaiḥ*
*sārasaiś cakravākaiś ca*
*cakorair valgu kūjitam*

*kadamba—kadamba* flowers; *campaka—campaka* flowers; *aśoka—aśoka* flowers; *karañja—karañja* flowers; *bakula—bakula* flowers; *āsanaiḥ*—by *āsana* trees; *kunda—kunda; mandāra—mandāra; kuṭajaiḥ*—and by *kuṭaja* trees; *cūta-potaiḥ*—by young mango trees; *alaṅkṛtam*—adorned; *kāraṇḍavaiḥ*—by *kāraṇḍava* ducks; *plavaiḥ*—by *plavas; haṁsaiḥ*—by swans; *kuraraiḥ*—by ospreys; *jala-kukkuṭaiḥ*—by waterfowl; *sārasaiḥ*—by cranes; *cakravākaiḥ*—by *cakravāka* birds; *ca*—and; *cakoraiḥ*—by *cakora* birds; *valgu*—pleasing; *kūjitam*—vibration of birds' sounds.

## TRANSLATION

**Lake Bindu-sarovara was adorned by flowering trees such as kadamba, campaka, aśoka, karañja, bakula, āsana, kunda, mandāra, kuṭaja and young mango trees. The air was filled with the pleasing notes of kāraṇḍava ducks, plavas, swans, ospreys, waterfowl, cranes, cakravākas and cakoras.**

## PURPORT

For most of the trees, flowers, fruits and birds mentioned here as surrounding Bindu-sarovara Lake, English synonyms cannot be found. All the trees mentioned are very pious in that they produce a nice aromatic flower, such as the *campaka*, *kadamba* and *bakula*. The sweet sounds of waterfowl and cranes made the surrounding area as pleasant as possible and created a very suitable spiritual atmosphere.

## TEXT 44

**तथैव हरिणैः क्रोडैः श्वाविद्गवयकुञ्जरैः ।**
**गोपुच्छैर्हरिभिर्मर्कैर्नकुलैर्नाभिभिर्वृतम् ॥४४॥**

*tathaiva hariṇaiḥ kroḍaiḥ*
*śvāvid-gavaya-kuñjaraiḥ*
*gopucchair haribhir markair*
*nakulair nābhibhir vṛtam*

*tathā eva*—likewise; *hariṇaiḥ*—by deer; *kroḍaiḥ*—by boars; *śvāvit*—porcupines; *gavaya*—a wild animal closely resembling the cow; *kuñjaraiḥ*—by elephants; *gopucchaiḥ*—by baboons; *haribhiḥ*—by lions; *markaiḥ*—by monkeys; *nakulaiḥ*—by mongooses; *nābhibhiḥ*—by musk deer; *vṛtam*—surrounded.

## TRANSLATION

**Its shores abounded with deer, boars, porcupines, gavayas, elephants, baboons, lions, monkeys, mongooses and musk deer.**

## PURPORT

Musk deer are not found in every forest, but only in places like Bindu-sarovara. They are always intoxicated by the aroma of musk secreted from their navels. *Gavayas*, the species of cow mentioned herein, bear a bunch of hair at the end of their tails. This bunch of hair is used in temple worship to fan the Deities. *Gavayas* are sometimes called *camarīs*, and they are considered very sacred. In India there are still gypsies or forest mercantile people who flourish by trading *kastūrī*, or musk, and the bunches of hair from the *camarīs*. These are always in great demand for the higher classes of Hindu population, and such business still goes on in large cities and villages in India.

## TEXTS 45–47

प्रविश्य तत्तीर्थवरमादिराजः सहात्मजः ।
ददर्श मुनिमासीनं तस्मिन् हुतहुताशनम् ॥४५॥
विद्योतमानं वपुषा तपस्युग्रयुजा चिरम् ।
नातिक्षामं भगवतः स्निग्धापाङ्गावलोकनात् ।
तद्व्याहृतामृतकलापीयूषश्रवणेन च ॥४६॥
प्रांशुं पद्मपलाशाक्षं जटिलं चीरवाससम् ।
उपसंश्रित्य मलिनं यथार्हणमसंस्कृतम् ॥४७॥

*praviśya tat tīrtha-varam*
*ādi-rājaḥ sahātmajaḥ*
*dadarśa munim āsīnaṁ*
*tasmin huta-hutāśanam*

*vidyotamānaṁ vapuṣā*
*tapasy ugra-yujā ciram*
*nātikṣāmaṁ bhagavataḥ*
*snigdhāpāṅgāvalokanāt*
*tad-vyāhṛtāmṛta-kalā-*
*pīyūṣa-śravaṇena ca*

*prāṁśuṁ padma-palāśākṣaṁ*
*jaṭilaṁ cīra-vāsasam*
*upasaṁśritya malinaṁ*
*yathārhaṇam asaṁskṛtam*

*praviśya*—entering; *tat*—that; *tīrtha-varam*—best of sacred places; *ādi-rājaḥ*—the first monarch (Svāyambhuva Manu); *saha-ātmajaḥ*—along with his daughter; *dadarśa*—saw; *munim*—the sage; *āsīnam*—sitting; *tasmin*—in the hermitage; *huta*—being offered oblations; *huta-aśanam*—the sacred fire; *vidyotamānam*—shining brilliantly; *vapuṣā*—by his body; *tapasi*—in penance; *ugra*—terribly; *yujā*—engaged in *yoga; ciram*—for a long time; *na*—not; *atikṣāmam*—very emaciated; *bhagavataḥ*—of the Lord; *snigdha*—affectionate; *apāṅga*—sidelong;

*avalokanāt*—from the glance; *tat*—of Him; *vyāhṛta*—from the words; *amṛta-kalā*—moonlike; *pīyūṣa*—the nectar; *śravaṇena*—by hearing; *ca*—and; *prāṁśum*—tall; *padma*—lotus flower; *palāśa*—petal; *akṣam*—eyes; *jaṭilam*—matted locks; *cīra-vāsasam*—having rags for clothes; *upasaṁśritya*—having approached; *malinam*—soiled; *yathā*—like; *arhaṇam*—gem; *asaṁskṛtam*—unpolished.

## TRANSLATION

**Entering that most sacred spot with his daughter and going near the sage, the first monarch, Svāyambhuva Manu, saw the sage sitting in his hermitage, having just propitiated the sacred fire by pouring oblations into it. His body shone most brilliantly; though he had engaged in austere penance for a long time, he was not emaciated, for the Lord had cast His affectionate sidelong glance upon him and he had also heard the nectar flowing from the moonlike words of the Lord. The sage was tall, his eyes were large, like the petals of a lotus, and he had matted locks on his head. He was clad in rags. Svāyambhuva Manu approached and saw him to be somewhat soiled, like an unpolished gem.**

## PURPORT

Here are some descriptions of a *brahmacārī-yogī*. In the morning, the first duty of a *brahmacārī* seeking spiritual elevation is *huta-hutāśana*, to offer sacrifical oblations to the Supreme Lord. Those engaged in *brahmacarya* cannot sleep until seven or nine o'clock in the morning. They must rise early in the morning, at least one and a half hours before the sun rises, and offer oblations, or in this age, they must chant the holy name of the Lord, Hare Kṛṣṇa. As referred to by Lord Caitanya, *kalau nāsty eva nāsty eva nāsty eva gatir anyathā:* there is no other alternative, no other alternative, no other alternative, in this age, to chanting the holy name of the Lord. The *brahmacārī* must rise early in the morning and, after placing himself, should chant the holy name of the Lord. From the very features of the sage, it appeared that he had undergone great austerities; that is the sign of one observing *brahmacarya*, the vow of celibacy. If one lives otherwise, it will be manifest in the lust visible in his face and body. The word *vidyotamānam* indicates that the *brahmacārī* feature showed in his body. That is the certificate that one has undergone great austerity in *yoga.* A drunkard or smoker or sex-monger can never be eligible to practice *yoga.* Generally *yogīs* look very skinny because of their not being comfortably situated, but Kardama Muni was not emaciated, for he had seen the Supreme Personality of Godhead face to face. Here the word *snigdhāpāṅgāvalokanāt* means that he was fortunate enough to see the Supreme Lord face to face. He looked healthy because he had directly received the nectarean sound vibrations from the lotus lips of the Personality of Godhead. Similarly, one who hears the transcendental sound vibration of the holy name of the Lord, Hare Kṛṣṇa, also improves in health. We have actually seen that many *brahmacārīs* and *gṛhasthas* connected with the International Society for Krishna Consciousness have improved in health, and a luster has come to their faces. It is essential that a *brahmacārī* engaged in spiritual advancement look very healthy and lustrous. The comparison of the sage to an unpolished gem is very appropriate. Even if a gem just taken from a mine looks unpolished, the luster of the gem cannot be stopped. Similarly, although Kardama was not properly dressed and his body was not properly cleansed, his overall appearance was gemlike.

## TEXT 48

अथोटजमुपायातं नृदेवं प्रणतं पुरः ।
सपर्यया पर्यगृह्णात्प्रतिनन्द्यानुरूपया ॥४८॥

*athoṭajam upāyātaṁ*
*nṛdevaṁ praṇataṁ puraḥ*
*saparyayā paryagṛhṇāt*
*pratinandyānurūpayā*

*atha*—then; *uṭajam*—the hermitage; *upāyātam*—approached; *nṛdevam*—the monarch; *praṇatam*—bowed down; *puraḥ*—in front; *saparyayā*—with honor; *paryagṛhṇāt*—received him; *pratinandya*—greeting him; *anurūpayā*—befitting the King's position.

## TRANSLATION

**Seeing that the monarch had come to his hermitage and was bowing before him, the sage greeted him with benediction and received him with due honor.**

## PURPORT

Emperor Svāyambhuva Manu not only approached the cottage of dried leaves possessed by the hermit Kardama but also offered respectful obeisances unto him. Similarly, it was the duty of the hermit to offer blessings to kings who used to approach his hermitage in the jungle.

## TEXT 49

गृहीतार्हणमासीनं संयतं प्रीणयन्मुनिः ।
स्मरन् भगवदादेशमित्याह श्लक्ष्णया गिरा ॥४९॥

*gṛhītārhaṇam āsīnaṁ*
*saṁyataṁ prīṇayan muniḥ*
*smaran bhagavad-ādeśam*
*ity āha ślakṣṇayā girā*

*gṛhīta*—received; *arhaṇam*—honor; *āsīnam*—seated; *saṁyatam*—remained silent; *prīṇayan*—delighting; *muniḥ*—the sage; *smaran*—remembering; *bhagavat*—of the Lord; *ādeśam*—the order; *iti*—thus; *āha*—spoke; *ślakṣṇayā*—sweet; *girā*—with a voice.

## TRANSLATION

**After receiving the sage's attention, the King sat down and was silent. Recalling the instructions of the Lord, Kardama then spoke to the King as follows, delighting him with his sweet accents.**

## TEXT 50

नूनं चङ्क्रमणं देव सतां संरक्षणाय ते ।
वधाय चासतां यस्त्वं हरेः शक्तिर्हि पालिनी ॥५०॥

*nūnaṁ caṅkramaṇaṁ deva*
*satāṁ saṁrakṣaṇāya te*
*vadhāya cāsatāṁ yas tvaṁ*
*hareḥ śaktir hi pālinī*

*nūnam*—surely; *caṅkramaṇam*—the tour; *deva*—O lord; *satām*—of the virtuous; *saṁrakṣaṇāya*—for the protection; *te*—your; *vadhāya*—for killing; *ca*—and; *asatām*—of the demons; *yaḥ*—the person who; *tvam*—you; *hareḥ*—of the Supreme Personality of Godhead; *śaktiḥ*—the energy; *hi*—since; *pālinī*—protecting.

## TRANSLATION

**The tour you have undertaken, O lord, is surely intended to protect the virtuous and kill the demons, since you embody the protecting energy of Śrī Hari.**

## PURPORT

It appears from many Vedic literatures, especially histories like *Śrīmad-Bhāgavatam* and the *Purāṇas*, that the pious kings of old used to tour their kingdoms in order to give protection to the pious citizens and to chastise or kill the impious. Sometimes they used to kill animals in the forests to practice the killing art because without such practice they would not be able to kill the undesirable elements. *Kṣatriyas* are allowed to commit violence in that way because violence for a good purpose is a part of their duty. Here two terms are clearly mentioned: *vadhāya*, "for the purpose of killing," and *asatām*, "those who are undesirable." The protecting energy of the king is supposed to be the energy of the Supreme Lord. In *Bhagavad-gītā* (4.8) the Lord says, *paritrāṇāya sādhūnāṁ vināśāya ca duṣkṛtām.* The Lord descends to give protection to the pious and to kill the demons. The potency, therefore, to give protection to the pious and kill the demons or undesirables is directly an energy from the Supreme Lord, and the king or the chief executive of the state is supposed to possess such energy. In this age it is very difficult to find such a head of state who is expert in killing the undesirables. Modern heads of state sit very nicely in their palaces and try without reason to kill innocent persons.

## TEXT 51

योऽर्केन्द्वग्नीन्द्रवायूनां यमधर्मप्रचेतसाम् ।
रूपाणि स्थान आधत्से तस्मै शुक्लाय ते नमः ॥५१॥

*yo 'rkendv-agnīndra-vāyūnāṁ*
*yama-dharma-pracetasām*
*rūpāṇi sthāna ādhatse*
*tasmai śuklāya te namaḥ*

*yaḥ*—you who; *arka*—of the sun; *indu*—of the moon; *agni*—of Agni, the fire-god; *indra*—of Indra, the lord of heaven; *vāyūnām*—of Vāyu, the wind-god; *yama*—of Yama, the god of punishment; *dharma*—of Dharma, the god of piety; *pracetasām*—and of Varuṇa, the god of the waters; *rūpāṇi*—the forms; *sthāne*—when necessary; *ādhatse*—you assume; *tasmai*—unto Him; *śuklāya*—unto Lord Viṣṇu; *te*—unto you; *namaḥ*—obeisances.

## TRANSLATION

**You assume, when necessary, the part of the sun-god; the moon-god; Agni, the god of fire; Indra, the lord of paradise; Vāyu, the wind-god; Yama, the god of punishment; Dharma, the god of piety; and Varuṇa, the god presiding over the waters. All obeisances to you, who are none other than Lord Viṣṇu!**

## PURPORT

Since the sage Kardama was a *brāhmaṇa* and Svāyambhuva was a *kṣatriya*, the sage was not supposed to offer obeisances to the King because socially his position was greater than the King's. But he offered his obeisances to Svāyambhuva Manu because as Manu, king and emperor, he was the representative of the Supreme Lord. The Supreme Lord is always worshipable, regardless of whether one is a *brāhmaṇa*, a *kṣatriya* or a *śūdra*. As the representative of the Supreme Lord, the King deserved respectful obeisances from everyone.

## TEXTS 52–54

न यदा रथमास्थाय जैत्रं मणिगणार्पितम् ।
विस्फूर्जच्चण्डकोदण्डो रथेन त्रासयन्नघान् ।।५२।।
स्वसैन्यचरणक्षुण्णं वेपयन्मण्डलं भुवः ।
विकर्षन् बृहतीं सेनां पर्यटस्यंशुमानिव ।।५३।।

तदैव सेतवः सर्वे वर्णाश्रमनिबन्धनाः ।
भगवद्रचिता राजन् भिद्येरन् बत दस्युभिः ॥५४॥

*na yadā ratham āsthāya*
*jaitraṁ maṇi-gaṇārpitam*
*visphūrjac-caṇḍa-kodaṇḍo*
*rathena trāsayann aghān*

*sva-sainya-caraṇa-kṣuṇṇaṁ*
*vepayan maṇḍalaṁ bhuvaḥ*
*vikarṣan bṛhatīṁ senāṁ*
*paryaṭasy aṁśumān iva*

*tadaiva setavaḥ sarve*
*varṇāśrama-nibandhanāḥ*
*bhagavad-racitā rājan*
*bhidyeran bata dasyubhiḥ*

*na*—not; *yadā*—when; *ratham*—the chariot; *āsthāya*—having mounted; *jaitram*—victorious; *maṇi*—of jewels; *gaṇa*—with clusters; *arpitam*—bedecked; *visphūrjat*—twanging; *caṇḍa*—a fearful sound just to punish the criminals; *kodaṇḍaḥ*—bow; *rathena*—by the presence of such a chariot; *trāsayan*—threatening; *aghān*—all the culprits; *sva-sainya*—of your soldiers; *caraṇa*—by the feet; *kṣuṇṇam*—trampled; *vepayan*—causing to tremble; *maṇḍalam*—the globe; *bhuvaḥ*—of the earth; *vikarṣan*—leading; *bṛhatīm*—huge; *senām*—army; *paryaṭasi*—you roam about; *aṁśumān*—the brilliant sun; *iva*—like; *tadā*—then; *eva*—certainly; *setavaḥ*—religious codes; *sarve*—all; *varṇa*—of *varṇas; āśrama*—of *āśramas; nibandhanāḥ*—obligations; *bhagavat*—by the Lord; *racitāḥ*—created; *rājan*—O King; *bhidyeran*—they would be broken; *bata*—alas; *dasyubhiḥ*—by rogues.

## TRANSLATION

**If you did not mount your victorious jeweled chariot, whose mere presence threatens culprits, if you did not produce fierce sounds by the twanging of your bow, and if you did not roam about the world like the brilliant sun, leading a huge army whose**

**trampling feet cause the globe of the earth to tremble, then all the moral laws governing the varṇas and āśramas created by the Lord Himself would be broken by the rogues and rascals.**

## PURPORT

It is the duty of a responsible king to protect the social and spiritual orders in human society. The spiritual orders are divided into four *āśramas—brahmacarya, gṛhastha, vānaprastha* and *sannyāsa*—and the social orders, according to work and qualification, are made up of the *brāhmaṇas*, the *kṣatriyas*, the *vaiśyas* and the *śūdras*. These social orders, according to the different grades of work and qualification, are described in *Bhagavad-gītā*. Unfortunately, for want of proper protection by responsible kings, the system of social and spiritual orders has now become a hereditary caste system. But this is not the actual system. Human society means that society which is making progress toward spiritual realization. The most advanced human society was known as *ārya; ārya* refers to those who are advancing. So the question is, "Which society is advancing?" Advancement does not mean creating material "necessities" unnecessarily and thus wasting human energy in aggravation over so-called material comforts. Real advancement is advancement toward spiritual realization, and the community which acted toward this end was known as the Āryan civilization. The intelligent men, the *brāhmaṇas*, as exemplified by Kardama Muni, were engaged in advancing the spiritual cause, and *kṣatriyas* like Emperor Svāyambhuva used to rule the country and insure that all facilities for spiritual realization were nicely provided. It is the duty of the king to travel all over the country and see that everything is in order. Indian civilization on the basis of the four *varṇas* and *āśramas* deteriorated because of her dependency on foreigners, or those who did not follow the civilization of *varṇāśrama*. Thus the *varṇāśrama* system has now been degraded into the caste system.

The institution of four *varṇas* and four *āśramas* is confirmed herewith to be *bhagavad-racita*, which means "designed by the Supreme Personality of Godhead." In *Bhagavad-gītā* this is also confirmed: *cātur-varṇyaṁ mayā sṛṣṭam.* The Lord says that the institution of four *varṇas* and four *āśramas* "is created by Me." Anything created by the Lord cannot be closed or covered. The divisions of *varṇas* and *āśramas* will continue to exist, either in their original form or in degraded form, but because they are created by the Lord, the Supreme Personality of Godhead, they cannot be extinguished. They are like the sun, a creation of God, and therefore will remain. Either covered by clouds or in a clear sky, the sun will continue to exist. Similarly, when the *varṇāśrama* system becomes degraded, it appears as a hereditary caste system, but in every society there is an intelligent class of men, a martial class, a mercantile class and a laborer class. When they are regulated for cooperation among communities according to the Vedic principles, then there is peace and spiritual advancement. But when there is hatred and malpractice and mutual mistrust in the caste system, the whole system becomes degraded, and as stated herein, it creates a deplorable state. At the present moment, the entire world is in this deplorable condition because of giving rights to so many interests. This is due to the degradation of the four castes of *varṇas* and *āśramas.*

## TEXT 55

अधर्मश्च समेधेत लोलुपैर्व्यङ्कुशैर्नृभिः ।
शयाने त्वयि लोकोऽयं दस्युग्रस्तो विनङ्क्ष्यति ॥५५॥

*adharmaś ca samedheta*
*lolupair vyaṅkuśair nṛbhiḥ*
*śayāne tvayi loko 'yaṁ*
*dasyu-grasto vinaṅkṣyati*

*adharmaḥ*—unrighteousness; *ca*—and; *samedheta*—would flourish; *lolupaiḥ*—simply hankering after money; *vyaṅkuśaiḥ*—uncontrolled; *nṛbhiḥ*—by men; *śayāne tvayi*—when you lie down for rest; *lokaḥ*—world; *ayam*—this; *dasyu*—by the miscreants; *grastaḥ*—attacked; *vinaṅkṣyati*—it will perish.

## TRANSLATION

**If you gave up all thought of the world's situation, unrighteousness would flourish, for men who hanker only after money would be unopposed. Such miscreants would attack, and the world would perish.**

## PURPORT

Because the scientific division of four *varṇas* and four *āśramas* is now being extinguished, the entire world is being governed by unwanted men who have no training in religion, politics or social order, and it is in a very deplorable condition. In the institution of four *varṇas* and four *āśramas* there are regular training principles for the different classes of men. Just as, in the modern age, there is a necessity for engineers, medical practioners and electricians, and they are properly trained in different scientific institutions, similarly, in former times, the higher social orders, namely the intelligent class (the *brāhmaṇas*), the ruling class (the *kṣatriyas*) and the mercantile class (the *vaiśyas*), were properly trained. *Bhagavad-gītā* describes the duties of the *brāhmaṇas, kṣatriyas, vaiśyas* and *śūdras*. When there is no such training, one simply claims that because he is born in a *brāhmaṇa* or *kṣatriya* family, he is therefore a *brāhmaṇa* or a *kṣatriya*, even though he performs the duties of a *śūdra*. Such undue claims to being a higher-caste man make the system of scientific social orders into a caste system, completely degrading the original system. Thus society is now in chaos, and there is neither peace nor prosperity. It is clearly stated herein that unless there is the vigilance of a strong king, impious, unqualified men will claim a certain status in society, and that will make the social order perish.

## TEXT 56

अथापि पृच्छे त्वां वीर यदर्थं त्वमिहागतः ।
तद्वयं निर्व्यलीकेन प्रतिपद्यामहे हृदा ॥५६॥

*athāpi pṛcche tvāṁ vīra*
*yad-arthaṁ tvam ihāgataḥ*
*tad vayaṁ nirvyalīkena*
*pratipadyāmahe hṛdā*

*atha api*—in spite of all this; *pṛcche*—I ask; *tvām*—you; *vīra*—O valiant King; *yat-artham*—the purpose; *tvam*—you; *iha*—here; *āgataḥ*—have come; *tat*—that; *vayam*—we; *nirvyalīkena*—without reservation; *pratipadyāmahe*—we shall carry out; *hṛdā*—with heart and soul.

## TRANSLATION

**In spite of all this, I ask you, O valiant King, the purpose for which you have come here. Whatever it may be, we shall carry it out without reservation.**

## PURPORT

When a guest comes to a friend's house, it is understood that there is some special purpose. Kardama Muni could understand that such a great king as Svāyambhuva, although traveling to inspect the condition of his kingdom, must have had some special purpose to come to his hermitage. Thus he prepared himself to fulfill the King's desire. Formerly it was customary that the sages used to go to the kings and the kings used to visit the sages in their hermitages; each was glad to fulfill the other's purpose. This reciprocal relationship is called *bhakti-kārya.* There is a nice verse describing the relationship of mutual beneficial interest between the *brāhmaṇa* and the *kṣatriya* (*kṣatraṁ dvijatvam*). *Kṣatram* means "the royal order," and *dvijatvam* means "the brahminical order." The two were meant for mutual interest. The royal order would give protection to the *brāhmaṇas* for the cultivation of spiritual advancement in society, and the *brāhmaṇas* would give their valuable instruction to the royal order on how the state and the citizens can gradually be elevated in spiritual perfection.

*Thus end the Bhaktivedanta purports of the Third Canto, Twenty-first Chapter, of the* Śrīmad-Bhāgavatam, *entitled "Conversation Between Manu and Kardama."*

# CHAPTER TWENTY-TWO

# The Marriage of Kardama Muni and Devahūti

## TEXT 1

मैत्रेय उवाच

एवमाविष्कृताशेषगुणकर्मोदयो मुनिम् ।
सव्रीड इव तं सम्राडुपारतमुवाच ह ॥ १ ॥

*maitreya uvāca*
*evam āviṣkṛtāśeṣa-*
*guṇa-karmodayo munim*
*savrīḍa iva taṁ samrāḍ*
*upāratam uvāca ha*

*maitreyaḥ*—the great sage Maitreya; *uvāca*—said; *evam*—thus; *āviṣkṛta*—having been described; *aśeṣa*—all; *guṇa*—of the virtues; *karma*—of the activities; *udayaḥ*—the greatness; *munim*—the great sage; *sa-vrīḍaḥ*—feeling modest; *iva*—as though; *tam*—him (Kardama); *samrāṭ*—Emperor Manu; *upāratam*—silent; *uvāca ha*—addressed.

### TRANSLATION

**Śrī Maitreya said: After describing the greatness of the Emperor's manifold qualities and activities, the sage became silent, and the Emperor, feeling modesty, addressed him as follows.**

## TEXT 2

मनुरुवाच

ब्रह्मासृजत्स्वमुखतो युष्मानात्मपरीप्सया ।
छन्दोमयस्तपोविद्यायोगयुक्तानलम्पटान् ॥ २ ॥

*manur uvāca*
*brahmāsṛjat sva-mukhato*
*yuṣmān ātma-parīpsayā*
*chandomayas tapo-vidyā-*
*yoga-yuktān alampaṭān*

*manuḥ*—Manu; *uvāca*—said; *brahmā*—Lord Brahmā; *asṛjat*—created; *sva-mukhataḥ*—from his face; *yuṣmān*—you (*brāhmaṇas*); *ātma-parīpsayā*—to protect himself by expanding; *chandaḥ-mayaḥ*—the form of the *Vedas; tapaḥ-vidyā-yoga-yuktān*—full of austerity, knowledge and mystic power; *alampaṭān*—averse to sense gratification.

## TRANSLATION

**Manu replied: To expand himself in Vedic knowledge, Lord Brahmā, the personified Veda, from his face created you, the brāhmaṇas, who are full of austerity, knowledge and mystic power and are averse to sense gratification.**

## PURPORT

The purpose of the *Vedas* is to propagate the transcendental knowledge of the Absolute Truth. The *brāhmaṇas* were created from the mouth of the Supreme Person, and therefore they are meant to spread the knowledge of the *Vedas* in order to spread the glories of the Lord. In *Bhagavad-gītā* also Lord Kṛṣṇa says that all the *Vedas* are meant for understanding the Supreme Personality of Godhead. It is especially mentioned here (*yoga-yuktān alampaṭān*) that *brāhmaṇas* are full of mystic power and are completely averse to sense gratification. Actually there are two kinds of occupations. One occupation, in the material world, is sense gratification, and the other occupation is spiritual activity—to satisfy the Lord by His glorification. Those who engage in sense gratification are called demons, and those who spread the glorification of the Lord or satisfy the transcendental senses of the Lord are called demigods. It is specifically mentioned here that the *brāhmaṇas* are created from the face of the cosmic personality, or *virāṭ-puruṣa;* similarly the *kṣatriyas* are said to be created from His arms, the *vaiśyas* are created from His waist, and the *śūdras* are created from His legs. *Brāhmaṇas* are especially meant for austerity, learning and knowledge and are averse to all kinds of sense gratification.

## TEXT 3

तत्त्राणायासृजच्चास्मान्दोःसहस्रात्सहस्रपात् ।
हृदयं तस्य हि ब्रह्म क्षत्रमङ्गं प्रचक्षते ॥ ३ ॥

*tat-trāṇāyāsṛjac cāsmān*
*doḥ-sahasrāt sahasra-pāt*
*hṛdayaṁ tasya hi brahma*
*kṣatram aṅgaṁ pracakṣate*

*tat-trāṇāya*—for the protection of the *brāhmaṇas; asṛjat*—created; *ca*—and; *asmān*—us (*kṣatriyas*); *doḥ-sahasrāt*—from His thousand arms; *sahasra-pāt*—the thousand-legged Supreme Being (the universal form); *hṛdayam*—heart; *tasya*—His; *hi*—for; *brahma*—*brāhmaṇas; kṣatram*—the *kṣatriyas; aṅgam*—arms; *pracakṣate*—are spoken of.

## TRANSLATION

**For the protection of the brāhmaṇas, the thousand-legged Supreme Being created us, the kṣatriyas, from His thousand arms. Hence the brāhmaṇas are said to be His heart and the kṣatriyas His arms.**

## PURPORT

*Kṣatriyas* are specifically meant to maintain the *brāhmaṇas* because if the *brāhmaṇas* are protected, then the head of civilization is protected. *Brāhmaṇas* are supposed to be the head of the social body; if the head is clear and has not gone mad, then everything is in proper position. The Lord is described thus: *namo brahmaṇya-devāya go-brāhmaṇa-hitāya ca.* The purport of this prayer is that the Lord specifically protects the *brāhmaṇas* and the cows, and then He protects all other members of society (*jagad-dhitāya*). It is His will that universal welfare work depends on the protection of cows and *brāhmaṇas;* thus brahminical culture and cow protection are the basic principles for human civilization.

*Kṣatriyas* are especially meant to protect the *brāhmaṇas*, as is the supreme will of the Lord: *go-brāhmaṇa-hitāya ca*. As, within the body, the heart is a very important part, so the *brāhmaṇas* are also the important element in human society. The *kṣatriyas* are more like the whole body; even though the whole body is bigger than the heart, the heart is more important.

## TEXT 4

अतो ह्यन्योन्यमात्मानं ब्रह्म क्षत्रं च रक्षतः ।
रक्षति स्माव्ययो देवः स यः सदसदात्मकः ॥ ४ ॥

*ato hy anyonyam ātmānaṁ*
*brahma kṣatraṁ ca rakṣataḥ*
*rakṣati smāvyayo devaḥ*
*sa yaḥ sad-asad-ātmakaḥ*

*ataḥ*—hence; *hi*—certainly; *anyonyam*—each other; *ātmānam*—the self; *brahma*—the *brāhmaṇas; kṣatram*—the *kṣatriyas; ca*—and; *rakṣataḥ*—protect; *rakṣati sma*—protects; *avyayaḥ*—immutable; *devaḥ*—the Lord; *saḥ*—He; *yaḥ*—who; *sat-asat-ātmakaḥ*—the form of the cause and effect.

## TRANSLATION

**That is why the brāhmaṇas and kṣatriyas protect each other, as well as themselves; and the Lord Himself, who is both the cause and effect and is yet immutable, protects them through each other.**

## PURPORT

The entire social structure of *varṇa* and *āśrama* is a cooperative system meant to uplift all to the highest platform of spiritual realization. The *brāhmaṇas* are intended to be protected by the *kṣatriyas*, and the *kṣatriyas* also are intended to be enlightened by the *brāhmaṇas*. When the *brāhmaṇas* and *kṣatriyas* cooperate nicely, the other subordinate divisions, the *vaiśyas*, or mercantile people, and the *śūdras*, or laborer class, automatically flourish. The entire elaborate system of Vedic society was therefore based on the importance of the *brāhmaṇas* and *kṣatriyas*.

The Lord is the real protector, but He is unattached to the affairs of protection. He creates *brāhmaṇas* for the protection of the *kṣatriyas*, and *kṣatriyas* for the protection of the *brāhmaṇas*. He remains aloof from all activities; therefore, He is called *nirvikāra*, "without activity." He has nothing to do. He is so great that He does not perform action personally, but His energies act. The *brāhmaṇas* and *kṣatriyas*, and anything that we see, are different energies acting upon one another.

Although individual souls are all different, the Superself, or Supersoul, is the Supreme Personality of Godhead. Individually one's self may differ from others in certain qualities and may engage in different activities, such as those of a *brāhmaṇa, kṣatriya* or *vaiśya*, but when there is complete cooperation among different individual souls, the Supreme Personality of Godhead as Supersoul, Paramātmā, being one in every individual soul, is pleased and gives them all protection. As stated before, the *brāhmaṇas* are produced from the mouth of the Lord, and the *kṣatriyas* are produced from the chest or arms of the Lord. If the different castes or social sections, although apparently differently occupied in different activities, nevertheless act in full cooperation, then the Lord is pleased. This is the idea of the institution of four *varṇas* and four *āśramas*. If the members of different *āśramas* and *varṇas* cooperate fully in Kṛṣṇa consciousness, then society is well protected by the Lord, without doubt.

In *Bhagavad-gītā* it is stated that the Lord is the proprietor of all different bodies. The individual soul is the proprietor of his individual body, but the Lord clearly states, "My dear Bhārata, you must know that I am also *kṣetra-jña.*" *Kṣetra-jña* means "the knower or proprietor of the body." The individual soul is the proprietor of the individual body, but the Supersoul, the Personality of Godhead, Kṛṣṇa, is the proprietor of all bodies everywhere. He is the proprietor not only of human bodies but of birds, beasts and all other entities, not only on this planet but on other planets also. He is the supreme proprietor; therefore He does not become divided by protecting the different individual souls. He remains one and the same. That the sun appears on top of everyone's head when at the meridian does not imply that the sun becomes divided. One man thinks that the sun is on his head only, whereas five thousand miles away another man is thinking that the sun is only on his head. Similarly, the Supersoul, the Supreme Personality of Godhead, is one, but He appears to individually oversee each individual soul. This does not mean that the individual soul and the Supersoul are one. They are one in quality, as spirit soul, but the individual soul and Supersoul are different.

## TEXT 5

तव सन्दर्शनादेवच्छिन्ना मे सर्वसंशयाः ।
यत्स्वयं भगवान् प्रीत्या धर्ममाह रिरक्षिषोः ॥ ५ ॥

*tava sandarśanād eva*
*cchinnā me sarva-saṁśayāḥ*
*yat svayaṁ bhagavān prītyā*
*dharmam āha rirakṣiṣoḥ*

*tava*—your; *sandarśanāt*—by sight; *eva*—only; *chinnāḥ*—resolved; *me*—my; *sarva-saṁśayāḥ*—all doubts; *yat*—inasmuch as; *svayam*—personally; *bhagavān*—Your Lordship; *prītyā*—lovingly; *dharmam*—duty; *āha*—explained; *rirakṣiṣoḥ*—of a king anxious to protect his subjects.

## TRANSLATION

**Now I have resolved all my doubts simply by meeting you, for Your Lordship has very kindly and clearly explained the duty of a king who desires to protect his subjects.**

## PURPORT

Manu described herewith the result of seeing a great saintly person. Lord Caitanya says that one should always try to associate with saintly persons because if one establishes a proper association with a saintly person, even for a moment, one attains all perfection. Somehow or other, if one meets a saintly person and achieves his favor, then the entire mission of one's human life is fulfilled. In our personal experience we have actual proof of this statement of Manu. Once we had the opportunity to meet Viṣṇupāda Śrī Śrīmad Bhaktisiddhānta Sarasvatī Gosvāmī Mahārāja, and on first sight he requested this humble self to preach his message in the Western countries. There was no preparation for this, but somehow or other he desired it, and by his grace we are now engaged in executing his order, which has given us a transcendental occupation and has saved and liberated us from the occupation of material activities. Thus it is actually a fact that if one meets a saintly person completely engaged in transcendental duties and achieves his favor, then one's life mission becomes complete. What is not possible to achieve in thousands of lives can be achieved in one moment if there is an opportunity to meet a saintly person. It is therefore enjoined in Vedic literature that one should always try to associate with saintly persons and try to disassociate oneself from the common man, because by one word of a saintly person one can be liberated from material entanglement. A saintly person has the power, because of his spiritual advancement, to give immediate liberation to the conditioned soul. Here Manu admits that all his doubts are now over because Kardama has very kindly described the different duties of individual souls.

## TEXT 6

दिष्ट्या मे भगवान् दृष्टो दुर्दर्शो योऽकृतात्मनाम् ।
दिष्ट्या पादरजः स्पृष्टं शीर्ष्णा मे भवतः शिवम् ॥६॥

*diṣṭyā me bhagavān dṛṣṭo*
*durdarśo yo 'kṛtātmanām*
*diṣṭyā pāda-rajaḥ spṛṣṭaṁ*
*śīrṣṇā me bhavataḥ śivam*

*diṣṭyā*—by good fortune; *me*—my; *bhagavān*—all-powerful; *dṛṣṭaḥ*—is seen; *durdarśaḥ*—not easily seen; *yaḥ*—who; *akṛta-ātmanām*—of those who have not controlled the mind and senses; *diṣṭyā*—by my good fortune; *pāda-rajaḥ*—the dust of the feet; *spṛṣṭam*—is touched; *śīrṣṇā*—by the head; *me*—my; *bhavataḥ*—your; *śivam*—causing all auspiciousness.

## TRANSLATION

**It is my good fortune that I have been able to see you, for you cannot easily be seen by persons who have not subdued the mind**

**or controlled the senses. I am all the more fortunate to have touched with my head the blessed dust of your feet.**

## PURPORT

The perfection of transcendental life can be achieved simply by touching the holy dust of the lotus feet of a holy man. In the *Bhāgavatam* it is said, *mahat-pāda-rajo-'bhiṣekam*, which means to be blessed by the holy dust of the lotus feet of a *mahat*, a great devotee. As stated in *Bhagavad-gītā*, *mahātmānas tu:* those who are great souls are under the spell of spiritual energy, and their symptom is that they fully engage in Kṛṣṇa consciousness for the service of the Lord. Therefore they are called *mahat.* Unless one is fortunate enough to have the dust of the lotus feet of a *mahātmā* on one's head, there is no possibility of perfection in spiritual life.

The *paramparā* system of disciplic succession is very important as a means of spiritual success. One becomes a *mahat* by the grace of his *mahat* spiritual master. If one takes shelter of the lotus feet of a great soul, there is every possibility of one's also becoming a great soul. When Mahārāja Rahūgaṇa asked Jaḍa Bharata about his wonderful achievement of spiritual success, he replied to the King that spiritual success is not possible simply by following the rituals of religion or simply by converting oneself into a *sannyāsī* or offering sacrifices as recommended in the scriptures. These methods are undoubtedly helpful for spiritual realization, but the real effect is brought about by the grace of a *mahātmā.* In Viśvanātha Cakravartī Ṭhākura's eight stanzas of prayer to the spiritual master, it is clearly stated that simply by satisfying the spiritual master one can achieve the supreme success in life, and in spite of executing all ritualistic performances, if one cannot satisfy the spiritual master, one has no access to spiritual perfection. Here the word *akṛtātmanām* is very significant. *Ātmā* means "body," "soul," or "mind," and *akṛtātmā* means the common man, who cannot control the senses or the mind. Because the common man is unable to control the senses and the mind, it is his duty to seek the shelter of a great soul or a great devotee of the Lord and just try to please him. That will make his life perfect. A common man cannot rise to the topmost stage of spiritual perfection simply by following the rituals and religious principles. He has to take shelter of a bona fide spiritual master and work under his direction faithfully and sincerely; then he becomes perfect, without a doubt.

## TEXT 7

दिष्ट्या त्वयानुशिष्टोऽहं कृतश्चानुग्रहो महान् ।
अपावृतैः कर्णरन्ध्रैर्जुष्टा दिष्ट्योशतीर्गिरः ॥ ७ ॥

*diṣṭyā tvayānuśiṣṭo 'haṁ*
*kṛtaś cānugraho mahān*
*apāvṛtaiḥ karṇa-randhrair*
*juṣṭā diṣṭyośatīr giraḥ*

*diṣṭyā*—luckily; *tvayā*—by you; *anuśiṣṭaḥ*—instructed; *aham*—I; *kṛtaḥ*—bestowed; *ca*—and; *anugrahaḥ*—favor; *mahān*—great; *apāvṛtaiḥ*—open; *karṇa-randhraiḥ*—with the holes of the ears; *juṣṭāḥ*—received; *diṣṭyā*—by good fortune; *uśatīḥ*—pure; *giraḥ*—words.

## TRANSLATION

**I have fortunately been instructed by you, and thus great favor has been bestowed upon me. I thank God that I have listened with open ears to your pure words.**

## PURPORT

Śrīla Rūpa Gosvāmī has given directions, in his *Bhakti-rasāmṛta-sindhu*, on how to accept a bona fide spiritual master and how to deal with him. First, the desiring candidate must find a bona fide spiritual master, and then he must very eagerly receive instructions from him and execute them. This is reciprocal service. A bona fide spiritual master or saintly person always desires to elevate a common man who comes to him. Because everyone is under the delusion of *māyā* and is forgetful of his prime duty, Kṛṣṇa consciousness, a saintly person always desires that everyone become a saintly person. It is the function of a saintly person to invoke Kṛṣṇa consciousness in every forgetful common man.

Manu said that since he was advised and instructed by Kardama Muni, he was very much favored. He considered himself lucky to receive the message by aural reception. It is especially mentioned here that one should be very inquisitive to hear with open ears from the authorized source of the bona fide spiritual master. How is one to receive? One should receive the transcendental message by aural reception. The word *karṇa-randhraiḥ* means "through the holes of the ears." The favor of the spiritual master is not received through any other part of the body but the ears. This does not mean, however, that the spiritual master gives a particular type of *mantra* through the ears in exchange for some dollars and if the man meditates on that he achieves perfection and becomes God within six months. Such reception through the ears is bogus. The real fact is that a bona fide spiritual master knows the nature of a particular man and what sort of duties he can perform in Kṛṣṇa consciousness, and he instructs him in that way. He instructs him through the ear, not privately, but publicly. "You are fit for such and such work in Kṛṣṇa consciousness. You can act in this way." One person is advised to act in Kṛṣṇa consciousness by working in the Deities' room, another is advised to act in Kṛṣṇa consciousness by performing editorial work, another is advised to do preaching work, and another is advised to carry out Kṛṣṇa consciousness in the cooking department. There are different departments of activity in Kṛṣṇa consciousness, and a spiritual master, knowing the particular ability of a particular man, trains him in such a way that by his tendency to act he becomes perfect. *Bhagavad-gītā* makes it clear that one can attain the highest perfection of spiritual life simply by offering service according to his ability, just as Arjuna served Kṛṣṇa by his ability in the military art. Arjuna offered his service fully as a military man, and he became perfect. Similarly, an artist can attain perfection simply by performing artistic work under the direction of the spiritual master. If one is a literary man, he can write articles and poetry for the service of the Lord under the direction of the spiritual master. One has to receive the message of the spiritual master regarding how to act in one's capacity, for the spiritual master is expert in giving such instructions.

This combination, the instruction of the spiritual master and the faithful execution of the instruction by the disciple, makes the entire process perfect. Śrīla Viśvanātha Cakravartī Ṭhākura describes in his explanation of the verse in *Bhagavad-gītā*, *vyavasāyātmikā buddhiḥ*, that one who wants to be certain to achieve spiritual success must take the instruction from the spiritual master as to what his particular function is. He should faithfully try to execute that particular instruction and should consider that his life and soul. The faithful execution of the instruction which he receives from the spiritual master is the only duty of a disciple, and that will bring him perfection. One should be very careful to receive the message from the spiritual master through the ears and execute it faithfully. That will make one's life successful.

## TEXT 8

स भवान्दुहितृस्नेहपरिक्लिष्टात्मनो मम ।
श्रोतुमर्हसि दीनस्य श्रावितं कृपया मुने ॥ ८ ॥

*sa bhavān duhitṛ-sneha-*
*parikliṣṭātmano mama*
*śrotum arhasi dīnasya*
*śrāvitaṁ kṛpayā mune*

*saḥ*—yourself; *bhavān*—Your Honor; *duhitṛ-sneha*—by affection for my daughter; *parikliṣṭa-ātmanaḥ*—whose mind is agitated; *mama*—my; *śrotum*—to listen; *arhasi*—be pleased; *dīnasya*—of my humble self; *śrāvitam*—to the prayer; *kṛpayā*—graciously; *mune*—O sage.

## TRANSLATION

**O great sage, graciously be pleased to listen to the prayer of my humble self, for my mind is troubled by affection for my daughter.**

## PURPORT

When a disciple is perfectly in consonance with the spiritual master, having received his message and executed it perfectly and sincerely, he has a right to ask a particular favor from the spiritual master. Generally a pure devotee of the Lord or a pure disciple of a bona fide spiritual master does not ask any favor either from the Lord or the spiritual master, but even if there is a need to ask a favor from the spiritual master, one cannot ask that favor without satisfying him fully.

Svāyambhuva Manu wanted to disclose his mind regarding the function he wanted to execute due to affection for his daughter.

## TEXT 9

प्रियव्रतोत्तानपदोः स्वसेयं दुहिता मम ।
अन्विच्छति पतिं युक्तं वयःशीलगुणादिभिः ॥ ९ ॥

*priyavratottānapadoḥ*
*svaseyaṁ duhitā mama*
*anvicchati patiṁ yuktaṁ*
*vayaḥ-śīla-guṇādibhiḥ*

*priyavrata-uttānapadoḥ*—of Priyavrata and Uttānapāda; *svasā*—sister; *iyam*—this; *duhitā*—daughter; *mama*—my; *anvicchati*—is seeking; *patim*—husband; *yuktam*—suited; *vayaḥ-śīla-guṇa-ādibhiḥ*—by age, character, good qualities, etc.

## TRANSLATION

**My daughter is the sister of Priyavrata and Uttānapāda. She is seeking a suitable husband in terms of age, character and good qualities.**

## PURPORT

The grown-up daughter of Svāyambhuva Manu, Devahūti, had good character and was well qualified; therefore she was searching for a suitable husband just befitting her age, qualities and character. The purpose of Manu's introducing his daughter as the sister of Priyavrata and Uttānapāda, two great kings, was to convince the sage that the girl came from a great family. She was his daughter and at the same time the sister of *kṣatriyas;* she did not come from a lower-class family. Manu therefore offered her to Kardama as just suitable for his purpose. It is clear that although the daughter was mature in age and qualities, she did not go out and find her husband independently. She expressed her desire for a suitable husband corresponding to her character, age and quality, and the father himself, out of affection for his daughter, took charge of finding such a husband.

### TEXT 10

यदा तु भवतः शीलश्रुतरूपवयोगुणान् ।
अशृणोन्नारदादेषा त्वय्यासीत्कृतनिश्चया ॥१०॥

*yadā tu bhavataḥ śīla-*
*śruta-rūpa-vayo-guṇān*
*aśṛṇon nāradād eṣā*
*tvayy āsīt kṛta-niścayā*

*yadā*—when; *tu*—but; *bhavataḥ*—your; *śīla*—noble character; *śruta*—learning; *rūpa*—beautiful appearance; *vayaḥ*—youth; *guṇān*—virtues; *aśṛṇot*—heard; *nāradāt*—from Nārada Muni; *eṣā*—Devahūti; *tvayi*—in you; *āsīt*—became; *kṛta-niścayā*—fixed in determination.

### TRANSLATION

**The moment she heard from the sage Nārada of your noble character, learning, beautiful appearance, youth and other virtues, she fixed her mind upon you.**

### PURPORT

The girl Devahūti did not personally see Kardama Muni, nor did she personally experience his character or qualities, since there was no social intercourse by which she could gain such understanding. But she heard about Kardama Muni from the authority of Nārada Muni. Hearing from an authority is a better experience than gaining personal understanding. She heard from Nārada Muni that Kardama Muni was just fit to be her husband; therefore she became fixed in her heart that she would marry him, and she expressed her desire to her father, who therefore brought her before him.

### TEXT 11

तत्प्रतीच्छ द्विजाग्र्येमां श्रद्धयोपहृतां मया ।
सर्वात्मनानुरूपां ते गृहमेधिषु कर्मसु ॥११॥

*tat pratīccha dvijāgryemāṁ*
*śraddhayopahṛtāṁ mayā*

*sarvātmanānurūpāṁ te*
*gṛhamedhiṣu karmasu*

*tat*—therefore; *pratīccha*—please accept; *dvija-agrya*—O best of the *brāhmaṇas; imām*—her; *śraddhayā*—with faith; *upahṛtām*—offered as a presentation; *mayā*—by me; *sarva-ātmanā*—in every way; *anu-rūpām*—suitable; *te*—for you; *gṛha-medhiṣu*—in the household; *kar-masu*—duties.

## TRANSLATION

**Therefore please accept her, O chief of the brāhmaṇas, for I offer her with faith and she is in every respect fit to be your wife and take charge of your household duties.**

## PURPORT

The words *gṛhamedhiṣu karmasu* mean "in household duties." Another word is also used here: *sarvātmanānurūpām.* The purport is that a wife should not only be equal to her husband in age, character and qualities, but must be helpful to him in his household duties. The household duty of a man is not to satisfy his sense gratification, but to remain with a wife and children and at the same time attain advancement in spiritual life. One who does not do so is not a householder but a *gṛhamedhī.* Two words are used in Sanskrit literature; one is *gṛhastha,* and the other is *gṛhamedhī.* The difference between *gṛhamedhī* and *gṛhastha* is that *gṛhastha* is also an *āśrama,* or spiritual order, but if one simply satisfies his senses as a householder, then he is a *gṛhamedhī.* For a *gṛhamedhī,* to accept a wife means to satisfy the senses, but for a *gṛhastha* a qualified wife is an assistant in every respect for advancement in spiritual activities. It is the duty of the wife to take charge of household affairs and not to compete with the husband. A wife is meant to help, but she cannot help her husband unless he is completely equal to her in age, character and quality.

## TEXT 12

उद्यतस्य हि कामस्य प्रतिवादो न शस्यते ।
अपि निर्मुक्तसङ्गस्य कामरक्तस्य किं पुनः ॥१२॥

*udyatasya hi kāmasya*
*prativādo na śasyate*
*api nirmukta-saṅgasya*
*kāma-raktasya kiṁ punaḥ*

*udyatasya*—which has come of itself; *hi*—in fact; *kāmasya*—of material desire; *prativādaḥ*—the denial; *na*—not; *śasyate*—to be praised; *api*—even; *nirmukta*—of one who is free; *saṅgasya*—from attachment; *kāma*—to sensual pleasures; *raktasya*—of one addicted; *kim punaḥ*—how much less.

## TRANSLATION

**To deny an offering that has come of itself is not commendable even for one absolutely free from all attachment, much less one addicted to sensual pleasure.**

## PURPORT

In material life everyone is desirous of sense gratification; therefore, a person who gets an object of sense gratification without endeavor should not refuse to accept it. Kardama Muni was not meant for sense gratification, yet he aspired to marry and prayed to the Lord for a suitable wife. This was known to Svāyambhuva Manu. He indirectly convinced Kardama Muni: "You desire a suitable wife like my daughter, and she is now present before you. You should not reject the fulfillment of your prayer; you should accept my daughter."

## TEXT 13

य उद्यतमनादृत्य कीनाशमभियाचते ।
क्षीयते तद्यशः स्फीतं मानश्चावज्ञया हतः ॥१३॥

*ya udyatam anādṛtya*
*kīnāśam abhiyācate*
*kṣīyate tad-yaśaḥ sphītaṁ*
*mānaś cāvajñayā hataḥ*

*yaḥ*—who; *udyatam*—an offering; *anādṛtya*—rejecting; *kīnāśam*—from a miser; *abhiyācate*—begs; *kṣīyate*—is lost; *tat*—his; *yaśaḥ*—

reputation; *sphītam*—widespread; *mānaḥ*—honor; *ca*—and; *avajñayā*—by neglectful behavior; *hataḥ*—destroyed.

## TRANSLATION

**One who rejects an offering that comes of its own accord but later begs a boon from a miser thus loses his widespread reputation, and his pride is humbled by the neglectful behavior of others.**

## PURPORT

The general procedure of Vedic marriage is that a father offers his daughter to a suitable boy. That is a very respectable marriage. A boy should not go to the girl's father and ask for the hand of his daughter in marriage. That is considered to be humbling one's respectable position. Svāyambhuva Manu wanted to convince Kardama Muni, since he knew that the sage wanted to marry a suitable girl: "I am offering just such a suitable wife. Do not reject the offer, or else, because you are in need of a wife, you will have to ask for such a wife from someone else, who may not behave with you so well. In that case your position will be humbled."

Another feature of this incident is that Svāyambhuva Manu was the emperor, but he went to offer his qualified daughter to a poor *brāhmaṇa*. Kardama Muni had no worldly possessions—he was a hermit living in the forest—but he was advanced in culture. Therefore, in offering one's daughter to a person, the culture and quality are counted as prominent, not wealth or any other material consideration.

## TEXT 14

अहं त्वाश्रृणवं विद्वन् विवाहार्थं समुद्यतम् ।
अतस्त्वमुपकुर्वाणः प्रत्तां प्रतिगृहाण मे ॥१४॥

*ahaṁ tvāśṛṇavaṁ vidvan*
*vivāhārthaṁ samudyatam*
*atas tvam upakurvāṇaḥ*
*prattāṁ pratigṛhāṇa me*

*aham*—I; *tvā*—you; *aśṛṇavam*—heard; *vidvan*—O wise man; *vivāha-artham*—for the sake of marriage; *samudyatam*—prepared; *ataḥ*—hence; *tvam*—you; *upakurvāṇaḥ*—not taken a vow of perpetual celibacy; *prattām*—offered; *pratigṛhāṇa*—please accept; *me*—of me.

## TRANSLATION

**Svāyambhuva Manu continued: O wise man, I heard that you were prepared to marry. Please accept her hand, which is being offered to you by me, since you have not taken a vow of perpetual celibacy.**

## PURPORT

The principle of *brahmacarya* is celibacy. There are two kinds of *brahmacārīs*. One is called *naiṣṭhika-brahmacārī*, which means one who takes a vow of celibacy for his whole life, whereas the other, the *upakurvāṇa-brahmacārī*, is a *brahmacārī* who takes the vow of celibacy up to a certain age. For example, he may take the vow to remain celibate up to twenty-five years of age; then, with the permission of his spiritual master, he enters married life. *Brahmacarya* is student life, the beginning of life in the spiritual orders, and the principle of *brahmacarya* is celibacy. Only a householder can indulge in sense gratification or sex life, not a *brahmacārī*. Svāyambhuva Manu requested Kardama Muni to accept his daughter, since Kardama had not taken the vow of *naiṣṭhika-brahmacarya*. He was willing to marry, and the suitable daughter of a high royal family was presented.

## TEXT 15

ऋषिरुवाच

बाढमुद्वोढुकामोऽहमप्रत्ता च तवात्मजा ।
आवयोरनुरूपोऽसावाद्यो वैवाहिको विधिः ॥१५॥

*ṛṣir uvāca*
*bāḍham udvoḍhu-kāmo 'ham*
*aprattā ca tavātmajā*

*āvayor anurūpo 'sāv*
*ādyo vaivāhiko vidhiḥ*

*ṛṣiḥ*—the great sage Kardama; *uvāca*—said; *bāḍham*—very well; *ud-voḍhu-kāmaḥ*—desirous to marry; *aham*—I; *aprattā*—not promised to anyone else; *ca*—and; *tava*—your; *ātma-jā*—daughter; *āvayoḥ*—of us two; *anurūpaḥ*—proper; *asau*—this; *ādyaḥ*—first; *vaivāhikaḥ*—of marriage; *vidhiḥ*—ritualistic ceremony.

## TRANSLATION

**The great sage replied: Certainly I have a desire to marry, and your daughter has not yet married or given her word to anyone. Therefore our marriage according to the Vedic system can take place.**

## PURPORT

There were many considerations by Kardama Muni before accepting the daughter of Svāyambhuva Manu. Most important is that Devahūti had first of all fixed her mind on marrying him. She did not choose to have any other man as her husband. That is a great consideration because female psychology dictates that when a woman offers her heart to a man for the first time, it is very difficult for her to take it back. Also, she had not married before; she was a virgin girl. All these considerations convinced Kardama Muni to accept her. Therefore he said, "Yes, I shall accept your daughter under religious regulations of marriage." There are different kinds of marriages, of which the first-class marriage is held by inviting a suitable bridegroom for the daughter and giving her in charity, well dressed and well decorated with ornaments, along with a dowry according to the means of the father. There are other kinds of marriage, such as *gāndharva* marriage and marriage by love, which are also accepted as marriage. Even if one is forcibly kidnapped and later on accepted as a wife, that is also accepted. But Kardama Muni accepted the first-class way of marriage because the father was willing and the daughter was qualified. She had never offered her heart to anyone else. All these considerations made Kardama Muni agree to accept the daughter of Svāyambhuva Manu.

## TEXT 16

कामः स भूयान्नरदेव तेऽस्याः
पुत्र्याः समाम्नायविधौ प्रतीतः ।
क एव ते तनयां नाद्रियेत
स्वयैव कान्त्या क्षिपतीमिव श्रियम् ॥१६॥

*kāmaḥ sa bhūyān naradeva te 'syāḥ*
*putryāḥ samāmnāya-vidhau pratītaḥ*
*ka eva te tanayāṁ nādriyeta*
*svayaiva kāntyā kṣipatīm iva śriyam*

*kāmaḥ*—desire; *saḥ*—that; *bhūyāt*—let it be fulfilled; *nara-deva*—O King; *te*—your; *asyāḥ*—this; *putryāḥ*—of the daughter; *samāmnāya-vidhau*—in the process of the Vedic scriptures; *pratītaḥ*—recognized; *kaḥ*—who; *eva*—in fact; *te*—your; *tanayām*—daughter; *na ādriyeta*—would not adore; *svayā*—by her own; *eva*—alone; *kāntyā*—bodily luster; *kṣipatīm*—excelling; *iva*—as if; *śriyam*—ornaments.

## TRANSLATION

**Let your daughter's desire for marriage, which is recognized in the Vedic scriptures, be fulfilled. Who would not accept her hand? She is so beautiful that by her bodily luster alone she excels the beauty of her ornaments.**

## PURPORT

Kardama Muni wanted to marry Devahūti in the recognized manner of marriage prescribed in the scriptures. As stated in the Vedic scriptures, the first-class process is to call the bridegroom to the home of the bride and hand her to him in charity with a dowry of necessary ornaments, gold, furniture and other household paraphernalia. This form of marriage is prevalent among higher-class Hindus even today and is declared in the *śāstras* to confer great religious merit on the bride's father. To give a daughter in charity to a suitable son-in-law is considered to be one of the pious activities of a householder. There are eight forms of marriage mentioned in the scripture *Manu-smṛti*, but only one process of marriage, *brāhma* or *rājasika* marriage, is now current. Other kinds of marriage—by love, by exchange of garlands or by kidnapping the bride—are now forbidden in this Kali age. Formerly, *kṣatriyas* would, at their pleasure, kidnap a princess from another royal house, and there would be a fight between the *kṣatriya* and the girl's family; then, if the kidnapper was the winner, the girl would be offered to him for marriage. Even Kṛṣṇa married Rukmiṇī by that process, and some of His sons and grandsons also married by kidnapping. Kṛṣṇa's grandsons kidnapped Duryodhana's daughter, which caused a fight between the Kuru and Yadu families. Afterward, an adjustment was made by the elderly members of the Kuru family. Such marriages were current in bygone ages, but at the present moment they are impossible because the strict principles of *kṣatriya* life have practically been abolished. Since India has become dependent on foreign countries, the particular influences of her social orders have been lost; now, according to the scriptures, everyone is a *śūdra*. The so-called *brāhmaṇas*, *kṣatriyas* and *vaiśyas* have forgotten their traditional activities, and in the absence of these activities they are called *śūdras*. It is said in the scriptures, *kalau śūdra-sambhavaḥ*. In the age of Kali everyone will be like *śūdras*. The traditional social customs are not followed in this age, although formerly they were followed strictly.

## TEXT 17

यां हर्म्यपृष्ठे क्वणदङ्घ्रिशोभां
विक्रीडतीं कन्दुकविह्वलाक्षीम् ।
विश्वावसुर्न्यपतत्स्वाद्विमाना-
द्विलोक्य सम्मोहविमूढचेताः ॥१७॥

*yāṁ harmya-pṛṣṭhe kvaṇad-aṅghri-śobhāṁ*
*vikrīḍatīṁ kanduka-vihvalākṣīm*
*viśvāvasur nyapatat svād vimānād*
*vilokya sammoha-vimūḍha-cetāḥ*

*yām*—whom; *harmya-pṛṣṭhe*—on the roof of the palace; *kvaṇat-aṅghri-śobhām*—whose beauty was heightened by the tinkling ornaments on her feet; *vikrīḍatīm*—playing; *kanduka-vihvala-akṣīm*—with eyes bewildered, following her ball; *viśvāvasuḥ*—Viśvāvasu; *nyapatat*—fell down; *svāt*—from his own; *vimānāt*—from the airplane; *vilokya*—seeing; *sammoha-vimūḍha-cetāḥ*—whose mind was stupefied.

## TRANSLATION

**I have heard that Viśvāvasu, the great Gandharva, his mind stupefied with infatuation, fell from his airplane after seeing your daughter playing with a ball on the roof of the palace, for she was indeed beautiful with her tinkling ankle bells and her eyes moving to and fro.**

## PURPORT

It is understood that not only at the present moment but in those days also there were skyscrapers. Herein we find the word *harmya-pṛṣṭhe. Harmya* means "a very big palatial building." *Svād vimānāt* means "from his own airplane." It is suggested that private airplanes or helicopters were also current in those days. The Gandharva Viśvāvasu, while flying in the sky, could see Devahūti playing ball on the roof of the palace. Ball playing was also current, but aristocratic girls would not play in a public place. Ball playing and other such pleasures were not meant for ordinary women and girls; only princesses like Devahūti could indulge in such sports. It is described here that she was seen from the flying airplane. This indicates that the palace was very high, otherwise how could one see her from an airplane? The vision was so distinct that the Gandharva Viśvāvasu was bewildered by her beauty and by hearing the sound of her ankle bangles, and being captivated by the sound and beauty, he fell down. Kardama Muni mentioned the incident as he had heard it.

## TEXT 18

तां प्रार्थयन्तीं ललनाललाम-
मसेवितश्रीचरणैरदृष्टाम् ।

वत्सां मनोरुच्चपदः स्वसारं
को नानुमन्येत बुधोऽभियाताम् ॥१८॥

*tāṁ prārthayantīṁ lalanā-lalāmam*
*asevita-śrī-caraṇair adṛṣṭām*
*vatsāṁ manor uccapadaḥ svasāraṁ*
*ko nānumanyeta budho 'bhiyātām*

*tām*—her; *prārthayantīm*—seeking; *lalanā-lalāmam*—the ornament of women; *asevita-śrī-caraṇaiḥ*—by those who have not worshiped the feet of Lakṣmī; *adṛṣṭām*—not seen; *vatsām*—beloved daughter; *manoḥ*—of Svāyambhuva Manu; *uccapadaḥ*—of Uttānapāda; *svasāram*—sister; *kaḥ*—what; *na anumanyeta*—would not welcome; *budhaḥ*—wise man; *abhiyātām*—who has come of her own accord.

## TRANSLATION

**What wise man would not welcome her, the very ornament of womanhood, the beloved daughter of Svāyambhuva Manu and sister of Uttānapāda? Those who have not worshiped the gracious feet of the goddess of fortune cannot even perceive her, yet she has come of her own accord to seek my hand.**

## PURPORT

Kardama Muni praised the beauty and qualification of Devahūti in different ways. Devahūti was actually the ornament of all ornamented beautiful girls. A girl becomes beautiful by putting ornaments on her body, but Devahūti was more beautiful than the ornaments; she was considered the ornament of the ornamented beautiful girls. Demigods and Gandharvas were attracted by her beauty. Kardama Muni, although a great sage, was not a denizen of the heavenly planets, but it is mentioned in the previous verse that Viśvāvasu, who came from heaven, was also attracted by the beauty of Devahūti. Besides her personal beauty, she was the daughter of Emperor Svāyambhuva and sister of King Uttānapāda. Who could refuse the hand of such a girl?

## TEXT 19

अतो भजिष्ये समयेन साध्वीं
यावत्तेजो बिभृयादात्मनो मे ।
अतो धर्मान् पारमहंस्यमुख्यान्
शुक्लप्रोक्तान् बहु मन्येऽविहिंस्रान् ॥१९॥

*ato bhajiṣye samayena sādhvīṁ*
*yāvat tejo bibhṛyād ātmano me*
*ato dharmān pāramahaṁsya-mukhyān*
*śukla-proktān bahu manye 'vihiṁsrān*

*ataḥ*—therefore; *bhajiṣye*—I shall accept; *samayena*—on the conditions; *sādhvīm*—the chaste girl; *yāvat*—until; *tejaḥ*—semen; *bibhṛyāt*—may bear; *ātmanaḥ*—from my body; *me*—my; *ataḥ*—thereafter; *dharmān*—the duties; *pāramahaṁsya-mukhyān*—of the best of the *paramahaṁsas; śukla-proktān*—spoken by Lord Viṣṇu; *bahu*—much; *manye*—I shall consider; *avihiṁsrān*—free from envy.

## TRANSLATION

**Therefore I shall accept this chaste girl as my wife, on the condition that after she bears semen from my body, I shall accept the life of devotional service accepted by the most perfect human beings. That process was described by Lord Viṣṇu. It is free from envy.**

## PURPORT

Kardama Muni expressed his desire for a very beautiful wife to Emperor Svāyambhuva and accepted the Emperor's daughter for marriage. Kardama Muni was in the hermitage practicing complete celibacy as a *brahmacārī*, and although he had the desire to marry, he did not want to be a householder for the whole span of his life because he was conversant with the Vedic principles of human life. According to Vedic principles, the first part of life should be utilized in *brahmacarya* for the development of character and spiritual qualities. In the next part of life, one may accept a wife and beget children, but one should not beget children like cats and dogs.

Kardama Muni desired to beget a child who would be a ray of the Supreme Personality of Godhead. One should beget a child who can perform the duties of Viṣṇu, otherwise there is no need to produce children. There are two kinds of children born of good fathers: one is educated in Kṛṣṇa consciousness so that he can be delivered from the clutches of *māyā* in that very life, and the other is a ray of the Supreme Personality of Godhead and teaches the world the ultimate goal of life. As will be described in later chapters, Kardama Muni begot such a child—Kapila, the incarnation of the Personality of Godhead who enunciated the philosophy of Sāṅkhya. Great householders pray to God to send His representative so that there may be an auspicious movement in human society. This is one reason to beget a child. Another reason is that a highly enlightened parent can train a child in Kṛṣṇa consciousness so that the child will not have to come back again to this miserable world. Parents should see to it that the child born of them does not enter the womb of a mother again. Unless one can train a child for liberation in that life, there is no need to marry or produce children. If human society produces children like cats and dogs for the disturbance of social order, then the world becomes hellish, as it has in this age of Kali. In this age, neither parents nor their children are trained; both are animalistic and simply eat, sleep, mate, defend, and gratify their senses. This disorder in social life cannot bring peace to human society. Kardama Muni explains beforehand that he would not associate with the girl Devahūti for the whole duration of his life. He would simply associate with her until she had a child. In other words, sex life should be utilized only to produce a nice child, not for any other purpose. Human life is especially meant for complete devotion to the service of the Lord. That is the philosophy of Lord Caitanya.

After fulfilling his responsibility to produce a nice child, one should take *sannyāsa* and engage in the perfectional *paramahaṁsa* stage. *Paramahaṁsa* refers to the most highly elevated perfectional stage of life. There are four stages within *sannyāsa* life, and *paramahaṁsa* is the highest order. The *Śrīmad-Bhāgavatam* is called the *paramahaṁsa-saṁhitā*, the treatise for the highest class of human beings. The *paramahaṁsa* is free from envy. In other stages, even in the householder stage of life, there is competition and envy, but since the activities of the human being in the *paramahaṁsa* stage are completely engaged in Kṛṣṇa consciousness, or devotional service, there is no scope for envy. In the same order as Kardama Muni, about one hundred years ago, Ṭhākura Bhaktivinoda also wanted to beget a child who could preach the philosophy and teachings of Lord Caitanya to the fullest extent. By his prayers to the Lord he had as his child Bhaktisiddhānta Sarasvatī Gosvāmī Mahārāja, who at the present moment is preaching the philosophy of Lord Caitanya throughout the entire world through his bona fide disciples.

## TEXT 20

यतोऽभवद्विश्वमिदं विचित्रं
संस्थास्यते यत्र च वावतिष्ठते ।
प्रजापतीनां पतिरेष मह्यं
परं प्रमाणं भगवाननन्तः ॥२०॥

*yato 'bhavad viśvam idaṁ vicitraṁ*
*saṁsthāsyate yatra ca vāvatiṣṭhate*
*prajāpatīnāṁ patir eṣa mahyaṁ*
*paraṁ pramāṇaṁ bhagavān anantaḥ*

*yataḥ*—from whom; *abhavat*—emanated; *viśvam*—creation; *idam*—this; *vicitram*—wonderful; *saṁsthāsyate*—will dissolve; *yatra*—in whom; *ca*—and; *vā*—or; *avatiṣṭhate*—presently exists; *prajā-patī-nām*—of the Prajāpatis; *patiḥ*—the Lord; *eṣaḥ*—this; *mahyam*—to me; *param*—highest; *pramāṇam*—authority; *bhagavān*—Supreme Lord; *anantaḥ*—unlimited.

## TRANSLATION

**The highest authority for me is the unlimited Supreme Personality of Godhead, from whom this wonderful creation emanates and in whom its sustenance and dissolution rest. He is the origin of all Prajāpatis, the personalities meant to produce living entities in this world.**

## PURPORT

Kardama Muni was ordered by his father, Prajāpati, to produce children. In the beginning of creation the Prajāpatis were meant to produce the large population which was to reside in the planets of the gigantic universe. But Kardama Muni said that although his father was Prajāpati, who desired him to produce children, actually his origin was the Supreme Personality of Godhead, Viṣṇu, because Viṣṇu is the origin of everything; He is the actual creator of this universe, He is the actual maintainer, and when everything is annihilated, it rests in Him only. That is the conclusion of *Śrīmad-Bhāgavatam.* For creation, maintenance and annihilation there are the three deities Brahmā, Viṣṇu and Maheśvara (Śiva), but Brahmā and Maheśvara are qualitative expansions of Viṣṇu. Viṣṇu is the central figure. Viṣṇu, therefore, takes charge of maintenance. No one can maintain the whole creation but He. There are innumerable entities, and they have innumerable demands; no one but Viṣṇu can fulfill the unnumerable demands of all the innumerable living entities. Brahmā is ordered to create, and Śiva is ordered to annihilate. The middle function, maintenance, is taken charge of by Viṣṇu. Kardama Muni knew very well, by his power in progressive spiritual life, that Viṣṇu, the Personality of Godhead, was his worshipable Deity. Whatever Viṣṇu desired was his duty, and nothing else. He was not prepared to beget a number of children. He would beget only one child, who would help the mission of Viṣṇu. As stated in *Bhagavad-gītā,* whenever there is a discrepancy in the discharge of religious principles, the Lord descends on the surface of the earth to protect religious principles and to annihilate the miscreants.

Marrying and begetting a child is considered to liquidate one's debts to the family in which one is born. There are many debts which are imposed upon a child just after his birth. There are debts to the family in which one is born, debts to the demigods, debts to the Pitās, debts to the *ṛṣis,* etc. But if someone engages only in the service of the Supreme Lord, the Personality of Godhead, who is actually worshipable, then even without trying to liquidate other debts, one becomes free from all obligations. Kardama Muni preferred to devote his life as a servant of the Lord in *paramahaṁsa* knowledge and to beget a child only for that purpose, not to beget numberless children to fill up the vacancies in the universe.

## TEXT 21

मैत्रेय उवाच
स उग्रधन्वन्नियदेवाबभाषे
आसीच्च तूष्णीमरविन्दनाभम् ।
धियोपगृह्णन् स्मितशोभितेन
मुखेन चेतो लुलुभे देवहूत्याः ॥२१॥

*maitreya uvāca*
*sa ugra-dhanvann iyad evābabhāṣe*
*āsīc ca tūṣṇīm aravinda-nābham*
*dhiyopagṛhṇan smita-śobhitena*
*mukhena ceto lulubhe devahūtyāḥ*

*maitreyaḥ*—the great sage Maitreya; *uvāca*—said; *saḥ*—he (Kardama); *ugra-dhanvan*—O great warrior Vidura; *iyat*—this much; *eva*—only; *ābabhāṣe*—spoke; *āsīt*—became; *ca*—and; *tūṣṇīm*—silent; *aravinda-nābham*—Lord Viṣṇu (whose navel is adorned by a lotus); *dhiyā*—by thought; *upagṛhṇan*—seizing; *smita-śobhitena*—beautified by his smile; *mukhena*—by his face; *cetaḥ*—the mind; *lulubhe*—was captivated; *devahūtyāḥ*—of Devahūti.

## TRANSLATION

**Śrī Maitreya said: O great warrior Vidura, the sage Kardama said this much only and then became silent, thinking of his worshipable Lord Viṣṇu, who has a lotus on His navel. As he silently smiled, his face captured the mind of Devahūti, who began to meditate upon the great sage.**

## PURPORT

It appears that Kardama Muni was fully absorbed in Kṛṣṇa consciousness because as soon as he became silent, he at once began to think of Lord Viṣṇu. That is the way of Kṛṣṇa consciousness. Pure devotees are so absorbed in thought of Kṛṣṇa that they have no other engagement; although they may seem to think or act otherwise, they are always thinking of Kṛṣṇa. The smile of such a Kṛṣṇa conscious person is so attractive that simply by smiling he wins so many admirers, disciples and followers.

## TEXT 22

सोऽनु ज्ञात्वा व्यवसितं महिष्या दुहितुः स्फुटम् ।
तस्मै गुणगणाढ्याय ददौ तुल्यां प्रहर्षितः ॥२२॥

*so 'nu jñātvā vyavasitaṁ*
*mahiṣyā duhituḥ sphuṭam*
*tasmai guṇa-gaṇāḍhyāya*
*dadau tulyāṁ praharṣitaḥ*

*saḥ*—he (Emperor Manu); *anu*—afterward; *jñātvā*—having known; *vyavasitam*—the fixed decision; *mahiṣyāḥ*—of the Queen; *duhituḥ*—of his daughter; *sphuṭam*—clearly; *tasmai*—to him; *guṇa-gaṇa-āḍhyāya*—who was endowed with a host of virtues; *dadau*—gave away; *tulyām*—who was equal (in good qualities); *praharṣitaḥ*—extremely pleased.

### TRANSLATION

**After having unmistakably known the decision of the Queen, as well as that of Devahūti, the Emperor most gladly gave his daughter to the sage, whose host of virtues was equaled by hers.**

## TEXT 23

शतरूपा महाराज्ञी पारिबर्हान्महाधनान् ।
दम्पत्योः पर्यदात्प्रीत्या भूषावासः परिच्छदान् ॥२३॥

*śatarūpā mahā-rājñī*
*pāribarhān mahā-dhanān*
*dampatyoḥ paryadāt prītyā*
*bhūṣā-vāsaḥ paricchadān*

*śatarūpā*—Empress Śatarūpā; *mahā-rājñī*—the Empress; *pāribar-hān*—dowry; *mahā-dhanān*—valuable presents; *dam-patyoḥ*—to the bride and bridegroom; *paryadāt*—gave; *prītyā*—out of affection;

*bhūṣā*—ornaments; *vāsaḥ*—clothes; *paricchadān*—articles for household use.

## TRANSLATION

**Empress Śatarūpā lovingly gave most valuable presents, suitable for the occasion, such as jewelry, clothes and household articles, in dowry to the bride and bridegroom.**

## PURPORT

The custom of giving one's daughter in charity with a dowry is still current in India. The gifts are given according to the position of the father of the bride. *Pāribarhān mahā-dhanān* means the dowry which must be awarded to the bridegroom at the time of marriage. Here *mahā-dhanān* means greatly valuable gifts befitting the dowry of an empress. The words *bhūṣā-vāsaḥ paricchadān* also appear here. *Bhūṣā* means "ornaments," *vāsaḥ* means "clothing," and *paricchadān* means "various household articles." All things befitting the marriage ceremony of an emperor's daughter were awarded to Kardama Muni, who was until now observing celibacy as a *brahmacārī*. The bride, Devahūti, was very richly dressed with ornaments and clothing.

In this way Kardama Muni was married with full opulence to a qualified wife and was endowed with the necessary paraphernalia for household life. In the Vedic way of marriage such a dowry is still given to the bridegroom by the father of the bride; even in poverty-stricken India there are marriages where hundreds and thousands of rupees are spent for a dowry. The dowry system is not illegal, as some have tried to prove. The dowry is a gift given to the daughter by the father to show good will, and it is compulsory. In rare cases where the father is completely unable to give a dowry, it is enjoined that he must at least give a fruit and a flower. As stated in *Bhagavad-gītā*, God can also be pleased even by a fruit and a flower. When there is financial inability and no question of accumulating a dowry by another means, one can give a fruit and flower for the satisfaction of the bridegroom.

## TEXT 24

प्रत्तां दुहितरं सम्राट् सदृक्षाय गतव्यथः ।
उपगुह्य च बाहुभ्यामौत्कण्ठ्योन्मथिताशयः ॥२४॥

*prattāṁ duhitaraṁ samrāṭ*
*sadṛkṣāya gata-vyathaḥ*
*upaguhya ca bāhubhyām*
*autkaṇṭhyonmathitāśayaḥ*

*prattām*—who was given; *duhitaram*—daughter; *samrāṭ*—the Emperor (Manu); *sadṛkṣāya*—unto a suitable person; *gata-vyathaḥ*—relieved of his responsibility; *upaguhya*—embracing; *ca*—and; *bāhubhyām*—with his two arms; *autkaṇṭhya-unmathita-āśayaḥ*—having an anxious and agitated mind.

## TRANSLATION

**Thus relieved of his responsibility by handing over his daughter to a suitable man, Svāyambhuva Manu, his mind agitated by feelings of separation, embraced his affectionate daughter with both his arms.**

## PURPORT

A father always remains in anxiety until he can hand over his grown-up daughter to a suitable boy. A father and mother's responsibility for children continues until they marry them to suitable spouses; when the father is able to perform that duty, he is relieved of his responsibility.

## TEXT 25

अशक्नुवंस्तद्विरहं मुञ्चन् बाष्पकलां मुहुः ।
आसिञ्चदम्ब वत्सेति नेत्रोदैर्दुहितुः शिखाः ॥२५॥

*aśaknuvaṁs tad-virahaṁ*
*muñcan bāṣpa-kalāṁ muhuḥ*
*āsiñcad amba vatseti*
*netrodair duhituḥ śikhāḥ*

*aśaknuvan*—being unable to bear; *tat-viraham*—separation from her; *muñcan*—shedding; *bāṣpa-kalām*—tears; *muhuḥ*—again and again; *āsiñcat*—he drenched; *amba*—my dear mother; *vatsa*—my dear daughter; *iti*—thus; *netra-udaiḥ*—by the water from his eyes; *duhituḥ*—of his daughter; *śikhāḥ*—the locks of hair.

## TRANSLATION

**The Emperor was unable to bear the separation of his daughter. Therefore tears poured from his eyes again and again, drenching his daughter's head as he cried, "My dear mother! My dear daughter!"**

## PURPORT

The word *amba* is significant. A father sometimes addresses his daughter in affection as "mother" and sometimes as "my darling." The feeling of separation occurs because until the daughter is married she remains the daughter of the father, but after her marriage she is no longer claimed as a daughter in the family; she must go to the husband's house, for after marriage she becomes the property of the husband. According to *Manu-saṁhitā,* a woman is never independent. She must remain the property of the father while she is not married, and she must remain the property of the husband until she is elderly and has grown-up children of her own. In old age, when the husband has taken *sannyāsa* and left home, she remains the property of the sons. A woman is always dependent, either upon the father, husband or elderly sons. That will be exhibited in the life of Devahūti. Devahūti's father handed over responsibility for her to the husband, Kardama Muni, and in the same way, Kardama Muni also left home, giving the responsibility to his son, Kapiladeva. This narration will describe these events one after another.

## TEXTS 26–27

आमन्त्र्य तं मुनिवरमनुज्ञातः सहानुगः ।
प्रतस्थे रथमारुह्य सभार्यः स्वपुरं नृपः ॥२६॥
उभयोर्ऋषिकुल्यायाः सरस्वत्याः सुरोधसोः ।
ऋषीणामुपशान्तानां पश्यन्नाश्रमसम्पदः ॥२७॥

*āmantrya taṁ muni-varam*
*anujñātaḥ sahānugaḥ*

*pratasthe ratham āruhya*
*sabhāryaḥ sva-puraṁ nṛpaḥ*

*ubhayor ṛṣi-kulyāyāḥ*
*sarasvatyāḥ surodhasoḥ*
*ṛṣīṇām upaśāntānāṁ*
*paśyann āśrama-sampadaḥ*

*āmantrya*—taking permission to go; *tam*—from him (Kardama); *muni-varam*—from the best of sages; *anujñātaḥ*—being permitted to leave; *saha-anugaḥ*—along with his retinue; *pratasthe*—started for; *ratham āruhya*—mounting his chariot; *sa-bhāryaḥ*—along with his wife; *sva-puram*—his own capital; *nṛpaḥ*—the Emperor; *ubhayoḥ*—on both; *ṛṣi-kulyāyāḥ*—agreeable to the sages; *sarasvatyāḥ*—of the River Sarasvatī; *su-rodhasoḥ*—the charming banks; *ṛṣīṇām*—of the great sages; *upaśāntānām*—tranquil; *paśyan*—seeing; *āśrama-sampadaḥ*—the prosperity of the beautiful hermitages.

## TRANSLATION

**After asking and obtaining the great sage's permission to leave, the monarch mounted his chariot with his wife and started for his capital, followed by his retinue. Along the way he saw the prosperity of the tranquil seers' beautiful hermitages on both the charming banks of the Sarasvatī, the river so agreeable to saintly persons.**

## PURPORT

As cities are constructed in the modern age with great engineering and architectural craftsmanship, so in days gone by there were neighborhoods called *ṛṣi-kulas*, where great saintly persons resided. In India there are still many magnificent places for spiritual understanding; there are many *ṛṣis* and saintly persons living in nice cottages on the banks of the Ganges and Yamunā for purposes of spiritual cultivation. While passing through the *ṛṣi-kulas* the King and his party were very much satisfied with the beauty of the cottages and hermitages. It is stated here, *paśyann āśrama-sampadaḥ.* The great sages had no skyscrapers, but the hermitages were so beautiful that the King was very much pleased at the sight.

## TEXT 28

तमायान्तमभिप्रेत्य ब्रह्मावर्तात्प्रजाः पतिम् ।
गीतसंस्तुतिवादित्रैः प्रत्युदीयुः प्रहर्षिताः ॥२८॥

*tam āyāntam abhipretya*
*brahmāvartāt prajāḥ patim*
*gīta-saṁstuti-vāditraiḥ*
*pratyudīyuḥ praharṣitāḥ*

*tam*—him; *āyāntam*—who was arriving; *abhipretya*—knowing of; *brahmāvartāt*—from Brahmāvarta; *prajāḥ*—his subjects; *patim*—their lord; *gīta-saṁstuti-vāditraiḥ*—with songs, praise and instrumental music; *pratyudīyuḥ*—came forward to greet; *praharṣitāḥ*—overjoyed.

## TRANSLATION

**Overjoyed to know of his arrival, his subjects came forth from Brahmāvarta to greet their returning lord with songs, prayers and musical instruments.**

## PURPORT

It is the custom of the citizens of a kingdom's capital to receive the king when he returns from a tour. There is a similar description when Kṛṣṇa returned to Dvārakā after the Battle of Kurukṣetra. At that time He was received by all classes of citizens at the gate of the city. Formerly, capital cities were surrounded by walls, and there were different gates for regular entrance. Even in Delhi today there are old gates, and some other old cities have such gates where citizens would gather to receive the king. Here also the citizens of Barhiṣmatī, the capital of Brahmāvarta, the kingdom of Svāyambhuva, came nicely dressed to receive the Emperor with decorations and musical instruments.

## TEXTS 29–30

बर्हिष्मती नाम पुरी सर्वसम्पत्समन्विता ।
न्यपतन् यत्र रोमाणि यज्ञस्याङ्गं विधुन्वतः ॥२९॥
कुशाः काशास्त एवासन् शश्वद्धरितवर्चसः ।
ऋषयो यैः पराभाव्य यज्ञघ्नान् यज्ञमीजिरे ॥३०॥

*barhiṣmatī nāma purī*
*sarva-sampat-samanvitā*
*nyapatan yatra romāṇi*
*yajñasyāṅgaṁ vidhunvataḥ*

*kuśāḥ kāśās ta evāsan*
*śaśvad-dharita-varcasaḥ*
*ṛṣayo yaiḥ parābhāvya*
*yajña-ghnān yajñam ījire*

*barhiṣmatī*—Barhiṣmatī; *nāma*—named; *purī*—city; *sarva-sampat*—all kinds of wealth; *samanvitā*—full of; *nyapatan*—fell down; *yatra*—where; *romāṇi*—the hairs; *yajñasya*—of Lord Boar; *aṅgam*—His body; *vidhunvataḥ*—shaking; *kuśāḥ*—*kuśa* grass; *kāśāḥ*—*kāśa* grass; *te*—they; *eva*—certainly; *āsan*—became; *śaśvat-harita*—of evergreen; *varcasaḥ*—having the color; *ṛṣayaḥ*—the sages; *yaiḥ*—by which; *parābhāvya*—defeating; *yajña-ghnān*—the disturbers of the sacrificial performances; *yajñam*—Lord Viṣṇu; *ījire*—they worshiped.

## TRANSLATION

**The city of Barhiṣmatī, rich in all kinds of wealth, was so called because Lord Viṣṇu's hair dropped there from His body when He manifested Himself as Lord Boar. As He shook His body, this very hair fell and turned into blades of evergreen kuśa grass and kāśa [another kind of grass used for mats], by means of which the sages worshiped Lord Viṣṇu after defeating the demons who had interfered with the performance of their sacrifices.**

## PURPORT

Any place directly connected with the Supreme Lord is called *pīṭha-sthāna.* Barhiṣmatī, the capital of Svāyambhuva Manu, was exalted not because the city was very rich in wealth and opulence, but because the hairs of Lord Varāha fell at this very spot. These hairs of the Lord later grew as green grass, and the sages used to worship the Lord with that grass after the time when the Lord killed the demon Hiraṇyākṣa. *Yajña* means Viṣṇu, the Supreme Personality of Godhead. In *Bhagavad-gītā, karma* is described as *yajñārtha. Yajñārtha-karma* means "work done only for the satisfaction of Viṣṇu." If something is done for sense gratification or any other purpose, it will be binding upon the worker. If one wants to be freed from the reaction of his work, he must perform everything for the satisfaction of Viṣṇu, or Yajña. In the capital of Svāyambhuva Manu, Barhiṣmatī, these particular functions were being performed by the great sages and saintly persons.

## TEXT 31

कुशकाशमयं बर्हिरास्तीर्य भगवान्मनुः ।
अयजद्यज्ञपुरुषं लब्धा स्थानं यतो भुवम् ॥३१॥

*kuśa-kāśamayaṁ barhir*
*āstīrya bhagavān manuḥ*
*ayajad yajña-puruṣaṁ*
*labdhā sthānaṁ yato bhuvam*

*kuśa*—of *kuśa* grass; *kāśa*—and of *kāśa* grass; *mayam*—made; *barhiḥ*—a seat; *āstīrya*—having spread; *bhagavān*—the greatly fortunate; *manuḥ*—Svāyambhuva Manu; *ayajat*—worshiped; *yajña-puruṣam*—Lord Viṣṇu; *labdhā*—had achieved; *sthānam*—the abode; *yataḥ*—from whom; *bhuvam*—the earth.

## TRANSLATION

**Manu spread a seat of kuśas and kāśas and worshiped the Lord, the Personality of Godhead, by whose grace he had obtained the rule of the terrestrial globe.**

## PURPORT

Manu is the father of mankind, and therefore from *Manu* comes the word *man*, or, in Sanskrit, *manuṣya.* Those who are in a better position in the world, having sufficient wealth, should especially take lessons from Manu, who acknowledged his kingdom and opulence to be gifts from the Supreme Personality of Godhead and thus always engaged in devotional service. Similarly, the descendants of Manu, or human beings, especially those who are situated in a well-to-do condition, must consider that whatever riches they have are gifts from the Supreme Personality of Godhead. Those riches should be utilized for the service of the Lord in sacrifices performed to please Him. That is the way of utilizing wealth and opulence. No one can achieve wealth, opulence, good birth, a beautiful body or nice education without the mercy of the Supreme Lord. Therefore, those who are in possession of such valuable facilities must acknowledge their gratefulness to the Lord by worshiping Him and offering what they have received from Him. When such acknowledgment is given, either by a family, nation or society, their abode becomes almost like Vaikuṇṭha, and it becomes free from the operation of the threefold miseries of this material world. In the modern age the mission of Kṛṣṇa consciousness is for everyone to acknowledge the supremacy of Lord Kṛṣṇa; whatever one has in his possession must be considered a gift by the grace of the Lord. Everyone, therefore, should engage in devotional service through Kṛṣṇa consciousness. If one wants to be happy and peaceful in his position, either as a householder or citizen or member of human society, one must promote devotional service for the pleasure of the Lord.

## TEXT 32

बर्हिष्मतीं नाम विभुर्यां निर्विश्य समावसत् ।
तस्यां प्रविष्टो भवनं तापत्रयविनाशनम् ॥३२॥

*barhiṣmatīṁ nāma vibhur*
*yāṁ nirviśya samāvasat*
*tasyāṁ praviṣṭo bhavanaṁ*
*tāpa-traya-vināśanam*

*barhiṣmatīm*—the city Barhiṣmatī; *nāma*—named; *vibhuḥ*—the very powerful Svāyambhuva Manu; *yām*—which; *nirviśya*—having entered; *samāvasat*—he lived in previously; *tasyām*—in that city; *praviṣṭaḥ*—entered; *bhavanam*—the palace; *tāpa-traya*—the threefold miseries; *vināśanam*—destroying.

## TRANSLATION

**Having entered the city of Barhiṣmatī, in which he had previously lived, Manu entered his palace, which was filled with an atmosphere that eradicated the three miseries of material existence.**

## PURPORT

The material world, or material existential life, is filled with threefold miseries: miseries pertaining to the body and mind, miseries pertaining to natural disturbances and miseries inflicted by other living entities. Human society is meant to create a spiritual atmosphere by spreading the spirit of Kṛṣṇa consciousness. The miseries of material existence cannot affect the status of Kṛṣṇa consciousness. It is not that the miseries of the material world completely vanish when one takes to Kṛṣṇa consciousness, but for one who is Kṛṣṇa conscious the miseries of material existence have no effect. We cannot stop the miseries of the material atmosphere, but Kṛṣṇa consciousness is the antiseptic method to protect us from being affected by the miseries of material existence. For a Kṛṣṇa conscious person, both living in heaven and living in hell are equal. How Svāyambhuva Manu created an atmosphere wherein he was not affected by material miseries is explained in the following verses.

## TEXT 33

सभार्यः सप्रजः कामान् बुभुजेऽन्याविरोधतः ।
सङ्गीयमानसत्कीर्तिः सस्त्रीभिः सुरगायकैः ।
प्रत्यूषेष्वनुबद्धेन हृदा शृण्वन् हरेः कथाः ॥३३॥

*sabhāryaḥ saprajaḥ kāmān*
*bubhuje 'nyāvirodhataḥ*

*saṅgīyamāna-sat-kīrtiḥ*
*sastrībhiḥ sura-gāyakaiḥ*
*praty-ūṣeṣv anubaddhena*
*hṛdā śṛṇvan hareḥ kathāḥ*

*sa-bhāryaḥ*—along with his wife; *sa-prajaḥ*—along with his subjects; *kāmān*—the necessities of life; *bubhuje*—he enjoyed; *anya*—from others; *avirodhataḥ*—without disturbance; *saṅgīyamāna*—being praised; *sat-kīrtiḥ*—reputation for pious activities; *sa-strībhiḥ*—along with their wives; *sura-gāyakaiḥ*—by celestial musicians; *prati-ūṣeṣu*—at every dawn; *anubaddhena*—being attached; *hṛdā*—with the heart; *śṛṇvan*—listening to; *hareḥ*—of Lord Hari; *kathāḥ*—the topics.

## TRANSLATION

**Emperor Svāyambhuva Manu enjoyed life with his wife and subjects and fulfilled his desires without being disturbed by unwanted principles contrary to the process of religion. Celestial musicians and their wives sang in chorus about the pure reputation of the Emperor, and early in the morning, every day, he used to listen to the pastimes of the Supreme Personality of Godhead with a loving heart.**

## PURPORT

Human society is actually meant for realization of perfection in Kṛṣṇa consciousness. There is no restriction against living with a wife and children, but life should be so conducted that one may not go against the principles of religion, economic development, regulated sense enjoyment and, ultimately, liberation from material existence. The Vedic principles are designed in such a way that the conditioned souls who have come to this material existence may be guided in fulfilling their material desires and at the same time be liberated and go back to Godhead, back home.

It is understood that Emperor Svāyambhuva Manu enjoyed his household life by following these principles. It is stated here that early in the morning there were musicians who used to sing with musical instruments about the glories of the Lord, and the Emperor, with his family, personally used to hear about the pastimes of the Supreme Person. This custom is still prevalent in India in some of the royal families and temples. Professional musicians sing with *śahnāīs*, and the sleeping members of the house gradually get up from their beds in a pleasing atmosphere. During bedtime also the singers sing songs in relationship with the pastimes of the Lord, with *śahnāī* accompaniment, and the householders gradually fall asleep remembering the glories of the Lord. In every house, in addition to the singing program, there is an arrangement for *Bhāgavatam* lectures in the evening; family members sit down, hold Hare Kṛṣṇa *kīrtana*, hear narrations from *Śrīmad-Bhāgavatam* and *Bhagavad-gītā* and enjoy music before going to bed. The atmosphere created by this *saṅkīrtana* movement lives in their hearts, and while sleeping they also dream of the singing and glorification of the Lord. In such a way, perfection of Kṛṣṇa consciousness can be attained. This practice is very old, as learned from this verse of *Śrīmad-Bhāgavatam;* millions of years ago, Svāyambhuva Manu used to avail himself of this opportunity to live householder life in the peace and prosperity of a Kṛṣṇa consciousness atmosphere.

As far as temples are concerned, in each and every royal palace or rich man's house, inevitably there is a nice temple, and the members of the household rise early in the morning and go to the temple to see the *maṅgalārātrika* ceremony. The *maṅgalārātrika* ceremony is the first worship of the morning. In the *ārātrika* ceremony a light is offered in circles before the Deities, as are a conchshell and flowers and a fan. The Lord is supposed to rise early in the morning and take some light refreshment and give audience to the devotees. The devotees then go back to the house or sing the glories of the Lord in the temple. The early morning ceremony still takes place in Indian temples and palaces. Temples are meant for the assembly of the general public. Temples within palaces are especially for the royal families, but in many of these palace temples the public is also allowed to visit. The temple of the King of Jaipur is situated within the palace, but the public is allowed to assemble; if one goes there, he will see that the temple is always crowded with at least five hundred devotees. After the *maṅgalārātrika* ceremony they sit down together and sing the glories of the Lord with musical instruments and thus enjoy life. Temple worship by the royal family is also mentioned in *Bhagavad-gītā*, where it is stated that those who fail to achieve success in the *bhakti-yoga* principles within one life are given a chance to take birth in the next life in a family of rich men or in a royal family or family of learned *brāhmaṇas* or devotees. If one gets the opportunity to take birth in these families, he can achieve the facilities of a Kṛṣṇa conscious atmosphere without difficulty. A child born in that Kṛṣṇa atmosphere is sure to develop Kṛṣṇa consciousness. The perfection which he failed to attain in his last life is again offered in this life, and he can make himself perfect without fail.

## TEXT 34

निष्णातं योगमायासु मुनिं स्वायम्भुवं मनुम् ।
यदाभ्रंशयितुं भोगा न शेकुर्भगवत्परम् ॥३४॥

*niṣṇātaṁ yogamāyāsu*
*muniṁ svāyambhuvaṁ manum*
*yad ābhraṁśayituṁ bhogā*
*na śekur bhagavat-param*

*niṣṇātam*—absorbed; *yoga-māyāsu*—in temporary enjoyment; *munim*—who was equal to a saint; *svāyambhuvam*—Svāyambhuva; *manum*—Manu; *yat*—from which; *ābhraṁśayitum*—to cause to deviate; *bhogāḥ*—material enjoyments; *na*—not; *śekuḥ*—were able; *bhagavat-param*—who was a great devotee of the Supreme Personality of Godhead.

## TRANSLATION

**Thus Svāyambhuva Manu was a saintly king. Although absorbed in material happiness, he was not dragged to the lowest grade of life, for he always enjoyed his material happiness in a Kṛṣṇa conscious atmosphere.**

## PURPORT

The kingly happiness of material enjoyment generally drags one to the lowest grade of life, namely degradation to animal life, because of unrestricted sense enjoyment. But Svāyambhuva Manu was considered as good as a saintly sage because the atmosphere created in his kingdom and home was completely Kṛṣṇa conscious. The case is similar with the conditioned souls in general; they have come into this material life for sense gratification, but if they are able to create a Kṛṣṇa conscious atmosphere, as depicted here or as prescribed in revealed scriptures, by temple worship and household Deity worship, then in spite of their material enjoyment they can make advancement in pure Kṛṣṇa consciousness without a doubt. At the present moment, modern civilization is too much attached to the material way of life, or sense gratification. Therefore, the Kṛṣṇa consciousness movement can give the people in general the best opportunity to utilize their human life in the midst of material enjoyment. Kṛṣṇa consciousness does not stop them in their propensity for material enjoyment, but simply regulates their habits in the life of sense enjoyment. In spite of their enjoying the material advantages, they can be liberated in this very life by practicing Kṛṣṇa consciousness by the simple method of chanting the holy names of the Lord—Hare Kṛṣṇa, Hare Kṛṣṇa, Kṛṣṇa Kṛṣṇa, Hare Hare/ Hare Rāma, Hare Rāma, Rāma Rāma, Hare Hare.

## TEXT 35

अयातयामास्तस्यासन् यामाः स्वान्तरयापनाः ।
शृण्वतो ध्यायतो विष्णोः कुर्वतो ब्रुवतः कथाः ॥३५॥

*ayāta-yāmās tasyāsan*
*yāmāḥ svāntara-yāpanāḥ*
*śṛṇvato dhyāyato viṣṇoḥ*
*kurvato bruvataḥ kathāḥ*

*ayāta-yāmāḥ*—time never lost; *tasya*—of Manu; *āsan*—were; *yāmāḥ*—the hours; *sva-antara*—his duration of life; *yāpanāḥ*—bringing to an end; *śṛṇvataḥ*—hearing; *dhyāyataḥ*—contemplating; *viṣṇoḥ*—of Lord Viṣṇu; *kurvataḥ*—acting; *bruvataḥ*—speaking; *kathāḥ*—the topics.

## TRANSLATION

**Consequently, although his duration of life gradually came to an end, his long life, consisting of a Manvantara era, was not spent in**

**vain, since he ever engaged in hearing, contemplating, writing down and chanting the pastimes of the Lord.**

## PURPORT

As freshly prepared food is very tasteful but if kept for three or four hours becomes stale and tasteless, so the existence of material enjoyment can endure as long as life is fresh, but at the fag end of life everything becomes tasteless, and everything appears to be vain and painful. The life of Emperor Svāyambhuva Manu, however, was not tasteless; as he grew older, his life remained as fresh as in the beginning because of his continued Kṛṣṇa consciousness. The life of a man in Kṛṣṇa consciousness is always fresh. It is said that the sun rises in the morning and sets in the evening and its business is to reduce the duration of everyone's life. But the sunrise and sunset cannot diminish the life of one who engages in Kṛṣṇa consciousness. Svāyambhuva Manu's life did not become stale after some time, for he engaged himself always in chanting about and meditating upon Lord Viṣṇu. He was the greatest *yogī* because he never wasted his time. It is especially mentioned here, *viṣṇoḥ kurvato bruvataḥ kathāḥ*. When he talked, he talked only of Kṛṣṇa and Viṣṇu, the Personality of Godhead; when he heard something, it was about Kṛṣṇa; when he meditated, it was upon Kṛṣṇa and His activities.

It is stated that his life was very long, seventy-one *yugas*. One *yuga* is completed in 4,320,000 years, seventy-one of such *yugas* is the duration of the life of a Manu, and fourteen such Manus come and go in one day of Brahmā. For the entire duration of his life—4,320,000 X 71 years—Manu engaged in Kṛṣṇa consciousness by chanting, hearing, talking about and meditating upon Kṛṣṇa. Therefore, his life was not wasted, nor did it become stale.

## TEXT 36

स एवं स्वान्तरं निन्ये युगानामेकसप्ततिम् ।
वासुदेवप्रसङ्गेन परिभूतगतित्रयः ॥३६॥

*sa evaṁ svāntaraṁ ninye*
*yugānām eka-saptatim*

*vāsudeva-prasaṅgena*
*paribhūta-gati-trayaḥ*

*saḥ*—he (Svāyambhuva Manu); *evam*—thus; *sva-antaram*—his own period; *ninye*—passed; *yugānām*—of the cycles of four ages; *eka-saptatim*—seventy-one; *vāsudeva*—with Vāsudeva; *prasaṅgena*—by topics connected; *paribhūta*—transcended; *gati-trayaḥ*—the three destinations.

## TRANSLATION

**He passed his time, which lasted seventy-one cycles of the four ages [71 X 4,320,000 years], always thinking of Vāsudeva and always engaged in matters regarding Vāsudeva. Thus he transcended the three destinations.**

## PURPORT

The three destinations are meant for persons who are under the control of the three modes of material nature. These destinations are sometimes described as the awakened, dreaming and unconscious stages. In *Bhagavad-gītā* the three destinations are described as the destinations of persons in the modes of goodness, passion and ignorance. It is stated in the *Gītā* that those who are in the mode of goodness are promoted to better living conditions in higher planets, and those who are in the mode of passion remain within this material world on the earth or on heavenly planets, but those who are in the mode of ignorance are degraded to an animal life on planets where life is lower than human. But one who is Kṛṣṇa conscious is above these three modes of material nature. It is stated in *Bhagavad-gītā* that anyone who engages in devotional service to the Lord automatically becomes transcendental to the three destinations of material nature and is situated in the *brahma-bhūta*, or self-realized, stage. Although Svāyambhuva Manu, the ruler of this material world, appeared to be absorbed in material happiness, he was neither in the mode of goodness nor in the modes of passion or ignorance, but in the transcendental stage.

Therefore, one who fully engages in devotional service is always liberated. Bilvamaṅgala Ṭhākura, a great devotee of the Lord, stated: "If I have unflinching devotion to the lotus feet of Kṛṣṇa, then Mother Liberation is always engaged in my service. The complete perfection of material enjoyment, religion and economic development is at my command." People are after *dharma, artha, kāma* and *mokṣa.* Generally they perform religious activities to achieve some material gain, and they engage in material activity for sense gratification. After being frustrated in material sense gratification, one wants to be liberated and become one with the Absolute Truth. These four principles form the transcendental path for the less intelligent. Those who are actually intelligent engage in Kṛṣṇa consciousness, not caring for these four principles of the transcendental method. They at once elevate themselves to the transcendental platform which is above liberation. Liberation is not a very great achievement for a devotee, to say nothing of the results of ritualistic performances in religion, economic development or the materialistic life of sense gratification. Devotees do not care for these. They are situated always on the transcendental platform of the *brahma-bhūta* stage of self-realization.

## TEXT 37

शारीरा मानसा दिव्या वैयासे ये च मानुषाः ।
भौतिकाश्च कथं क्लेशा बाधन्ते हरिसंश्रयम् ॥३७॥

*śārīrā mānasā divyā*
*vaiyāse ye ca mānuṣāḥ*
*bhautikāś ca kathaṁ kleśā*
*bādhante hari-saṁśrayam*

*śārīrāḥ*—pertaining to the body; *mānasāḥ*—pertaining to the mind; *divyāḥ*—pertaining to supernatural powers (demigods); *vaiyāse*—O Vidura; *ye*—those; *ca*—and; *mānuṣāḥ*—pertaining to other men; *bhautikāḥ*—pertaining to other living beings; *ca*—and; *katham*—how; *kleśāḥ*—miseries; *bādhante*—can trouble; *hari-saṁśrayam*—one who has taken shelter of Lord Kṛṣṇa.

## TRANSLATION

**Therefore, O Vidura, how can persons completely under the shelter of Lord Kṛṣṇa in devotional service be put into miseries**

**pertaining to the body, the mind, nature, and other men and living creatures?**

## PURPORT

Every living entity within this material world is always afflicted by some kind of miseries, pertaining either to the body, the mind or natural disturbances. Distresses due to cold in winter and severe heat in summer always inflict miseries on the living entities in this material world, but one who has completely taken shelter of the lotus feet of the Lord in Kṛṣṇa consciousness is in the transcendental stage; he is not disturbed by any miseries, either due to the body, the mind, or natural disturbances of summer and winter. He is transcendental to all these miseries.

## TEXT 38

यः पृष्टो मुनिभिः प्राह धर्मान्नानाविधाञ्छुभान् ।
नृणां वर्णाश्रमाणां च सर्वभूतहितः सदा ॥३८॥

*yaḥ pṛṣṭo munibhiḥ prāha*
*dharmān nānā-vidāñ chubhān*
*nṛṇāṁ varṇāśramāṇāṁ ca*
*sarva-bhūta-hitaḥ sadā*

*yaḥ*—who; *pṛṣṭaḥ*—being questioned; *munibhiḥ*—by the sages; *prāha*—spoke; *dharmān*—the duties; *nānā-vidhān*—many varieties; *śubhān*—auspicious; *nṛṇām*—of human society; *varṇa-āśramāṇām*—of the *varṇas* and *āśramas; ca*—and; *sarva-bhūta*—for all living beings; *hitaḥ*—who does welfare; *sadā*—always.

## TRANSLATION

**In reply to questions asked by certain sages, he [Svāyambhuva Manu], out of compassion for all living entities, taught the diverse sacred duties of men in general and the different varṇas and āśramas.**

## TEXT 39

एतत्त आदिराजस्य मनोश्चरितमद्भुतम् ।
वर्णितं वर्णनीयस्य तदपत्योदयं शृणु ॥३९॥

*etat ta ādi-rājasya*
*manoś caritam adbhutam*
*varṇitaṁ varṇanīyasya*
*tad-apatyodayaṁ śṛṇu*

*etat*—this; *te*—unto you; *ādi-rājasya*—of the first emperor; *manoḥ*—of Svāyambhuva Manu; *caritam*—the character; *adbhutam*—wonderful; *varṇitam*—described; *varṇanīyasya*—whose reputation is worthy of description; *tat-apatya*—of his daughter; *udayam*—to the flourishing; *śṛṇu*—please listen.

## TRANSLATION

**I have spoken to you of the wonderful character of Svāyambhuva Manu, the original king, whose reputation is worthy of description. Please hear as I speak of the flourishing of his daughter Devahūti.**

*Thus end the Bhaktivedanta purports of the Third Canto, Twenty-second Chapter, of the* Śrīmad-Bhāgavatam, *entitled "The Marriage of Kardama Muni and Devahūti."*

## CHAPTER TWENTY-THREE

# Devahūti's Lamentation

### TEXT 1

मैत्रेय उवाच
पितृभ्यां प्रस्थिते साध्वी पतिमिङ्गितकोविदा ।
नित्यं पर्यचरत्प्रीत्या भवानीव भवं प्रभुम् ॥ १ ॥

*maitreya uvāca*
*pitṛbhyāṁ prasthite sādhvī*
*patim iṅgita-kovidā*
*nityaṁ paryacarat prītyā*
*bhavānīva bhavaṁ prabhum*

*maitreyaḥ uvāca*—Maitreya said; *pitṛbhyām*—by the parents; *prasthite*—at the departure; *sādhvī*—the chaste woman; *patim*—her husband; *iṅgita-kovidā*—understanding the desires; *nityam*—constantly; *paryacarat*—she served; *prītyā*—with great love; *bhavānī*—the goddess Pārvatī; *iva*—like; *bhavam*—Lord Śiva; *prabhum*—her lord.

### TRANSLATION

**Maitreya continued: After the departure of her parents, the chaste woman Devahūti, who could understand the desires of her husband, served him constantly with great love, as Bhavānī, the wife of Lord Śiva, serves her husband.**

### PURPORT

The specific example of Bhavānī is very significant. *Bhavānī* means the wife of Bhava, or Lord Śiva. Bhavānī, or Pārvatī, the daughter of the King of the Himalayas, selected Lord Śiva, who appears to be just like a beggar, as her husband. In spite of her being a princess, she undertook all kinds of tribulations to associate with Lord Śiva, who did not even have a house, but was sitting underneath the trees and passing his time in meditation. Although Bhavānī was the daughter of a very great king, she used to serve Lord Śiva just like a poor woman. Similarly, Devahūti was the daughter of an emperor, Svāyambhuva Manu, yet she preferred to accept Kardama Muni as her husband. She served him with great love and affection, and she knew how to please him. Therefore, she is designated here as *sādhvī*, which means "a chaste, faithful wife." Her rare example is the ideal of Vedic civilization. Every woman is expected to be as good and chaste as Devahūti or Bhavānī. Today in Hindu society, unmarried girls are still taught to worship Lord Śiva with the idea that they may get husbands like him. Lord Śiva is the ideal husband, not in the sense of riches or sense gratification, but because he is the greatest of all devotees. *Vaiṣṇavānāṁ yathā śambhuḥ:* Śambhu, or Lord Śiva, is the ideal Vaiṣṇava. He constantly meditates upon Lord Rāma and chants Hare Rāma, Hare Rāma, Rāma Rāma, Hare Hare. Lord Śiva has a Vaiṣṇava *sampradāya*, which is called the Viṣṇusvāmi-sampradāya. Unmarried girls worship Lord Śiva so that they can expect a husband who is as good a Vaiṣṇava as he. The girls are not taught to select a husband who is very rich or very opulent for material sense gratification; rather, if a girl is fortunate enough to get a husband as good as Lord Śiva in devotional service, then her life becomes perfect. The wife is dependent on the husband, and if the husband is a Vaiṣṇava, then naturally she shares the devotional service of the husband because she renders him service. This reciprocation of service and love between husband and wife is the ideal of a householder's life.

## TEXT 2

**विश्रम्भेणात्मशौचेन गौरवेण दमेन च ।**
**शुश्रूषया सौहृदेन वाचा मधुरया च भोः ॥ २ ॥**

*viśrambheṇātma-śaucena*
*gauraveṇa damena ca*
*śuśrūṣayā sauhṛdena*
*vācā madhurayā ca bhoḥ*

*viśrambheṇa*—with intimacy; *ātma-śaucena*—with purity of mind and body; *gauraveṇa*—with great respect; *damena*—with control of the senses; *ca*—and; *śuśrūṣayā*—with service; *sauhṛdena*—with love; *vācā*—with words; *madhurayā*—sweet; *ca*—and; *bhoḥ*—O Vidura.

## TRANSLATION

**O Vidura, Devahūti served her husband with intimacy and great respect, with control of the senses, with love and with sweet words.**

## PURPORT

Here two words are very significant. Devahūti served her husband in two ways, *viśrambheṇa* and *gauraveṇa.* These are two important processes in serving the husband or the Supreme Personality of Godhead. *Viśrambheṇa* means "with intimacy," and *gauraveṇa* means "with great reverence." The husband is a very intimate friend; therefore, the wife must render service just like an intimate friend, and at the same time she must understand that the husband is superior in position, and thus she must offer him all respect. A man's psychology and woman's psychology are different. As constituted by bodily frame, a man always wants to be superior to his wife, and a woman, as bodily constituted, is naturally inferior to her husband. Thus the natural instinct is that the husband wants to post himself as superior to the wife, and this must be observed. Even if there is some wrong on the part of the husband, the wife must tolerate it, and thus there will be no misunderstanding between husband and wife. *Viśrambheṇa* means "with intimacy," but it must not be familiarity that breeds contempt. According to the Vedic civilization, a wife cannot call her husband by name. In the present civilization the wife calls her husband by name, but in Hindu civilization she does not. Thus the inferiority and superiority complexes are recognized. *Damena ca:* a wife has to learn to control herself even if there is a misunderstanding. *Sauhṛdena vācā madhurayā* means always desiring good for the husband and speaking to him with sweet words. A person becomes agitated by so many material contacts in the outside world; therefore, in his home life he must be treated by his wife with sweet words.

## TEXT 3

विसृज्य कामं दम्भं च द्वेषं लोभमघं मदम् ।
अप्रमत्तोद्यता नित्यं तेजीयांसमतोषयत् ॥ ३ ॥

*visṛjya kāmaṁ dambhaṁ ca*
*dveṣaṁ lobham aghaṁ madam*
*apramattodyatā nityaṁ*
*tejīyāṁsam atoṣayat*

*visṛjya*—giving up; *kāmam*—lust; *dambham*—pride; *ca*—and; *dveṣam*—envy; *lobham*—greed; *agham*—sinful activities; *madam*—vanity; *apramattā*—sane; *udyatā*—laboring diligently; *nityam*—always; *tejīyāṁsam*—her very powerful husband; *atoṣayat*—she pleased.

## TRANSLATION

**Working sanely and diligently, she pleased her very powerful husband, giving up all lust, pride, envy, greed, sinful activities and vanity.**

## PURPORT

Here are some of the qualities of a great husband's great wife. Kardama Muni is great by spiritual qualification. Such a husband is called *tejīyāṁsam*, most powerful. Although a wife may be equal to her husband in advancement in spiritual consciousness, she should not be vainly proud. Sometimes it happens that the wife comes from a very rich family, as did Devahūti, the daughter of Emperor Svāyambhuva Manu. She could have been very proud of her parentage, but that is forbidden. The wife should not be proud of her parental position. She must always be submissive to the husband and must give up all vanity. As soon as the wife becomes proud of her parentage, her pride creates great misunderstanding between the husband and wife, and their nuptial life is ruined. Devahūti was very careful about that, and therefore it is said here that she gave up pride completely. Devahūti was not unfaithful. The most sinful activity for a wife is to accept another husband or another lover. Cāṇakya Paṇḍita has described four kinds of enemies at home. If the father is in debt he is considered to be an enemy; if the mother has selected another husband in the presence of her grown-up children, she is considered to be an enemy; if a wife does not live well with her husband but deals very roughly, then she is an enemy; and if a son is a fool, he is also an enemy. In family life, father, mother, wife and children are assets, but if the wife or mother accepts another husband in the presence of her husband or son, then, according to Vedic civilization, she is considered an enemy. A chaste and faithful woman must not practice adultery—that is a greatly sinful act.

## TEXTS 4–5

स वै देवर्षिवर्यस्तां मानवीं समनुव्रताम् ।
दैवाद्गरीयसः पत्युराशासानां महाशिषः ॥ ४ ॥
कालेन भूयसा क्षामां कर्शितां व्रतचर्यया ।
प्रेमगद्गदया वाचा पीडितः कृपयाब्रवीत् ॥ ५ ॥

*sa vai devarṣi-varyas tāṁ*
*mānavīṁ samanuvratām*
*daivād garīyasaḥ patyur*
*āśāsānāṁ mahāśiṣaḥ*

*kālena bhūyasā kṣāmāṁ*
*karśitāṁ vrata-caryayā*
*prema-gadgadayā vācā*
*pīḍitaḥ kṛpayābravīt*

*saḥ*—he (Kardama); *vai*—certainly; *deva-ṛṣi*—of the celestial sages; *varyaḥ*—the foremost; *tām*—her; *mānavīm*—the daughter of Manu; *samanuvratām*—fully devoted; *daivāt*—than providence; *garīyasaḥ*—who was greater; *patyuḥ*—from her husband; *āśāsānām*—expecting; *mahā-āśiṣaḥ*—great blessings; *kālena bhūyasā*—for a long time; *kṣāmām*—weak; *karśitām*—emaciated; *vrata-caryayā*—by religious observances; *prema*—with love; *gadgadayā*—stammering; *vācā*—with a voice; *pīḍitaḥ*—overcome; *kṛpayā*—with compassion; *abravīt*—he said.

## TRANSLATION

**The daughter of Manu, who was fully devoted to her husband, looked upon him as greater even than providence. Thus she expected great blessings from him. Having served him for a long**

**time, she grew weak and emaciated due to her religious observances. Seeing her condition, Kardama, the foremost of celestial sages, was overcome with compassion and spoke to her in a voice choked with great love.**

## PURPORT

The wife is expected to be of the same category as the husband. She must be prepared to follow the principles of the husband, and then there will be happy life. If the husband is a devotee and the wife is materialistic, there cannot be any peace in the home. The wife must see the tendencies of the husband and must be prepared to follow him. From *Mahābhārata* we learn that when Gāndhārī understood that her would-be husband, Dhṛtarāṣṭra, was blind, she immediately began to practice blindness herself. Thus she covered her eyes and played the part of a blind woman. She decided that since her husband was blind, she must also act like a blind woman, otherwise she would be proud of her eyes, and her husband would be seen as inferior. The word *samanuvrata* indicates that it is the duty of a wife to adopt the special circumstances in which the husband is situated. Of course, if the husband is as great as Kardama Muni, then a very good result accrues from following him. But even if the husband is not a great devotee like Kardama Muni, it is the wife's duty to adapt herself according to his mentality. That makes married life very happy. It is also mentioned herein that by following the strict vows of a chaste woman, Princess Devahūti became very skinny, and therefore her husband became compassionate. He knew that she was the daughter of a great king and yet was serving him just like an ordinary woman. She was reduced in health by such activities, and he became compassionate and addressed her as follows.

## TEXT 6

कर्दम उवाच

तुष्टोऽहमद्य तव मानवि मानदायाः
शुश्रूषया परमया परया च भक्त्या ।
यो देहिनामयमतीव सुहृत्स देहो
नावेक्षितः समुचितः क्षपितुं मदर्थे ॥ ६ ॥

*kardama uvāca*
*tuṣṭo 'ham adya tava mānavi mānadāyāḥ*
*śuśrūṣayā paramayā parayā ca bhaktyā*
*yo dehinām ayam atīva suhṛt sa deho*
*nāvekṣitaḥ samucitaḥ kṣapituṁ mad-arthe*

*kardamaḥ uvāca*—the great sage Kardama said; *tuṣṭaḥ*—pleased; *aham*—I am; *adya*—today; *tava*—with you; *mānavi*—O daughter of Manu; *māna-dāyāḥ*—who are respectful; *śuśrūṣayā*—by the service; *paramayā*—most excellent; *parayā*—highest; *ca*—and; *bhaktyā*—by the devotion; *yaḥ*—that which; *dehinām*—to the embodied; *ayam*—this; *atīva*—extremely; *suhṛt*—dear; *saḥ*—that; *dehaḥ*—body; *na*—not; *avekṣitaḥ*—taken care of; *samucitaḥ*—properly; *kṣapitum*—to expend; *mat-arthe*—on my account.

## TRANSLATION

**Kardama Muni said: O respectful daughter of Svāyambhuva Manu, today I am very much pleased with you for your great devotion and most excellent loving service. Since the body is so dear to embodied beings, I am astonished that you have neglected your own body to use it on my behalf.**

## PURPORT

It is indicated here that one's body is very dear, yet Devahūti was so faithful to her husband that not only did she serve him with great devotion, service and respect, but she did not even care for her own health. That is called selfless service. It appears that Devahūti had no sense pleasure, even with her husband, otherwise she would not have deteriorated in health. Acting to facilitate Kardama Muni's engagement in spiritual elevation, she continually assisted him, not caring for bodily comfort. It is the duty of a faithful and chaste wife to help her husband in every respect, especially when the husband is engaged in Kṛṣṇa consciousness. In this case, the husband also amply rewarded the wife. This is not to be expected by a woman who is the wife of an ordinary person.

## TEXT 7

ये मे स्वधर्मनिरतस्य तपःसमाधि-
विद्यात्मयोगविजिता भगवत्प्रसादाः ।
तानेव ते मदनुसेवनयावरुद्धान्
दृष्टिं प्रपश्य वितराम्यभयानशोकान् ॥ ७ ॥

*ye me sva-dharma-niratasya tapaḥ-samādhi-*
*vidyātma-yoga-vijitā bhagavat-prasādāḥ*
*tān eva te mad-anusevanayāvaruddhān*
*dṛṣṭiṁ prapaśya vitarāmy abhayān aśokān*

*ye*—those which; *me*—by me; *sva-dharma*—own religious life; *niratasya*—fully occupied with; *tapaḥ*—in austerity; *samādhi*—in meditation; *vidyā*—in Kṛṣṇa consciousness; *ātma-yoga*—by fixing the mind; *vijitāḥ*—achieved; *bhagavat-prasādāḥ*—the blessings of the Lord; *tān*—them; *eva*—even; *te*—by you; *mat*—to me; *anusevanayā*—by devoted service; *avaruddhān*—obtained; *dṛṣṭim*—transcendental vision; *prapaśya*—just see; *vitarāmi*—I am giving; *abhayān*—which are free from fear; *aśokān*—which are free from lamentation.

## TRANSLATION

**Kardama Muni continued: I have achieved the blessings of the Lord in discharging my own religious life of austerity, meditation and Kṛṣṇa consciousness. Although you have not yet experienced these achievements, which are free from fear and lamentation, I shall offer them all to you because you are engaged in my service. Now just look at them. I am giving you the transcendental vision to see how nice they are.**

## PURPORT

Devahūti engaged only in the service of Kardama Muni. She was not supposed to be so advanced in austerity, ecstasy, meditation or Kṛṣṇa consciousness, but, imperceptibly, she was sharing her husband's achievements, which she could neither see nor experience. Automatically she achieved these graces of the Lord.

What are the graces of the Lord? It is stated here that the graces of the Lord are *abhaya*, free from fearfulness. In the material world, if someone accumulates a million dollars, he is always full of fear because he is always thinking, "What if the money is lost?" But the benediction of the Lord, *bhagavat-prasāda*, is never to be lost. It is simply to be enjoyed. There is no question of loss. One simply gains and enjoys gaining. *Bhagavad-gītā* also confirms this: when one achieves the grace of the Lord, the result is that *sarva-duḥkhāni*, all distresses, are destroyed. When situated in the transcendental position, one is freed from the two kinds of material diseases—hankering and lamentation. This is also stated in *Bhagavad-gītā*. After devotional life begins, we can achieve the full result of love of Godhead. Love of Kṛṣṇa is the highest perfection of *bhagavat-prasāda*, or divine mercy. This transcendental achievement is so greatly valuable that no material happiness can compare to it. Prabodhānanda Sarasvatī said that if one achieves the grace of Lord Caitanya he becomes so great that he does not care a fig even for the demigods, he thinks of monism as hellish, and for him the perfection of controlling the senses is as easy as anything. Heavenly pleasures become to him no more than stories. Actually, there is no comparison between material happiness and transcendental happiness.

By the grace of Kardama Muni, Devahūti experienced actual realization simply by serving. We get a similar example in the life of Nārada Muni. In his previous life, Nārada was a maidservant's son, but his mother was engaged in the service of great devotees. He got the opportunity to serve the devotees, and simply by eating the remnants of their foodstuff and carrying out their orders he became so elevated that in his next life he became the great personality Nārada. For spiritual achievement the easiest path is to take shelter of a bona fide spiritual master and to serve him with heart and soul. That is the secret of success. As stated by Viśvanātha Cakravartī Ṭhākura in his eight stanzas of prayer to the spiritual master, *yasya prasādād bhagavat-prasādaḥ:* by serving or receiving the grace of the spiritual master, one receives the grace of the Supreme Lord. By serving her devotee husband, Kardama Muni, Devahūti shared in his achievements. Similarly, a sincere disciple, simply by serving a bona fide spiritual master, can achieve all the mercy of the Lord and the spiritual master simultaneously.

## TEXT 8

अन्ये पुनर्भगवतो भ्रुव उद्विजृम्भ-
विभ्रंशितार्थरचनाः किमुरुक्रमस्य ।
सिद्धासि भुङ्क्ष्व विभवान्निजधर्मदोहान्
दिव्यान्नरैर्दुरधिगान्नृपविक्रियाभिः ॥ ८ ॥

*anye punar bhagavato bhruva udvijṛmbha-*
*vibhraṁśitārtha-racanāḥ kim urukramasya*
*siddhāsi bhuṅkṣva vibhavān nija-dharma-dohān*
*divyān narair duradhigān nṛpa-vikriyābhiḥ*

*anye*—others; *punaḥ*—again; *bhagavataḥ*—of the Lord; *bhruvaḥ*—of the eyebrows; *udvijṛmbha*—by the movement; *vibhraṁśita*—annihilated; *artha-racanāḥ*—material achievements; *kim*—what use; *urukramasya*—of Lord Viṣṇu (far-stepping); *siddhā*—successful; *asi*—you are; *bhuṅkṣva*—enjoy; *vibhavān*—the gifts; *nija-dharma*—by your own principles of devotion; *dohān*—gained; *divyān*—transcendental; *naraiḥ*—by persons; *duradhigān*—difficult to obtain; *nṛpa-vikriyābhiḥ*—proud of aristocracy.

## TRANSLATION

**Kardama Muni continued: What is the use of enjoyments other than the Lord's grace? All material achievements are subject to be annihilated simply by a movement of the eyebrows of Lord Viṣṇu, the Supreme Personality of Godhead. By your principles of devotion to your husband, you have achieved and can enjoy transcendental gifts very rarely obtained by persons proud of aristocracy and material possessions.**

## PURPORT

Lord Caitanya recommended that the greatest achievement of human life is to achieve the grace of the Lord, love of God. He said, *premā pumartho mahān:* to achieve love of Godhead is the highest perfection of life. The same perfection is recommended by Kardama Muni to his wife. His wife belonged to a very aristocratic royal family. Generally, those who are very materialistic or who possess material wealth and prosperity are unable to appreciate the value of transcendental love of God. Although Devahūti was a princess coming from a very great royal family, fortunately she was under the supervision of her great husband, Kardama Muni, who offered her the best gift which can be bestowed in human life—the grace of the Lord, or love of God. This grace of the Lord was achieved by Devahūti by the good will and satisfaction of her husband. She served her husband, who was a great devotee and saintly person, with great sincerity, love, affection and service, and Kardama Muni was satisfied. He willingly gave love of God, and he recommended that she accept it and enjoy it because he had already achieved it.

Love of God is not an ordinary commodity. Caitanya Mahāprabhu was worshiped by Rūpa Gosvāmī because He distributed love of God, *kṛṣṇa-premā*, to everyone. Rūpa Gosvāmī praised Him as *mahā-vadānya*, a greatly munificent personality, because He was freely distributing to everyone love of Godhead, which is achieved by wise men only after many, many births. *Kṛṣṇa-premā*, Kṛṣṇa consciousness, is the highest gift which can be bestowed on anyone whom we presume to love.

One word used in this verse, *nija-dharma-dohān*, is very significant. Devahūti, as the wife of Kardama Muni, achieved an invaluable gift from her husband because she was very faithful to him. For a woman the first principle of religion is to be faithful to her husband. If, fortunately, the husband is a great personality, then the combination is perfect, and the lives of both the wife and the husband are at once fulfilled.

## TEXT 9

एवं ब्रुवाणमबलाखिलयोगमाया-
विद्याविचक्षणमवेक्ष्य गताधिरासीत् ।
सम्प्रश्रयप्रणयविह्वलया गिरेषद्-
व्रीडावलोकविलसद्धसिताननाह ॥ ९ ॥

*evaṁ bruvāṇam abalākhila-yogamāyā-*
*vidyā-vicakṣaṇam avekṣya gatādhir āsīt*
*sampraśraya-praṇaya-vihvalayā gireṣad-*
*vrīḍāvaloka-vilasad-dhasitānanāha*

*evam*—thus; *bruvāṇam*—speaking; *abalā*—the woman; *akhila*—all; *yoga-māyā*—of transcendental science; *vidyā-vicakṣaṇam*—excelling in knowledge; *avekṣya*—after hearing; *gata-ādhiḥ*—satisfied; *āsīt*—she became; *sampraśraya*—with humility; *praṇaya*—and with love; *vihvalayā*—choked up; *girā*—with a voice; *īṣat*—slightly; *vrīḍā*—bashful; *avaloka*—with a glance; *vilasat*—shining; *hasita*—smiling; *ānanā*—her face; *āha*—she spoke.

## TRANSLATION

**Upon hearing the speaking of her husband, who excelled in knowledge of all kinds of transcendental science, innocent Devahūti was very satisfied. Her smiling face shining with a slightly bashful glance, she spoke in a choked voice because of great humility and love.**

## PURPORT

It is said that if one is already engaged in Kṛṣṇa consciousness and is rendering transcendental loving service to the Lord, then it can be supposed that he has finished all the recommended courses of austerity, penance, religion, sacrifice, mystic *yoga* and meditation. Devahūti's husband was so expert in the transcendental science that there was nothing for him to argue about, and when she heard him speak she was confident that since he was very much advanced in devotional service he had already surpassed all transcendental educational activities. She had no doubt about the gifts offered by her husband; she knew that he was expert in offering such gifts, and when she understood that he was offering the greatest gift, she was very satisfied. She was overwhelmed with ecstatic love, and therefore she could not reply; then, with faltering language, just like an attractive wife, she spoke the following words.

## TEXT 10

देवहूतिरुवाच

राद्धं बत द्विजवृषैतदमोघयोग-

मायाधिपे त्वयि विभो तदवैमि भर्तः ।

यस्तेऽभ्यधायि समयः सकृदङ्गसङ्गो
भूयाद्गरीयसि गुणः प्रसवः सतीनाम् ॥१०॥

*devahūtir uvāca*
*rāddhaṁ bata dvija-vṛṣaitad amogha-yoga-*
*māyādhipe tvayi vibho tad avaimi bhartaḥ*
*yas te 'bhyadhāyi samayaḥ sakṛd aṅga-saṅgo*
*bhūyād garīyasi guṇaḥ prasavaḥ satīnām*

*devahūtiḥ uvāca*—Devahūti said; *rāddham*—it has been achieved; *bata*—indeed; *dvija-vṛṣa*—O best of the *brāhmaṇas; etat*—this; *amogha*—infallible; *yoga-māyā*—of mystic powers; *adhipe*—the master; *tvayi*—in you; *vibho*—O great one; *tat*—that; *avaimi*—I know; *bhartaḥ*—O husband; *yaḥ*—that which; *te*—by you; *abhyadhāyi*—was given; *samayaḥ*—promise; *sakṛt*—once; *aṅga-saṅgaḥ*—bodily union; *bhūyāt*—may be; *garīyasi*—when very glorious; *guṇaḥ*—a great quality; *prasavaḥ*—progeny; *satīnām*—of chaste women.

## TRANSLATION

**Śrī Devahūti said: My dear husband, O best of brāhmaṇas, I know that you have achieved perfection and are the master of all the infallible mystic powers because you are under the protection of yogamāyā, the transcendental nature. But you once made a promise that our bodily union should now fulfill, since children are a great quality for a chaste woman who has a glorious husband.**

## PURPORT

Devahūti expressed her happiness by uttering the word *bata,* for she knew that her husband was in a highly elevated, transcendental position and was under the shelter of *yogamāyā.* As stated in *Bhagavad-gītā,* those who are great souls, *mahātmās,* are not under the control of the material energy. The Supreme Lord has two energies, material and spiritual. The living entities are marginal energy. As marginal energy, a person may be under the control of the material energy or the spiritual energy (*yogamāyā*). Kardama Muni was a great soul, and therefore he was under the spiritual energy, which means that he was directly connected with the Supreme Lord. The symptom of this is Kṛṣṇa consciousness, constant engagement in devotional service. This was known to Devahūti, yet she was anxious to have a son by bodily union with the sage. She reminded her husband of his promise to her parents: "I will remain only until the time of Devahūti's pregnancy." She reminded him that for a chaste woman to have a child by a great personality is most glorious. She wanted to be pregnant, and she prayed for that. The word *strī* means "expansion." By bodily union of the husband and wife their qualities are expanded: children born of good parents are expansions of the parents' personal qualifications. Both Kardama Muni and Devahūti were spiritually enlightened; therefore she desired from the beginning that first she be pregnant and then she be empowered with the achievement of God's grace and love of God. For a woman it is a great ambition to have a son of the same quality as a highly qualified husband. Since she had the opportunity to have Kardama Muni as her husband, she also desired to have a child by bodily union.

## TEXT 11

तत्रेतिकृत्यमुपशिक्ष यथोपदेशं
येनैष मे कर्शितोऽतिरिरंसयात्मा ।
सिद्ध्येत ते कृतमनोभवधर्षिताया
दीनस्तदीश भवनं सदृशं विचक्ष्व ॥११॥

*tatreti-kṛtyam upaśikṣa yathopadeśaṁ*
*yenaiṣa me karśito 'tiriraṁsayātmā*
*siddhyeta te kṛta-manobhava-dharṣitāyā*
*dīnas tad īśa bhavanaṁ sadṛśaṁ vicakṣva*

*tatra*—in that; *iti-kṛtyam*—what is necessary to be done; *upaśikṣa*—perform; *yathā*—according to; *upadeśam*—instruction in scripture; *yena*—by which; *eṣaḥ*—this; *me*—my; *karśitaḥ*—emaciated; *atiriraṁsayā*—due to intense passion not being satisfied; *ātmā*—body; *siddhyeta*—it may be rendered fit; *te*—for you; *kṛta*—excited; *manaḥ-bhava*—by emotion; *dharṣitāyāḥ*—who am struck; *dīnaḥ*—poor; *tat*—

therefore; *īśa*—O my dear lord; *bhavanam*—house; *sadṛśam*—suitable; *vicakṣva*—please think of.

## TRANSLATION

**Devahūti continued: My dear lord, I am struck by excited emotion for you. Therefore kindly make what arrangements must be made according to the scriptures so that my skinny body, emaciated through unsatisfied passion, may be rendered fit for you. Also, my lord, please think of a suitable house for this purpose.**

## PURPORT

The Vedic literatures are not only full of spiritual instruction but are also instructive in how to prosecute material existence very nicely, with the ultimate aim of spiritual perfection. Devahūti asked her husband, therefore, how to prepare herself for sex life according to the Vedic instructions. Sex life is especially meant for having good children. The circumstances for creating good children are mentioned in *kāma-śāstra*, the scripture in which suitable arrangements are prescribed for factually glorious sex life. Everything needed is mentioned in the scriptures—what sort of house and decorations there should be, what sort of dress the wife should have, how she should be decorated with ointments, scents and other attractive features, etc. With these requisites fulfilled, the husband will be attracted by her beauty, and a favorable mental situation will be created. The mental situation at the time of sex life may then be transferred into the womb of the wife, and good children can come out of that pregnancy. Here is a special reference to Devahūti's bodily features. Because she had become skinny, she feared that her body might have no attraction for Kardama. She wanted to be instructed how to improve her bodily condition in order to attract her husband. Sexual intercourse in which the husband is attracted to the wife is sure to produce a male child, but sexual intercourse based on attraction of the wife for the husband may produce a girl. That is mentioned in the *Āyur-veda*. When the passion of the woman is greater, there is a chance of a girl's being born. When the passion of the man is greater, then there is the possibility of a son. Devahūti wanted the passion of her husband to be increased by the arrangement mentioned in the *kāma-śāstra*. She wanted him to instruct her in that way, and she also requested that he arrange for a suitable house because the hermitage in which Kardama Muni was living was very simple and completely in the mode of goodness, and there was less possibility of passion's being aroused in his heart.

## TEXT 12

मैत्रेय उवाच
प्रियायाः प्रियमन्विच्छन् कर्दमो योगमास्थितः ।
विमानं कामगं क्षत्तस्तर्ह्येवाविरचीकरत् ॥१२॥

*maitreya uvāca*
*priyāyāḥ priyam anvicchan*
*kardamo yogam āsthitaḥ*
*vimānaṁ kāma-gaṁ kṣattas*
*tarhy evāviracīkarat*

*maitreyaḥ*—the great sage Maitreya; *uvāca*—said; *priyāyāḥ*—of his beloved wife; *priyam*—the pleasure; *anvicchan*—seeking; *kardamaḥ*—the sage Kardama; *yogam*—yogic power; *āsthitaḥ*—exercised; *vimānam*—an airplane; *kāma-gam*—moving at will; *kṣattaḥ*—O Vidura; *tarhi*—instantly; *eva*—quite; *āviracīkarat*—he produced.

## TRANSLATION

**Maitreya continued: O Vidura, seeking to please his beloved wife, the sage Kardama exercised his yogic power and instantly produced an aerial mansion that could travel at his will.**

## PURPORT

Here the words *yogam āsthitaḥ* are significant. The sage Kardama was completely perfect in *yoga.* As the result of real *yoga* practice there are eight kinds of perfection: the *yogī* can become smaller than the smallest, greater than the greatest or lighter than the lightest, he can achieve anything he likes, he can create even a planet, he can establish influence over anyone, etc. In this way yogic perfection is achieved, and after this one can achieve the perfection of spiritual life. Thus it was not very wonderful for Kardama Muni to create a mansion in the air, according to his own desire, to fulfill the desire of his beloved wife. He at once created the palace, which is described in the following verses.

## TEXT 13

सर्वकामदुघं दिव्यं सर्वरत्नसमन्वितम् ।
सर्वर्द्ध्युपचयोदर्कं मणिस्तम्भैरुपस्कृतम् ॥१३॥

*sarva-kāma-dughaṁ divyaṁ*
*sarva-ratna-samanvitam*
*sarvarddhy-upacayodarkaṁ*
*maṇi-stambhair upaskṛtam*

*sarva*—all; *kāma*—desires; *dugham*—yielding; *divyam*—wonderful; *sarva-ratna*—all sorts of jewels; *samanvitam*—bedecked with; *sarva*—all; *ṛddhi*—of wealth; *upacaya*—increase; *udarkam*—gradual; *maṇi*—of precious stones; *stambhaiḥ*—with pillars; *upaskṛtam*—adorned.

## TRANSLATION

**It was a wonderful structure, bedecked with all sorts of jewels, adorned with pillars of precious stones, and capable of yielding whatever one desired. It was equipped with every form of furniture and wealth, which tended to increase in the course of time.**

## PURPORT

The castle created in the sky by Kardama Muni may be called "a castle in the air," but by his mystic power of *yoga* Kardama Muni actually constructed a huge castle in the air. To our feeble imagination, a castle in the sky is an impossibility, but if we scrutinizingly consider the matter we can understand that it is not impossible at all. If the Supreme Personality of Godhead can create so many planets, carrying millions of castles in the air, a perfect *yogī* like Kardama Muni can easily construct one castle in the air. The castle is described as *sarva-kāma-dugham*, "yielding whatever one desired." It was full of jewels. Even the pillars were made of pearls and valuable stones. These valuable jewels and stones were not subject to deterioration, but were everlastingly and increasingly opulent. We sometimes hear of castles thus bedecked on the surface of this earth also. The castles constructed by Lord Kṛṣṇa for His 16,108 wives were so bedecked with jewels that there was no need of lamplight during the night.

## TEXTS 14–15

दिव्योपकरणोपेतं सर्वकालसुखावहम् ।
पट्टिकाभिः पताकाभिर्विचित्राभिरलंकृतम् ॥१४॥
स्रग्भिर्विचित्रमाल्याभिर्मञ्जुशिञ्जत्षडङ्घ्रिभिः ।
दुकूलक्षौमकौशेयैर्नानावस्त्रैर्विराजितम् ॥१५॥

*divyopakaraṇopetaṁ*
*sarva-kāla-sukhāvaham*
*paṭṭikābhiḥ patākābhir*
*vicitrābhir alaṅkṛtam*

*sragbhir vicitra-mālyābhir*
*mañju-śiñjat-ṣaḍ-aṅghribhiḥ*
*dukūla-kṣauma-kauśeyair*
*nānā-vastrair virājitam*

*divya*—wonderful; *upakaraṇa*—with paraphernalia; *upetam*—equipped; *sarva-kāla*—in all seasons; *sukha-āvaham*—bringing happiness; *paṭṭikābhiḥ*—with festoons; *patākābhiḥ*—with flags; *vicitrābhiḥ*—of various colors and fabrics; *alaṅkṛtam*—decorated; *sragbhiḥ*—with wreaths; *vicitra-mālyābhiḥ*—with charming flowers; *mañju*—sweet; *śiñjat*—humming; *ṣaṭ-aṅghribhiḥ*—with bees; *dukūla*—fine cloth; *kṣauma*—linen; *kauśeyaiḥ*—of silk cloth; *nānā*—various; *vastraiḥ*—with tapestries; *virājitam*—embellished.

## TRANSLATION

**The castle was fully equipped with all necessary paraphernalia, and it was pleasing in all seasons. It was decorated all around with flags, festoons and artistic work of variegated colors. It was further embellished with wreaths of charming flowers that attracted**

**sweetly humming bees and with tapestries of linen, silk and various other fabrics.**

## TEXT 16

उपर्युपरि विन्यस्तनिलयेषु पृथक्पृथक् ।
क्षिप्तैः कशिपुभिः कान्तं पर्यङ्कव्यजनासनैः ॥१६॥

*upary upari vinyasta-*
*nilayeṣu pṛthak pṛthak*
*kṣiptaiḥ kaśipubhiḥ kāntaṁ*
*paryaṅka-vyajanāsanaiḥ*

*upari upari*—one upon another; *vinyasta*—placed; *nilayeṣu*—in stories; *pṛthak pṛthak*—separately; *kṣiptaiḥ*—arranged; *kaśipubhiḥ*—with beds; *kāntam*—charming; *paryaṅka*—couches; *vyajana*—fans; *āsanaiḥ*—with seats.

## TRANSLATION

**The palace looked charming, with beds, couches, fans and seats, all separately arranged in seven stories.**

## PURPORT

It is understood from this verse that the castle had many stories. The words *upary upari vinyasta* indicate that skyscrapers are not newly invented. Even in those days, millions of years ago, the idea of building many-storied houses was current. They contained not merely one or two rooms, but many different apartments, and each was completely decorated with cushions, bedsteads, sitting places and carpets.

## TEXT 17

तत्र तत्र विनिक्षिप्तनानाशिल्पोपशोभितम् ।
महामरकतस्थल्या जुष्टं विद्रुमवेदिभिः ॥१७॥

*tatra tatra vinikṣipta-*
*nānā-śilpopaśobhitam*

*mahā-marakata-sthalyā*
*juṣṭaṁ vidruma-vedibhiḥ*

*tatra tatra*—here and there; *vinikṣipta*—placed; *nānā*—various; *śilpa*—by artistic engravings; *upaśobhitam*—extraordinarily beautiful; *mahā-marakata*—of great emeralds; *sthalyā*—with a floor; *juṣṭam*—furnished; *vidruma*—of coral; *vedibhiḥ*—with raised platforms (daises).

## TRANSLATION

**Its beauty was enhanced by artistic engravings here and there on the walls. The floor was of emerald, with coral daises.**

## PURPORT

At the present moment people are very proud of their architectural art, yet floors are generally decorated with colored cement. It appears, however, that the castle constructed by the yogic powers of Kardama Muni had floors of emerald with coral daises.

## TEXT 18

द्वाःसु विद्रुमदेहल्या भातं वज्रकपाटवत् ।
शिखरेष्विन्द्रनीलेषु हेमकुम्भैरधिश्रितम् ॥१८॥

*dvāḥsu vidruma-dehalyā*
*bhātaṁ vajra-kapāṭavat*
*śikhareṣv indranīleṣu*
*hema-kumbhair adhiśritam*

*dvāḥsu*—in the entrances; *vidruma*—of coral; *dehalyā*—with a threshold; *bhātam*—beautiful; *vajra*—bedecked with diamonds; *kapāṭa-vat*—having doors; *śikhareṣu*—on the domes; *indra-nīleṣu*—of sapphires; *hema-kumbhaiḥ*—with gold pinnacles; *adhiśritam*—crowned.

## TRANSLATION

**The palace was very beautiful, with its coral thresholds at the entrances and its doors bedecked with diamonds. Gold pinnacles crowned its domes of sapphire.**

## TEXT 19

चक्षुष्मत्पद्मरागाग्र्यैर्वज्रभित्तिषु निर्मितैः ।
जुष्टं विचित्रवैतानैर्महार्हैर्हेमतोरणैः ॥१९॥

*cakṣuṣmat padmarāgāgryair*
*vajra-bhittiṣu nirmitaiḥ*
*juṣṭaṁ vicitra-vaitānair*
*mahārhair hema-toraṇaiḥ*

*cakṣuḥ-mat*—as if possessed of eyes; *padma-rāga*—with rubies; *agryaiḥ*—choicest; *vajra*—of diamond; *bhittiṣu*—on the walls; *nirmitaiḥ*—set; *juṣṭam*—furnished; *vicitra*—various; *vaitānaiḥ*—with canopies; *mahā-arhaiḥ*—greatly valuable; *hema-toraṇaiḥ*—with gates of gold.

## TRANSLATION

**With the choicest rubies set in its diamond walls, it appeared as though possessed of eyes. It was furnished with wonderful canopies and greatly valuable gates of gold.**

## PURPORT

Artistic jewelry and decorations giving the appearance of eyes are not imaginary. Even in recent times the Mogul emperors constructed their palaces with decorations of jeweled birds with eyes made of valuable stones. The stones have been taken away by the authorities, but the decorations are still present in some of the castles constructed by the Mogul emperors in New Delhi. The royal palaces were built with jewels and rare stones resembling eyes, and thus at night they would give off reflective light without need of lamps.

## TEXT 20

हंसपारावतव्रातैस्तत्र तत्र निकूजितम् ।
कृत्रिमान् मन्यमानैः स्वानधिरुह्याधिरुह्य च ॥२०॥

*haṁsa-pārāvata-vrātais*
*tatra tatra nikūjitam*

*kṛtrimān manyamānaiḥ svān*
*adhiruhyādhiruhya ca*

*haṁsa*—of swans; *pārāvata*—of pigeons; *vrātaiḥ*—with multitudes; *tatra tatra*—here and there; *nikūjitam*—vibrated; *kṛtrimān*—artificial; *manyamānaiḥ*—thinking; *svān*—belonging to their own kind; *adhiruhya adhiruhya*—rising repeatedly; *ca*—and.

### TRANSLATION

**Here and there in that palace were multitudes of live swans and pigeons, as well as artificial swans and pigeons so lifelike that the real swans rose above them again and again, thinking them live birds like themselves. Thus the palace vibrated with the sounds of these birds.**

### TEXT 21

विहारस्थानविश्रामसंवेशप्राङ्गणाजिरैः ।
यथोपजोषं रचितैर्विस्मापनमिवात्मनः ॥२१॥

*vihāra-sthāna-viśrāma-*
*saṁveśa-prāṅgaṇājiraiḥ*
*yathopajoṣaṁ racitair*
*vismāpanam ivātmanaḥ*

*vihāra-sthāna*—pleasure grounds; *viśrāma*—resting chambers; *saṁveśa*—bedrooms; *prāṅgaṇa*—inner yards; *ajiraiḥ*—with outer yards; *yathā-upajoṣam*—according to comfort; *racitaiḥ*—which were designed; *vismāpanam*—causing astonishment; *iva*—indeed; *ātmanaḥ*—to himself (Kardama).

### TRANSLATION

**The castle had pleasure grounds, resting chambers, bedrooms and inner and outer yards designed with an eye to comfort. All this caused astonishment to the sage himself.**

## PURPORT

Kardama Muni, being a saintly person, was living in a humble hermitage, but when he saw the palace constructed by his yogic powers, which was full of resting rooms, rooms for sex enjoyment, and inner and outer yards, he himself was astonished. That is the way of a God-gifted person. A devotee like Kardama Muni exhibited such opulence by his yogic power at the request of his wife, but when the opulence was produced, he himself could not understand how such manifestations could be possible. When a *yogī's* power is exhibited, the *yogī* himself is sometimes astonished.

## TEXT 22

ईदृग्गृहं तत्पश्यन्तीं नातिप्रीतेन चेतसा ।
सर्वभूताशयाभिज्ञः प्रावोचत्कर्दमः स्वयम् ॥२२॥

*īdṛg gṛhaṁ tat paśyantīṁ*
*nātiprītena cetasā*
*sarva-bhūtāśayābhijñaḥ*
*prāvocat kardamaḥ svayam*

*īdṛk*—such; *gṛham*—house; *tat*—that; *paśyantīm*—looking at; *na atiprītena*—not much pleased; *cetasā*—with a heart; *sarva-bhūta*—of everyone; *āśaya-abhijñaḥ*—understanding the heart; *prāvocat*—he addressed; *kardamaḥ*—Kardama; *svayam*—personally.

## TRANSLATION

**When he saw Devahūti looking at the gigantic, opulent palace with a displeased heart, Kardama Muni could understand her feelings because he could study the heart of anyone. Thus he personally addressed his wife as follows.**

## PURPORT

Devahūti had spent a long time in the hermitage, not taking much care of her body. She was covered with dirt, and her clothing was not very nice. Kardama Muni was surprised that he could produce such a palace, and similarly his wife, Devahūti, was also astonished. How could she live in that opulent palace? Kardama Muni could understand her astonishment, and thus he spoke as follows.

## TEXT 23

निमज्ज्यास्मिन् ह्रदे भीरु विमानमिदमारुह ।
इदं शुक्लकृतं तीर्थमाशिषां यापकं नृणाम् ॥२३॥

*nimajjyāsmin hrade bhīru*
*vimānam idam āruha*
*idaṁ śukla-kṛtaṁ tīrtham*
*āśiṣāṁ yāpakaṁ nṛṇām*

*nimajjya*—after bathing; *asmin*—in this; *hrade*—in the lake; *bhīru*—O fearful one; *vimānam*—airplane; *idam*—this; *āruha*—ascend; *idam*—this; *śukla-kṛtam*—created by Lord Viṣṇu; *tīrtham*—sacred lake; *āśiṣām*—the desires; *yāpakam*—bestowing; *nṛṇām*—of human beings.

## TRANSLATION

**My dear Devahūti, you look very much afraid. First bathe in Lake Bindu-sarovara, created by Lord Viṣṇu Himself, which can grant all the desires of a human being, and then mount this airplane.**

## PURPORT

It is still the system to go to places of pilgrimage and take a bath in the water there. In Vṛndāvana the people take baths in the River Yamunā. In other places, such as Prayāga, they take baths in the River Ganges. The words *tīrtham āśiṣāṁ yāpakam* refer to the fulfillment of desires by bathing in a place of pilgrimage. Kardama Muni advised his good wife to bathe in Lake Bindu-sarovara so that she could revive the former beauty and luster of her body.

## TEXT 24

सा तद्भर्तुः समादाय वचः कुवलयेक्षणा ।
सरजं बिभ्रती वासो वेणीभूतांश्च मूर्धजान् ॥२४॥

*sā tad bhartuḥ samādāya*
*vacaḥ kuvalayekṣaṇā*
*sarajaṁ bibhratī vāso*
*veṇī-bhūtāṁś ca mūrdhajān*

*sā*—she; *tat*—then; *bhartuḥ*—of her husband; *samādāya*—accepting; *vacaḥ*—the words; *kuvalaya-īkṣaṇā*—the lotus-eyed; *sa-rajam*—dirty; *bibhratī*—wearing; *vāsaḥ*—clothing; *veṇī-bhūtān*—matted; *ca*—and; *mūrdha-jān*—hair.

## TRANSLATION

**The lotus-eyed Devahūti accepted the order of her husband. Because of her dirty dress and the locks of matted hair on her head, she did not look very attractive.**

## PURPORT

It appears that Devahūti's hair had remained uncombed for many years and had become complicated in tangles. In other words, she neglected her bodily dress and comforts to engage in the service of her husband.

## TEXT 25

अङ्गं च मलपङ्केन संछन्नं शबलस्तनम् ।
आविवेश सरस्वत्याः सरः शिवजलाशयम् ॥२५॥

*aṅgaṁ ca mala-paṅkena*
*sañchannaṁ śabala-stanam*
*āviveśa sarasvatyāḥ*
*saraḥ śiva-jalāśayam*

*aṅgam*—body; *ca*—and; *mala-paṅkena*—with dirt; *sañchannam*—covered; *śabala*—discolored; *stanam*—breasts; *āviveśa*—she entered; *sarasvatyāḥ*—of the River Sarasvatī; *saraḥ*—the lake; *śiva*—sacred; *jala*—waters; *āśayam*—containing.

## TRANSLATION

**Her body was coated with a thick layer of dirt, and her breasts were discolored. She dove, however, into the lake, which contained the sacred waters of the Sarasvatī.**

## TEXT 26

सान्तःसरसि वेश्मस्थाः शतानि दश कन्यकाः ।
सर्वाः किशोरवयसो ददर्शोत्पलगन्धयः ॥२६॥

*sāntaḥ sarasi veśma-sthāḥ*
*śatāni daśa kanyakāḥ*
*sarvāḥ kiśora-vayaso*
*dadarśotpala-gandhayaḥ*

*sā*—she; *antaḥ*—inside; *sarasi*—in the lake; *veśma-sthāḥ*—situated in a house; *śatāni daśa*—ten hundred; *kanyakāḥ*—girls; *sarvāḥ*—all; *kiśora-vayasaḥ*—in the prime of youth; *dadarśa*—she saw; *utpala*—like lotuses; *gandhayaḥ*—fragrant.

## TRANSLATION

**In a house inside the lake she saw one thousand girls, all in the prime of youth and fragrant like lotuses.**

## TEXT 27

तां दृष्ट्वा सहसोत्थाय प्रोचुः प्राञ्जलयः स्त्रियः ।
वयं कर्मकरीस्तुभ्यं शाधि नः करवाम किम् ॥२७॥

*tāṁ dṛṣṭvā sahasotthāya*
*procuḥ prāñjalayaḥ striyaḥ*
*vayaṁ karma-karīs tubhyaṁ*
*śādhi naḥ karavāma kim*

*tām*—her; *dṛṣṭvā*—seeing; *sahasā*—suddenly; *utthāya*—rising; *procuḥ*—they said; *prāñjalayaḥ*—with folded hands; *striyaḥ*—the damsels; *vayam*—we; *karma-karīḥ*—maidservants; *tubhyam*—for you; *śādhi*—please tell; *naḥ*—us; *karavāma*—we can do; *kim*—what.

## TRANSLATION

**Seeing her, the damsels suddenly rose and said with folded hands, "We are your maidservants. Tell us what we can do for you."**

## PURPORT

While Devahūti was thinking of what to do in that great palace in her dirty clothes, there were at once, by the yogic powers of Kardama Muni, one thousand maidservants prepared to serve her. They appeared before Devahūti within the water and presented themselves as her maidservants, simply awaiting her orders.

## TEXT 28

स्नानेन तां महार्हेण स्नापयित्वा मनस्विनीम् ।
दुकूले निर्मले नूत्ने ददुरस्यै च मानदाः ॥२८॥

*snānena tāṁ mahārheṇa*
*snāpayitvā manasvinīm*
*dukūle nirmale nūtne*
*dadur asyai ca mānadāḥ*

*snānena*—with bathing oils; *tām*—her; *mahā-arheṇa*—very costly; *snāpayitvā*—after bathing; *manasvinīm*—the virtuous wife; *dukūle*—in fine cloth; *nirmale*—spotless; *nūtne*—new; *daduḥ*—they gave; *asyai*—to her; *ca*—and; *māna-dāḥ*—the respectful girls.

## TRANSLATION

**The girls, being very respectful to Devahūti, brought her forth, and after bathing her with valuable oils and ointments, they gave her fine, new, spotless cloth to cover her body.**

## TEXT 29

भूषणानि परार्ध्यानि वरीयांसि द्युमन्ति च ।
अन्नं सर्वगुणोपेतं पानं चैवामृतासवम् ॥२९॥

*bhūṣaṇāni parārdhyāni*
*varīyāṁsi dyumanti ca*
*annaṁ sarva-guṇopetaṁ*
*pānaṁ caivāmṛtāsavam*

*bhūṣaṇāni*—ornaments; *para-ardhyāni*—most valuable; *varīyāṁsi*—very excellent; *dyumanti*—splendid; *ca*—and; *annam*—food; *sarva-guṇa*—all good qualities; *upetam*—containing; *pānam*—beverages; *ca*—and; *eva*—also; *amṛta*—sweet; *āsavam*—intoxicating.

## TRANSLATION

**They then decorated her with very excellent and valuable jewels, which shone brightly. Next they offered her food containing all good qualities, and a sweet, inebriating drink called āsavam.**

## PURPORT

*Āsavam* is an Āyur-vedic medical preparation; it is not a liquor. It is especially made from drugs and is meant to improve metabolism for the healthy condition of the body.

## TEXT 30

अथादर्शे स्वमात्मानं स्रग्विणं विरजाम्बरम् ।
विरजं कृतस्वस्त्ययनं कन्याभिर्बहुमानितम् ॥३०॥

*athādarśe svam ātmānaṁ*
*sragviṇaṁ virajāmbaram*
*virajaṁ kṛta-svastyayanaṁ*
*kanyābhir bahu-mānitam*

*atha*—then; *ādarśe*—in a mirror; *svam ātmānam*—her own reflection; *srak-viṇam*—adorned with a garland; *viraja*—unsullied; *am-*

*baram*—robes; *virajam*—freed from all bodily dirt; *kṛta-svasti-ayanam*—decorated with auspicious marks; *kanyābhiḥ*—by the maids; *bahu-mānitam*—very respectfully served.

## TRANSLATION

**Then in a mirror she beheld her own reflection. Her body was completely freed from all dirt, and she was adorned with a garland. Dressed in unsullied robes and decorated with auspicious marks of tilaka, she was served very respectfully by the maids.**

## TEXT 31

स्नातं कृतशिरःस्नानं सर्वाभरणभूषितम् ।
निष्कग्रीवं वलयिनं कूजत्काञ्चननूपुरम् ॥३१॥

*snātaṁ kṛta-śiraḥ-snānaṁ*
*sarvābharaṇa-bhūṣitam*
*niṣka-grīvaṁ valayinaṁ*
*kūjat-kāñcana-nūpuram*

*snātam*—bathed; *kṛta-śiraḥ*—including the head; *snānam*—bathing; *sarva*—all over; *ābharaṇa*—with ornaments; *bhūṣitam*—decorated; *niṣka*—a gold necklace with a locket; *grīvam*—on the neck; *valayi-nam*—with bangles; *kūjat*—tinkling; *kāñcana*—made of gold; *nū-puram*—ankle bells.

## TRANSLATION

**Her entire body, including her head, was completely bathed, and she was decorated all over with ornaments. She wore a special necklace with a locket. There were bangles on her wrists and tinkling anklets of gold about her ankles.**

## PURPORT

The word *kṛta-śiraḥ-snānam* appears here. According to the *smṛti-śāstra's* directions for daily duties, ladies are allowed to bathe daily up to the neck. The hair on the head does not necessarily have to be washed daily because the mass of wet hair may cause a cold. For ladies, therefore, taking a bath up to the neck is ordinarily prescribed, and they take a full bath only on certain occasions. On this occasion Devahūti took a full bath and washed her hair very nicely. When a lady takes an ordinary bath it is called *mala-snāna*, and when she takes a full bath, including the head, it is called *śiraḥ-snāna*. At this time she needs sufficient oil to smear on her head. That is the direction of the commentators of *smṛti-śāstra*.

## TEXT 32

श्रोण्योरध्यस्तया काञ्च्या काञ्चन्या बहुरत्नया ।
हारेण च महार्हेण रुचकेन च भूषितम् ॥३२॥

*śroṇyor adhyastayā kāñcyā*
*kāñcanyā bahu-ratnayā*
*hāreṇa ca mahārheṇa*
*rucakena ca bhūṣitam*

*śroṇyoḥ*—on the hips; *adhyastayā*—worn; *kāñcyā*—with a girdle; *kāñcanyā*—made of gold; *bahu-ratnayā*—decorated with numerous jewels; *hāreṇa*—with a pearl necklace; *ca*—and; *mahā-arheṇa*—precious; *rucakena*—with auspicious substances; *ca*—and; *bhūṣitam*—adorned.

## TRANSLATION

**About her hips she wore a girdle of gold, set with numerous jewels, and she was further adorned with a precious pearl necklace and auspicious substances.**

## PURPORT

Auspicious substances include saffron, *kuṅkuma* and sandalwood pulp. Before taking a bath there are other auspicious substances, such as turmeric mixed with mustard seed oil, which are smeared all over the body. All kinds of auspicious substances were used to bathe Devahūti from top to toe.

## TEXT 33

सुदता सुभ्रुवा श्लक्ष्णस्निग्धापाङ्गेन चक्षुषा ।
पद्मकोशस्पृधा नीलैरलकैश्च लसन्मुखम् ॥३३॥

*sudatā subhruvā ślakṣṇa-*
*snigdhāpāṅgena cakṣuṣā*
*padma-kośa-spṛdhā nīlair*
*alakaiś ca lasan-mukham*

*su-datā*—with beautiful teeth; *su-bhruvā*—with charming eyebrows; *ślakṣṇa*—lovely; *snigdha*—moist; *apāṅgena*—corners of eyes; *cakṣuṣā*—with eyes; *padma-kośa*—lotus buds; *spṛdhā*—defeating; *nīlaiḥ*—bluish; *alakaiḥ*—with curling hair; *ca*—and; *lasat*—shining; *mukham*—countenance.

### TRANSLATION

**Her countenance shone, with beautiful teeth and charming eyebrows. Her eyes, distinguished by lovely moist corners, defeated the beauty of lotus buds. Her face was surrounded by dark curling tresses.**

### PURPORT

According to Vedic culture, white teeth are very much appreciated. Devahūti's white teeth increased the beauty of her face and made it look like a lotus flower. When a face looks very attractive, the eyes are generally compared to lotus petals and the face to a lotus flower.

## TEXT 34

यदा सस्मार ऋषभमृषीणां दयितं पतिम् ।
तत्र चास्ते सह स्त्रीभिर्यत्रास्ते स प्रजापतिः ॥३४॥

*yadā sasmāra ṛṣabham*
*ṛṣīṇāṁ dayitaṁ patim*
*tatra cāste saha strībhir*
*yatrāste sa prajāpatiḥ*

*yadā*—when; *sasmāra*—she thought of; *ṛṣabham*—the foremost; *ṛṣīṇām*—among the *ṛṣis; dayitam*—dear; *patim*—husband; *tatra*—there; *ca*—and; *āste*—she was present; *saha*—along with; *strībhiḥ*—the maidservants; *yatra*—where; *āste*—was present; *saḥ*—he; *prajā-patiḥ*—the Prajāpati (Kardama).

## TRANSLATION

**When she thought of her great husband, the best of the sages, Kardama Muni, who was very dear to her, she, along with all the maidservants, at once appeared where he was.**

## PURPORT

It appears from this verse that in the beginning Devahūti thought herself to be dirty and dressed in a very niggardly way. When her husband asked her to enter the lake, she saw the maidservants, and they took care of her. Everything was done within the water, and as soon as she thought of her beloved husband, Kardama, she was brought before him without delay. These are some of the powers attained by perfect *yogīs;* they can immediately execute anything they desire.

## TEXT 35

भर्तुः पुरस्तादात्मानं स्त्रीसहस्रवृतं तदा ।
निशाम्य तद्योगगतिं संशयं प्रत्यपद्यत ॥३५॥

*bhartuḥ purastād ātmānaṁ*
*strī-sahasra-vṛtaṁ tadā*
*niśāmya tad-yoga-gatiṁ*
*saṁśayaṁ pratyapadyata*

*bhartuḥ*—of her husband; *purastāt*—in the presence; *ātmānam*—herself; *strī-sahasra*—by a thousand maids; *vṛtam*—surrounded; *tadā*—then; *niśāmya*—seeing; *tat*—his; *yoga-gatim*—yogic power; *saṁśayam pratyapadyata*—she was amazed.

## TRANSLATION

**She was amazed to find herself surrounded by a thousand maids in the presence of her husband and to witness his yogic power.**

## PURPORT

Devahūti saw everything miraculously done, yet when brought before her husband she could understand that it was all due to his great yogic mystic power. She understood that nothing was impossible for a *yogī* like Kardama Muni.

## TEXTS 36–37

स तां कृतमलस्नानां विभ्राजन्तीमपूर्ववत् ।
आत्मनो बिभ्रतीं रूपं संवीतरुचिरस्तनीम् ॥३६॥
विद्याधरीसहस्रेण सेव्यमानां सुवाससम् ।
जातभावो विमानं तदारोहयदमित्रहन् ॥३७॥

*sa tāṁ kṛta-mala-snānāṁ*
*vibhrājantīm apūrvavat*
*ātmano bibhratīṁ rūpaṁ*
*saṁvīta-rucira-stanīm*

*vidyādharī-sahasreṇa*
*sevyamānāṁ suvāsasam*
*jāta-bhāvo vimānaṁ tad*
*ārohayad amitra-han*

*saḥ*—the sage; *tām*—her (Devahūti); *kṛta-mala-snānām*—bathed clean; *vibhrājantīm*—shining forth; *apūrva-vat*—unprecedentedly; *ātmanaḥ*—her own; *bibhratīm*—possessing; *rūpam*—beauty; *saṁvīta*—girded; *rucira*—charming; *stanīm*—with breasts; *vidyādharī*—of Gandharva girls; *sahasreṇa*—by a thousand; *sevyamānām*—being waited upon; *su-vāsasam*—dressed in excellent robes; *jāta-bhāvaḥ*—struck with fondness; *vimānam*—airplane like a mansion; *tat*—that; *ārohayat*—he put her on board; *amitra-han*—O destroyer of the enemy.

## TRANSLATION

**The sage could see that Devahūti had washed herself clean and was shining forth as though no longer his former wife. She had regained her own original beauty as the daughter of a prince. Dressed in excellent robes, her charming breasts duly girded, she was waited upon by a thousand Gandharva girls. O destroyer of the enemy, his fondness for her grew, and he placed her on the aerial mansion.**

## PURPORT

Before her marriage, when Devahūti was brought by her parents before the sage Kardama, she was the perfectly beautiful princess, and Kardama Muni remembered her former beauty. But after her marriage, when she was engaged in the service of Kardama Muni, she neglected to care for her body like a princess, since there was no means for such care; her husband was living in a cottage, and since she was always engaged in serving him, her royal beauty disappeared, and she became just like an ordinary maidservant. Now, after being bathed by the Gandharva girls by the order of Kardama Muni's yogic power, she regained her beauty, and Kardama Muni felt attracted to the beauty she had shown before the marriage. The real beauty of a young woman is her breasts. When Kardama Muni saw the breasts of his wife so nicely decorated, increasing her beauty many times, he was attracted, even though he was a great sage. Śrīpāda Śaṅkarācārya has therefore warned the transcendentalists that one who is after transcendental realization should not be attracted by the raised breasts of a woman because they are nothing but an interaction of fat and blood within the body.

## TEXT 38

तस्मिन्नलुप्तमहिमा प्रिययानुरक्तो
विद्याधरीभिरुपचीर्णवपुर्विमाने ।
बभ्राज उत्कचकुमुद्गणवानपीच्य-
स्ताराभिरावृत इवोडुपतिर्नभःस्थः ॥३८॥

*tasminn alupta-mahimā priyayānurakto*
*vidyādharībhir upacīrṇa-vapur vimāne*

*babhrāja utkaca-kumud-gaṇavān apīcyas*
*tārābhir āvṛta ivoḍu-patir nabhaḥ-sthaḥ*

*tasmin*—in that; *alupta*—not lost; *mahimā*—glory; *priyayā*—with his beloved consort; *anuraktaḥ*—attached; *vidyādharībhiḥ*—by the Gandharva girls; *upacīrṇa*—waited upon; *vapuḥ*—his person; *vimāne*—on the airplane; *babhrāja*—he shone; *utkaca*—open; *kumut-gaṇa-vān*—the moon, which is followed by rows of lilies; *apīcyaḥ*—very charming; *tārābhiḥ*—by stars; *āvṛtaḥ*—surrounded; *iva*—as; *uḍu-patiḥ*—the moon (the chief of the stars); *nabhaḥ-sthaḥ*—in the sky.

## TRANSLATION

**Though seemingly attached to his beloved consort while served by the Gandharva girls, the sage did not lose his glory, which was mastery over his self. In the aerial mansion Kardama Muni with his consort shone as charmingly as the moon in the midst of the stars in the sky, which causes rows of lilies to open in ponds at night.**

## PURPORT

The mansion was in the sky, and therefore the comparison to the full moon and stars is very beautifully composed in this verse. Kardama Muni looked like the full moon, and the girls who surrounded his wife, Devahūti, seemed just like the stars. On a full-moon night the stars and the moon together form a beautiful constellation; similarly, in that aerial mansion in the sky, Kardama Muni with his beautiful wife and the damsels surrounding them appeared like the moon and stars on a full-moon night.

## TEXT 39

तेनाष्टलोकपविहारकुलाचलेन्द्र-
द्रोणीस्वनङ्गसखमारुतसौभगासु ।
सिद्धैर्नुतो द्युधुनिपातशिवस्वनासु
रेमे चिरं धनदवल्ललनावरूथी ॥३९॥

*tenāṣṭa-lokapa-vihāra-kulācalendra-*
*droṇīṣv anaṅga-sakha-māruta-saubhagāsu*
*siddhair nuto dyudhuni-pāta-śiva-svanāsu*
*reme ciraṁ dhanadaval-lalanā-varūthī*

*tena*—by that airplane; *aṣṭa-loka-pa*—of the predominating deities of the eight heavenly planets; *vihāra*—the pleasure grounds; *kula-acala-indra*—of the king of the mountains (Meru); *droṇīṣu*—in the valleys; *anaṅga*—of passion; *sakha*—the companions; *māruta*—with breezes; *saubhagāsu*—beautiful; *siddhaiḥ*—by the Siddhas; *nutaḥ*—being praised; *dyu-dhuni*—of the Ganges; *pāta*—of the downfall; *śiva-svanāsu*—vibrating with auspicious sounds; *reme*—he enjoyed; *ciram*—for a long time; *dhanada-vat*—like Kuvera; *lalanā*—by damsels; *varūthī*—surrounded.

## TRANSLATION

**In that aerial mansion he traveled to the pleasure valleys of Mount Meru, which were rendered all the more beautiful by cool, gentle, fragrant breezes that stimulated passion. In these valleys, the treasurer of the gods, Kuvera, surrounded by beautiful women and praised by the Siddhas, generally enjoys pleasure. Kardama Muni also, surrounded by the beautiful damsels and his wife, went there and enjoyed for many, many years.**

## PURPORT

Kuvera is one of the eight demigods who are in charge of different directions of the universe. It is said that Indra is in charge of the eastern side of the universe, where the heavenly planet, or paradise, is situated. Similarly, Agni is in charge of the southeastern portion of the universe; Yama, the demigod who punishes sinners, is in charge of the southern portion; Nirṛti is in charge of the southwestern part of the universe; Varuṇa, the demigod in charge of the waters, is in charge of the western portion; Vāyu, who controls the air and who has wings to travel in the air, is in charge of the northwestern part of the universe; and Kuvera, the treasurer of the demigods, is in charge of the northern part of the universe. All these demigods take pleasure in the valleys of Mount Meru, which is situated somewhere between the sun and the earth. In the aerial mansion, Kardama Muni traveled throughout the eight directions controlled by the different demigods described above, and as the demigods go to Mount Meru, he also went there to enjoy life. When one is surrounded by young, beautiful girls, sex stimulation naturally becomes prominent. Kardama Muni was sexually stimulated, and he enjoyed his wife for many, many years in that part of Mount Meru. But his sex indulgence was praised by many, many Siddhas, beings who have attained perfection, because it was intended to produce good progeny for the good of universal affairs.

## TEXT 40

वैश्रम्भके सुरसने नन्दने पुष्पभद्रके ।
मानसे चैत्ररथ्ये च स रेमे रामया रतः ॥४०॥

*vaiśrambhake surasane*
*nandane puṣpabhadrake*
*mānase caitrarathye ca*
*sa reme rāmayā rataḥ*

*vaiśrambhake*—in the Vaiśrambhaka garden; *surasane*—in Surasana; *nandane*—in Nandana; *puṣpabhadrake*—in Puṣpabhadraka; *mānase*—by the Mānasa-sarovara Lake; *caitrarathye*—in Caitrarathya; *ca*—and; *saḥ*—he; *reme*—enjoyed; *rāmayā*—by his wife; *rataḥ*—satisfied.

## TRANSLATION

**Satisfied by his wife, he enjoyed in that aerial mansion not only on Mount Meru but in different gardens known as Vaiśrambhaka, Surasana, Nandana, Puṣpabhadraka and Caitrarathya, and by the Mānasa-sarovara Lake.**

## TEXT 41

भ्राजिष्णुना विमानेन कामगेन महीयसा ।
वैमानिकानत्यशेत चरँल्लोकान् यथानिलः ॥४१॥

*bhrājiṣṇunā vimānena*
*kāma-gena mahīyasā*

*vaimānikān atyaśeta*
*caraḿl lokān yathānilaḥ*

*bhrājiṣṇunā*—splendid; *vimānena*—with the airplane; *kāma-gena*—which flew according to his desire; *mahīyasā*—very great; *vaimānikān*—the demigods in their airplanes; *atyaśeta*—he surpassed; *caran*—traveling; *lokān*—through the planets; *yathā*—like; *anilaḥ*—the air.

## TRANSLATION

**He traveled in that way through the various planets, as the air passes uncontrolled in every direction. Coursing through the air in that great and splendid aerial mansion, which could fly at his will, he surpassed even the demigods.**

## PURPORT

The planets occupied by the demigods are restricted to their own orbits, but Kardama Muni, by his yogic power, could travel all over the different directions of the universe without restriction. The living entities who are within the universe are called conditioned souls; that is, they are not free to move everywhere. We are inhabitants of this earthly globe; we cannot move freely to other planets. In the modern age, man is trying to go to other planets, but so far he has been unsuccessful. It is not possible to travel to any other planets because by the laws of nature even the demigods cannot move from one planet to another. But Kardama Muni, by his yogic power, could surpass the strength of the demigods and travel in space in all directions. The comparison here is very suitable. The words *yathā anilaḥ* indicate that as the air is free to move anywhere without restriction, so Kardama Muni unrestrictedly traveled in all directions of the universe.

## TEXT 42

किं दुरापादनं तेषां पुंसामुद्दामचेतसाम् ।
यैराश्रितस्तीर्थपदश्चरणो व्यसनात्ययः ॥४२॥

*kiṁ durāpādanaṁ teṣāṁ*
*puṁsām uddāma-cetasām*

*yair āśritas tīrtha-padaś*
*caraṇo vyasanātyayaḥ*

*kim*—what; *durāpādanam*—difficult to achieve; *teṣām*—for those; *puṁsām*—men; *uddāma-cetasām*—who are determined; *yaiḥ*—by whom; *āśritaḥ*—taken refuge; *tīrtha-padaḥ*—of the Supreme Personality of Godhead; *caraṇaḥ*—feet; *vyasana-atyayaḥ*—which vanquish dangers.

## TRANSLATION

**What is difficult to achieve for determined men who have taken refuge of the Supreme Personality of Godhead's lotus feet? His feet are the source of sacred rivers like the Ganges, which put an end to the dangers of mundane life.**

## PURPORT

The words *yair āśritas tīrtha-padaś caraṇaḥ* are significant here. The Supreme Personality of Godhead is known as *tīrtha-pāda.* The Ganges is called a sacred river because it emanates from the toe of Viṣṇu. The Ganges is meant to eradicate all the material distresses of the conditioned souls. For any living entity, therefore, who has taken shelter of the holy lotus feet of the Lord, nothing is impossible. Kardama Muni is special not because he was a great mystic, but because he was a great devotee. Therefore it is said here that for a great devotee like Kardama Muni, nothing is impossible. Although *yogīs* can perform wonderful feats, as Kardama has already displayed, Kardama was more than a *yogī* because he was a great devotee of the Lord; therefore he was more glorious than an ordinary *yogī.* As it is confirmed in *Bhagavad-gītā,* "Out of the many *yogīs,* he who is a devotee of the Lord is first class." For a person like Kardama Muni there is no question of being conditioned; he was already a liberated soul and better than the demigods, who are also conditioned. Although he was enjoying with his wife and many other women, he was above material, conditional life. Therefore the word *vyasanātyayaḥ* is used to indicate that he was beyond the position of a conditioned soul. He was transcendental to all material limitations.

## TEXT 43

प्रेक्षयित्वा भुवो गोलं पत्न्यै यावान् स्वसंस्थया ।
बह्वाश्चर्यं महायोगी स्वाश्रमाय न्यवर्तत ॥४३॥

*prekṣayitvā bhuvo golaṁ*
*patnyai yāvān sva-saṁsthayā*
*bahv-āścaryaṁ mahā-yogī*
*svāśramāya nyavartata*

*prekṣayitvā*—after showing; *bhuvaḥ*—of the universe; *golam*—the globe; *patnyai*—to his wife; *yāvān*—as much; *sva-saṁsthayā*—with its arrangements; *bahu-āścaryam*—full of many wonders; *mahā-yogī*—the great *yogī* (Kardama); *sva-āśramāya*—to his own hermitage; *nyavartata*—returned.

### TRANSLATION

**After showing his wife the globe of the universe and its different arrangements, full of many wonders, the great yogī Kardama Muni returned to his own hermitage.**

### PURPORT

All the planets are here described as *gola*, round. Every planet is round, and each planet is a different shelter, just like islands in the great ocean. Planets are sometimes called *dvīpa* or *varṣa.* This earth planet is called Bhārata-varṣa because it was ruled by King Bharata. Another significant word used in this verse is *bahv-āścaryam,* "many wonderful things." This indicates that the different planets are distributed all over the universe in the eight directions, and each and every one of them is wonderful in itself. Each planet has its particular climatic influences and particular types of inhabitants and is completely equipped with everything, including the beauty of the seasons. In the *Brahma-saṁhitā* (5.40) it is similarly stated, *vibhūti-bhinnam:* on each and every planet there are different opulences. It cannot be expected that one planet is exactly like another. By God's grace, by nature's law, each and every planet is made differently and has different wonderful features. All such wonders were personally experienced by Kardama Muni while he traveled with his wife, yet he could return again to his humble hermitage. He showed his princess-wife that although he was living in the hermitage, he had the power to go everywhere and do anything by mystic *yoga.* That is the perfection of *yoga.* One cannot become a perfect *yogī* simply by showing some sitting postures, nor by such sitting postures or so-called meditation can one become God, as is being advertised. Foolish persons are misled into believing that simply by some caricature of meditation and sitting postures one can become God within six months.

Here is the example of a perfect *yogī;* he could travel all over the universe. Similarly, there is a description of Durvāsā Muni, who also traveled in space. Actually, the perfect *yogī* can do that. But even if one can travel all over the universe and show wonderful feats like Kardama Muni, he cannot be compared to the Supreme Personality of Godhead, whose power and inconceivable energy can never be attained by any conditioned or liberated soul. By the actions of Kardama Muni we can understand that in spite of his immense mystic power, he remained a devotee of the Lord. That is the real position of every living entity.

## TEXT 44

विभज्य नवधात्मानं मानवीं सुरतोत्सुकाम् ।
रामां निरमयन् रेमे वर्षपूगान्मुहूर्तवत् ॥४४॥

*vibhajya navadhātmānaṁ*
*mānavīṁ suratotsukām*
*rāmāṁ niramayan reme*
*varṣa-pūgān muhūrtavat*

*vibhajya*—having divided; *nava-dhā*—into nine; *ātmānam*—himself; *mānavīm*—the daughter of Manu (Devahūti); *surata*—for sex life; *utsukām*—who was eager; *rāmām*—to his wife; *niramayan*—giving pleasure; *reme*—he enjoyed; *varṣa-pūgān*—for many years; *muhūrta-vat*—like a moment.

## TRANSLATION

**After coming back to his hermitage, he divided himself into nine personalities just to give pleasure to Devahūti, the daughter**

**of Manu, who was eager for sex life. In that way he enjoyed with her for many, many years, which passed just like a moment.**

### PURPORT

Here the daughter of Svāyambhuva Manu, Devahūti, is described as *suratotsuka.* After traveling with her husband all over the universe, in Mount Meru and the beautiful gardens of the heavenly kingdoms, she naturally became sexually stimulated, and in order to satisfy her sexual desire, Kardama Muni expanded himself into nine forms. Instead of one, he became nine, and nine persons had sexual intercourse with Devahūti for many, many years. It is understood that the sexual appetite of a woman is nine times greater than that of a man. That is clearly indicated here. Otherwise, Kardama Muni would have had no reason to expand himself into nine. Here is another example of yogic power. As the Supreme Personality of Godhead can expand Himself in millions of forms, a *yogī* can also expand up to nine forms, but not more than that. Another example is that of Saubhari Muni; he also expanded himself into eight forms. But however powerful a *yogī* may be, he cannot expand himself into more than eight or nine forms. The Supreme Personality of Godhead, however, can expand Himself into millions of forms, *ananta-rūpa*—innumerable, countless forms—as stated in the *Brahma-saṁhitā.* No one can compare to the Supreme Personality of Godhead by any conceivable energetic manifestation of power.

### TEXT 45

तस्मिन् विमान उत्कृष्टां शय्यां रतिकरीं श्रिता ।
न चाबुध्यत तं कालं पत्यापीच्येन सङ्गता ॥४५॥

*tasmin vimāna utkṛṣṭāṁ*
*śayyāṁ rati-karīṁ śritā*
*na cābudhyata taṁ kālaṁ*
*patyāpīcyena saṅgatā*

*tasmin*—in that; *vimāne*—airplane; *utkṛṣṭām*—excellent; *śayyām*—a bed; *rati-karīm*—increasing sexual desires; *śritā*—situated on; *na*—not;

*ca*—and; *abudhyata*—she noticed; *tam*—that; *kālam*—time; *patyā*—with her husband; *apīcyena*—most handsome; *saṅgatā*—in company.

## TRANSLATION

**In that aerial mansion, Devahūti, in the company of her handsome husband, situated on an excellent bed that increased sexual desires, could not realize how much time was passing.**

## PURPORT

Sex indulgence is so enjoyable for materialistic people that when they engage in such activities they forget how time is passing. Saint Kardama and Devahūti, in their sex indulgence, also forgot how time was passing by.

## TEXT 46

एवं योगानुभावेन दम्पत्यो रममाणयोः ।
शतं व्यतीयुः शरदः कामलालसयोर्मनाक् ॥४६॥

*evaṁ yogānubhāvena*
*dam-patyo ramamāṇayoḥ*
*śataṁ vyatīyuḥ śaradaḥ*
*kāma-lālasayor manāk*

*evam*—thus; *yoga-anubhāvena*—by yogic powers; *dam-patyoḥ*—the couple; *ramamāṇayoḥ*—while enjoying themselves; *śatam*—a hundred; *vyatīyuḥ*—passed; *śaradaḥ*—autumns; *kāma*—sexual pleasure; *lālasa-yoḥ*—who were eagerly longing for; *manāk*—like a short time.

## TRANSLATION

**While the couple, who eagerly longed for sexual pleasure, were thus enjoying themselves by virtue of mystic powers, a hundred autumns passed like a brief span of time.**

## TEXT 47

तस्यामाधत्त रेतस्तां भावयन्नात्मनात्मवित् ।
नोधा विधाय रूपं स्वं सर्वसङ्कल्पविद्विभुः ॥४७॥

*tasyām ādhatta retas tāṁ*
*bhāvayann ātmanātma-vit*
*nodhā vidhāya rūpaṁ svaṁ*
*sarva-saṅkalpa-vid vibhuḥ*

*tasyām*—in her; *ādhatta*—he deposited; *retaḥ*—semen; *tām*—her; *bhāvayan*—regarding; *ātmanā*—as half of himself; *ātma-vit*—a knower of spirit soul; *nodhā*—into nine; *vidhāya*—having divided; *rūpam*—body; *svam*—his own; *sarva-saṅkalpa-vit*—the knower of all desires; *vibhuḥ*—the powerful Kardama.

## TRANSLATION

**The powerful Kardama Muni was the knower of everyone's heart, and he could grant whatever one desired. Knowing the spiritual soul, he regarded her as half of his body. Dividing himself into nine forms, he impregnated Devahūti with nine discharges of semen.**

## PURPORT

Since Kardama Muni could understand that Devahūti wanted many children, at the first chance he begot nine children at one time. He is described here as *vibhu*, the most powerful master. By his yogic power he could at once produce nine daughters in the womb of Devahūti.

## TEXT 48

अतः सा सुषुवे सद्यो देवहूतिः स्त्रियः प्रजाः ।
सर्वास्ताश्चारुसर्वाङ्ग्यो लोहितोत्पलगन्धयः ॥४८॥

*ataḥ sā suṣuve sadyo*
*devahūtiḥ striyaḥ prajāḥ*
*sarvās tāś cāru-sarvāṅgyo*
*lohitotpala-gandhayaḥ*

*ataḥ*—then; *sā*—she; *suṣuve*—gave birth; *sadyaḥ*—on the same day; *devahūtiḥ*—Devahūti; *striyaḥ*—females; *prajāḥ*—progeny; *sarvāḥ*—all; *tāḥ*—they; *cāru-sarva-aṅgyaḥ*—charming in every limb; *lohita*—red; *utpala*—like the lotus; *gandhayaḥ*—fragrant.

## TRANSLATION

**Immediately afterward, on the same day, Devahūti gave birth to nine female children, all charming in every limb and fragrant with the scent of the red lotus flower.**

## PURPORT

Devahūti was too sexually excited, and therefore she discharged more ova, and nine daughters were born. It is said in the *smṛti-śāstra* as well as in the *Āyur-veda* that when the discharge of the male is greater, male children are begotten, but when the discharge of the female is greater, female children are begotten. It appears from the circumstances that Devahūti was more sexually excited, and therefore she had nine daughters at once. All the daughters, however, were very beautiful, and their bodies were nicely formed; each resembled a lotus flower and was fragrant like a lotus.

## TEXT 49

पतिं सा प्रव्रजिष्यन्तं तदालक्ष्योशतीबहिः ।
स्मयमाना विक्लवेन हृदयेन विदूयता ॥४९॥

*patiṁ sā pravrajiṣyantaṁ*
*tadālakṣyośatī bahiḥ*
*smayamānā viklavena*
*hṛdayena vidūyatā*

*patim*—her husband; *sā*—she; *pravrajiṣyantam*—going to leave home; *tadā*—then; *ālakṣya*—after seeing; *uśatī*—beautiful; *bahiḥ*—outwardly; *smayamānā*—smiling; *viklavena*—agitated; *hṛdayena*—with a heart; *vidūyatā*—being distressed.

## TRANSLATION

**When she saw her husband about to leave home, she smiled externally, but at heart she was agitated and distressed.**

## PURPORT

Kardama Muni finished his household affairs quickly by his mystic power. The building of the castle in the air, traveling all over the universe with his wife in the company of beautiful girls, and begetting of children were finished, and now, according to his promise to leave home for his real concern of spiritual realization after impregnating his wife, he was about to go away. Seeing her husband about to leave, Devahūti was very disturbed, but to satisfy her husband she was smiling. The example of Kardama Muni should be understood very clearly; a person whose main concern is Kṛṣṇa consciousness, even if he is entrapped in household life, should always be ready to leave household enticement as soon as possible.

## TEXT 50

लिखन्त्यधोमुखी भूमिं पदा नखमणिश्रिया ।
उवाच ललितां वाचं निरुध्याश्रुकलां शनैः ॥५०॥

*likhanty adho-mukhī bhūmiṁ*
*padā nakha-maṇi-śriyā*
*uvāca lalitāṁ vācaṁ*
*nirudhyāśru-kalāṁ śanaiḥ*

*likhantī*—scratching; *adhaḥ-mukhī*—her head bent down; *bhūmim*—the ground; *padā*—with her foot; *nakha*—nails; *maṇi*—gemlike; *śriyā*—with radiant; *uvāca*—she spoke; *lalitām*—charming; *vācam*—accents; *nirudhya*—suppressing; *aśru-kalām*—tears; *śanaiḥ*—slowly.

## TRANSLATION

**She stood and scratched the ground with her foot, which was radiant with the luster of her gemlike nails. Her head bent down, she spoke in slow yet charming accents, suppressing her tears.**

## PURPORT

Devahūti was so beautiful that her toenails appeared just like pearls, and as she scratched the ground it appeared as if pearls had been thrown on the ground. When a woman scratches the ground with her foot, it is a sign that her mind is very disturbed. These signs were sometimes exhibited by the *gopīs* before Kṛṣṇa. When the *gopīs* came in the dead of night and Kṛṣṇa asked them to return to their homes, the *gopīs* also scratched the ground like this because their minds were very disturbed.

## TEXT 51

देवहूतिरुवाच

सर्वं तद्भगवान्मह्यमुपोवाह प्रतिश्रुतम् ।
अथापि मे प्रपन्नाया अभयं दातुमर्हसि ॥५१॥

*devahūtir uvāca*
*sarvaṁ tad bhagavān mahyam*
*upovāha pratiśrutam*
*athāpi me prapannāyā*
*abhayaṁ dātum arhasi*

*devahūtiḥ*—Devahūti; *uvāca*—said; *sarvam*—all; *tat*—that; *bhagavān*—Your Lordship; *mahyam*—for me; *upovāha*—has been fulfilled; *pratiśrutam*—promised; *atha api*—yet; *me*—unto me; *prapannāyai*—unto one who has surrendered; *abhayam*—fearlessness; *dātum*—to give; *arhasi*—you deserve.

## TRANSLATION

**Śrī Devahūti said: My lord, you have fulfilled all the promises you gave me, yet because I am your surrendered soul, you should give me fearlessness too.**

## PURPORT

Devahūti requested her husband to grant her something without fear. As a wife, she was a fully surrendered soul to her husband, and it is the responsibility of the husband to give his wife fearlessness. How one awards fearlessness to his subordinate is mentioned in the Fifth Canto of *Śrīmad-Bhāgavatam.* One who cannot get free from the clutches of death is dependent, and he should not become a spiritual master, nor a husband, nor a kinsman, nor a father, nor a mother, etc. It is the duty of the superior to give fearlessness to the subordinate. To take charge of someone, therefore, either as father, mother, spiritual master, relative or husband, one must accept the responsibility to give his ward freedom from the fearful situation of material existence. Material existence is always fearful and full of anxiety. Devahūti is saying, "You have given me all sorts of material comforts by your yogic power, and since you are now prepared to go away, you must give me your last award so that I may get free from this material, conditional life."

## TEXT 52

ब्रह्मन्दुहितृभिस्तुभ्यं विमृग्याः पतयः समाः ।
कश्चित्स्यान्मे विशोकाय त्वयि प्रव्रजिते वनम् ॥५२॥

*brahman duhitṛbhis tubhyaṁ*
*vimṛgyāḥ patayaḥ samāḥ*
*kaścit syān me viśokāya*
*tvayi pravrajite vanam*

*brahman*—my dear *brāhmaṇa; duhitṛbhiḥ*—by the daughters themselves; *tubhyam*—for you; *vimṛgyāḥ*—to be found out; *patayaḥ*—husbands; *samāḥ*—suitable; *kaścit*—someone; *syāt*—there should be; *me*—my; *viśokāya*—for solace; *tvayi*—when you; *pravrajite*—departed; *vanam*—to the forest.

## TRANSLATION

**My dear brāhmaṇa, as far as your daughters are concerned, they will find their own suitable husbands and go away to their respective homes. But who will give me solace after your departure as a sannyāsī?**

## PURPORT

It is said that the father himself becomes the son in another form. The father and son are therefore considered to be nondifferent. A widow who has her son is actually not a widow, because she has the representative of her husband. Similarly, Devahūti is indirectly asking Kardama Muni to leave a representative so that in his absence she might be relieved of her anxieties by a suitable son. A householder is not expected to remain at home for all his days. After getting his sons and daughters married, a householder can retire from household life, leaving his wife in the charge of the grown-up sons. That is the social convention of the Vedic system. Devahūti is indirectly asking that in his absence from home there be at least one male child to give her relief from her anxieties. This relief means spiritual instruction. Relief does not mean material comforts. Material comforts will end with the end of the body, but spiritual instruction will not end; it will go on with the spirit soul. Instruction in spiritual advancement is necessary, but without having a worthy son, how could Devahūti advance in spiritual knowledge? It is the duty of the husband to liquidate his debt to his wife. The wife gives her sincere service to the husband, and he becomes indebted to her because one cannot accept service from his subordinate without giving him something in exchange. The spiritual master cannot accept service from a disciple without awarding him spiritual instruction. That is the reciprocation of love and duty. Thus Devahūti reminds her husband, Kardama Muni, that she has rendered him faithful service. Even considering the situation on the basis of liquidating his debt toward his wife, he must give a male child before he leaves. Indirectly, Devahūti requests her husband to remain at home a few days more, or at least until a male child is born.

## TEXT 53

एतावतालं कालेन व्यतिक्रान्तेन मे प्रभो ।
इन्द्रियार्थप्रसङ्गेन परित्यक्तपरात्मनः ॥५३॥

*etāvatālaṁ kālena*
*vyatikrāntena me prabho*
*indriyārtha-prasaṅgena*
*parityakta-parātmanaḥ*

*etāvatā*—so much; *alam*—for nothing; *kālena*—time; *vyatikrāntena*—passed by; *me*—my; *prabho*—O my lord; *indriya-artha*—sense gratification; *prasaṅgena*—in the matter of indulging; *parityakta*—disregarding; *para-ātmanaḥ*—knowledge of the Supreme Lord.

## TRANSLATION

**Until now we have simply wasted so much of our time in sense gratification, neglecting to cultivate knowledge of the Supreme Lord.**

## PURPORT

Human life is not meant to be wasted, like that of the animals, in sense gratificatory activities. Animals always engage in sense gratification—eating, sleeping, fearing and mating—but that is not the engagement of the human being, although, because of the material body, there is need of sense gratification according to a regulative principle. So, in effect, Devahūti said to her husband: "So far we have these daughters, and we have enjoyed material life in the aerial mansion, traveling all over the universe. These boons have come by your grace, but they have all been for sense gratification. Now there must be something for my spiritual advancement."

## TEXT 54

इन्द्रियार्थेषु सज्जन्त्या प्रसङ्गस्त्वयि मे कृतः ।
अजानन्त्या परं भावं तथाप्यस्त्वभयाय मे ॥५४॥

*indriyārtheṣu sajjantyā*
*prasaṅgas tvayi me kṛtaḥ*
*ajānantyā paraṁ bhāvaṁ*
*tathāpy astv abhayāya me*

*indriya-artheṣu*—to sense gratification; *sajjantyā*—being attached; *prasaṅgaḥ*—affinity; *tvayi*—for you; *me*—by me; *kṛtaḥ*—was done; *ajānantyā*—not knowing; *param bhāvam*—your transcendent situation; *tathā api*—nonetheless; *astu*—let it be; *abhayāya*—for fearlessness; *me*—my.

## TRANSLATION

**Not knowing your transcendental situation, I have loved you while remaining attached to the objects of the senses. Nonetheless, let the affinity I have developed for you rid me of all fear.**

## PURPORT

Devahūti is lamenting her position. As a woman, she had to love someone. Somehow or other, she came to love Kardama Muni, but without knowing of his spiritual advancement. Kardama Muni could understand Devahūti's heart; generally all women desire material enjoyment. They are called less intelligent because they are mostly prone to material enjoyment. Devahūti laments because her husband had given her the best kind of material enjoyment, but she did not know that he was so advanced in spiritual realization. Her plea was that even though she did not know the glories of her great husband, because she had taken shelter of him she must be delivered from material entanglement. Association with a great personality is most important. In *Caitanya-caritāmṛta* Lord Caitanya says that *sādhu-saṅga*, the association of a great saintly person, is very important, because even if one is not advanced in knowledge, simply by association with a great saintly person one can immediately make considerable advancement in spiritual life. As a woman, as an ordinary wife, Devahūti became attached to Kardama Muni in order to satisfy her sense enjoyment and other material necessities, but actually she associated with a great personality. Now she understood this, and she wanted to utilize the advantage of the association of her great husband.

## TEXT 55

सङ्गो यः संसृतेर्हेतुरसत्सु विहितोऽधिया ।
स एव साधुषु कृतो निःसङ्गत्वाय कल्पते ॥५५॥

*saṅgo yaḥ saṁsṛter hetur*
*asatsu vihito 'dhiyā*
*sa eva sādhuṣu kṛto*
*niḥsaṅgatvāya kalpate*

*saṅgaḥ*—association; *yaḥ*—which; *saṁsṛteḥ*—of the cycle of birth and death; *hetuḥ*—the cause; *asatsu*—with those engaged in sense gratification; *vihitaḥ*—done; *adhiyā*—through ignorance; *saḥ*—the same thing; *eva*—certainly; *sādhuṣu*—with saintly persons; *kṛtaḥ*—performed; *niḥsaṅgatvāya*—to liberation; *kalpate*—leads.

## TRANSLATION

**Association for sense gratification is certainly the path of bondage. But the same type of association, performed with a saintly person, leads to the path of liberation, even if performed without knowledge.**

## PURPORT

The association of a saintly person in any way bears the same result. For example, Lord Kṛṣṇa met many kinds of living entities, and some treated Him as an enemy, and some treated Him as an agent for sense gratification. It is generally said that the *gopīs* were attached to Kṛṣṇa for sense attractions, and yet they became first-class devotees of the Lord. Kaṁsa, Śiśupāla, Dantavakra and other demons, however, were related to Kṛṣṇa as enemies. But whether they associated with Kṛṣṇa as enemies or for sense gratification, out of fear or as pure devotees, they all got liberation. That is the result of association with the Lord. Even if one does not understand who He is, the results have the same efficacy. Association with a great saintly person also results in liberation, just as whether one goes toward fire knowingly or unknowingly, the fire will make one warm. Devahūti expressed her gratefulness, for although she wanted to associate with Kardama Muni only for sense gratification, because he was spiritually great she was sure to be liberated by his benediction.

## TEXT 56

नेह यत्कर्म धर्माय न विरागाय कल्पते ।
न तीर्थपदसेवायै जीवन्नपि मृतो हि सः ॥५६॥

*neha yat karma dharmāya*
*na virāgāya kalpate*
*na tīrtha-pada-sevāyai*
*jīvann api mṛto hi saḥ*

*na*—not; *iha*—here; *yat*—which; *karma*—work; *dharmāya*—for perfection of religious life; *na*—not; *virāgāya*—for detachment; *kal-*

*pate*—leads; *na*—not; *tīrtha-pada*—of the Lord's lotus feet; *sevāyai*—to devotional service; *jīvan*—living; *api*—although; *mṛtaḥ*—dead; *hi*—indeed; *saḥ*—he.

## TRANSLATION

**Anyone whose work is not meant to elevate him to religious life, anyone whose religious ritualistic performances do not raise him to renunciation, and anyone situated in renunciation that does not lead him to devotional service to the Supreme Personality of Godhead, must be considered dead, although he is breathing.**

## PURPORT

Devahūti's statement is that since she was attached to living with her husband for sense gratification, which does not lead to liberation from material entanglement, her life was simply a waste of time. Any work one performs that does not lead to the state of religious life is useless activity. Everyone is by nature inclined to some sort of work, and when that work leads one to religious life and religious life leads one to renunciation and renunciation leads one to devotional service, one attains the perfection of work. As stated in *Bhagavad-gītā*, any work that does not lead ultimately to the standard of devotional service is a cause of bondage in the material world. *Yajñārthāt karmaṇo 'nyatra loko 'yaṁ karma-bandhanaḥ.* Unless one is gradually elevated to the position of devotional service, beginning from his natural activity, he is to be considered a dead body. Work which does not lead one to the understanding of Kṛṣṇa consciousness is considered useless.

## TEXT 57

साहं भगवतो नूनं वञ्चिता मायया दृढम् ।
यत्त्वां विमुक्तिदं प्राप्य न मुमुक्षेय बन्धनात् ॥५७॥

*sāhaṁ bhagavato nūnaṁ*
*vañcitā māyayā dṛḍham*
*yat tvāṁ vimuktidaṁ prāpya*
*na mumukṣeya bandhanāt*

*sā*—that very person; *aham*—I am; *bhagavataḥ*—of the Lord; *nūnam*—surely; *vañcitā*—cheated; *māyayā*—by the illusory energy; *dṛḍham*—solidly; *yat*—because; *tvām*—you; *vimukti-dam*—who gives liberation; *prāpya*—having attained; *na mumukṣeya*—I have not sought liberation; *bandhanāt*—from material bondage.

## TRANSLATION

**My lord, surely I have been solidly cheated by the insurmountable illusory energy of the Supreme Personality of Godhead, for in spite of having obtained your association, which gives liberation from material bondage, I did not seek such liberation.**

## PURPORT

An intelligent man should utilize good opportunities. The first opportunity is the human form of life, and the second opportunity is to take birth in a suitable family where there is cultivation of spiritual knowledge; this is rarely obtained. The greatest opportunity is to have the association of a saintly person. Devahūti was conscious that she was born as the daughter of an emperor. She was sufficiently educated and cultured, and at last she got Kardama Muni, a saintly person and a great *yogī*, as her husband. Still, if she did not get liberation from the entanglement of material energy, then certainly she would be cheated by the insurmountable illusory energy. Actually, the illusory, material energy is cheating everyone. People do not know what they are doing when they worship the material energy in the form of goddess Kālī or Durgā for material boons. They ask, "Mother, give me great riches, give me a good wife, give me fame, give me victory." But such devotees of the goddess Māyā, or Durgā, do not know that they are being cheated by that goddess. Material achievement is actually no achievement because as soon as one is illusioned by the material gifts, he becomes more and more entangled, and there is no question of liberation. One should be intelligent enough to know how to utilize material assets for the purpose of spiritual realization. That is called *karma-yoga* or *jñāna-yoga*. Whatever we have we should use as service to the Supreme Person. It is advised in *Bhagavad-gītā, sva-karmaṇā tam abhyarcya:* one should try to worship the Supreme Personality of Godhead by one's assets. There are many forms of service to the Supreme Lord, and anyone can render service unto Him according to the best of his ability.

*Thus end the Bhaktivedanta purports of the Third Canto, Twenty-third Chapter, of the* Śrīmad-Bhāgavatam, *entitled "Devahūti's Lamentation."*

## CHAPTER TWENTY-FOUR

# The Renunciation of Kardama Muni

### TEXT 1

मैत्रेय उवाच

निर्वेदवादिनीमेवं मनोर्दुहितरं मुनिः ।
दयालुः शालिनीमाह शुक्लाभिव्याहृतं स्मरन् ॥ १ ॥

*maitreya uvāca*
*nirveda-vādinīm evaṁ*
*manor duhitaraṁ muniḥ*
*dayāluḥ śālinīm āha*
*śuklābhivyāhṛtaṁ smaran*

*maitreyaḥ*—the great sage Maitreya; *uvāca*—said; *nirveda-vādinīm*—who was speaking words full of renunciation; *evam*—thus; *manoḥ*—of Svāyambhuva Manu; *duhitaram*—to the daughter; *muniḥ*—the sage Kardama; *dayāluḥ*—merciful; *śālinīm*—who was worthy of praise; *āha*—replied; *śukla*—by Lord Viṣṇu; *abhivyāhṛtam*—what was said; *smaran*—recalling.

### TRANSLATION

**Recalling the words of Lord Viṣṇu, the merciful sage Kardama replied as follows to Svāyambhuva Manu's praiseworthy daughter, Devahūti, who was speaking words full of renunciation.**

### TEXT 2

ऋषिरुवाच

मा खिदो राजपुत्रीत्थमात्मानं प्रत्यनिन्दिते ।
भगवांस्तेऽक्षरो गर्भमदूरात्सम्प्रपत्स्यते ॥ २ ॥

*ṛṣir uvāca*
*mā khido rāja-putrīttham*
*ātmānaṁ praty anindite*
*bhagavāṁs te 'kṣaro garbham*
*adūrāt samprapatsyate*

*ṛṣiḥ uvāca*—the sage said; *mā khidaḥ*—do not be disappointed; *rāja-putri*—O princess; *ittham*—in this way; *ātmānam*—yourself; *prati*—toward; *anindite*—O praiseworthy Devahūti; *bhagavān*—the Supreme Personality of Godhead; *te*—your; *akṣaraḥ*—infallible; *garbham*—womb; *adūrāt*—without delay; *samprapatsyate*—will enter.

## TRANSLATION

**The sage said: Do not be disappointed with yourself, O princess. You are actually praiseworthy. The infallible Supreme Personality of Godhead will shortly enter your womb as your son.**

## PURPORT

Kardama Muni encouraged his wife not to be sorry, thinking herself unfortunate, because the Supreme Personality of Godhead, by His incarnation, was going to come from her body.

## TEXT 3

धृतव्रतासि भद्रं ते दमेन नियमेन च ।
तपोद्रविणदानैश्च श्रद्धया चेश्वरं भज ॥ ३ ॥

*dhṛta-vratāsi bhadraṁ te*
*damena niyamena ca*
*tapo-draviṇa-dānaiś ca*
*śraddhayā ceśvaraṁ bhaja*

*dhṛta-vratā asi*—you have undertaken sacred vows; *bhadram te*—may God bless you; *damena*—by control of the senses; *niyamena*—by religious observances; *ca*—and; *tapaḥ*—austerities; *draviṇa*—of money; *dānaiḥ*—by giving in charity; *ca*—and; *śraddhayā*—with great faith; *ca*—and; *īśvaram*—the Supreme Lord; *bhaja*—worship.

## TRANSLATION

**You have undertaken sacred vows. God will bless you. Hence you should worship the Lord with great faith, through sensory control, religious observances, austerities and gifts of your money in charity.**

## PURPORT

In order to spiritually advance or to achieve the mercy of the Lord, one must be self-controlled in the following manner: he must be restrained in sense gratification and must follow the rules and regulations of religious principles. Without austerity and penance and without sacrificing one's riches, one cannot achieve the mercy of the Supreme Lord. Kardama Muni advised his wife: "You have to factually engage in devotional service with austerity and penance, following the religious principles and giving charity. Then the Supreme Lord will be pleased with you, and He will come as your son."

## TEXT 4

स त्वयाराधितः शुक्लो वितन्वन्मामकं यशः।
छेत्ता ते हृदयग्रन्थिमौदर्यो ब्रह्मभावनः ॥ ४ ॥

*sa tvayārādhitaḥ śuklo*
*vitanvan māmakaṁ yaśaḥ*
*chettā te hṛdaya-granthim*
*audaryo brahma-bhāvanaḥ*

*saḥ*—He; *tvayā*—by you; *ārādhitaḥ*—being worshiped; *śuklaḥ*—the Personality of Godhead; *vitanvan*—spreading; *māmakam*—my; *yaśaḥ*—fame; *chettā*—He will cut; *te*—your; *hṛdaya*—of the heart; *granthim*—knot; *audaryaḥ*—your son; *brahma*—knowledge of Brahman; *bhāvanaḥ*—teaching.

## TRANSLATION

**The Personality of Godhead, being worshiped by you, will spread my name and fame. He will vanquish the knot of your heart by becoming your son and teaching knowledge of Brahman.**

## PURPORT

When the Supreme Personality of Godhead comes to disseminate spiritual knowledge for the benefit of all people, He generally descends as the son of a devotee, being pleased by the devotee's devotional service. The Supreme Personality of Godhead is the father of everyone. No one, therefore, is His father, but by His inconceivable energy He accepts some of the devotees as His parents and descendants. It is explained here that spiritual knowledge vanquishes the knot of the heart. Matter and spirit are knotted by false ego. This identification of oneself with matter, which is called *hṛdaya-granthi,* exists for all conditioned souls, and it becomes more and more tightened when there is too much affection for sex life. The explanation was given by Lord Ṛṣabha to His sons that this material world is an atmosphere of attraction between male and female. That attraction takes the shape of a knot in the heart, and by material affection it becomes still more tight. For people who hanker after material possessions, society, friendship and love, this knot of affection becomes very strong. It is only by *brahma-bhāvana*—the instruction by which spiritual knowledge is enhanced—that the knot in the heart is cut to pieces. No material weapon is needed to cut this knot, but it requires bona fide spiritual instruction. Kardama Muni instructed his wife, Devahūti, that the Lord would appear as her son and disseminate spiritual knowledge to cut the knot of material identification.

## TEXT 5

मैत्रेय उवाच
देवहूत्यपि संदेशं गौरवेण प्रजापतेः ।
सम्यक् श्रद्धाय पुरुषं कूटस्थमभजद्गुरुम् ॥ ५ ॥

*maitreya uvāca*
*devahūty api sandeśaṁ*
*gauraveṇa prajāpateḥ*
*samyak śraddhāya puruṣaṁ*
*kūṭa-stham abhajad gurum*

*maitreyaḥ uvāca*—Maitreya said; *devahūtī*—Devahūti; *api*—also; *sandeśam*—the direction; *gauraveṇa*—with great respect; *prajā-*

*pateḥ*—of Kardama; *samyak*—complete; *śraddhāya*—having faith in; *puruṣam*—the Supreme Personality of Godhead; *kūṭa-stham*—situated in everyone's heart; *abhajat*—worshiped; *gurum*—most worshipable.

## TRANSLATION

**Śrī Maitreya said: Devahūti was fully faithful and respectful toward the direction of her husband, Kardama, who was one of the Prajāpatis, or generators of human beings in the universe. O great sage, she thus began to worship the master of the universe, the Supreme Personality of Godhead, who is situated in everyone's heart.**

## PURPORT

This is the process of spiritual realization; one has to receive instruction from a bona fide spiritual master. Kardama Muni was Devahūti's husband, but because he instructed her on how to achieve spiritual perfection, he naturally became her spiritual master also. There are many instances wherein the husband becomes the spiritual master. Lord Śiva also is the spiritual master of his consort, Pārvatī. A husband should be so enlightened that he should become the spiritual master of his wife in order to enlighten her in the advancement of Kṛṣṇa consciousness. Generally *strī*, or woman, is less intelligent than man; therefore, if the husband is intelligent enough, the woman gets a great opportunity for spiritual enlightenment.

Here it is clearly said (*samyak śraddhāya*) that with great faith one should receive knowledge from the spiritual master and with great faith execute the performance of service. Śrīla Viśvanātha Cakravartī Ṭhākura, in his commentary on *Bhagavad-gītā*, has especially stressed the instruction of the spiritual master. One should accept the instruction of the spiritual master as one's life and soul. Whether one is liberated or not liberated, one should execute the instruction of the spiritual master with great faith. It is also stated that the Lord is situated in everyone's heart. One does not have to seek the Lord outside; He is already there. One simply has to concentrate on one's worship in good faith, as instructed by the bona fide spiritual master, and one's efforts will come out successfully. It is also clear that the Supreme Personality of Godhead does not appear as an ordinary child; He appears as He is. As stated in

*Bhagavad-gītā,* He appears by His own internal potency, *ātma-māyā.* And how does He appear? He appears when pleased by the worship of a devotee. A devotee may ask the Lord to appear as her son. The Lord is already sitting within the heart, and if He comes out from the body of a devotee it does not mean that the particular woman becomes His mother in the material sense. He is always there, but in order to please His devotee, He appears as her son.

## TEXT 6

तस्यां बहुतिथे काले भगवान्मधुसूदनः ।
कार्दमं वीर्यमापन्नो जज्ञेऽग्निरिव दारुणि ॥ ६ ॥

*tasyāṁ bahu-tithe kāle*
*bhagavān madhusūdanaḥ*
*kārdamaṁ vīryam āpanno*
*jajñe 'gnir iva dāruṇi*

*tasyām*—in Devahūti; *bahu-tithe kāle*—after many years; *bhagavān*—the Supreme Personality of Godhead; *madhu-sūdanaḥ*—the killer of the demon Madhu; *kārdamam*—of Kardama; *vīryam*—the semen; *āpannaḥ*—entered; *jajñe*—He appeared; *agniḥ*—fire; *iva*—like; *dāruṇi*—in wood.

## TRANSLATION

**After many, many years, the Supreme Personality of Godhead, Madhusūdana, the killer of the demon Madhu, having entered the semen of Kardama, appeared in Devahūti just as fire comes from wood in a sacrifice.**

## PURPORT

It is clearly stated here that the Lord is always the Supreme Personality of Godhead, although He appeared as the son of Kardama Muni. Fire is already present in wood, but by a certain process, fire is kindled. Similarly, God is all-pervading. He is everywhere, and since He may come out from everything, He appeared in His devotee's semen. Just as an ordinary living entity takes his birth by taking shelter of the semen of a certain living entity, the Supreme Personality of Godhead accepts the shelter of the semen of His devotee and comes out as His son. This manifests His full independence to act in any way, and it does not mean that He is an ordinary living entity forced to take birth in a certain type of womb. Lord Nṛsiṁha appeared from the pillar of Hiraṇyakaśipu's palace, Lord Varāha appeared from the nostril of Brahmā, and Lord Kapila appeared from the semen of Kardama, but this does not mean that the nostril of Brahmā or the pillar of Hiraṇyakaśipu's palace or the semen of Kardama Muni is the source of the appearance of the Lord. The Lord is always the Lord. *Bhagavān madhusūdanaḥ*—He is the killer of all kinds of demons, and He always remains the Lord, even if He appears as the son of a particular devotee. The word *kārdamam* is significant, for it indicates that the Lord had some devotional affection or relationship in devotional service with Kardama and Devahūti. But we should not mistakenly understand that He was born just like an ordinary living entity from the semen of Kardama Muni in the womb of Devahūti.

## TEXT 7

अवादयंस्तदा व्योम्नि वादित्राणि घनाघनाः ।
गायन्ति तं स्म गन्धर्वा नृत्यन्त्यप्सरसो मुदा ॥ ७ ॥

*avādayaṁs tadā vyomni*
*vāditrāṇi ghanāghanāḥ*
*gāyanti taṁ sma gandharvā*
*nṛtyanty apsaraso mudā*

*avādayan*—sounded; *tadā*—at that time; *vyomni*—in the sky; *vāditrāṇi*—musical instruments; *ghanāghanāḥ*—the rain clouds; *gāyanti*—sang; *tam*—to Him; *sma*—certainly; *gandharvāḥ*—the Gandharvas; *nṛtyanti*—danced; *apsarasaḥ*—the Apsarās; *mudā*—in joyful ecstasy.

## TRANSLATION

**At the time of His descent on earth, demigods in the form of raining clouds sounded musical instruments in the sky. The celestial musicians, the Gandharvas, sang the glories of the Lord,**

**while celestial dancing girls known as Apsarās danced in joyful ecstasy.**

## TEXT 8

पेतुः सुमनसो दिव्याः खेचरैरपवर्जिताः ।
प्रसेदुश्च दिशः सर्वा अम्भांसि च मनांसि च ॥ ८ ॥

*petuḥ sumanaso divyāḥ*
*khe-carair apavarjitāḥ*
*praseduś ca diśaḥ sarvā*
*ambhāṁsi ca manāṁsi ca*

*petuḥ*—fell; *sumanasaḥ*—flowers; *divyāḥ*—beautiful; *khe-caraiḥ*—by the demigods who fly in the sky; *apavarjitāḥ*—dropped; *praseduḥ*—became satisfied; *ca*—and; *diśaḥ*—directions; *sarvāḥ*—all; *ambhāṁsi*—waters; *ca*—and; *manāṁsi*—minds; *ca*—and.

## TRANSLATION

**At the time of the Lord's appearance, the demigods flying freely in the sky showered flowers. All the directions, all the waters and everyone's mind became very satisfied.**

## PURPORT

It is learned herewith that in the higher sky there are living entities who can travel through the air without being hampered. Although we can travel in outer space, we are hampered by so many impediments, but they are not. We learn from the pages of *Śrīmad-Bhāgavatam* that the inhabitants of the planet called Siddhaloka can travel in space from one planet to another without impediment. They showered flowers on the earth when Lord Kapila, the son of Kardama, appeared.

## TEXT 9

तत्कर्दमाश्रमपदं सरस्वत्या परिश्रितम् ।
स्वयम्भूः साकमृषिभिर्मरीच्यादिभिरभ्ययात् ॥ ९ ॥

*tat kardamāśrama-padaṁ*
*sarasvatyā pariśritam*
*svayambhūḥ sākam ṛṣibhir*
*marīcy-ādibhir abhyayāt*

*tat*—that; *kardama*—of Kardama; *āśrama-padam*—to the place of the hermitage; *sarasvatyā*—by the River Sarasvatī; *pariśritam*—surrounded; *svayambhūḥ*—Brahmā (the self-born); *sākam*—along with; *ṛṣibhiḥ*—the sages; *marīci*—the great sage Marīci; *ādibhiḥ*—and others; *abhyayāt*—he came there.

## TRANSLATION

**Brahmā, the first-born living being, went along with Marīci and other sages to the place of Kardama's hermitage, which was surrounded by the River Sarasvatī.**

## PURPORT

Brahmā is called Svayambhū because he is not born of any material father and mother. He is the first living creature and is born from the lotus which grows from the abdomen of the Supreme Personality of Godhead Garbhodakaśāyī Viṣṇu. Therefore he is called Svayambhū, self-born.

## TEXT 10

भगवन्तं परं ब्रह्म सत्त्वेनांशेन शत्रुहन् ।
तत्त्वसंख्यानविज्ञप्त्यै जातं विद्वानजः स्वराट् ॥१०॥

*bhagavantaṁ paraṁ brahma*
*sattvenāṁśena śatru-han*
*tattva-saṅkhyāna-vijñaptyai*
*jātaṁ vidvān ajaḥ svarāṭ*

*bhagavantam*—the Lord; *param*—supreme; *brahma*—Brahman; *sattvena*—having an uncontaminated existence; *aṁśena*—by a plenary portion; *śatru-han*—O killer of the enemy, Vidura; *tattva-saṅkhyāna*—

the philosophy of the twenty-four material elements; *vijñaptyai*—for explaining; *jātam*—appeared; *vidvān*—knowing; *ajaḥ*—the unborn (Lord Brahmā); *sva-rāṭ*—independent.

## TRANSLATION

**Maitreya continued: O killer of the enemy, the unborn Lord Brahmā, who is almost independent in acquiring knowledge, could understand that a portion of the Supreme Personality of Godhead, in His quality of pure existence, had appeared in the womb of Devahūti just to explain the complete state of knowledge known as sāṅkhya-yoga.**

## PURPORT

In *Bhagavad-gītā*, Fifteenth Chapter, it is stated that the Lord Himself is the compiler of *Vedānta-sūtra*, and He is the perfect knower of *Vedānta-sūtra*. Similarly, the Sāṅkhya philosophy is compiled by the Supreme Personality of Godhead in His appearance as Kapila. There is an imitation Kapila who has a Sāṅkhya philosophical system, but Kapila the incarnation of God is different from that Kapila. Kapila the son of Kardama Muni, in His system of Sāṅkhya philosophy, very explicitly explained not only the material world but also the spiritual world. Brahmā could understand this fact because he is *svarāṭ*, almost independent in receiving knowledge. He is called *svarāṭ* because he did not go to any school or college to learn but learned everything from within. Because Brahmā is the first living creature within this universe, he had no teacher; his teacher was the Supreme Personality of Godhead Himself, who is seated in the heart of every living creature. Brahmā acquired knowledge directly from the Supreme Lord within the heart; therefore he is sometimes called *svarāṭ* and *aja*.

Another important point is stated here. *Sattvenāṁśena:* when the Supreme Personality of Godhead appears, He brings with Him all His paraphernalia of Vaikuṇṭha; therefore His name, His form, His quality, His paraphernalia and His entourage all belong to the transcendental world. Real goodness is in the transcendental world. Here in the material world, the quality of goodness is not pure. Goodness may exist, but there must also be some tinges of passion and ignorance. In the spiritual world the unalloyed quality of goodness prevails; there the quality of goodness is called *śuddha-sattva,* pure goodness. Another name for *śuddha-sattva* is *vasudeva* because God is born from Vasudeva. Another meaning is that when one is purely situated in the qualities of goodness, he can understand the form, name, quality, paraphernalia and entourage of the Supreme Personality of Godhead. The word *aṁśena* also indicates that the Supreme Personality of Godhead, Kṛṣṇa, appeared as Kapiladeva in a portion of His portion. God expands either as *kalā* or as *aṁśa. Aṁśa* means "direct expansion," and *kalā* means "expansion of the expansion." There is no difference between the expansion, the expansion of the expansion, and the Supreme Personality of Godhead directly, as there is no difference between one candle and another—but still the candle from which the others are lit is called the original. Kṛṣṇa, therefore, is called the Parabrahman, or the ultimate Godhead and cause of all causes.

## TEXT 11

सभाजयन् विशुद्धेन चेतसा तच्चिकीर्षितम् ।
प्रहृष्यमाणैरसुभिः कर्दमं चेदमभ्यधात् ॥११॥

*sabhājayan viśuddhena*
*cetasā tac-cikīrṣitam*
*prahṛṣyamāṇair asubhiḥ*
*kardamaṁ cedam abhyadhāt*

*sabhājayan*—worshiping; *viśuddhena*—pure; *cetasā*—with a heart; *tat*—of the Supreme Personality of Godhead; *cikīrṣitam*—the intended activities; *prahṛṣyamāṇaiḥ*—gladdened; *asubhiḥ*—with senses; *kardamam*—to Kardama Muni; *ca*—and Devahūti; *idam*—this; *abhyadhāt*—spoke.

## TRANSLATION

**After worshiping the Supreme Lord with gladdened senses and a pure heart for His intended activities as an incarnation, Brahmā spoke as follows to Kardama and Devahūti.**

## PURPORT

As explained in *Bhagavad-gītā*, Fourth Chapter, anyone who understands the transcendental activities, the appearance and the disappearance of the Supreme Personality of Godhead is to be considered liberated. Brahmā, therefore, is a liberated soul. Although he is in charge of this material world, he is not exactly like the common living entity. Since he is liberated from the majority of the follies of the common living entities, he was in knowledge of the appearance of the Supreme Personality of Godhead, and he therefore worshiped the Lord's activities, and with a glad heart he also praised Kardama Muni because the Supreme Personality of Godhead, as Kapila, had appeared as his son. One who can become the father of the Supreme Personality of Godhead is certainly a great devotee. There is a verse spoken by a *brāhmaṇa* in which he says that he does not know what the *Vedas* and what the *Purāṇas* are, but while others might be interested in the *Vedas* or *Purāṇas*, he is interested in Nanda Mahārāja, who appeared as the father of Kṛṣṇa. The *brāhmaṇa* wanted to worship Nanda Mahārāja because the Supreme Personality of Godhead, as a child, crawled in the yard of his house. These are some of the good sentiments of devotees. If a recognized devotee brings forth the Supreme Personality of Godhead as his son, how he should be praised! Brahmā, therefore, not only worshiped the incarnation of Godhead Kapila but also praised His so-called father, Kardama Muni.

## TEXT 12

ब्रह्मोवाच

त्वया मेऽपचितिस्तात कल्पिता निर्व्यलीकतः ।
यन्मे सञ्जगृहे वाक्यं भवान्मानद मानयन् ॥१२॥

*brahmovāca*
*tvayā me 'pacitis tāta*
*kalpitā nirvyalīkataḥ*
*yan me sañjagṛhe vākyaṁ*
*bhavān mānada mānayan*

*brahmā*—Lord Brahmā; *uvāca*—said; *tvayā*—by you; *me*—my; *apacitiḥ*—worship; *tāta*—O son; *kalpitā*—is accomplished; *nirvyalīkataḥ*—

without duplicity; *yat*—since; *me*—my; *sañjagṛhe*—have completely accepted; *vākyam*—instructions; *bhavān*—you; *māna-da*—O Kardama (one who offers honor to others); *mānayan*—respecting.

## TRANSLATION

**Lord Brahmā said: My dear son Kardama, since you have completely accepted my instructions without duplicity, showing them proper respect, you have worshiped me properly. Whatever instructions you took from me you have carried out, and thereby you have honored me.**

## PURPORT

Lord Brahmā, as the first living entity within the universe, is supposed to be the spiritual master of everyone, and he is also the father, the creator, of all beings. Kardama Muni is one of the Prajāpatis, or creators of the living entities, and he is also a son of Brahmā. Brahmā praises Kardama because he carried out the orders of the spiritual master *in toto* and without cheating. A conditioned soul in the material world has the disqualification of cheating. He has four disqualifications: he is sure to commit mistakes, he is sure to be illusioned, he is prone to cheat others, and his senses are imperfect. But if one carries out the order of the spiritual master by disciplic succession, or the *paramparā* system, he overcomes the four defects. Therefore, knowledge received from the bona fide spiritual master is not cheating. Any other knowledge which is manufactured by the conditioned soul is cheating only. Brahmā knew well that Kardama Muni exactly carried out the instructions received from him and that he actually honored his spiritual master. To honor the spiritual master means to carry out his instructions word for word.

## TEXT 13

एतावत्येव शुश्रूषा कार्या पितरि पुत्रकैः ।
बाढमित्यनुमन्येत गौरवेण गुरोर्वचः ॥१३॥

*etāvaty eva śuśrūṣā*
*kāryā pitari putrakaiḥ*
*bāḍham ity anumanyeta*
*gauraveṇa guror vacaḥ*

*etāvatī*—to this extent; *eva*—exactly; *śuśrūṣā*—service; *kāryā*—ought to be rendered; *pitari*—to the father; *putrakaiḥ*—by the sons; *bāḍham iti*—accepting, "Yes, sir"; *anumanyeta*—he should obey; *gauraveṇa*—with due deference; *guroḥ*—of the *guru; vacaḥ*—commands.

## TRANSLATION

**Sons ought to render service to their father exactly to this extent. One should obey the command of his father or spiritual master with due deference, saying, "Yes, sir."**

## PURPORT

Two words in this verse are very important; one word is *pitari,* and another word is *guroḥ.* The son or disciple should accept the words of his spiritual master and father without hesitation. Whatever the father and the spiritual master order should be taken without argument: "Yes." There should be no instance in which the disciple or the son says, "This is not correct. I cannot carry it out." When he says that, he is fallen. The father and the spiritual master are on the same platform because a spiritual master is the second father. The higher classes are called *dvija,* twice-born. Whenever there is a question of birth, there must be a father. The first birth is made possible by the actual father, and the second birth is made possible by the spiritual master. Sometimes the father and the spiritual master may be the same man, and sometimes they are different men. In any case, the order of the father or the order of the spiritual master must be carried out without hesitation, with an immediate yes. There should be no argument. That is real service to the father and to the spiritual master. Viśvanātha Cakravartī Ṭhākura has stated that the order of the spiritual master is the life and soul of the disciples. As a man cannot separate his life from his body, a disciple cannot separate the order of the spiritual master from his life. If a disciple follows the instruction of the spiritual master in that way, he is sure to become perfect. This is confirmed in the *Upaniṣads:* the import of Vedic instruction is revealed automatically only to one who has implicit faith in the Supreme Personality of Godhead and in his spiritual master. One may be materially considered an illiterate man, but if he has faith in the spiritual master as well as in the Supreme Personality of Godhead, then the meaning of scriptural revelation is immediately manifested before him.

## TEXT 14

इमा दुहितरः सत्यस्तव वत्स सुमध्यमाः ।
सर्गमेतं प्रभावैः स्वैर्बृंहयिष्यन्त्यनेकधा ॥१४॥

*imā duhitaraḥ satyas*
*tava vatsa sumadhyamāḥ*
*sargam etaṁ prabhāvaiḥ svair*
*bṛṁhayiṣyanty anekadhā*

*imāḥ*—these; *duhitaraḥ*—daughters; *satyaḥ*—chaste; *tava*—your; *vatsa*—O my dear son; *su-madhyamāḥ*—thin-waisted; *sargam*—creation; *etam*—this; *prabhāvaiḥ*—by descendants; *svaiḥ*—their own; *bṛṁhayiṣyanti*—they will increase; *aneka-dhā*—in various ways.

## TRANSLATION

**Lord Brahmā then praised Kardama Muni's nine daughters, saying: All your thin-waisted daughters are certainly very chaste. I am sure they will increase this creation by their own descendants in various ways.**

## PURPORT

In the beginning of creation, Brahmā was concerned more or less with increasing the population, and when he saw that Kardama Muni had already begotten nine nice daughters, he was hopeful that through the daughters many children would come who would take charge of the creative principle of the material world. He was therefore happy to see them. The word *sumadhyamā* means "a good daughter of a beautiful woman." If she has a thin waist, a woman is considered very beautiful. All the daughters of Kardama Muni were of the same beautiful feature.

## TEXT 15

अतस्त्वमृषिमुख्येभ्यो यथाशीलं यथारुचि ।
आत्मजाः परिदेह्यद्य विस्तृणीहि यशो भुवि ॥१५॥

*atas tvam ṛṣi-mukhyebhyo*
*yathā-śīlaṁ yathā-ruci*

*ātmajāḥ paridehy adya*
*vistṛṇīhi yaśo bhuvi*

*ataḥ*—therefore; *tvam*—you; *ṛṣi-mukhyebhyaḥ*—unto the foremost sages; *yathā-śīlam*—according to temperament; *yathā-ruci*—according to taste; *ātma-jāḥ*—your daughters; *paridehi*—please give away; *adya*—today; *vistṛṇīhi*—spread; *yaśaḥ*—fame; *bhuvi*—over the universe.

## TRANSLATION

**Therefore, today please give away your daughters to the foremost of the sages, with due regard for the girls' temperaments and likings, and thereby spread your fame all over the universe.**

## PURPORT

The nine principal *ṛṣis*, or sages, are Marīci, Atri, Aṅgirā, Pulastya, Pulaha, Kratu, Bhṛgu, Vasiṣṭha and Atharvā. All these *ṛṣis* are most important, and Brahmā desired that the nine daughters already born of Kardama Muni be handed over to them. Here two words are used very significantly—*yathā-śīlam* and *yathā-ruci*. The daughters should be handed over to the respective *ṛṣis*, not blindly, but according to the combination of character and taste. That is the art of combining a man and woman. Man and woman should not be united simply on the consideration of sex life. There are many other considerations, especially character and taste. If the taste and character differ between the man and woman, their combination will be unhappy. Even about forty years ago, in Indian marriages, the taste and character of the boy and girl were first of all matched, and then they were allowed to marry. This was done under the direction of the respective parents. The parents used to astrologically determine the character and tastes of the boy and girl, and when they corresponded, the match was selected: "This girl and this boy are just suitable, and they should be married." Other considerations were less important. The same system was also advised in the beginning of the creation by Brahmā: "Your daughters should be handed over to the *ṛṣis* according to taste and character."

According to astrological calculation, a person is classified according to whether he belongs to the godly or demoniac quality. In that way the spouse was selected. A girl of godly quality should be handed over to a boy of godly quality. A girl of demoniac quality should be handed over to a boy of demoniac quality. Then they will be happy. But if the girl is demoniac and the boy is godly, then the combination is incompatible; they cannot be happy in such a marriage. At the present moment, because boys and girls are not married according to quality and character, most marriages are unhappy, and there is divorce.

It is foretold in the Twelfth Canto of the *Bhāgavatam* that in this age of Kali married life will be accepted on the consideration of sex only; when the boy and girl are pleased in sex, they get married, and when there is deficiency in sex, they separate. That is not actual marriage, but a combination of men and women like cats and dogs. Therefore, the children produced in the modern age are not exactly human beings. Human beings must be twice-born. A child is first born of a good father and mother, and then he is born again of the spiritual master and the *Vedas*. The first mother and father bring about his birth into the world; then the spiritual master and the *Vedas* become his second father and mother. According to the Vedic system of marriage for producing children, every man and woman was enlightened in spiritual knowledge, and at the time of their combination to produce a child, everything was scrutinizingly and scientifically done.

## TEXT 16

वेदाहमाद्यं पुरुषमवतीर्णं स्वमायया ।
भूतानां शेवधिं देहं बिभ्राणं कपिलं मुने ॥१६॥

*vedāham ādyaṁ puruṣam*
*avatīrṇaṁ sva-māyayā*
*bhūtānāṁ śevadhiṁ dehaṁ*
*bibhrāṇaṁ kapilaṁ mune*

*veda*—know; *aham*—I; *ādyam*—the original; *puruṣam*—enjoyer; *avatīrṇam*—incarnated; *sva-māyayā*—by His own internal energy; *bhūtānām*—of all the living entities; *śevadhim*—the bestower of all desired, who is just like a vast treasure; *deham*—the body; *bibhrāṇam*—assuming; *kapilam*—Kapila Muni; *mune*—O sage Kardama.

## TRANSLATION

**O Kardama, I know that the original Supreme Personality of Godhead has now appeared as an incarnation by His internal energy. He is the bestower of all desired by the living entities, and He has now assumed the body of Kapila Muni.**

## PURPORT

In this verse we find the words *puruṣam avatīrṇaṁ sva-māyayā.* The Supreme Personality of Godhead is everlastingly, eternally the form of *puruṣa*, the predominator or enjoyer, and when He appears He never accepts anything of this material energy. The spiritual world is a manifestation of His personal, internal potency, whereas the material world is a manifestation of His material, or differentiated, energy. The word *sva-māyayā*, "by His own internal potency," indicates that whenever the Supreme Personality of Godhead descends, He comes in His own energy. He may assume the body of a human being, but that body is not material. In *Bhagavad-gītā*, therefore, it is clearly stated that only fools and rascals, *mūḍhas*, consider the body of Kṛṣṇa to be the body of a common human being. The word *śevadhim* means that He is the original bestower of all the necessities of life upon the living entities. In the *Vedas* also it is stated that He is the chief living entity and that He bestows all the desired necessities of other living entities. Because He is the bestower of the necessities of all others, He is called God. The Supreme is also a living entity; He is not impersonal. As we are individual, the Supreme Personality of Godhead is also individual—but He is the supreme individual. That is the difference between God and the ordinary living entities.

## TEXT 17

**ज्ञानविज्ञानयोगेन कर्मणामुद्धरन् जटाः ।**
**हिरण्यकेशः पद्माक्षः पद्ममुद्रापदाम्बुजः ॥१७॥**

*jñāna-vijñāna-yogena*
*karmaṇām uddharan jaṭāḥ*
*hiraṇya-keśaḥ padmākṣaḥ*
*padma-mudrā-padāmbujaḥ*

*jñāna*—of scriptural knowledge; *vijñāna*—and application; *yogena*—by means of mystic *yoga; karmaṇām*—of material actions; *uddharan*—uprooting; *jaṭāḥ*—the roots; *hiraṇya-keśaḥ*—golden hair; *padma-akṣaḥ*—lotus-eyed; *padma-mudrā*—marked with the sign of the lotus; *pada-ambujaḥ*—having lotus feet.

## TRANSLATION

**By mystic yoga and the practical application of knowledge from the scriptures, Kapila Muni, who is characterized by His golden hair, His eyes just like lotus petals and His lotus feet, which bear the marks of lotus flowers, will uproot the deep-rooted desire for work in this material world.**

## PURPORT

In this verse the activities and bodily features of Kapila Muni are very nicely described. The activities of Kapila Muni are forecast herein: He will present the philosophy of Sāṅkhya in such a way that by studying His philosophy people will be able to uproot the deep-rooted desire for *karma*, fruitive activities. Everyone in this material world engages in achieving the fruits of his labor. A man tries to be happy by achieving the fruits of his own honest labor, but actually he becomes more and more entangled. One cannot get out of this entanglement unless he has perfect knowledge, or devotional service.

Those who are trying to get out of the entanglement by speculation are also doing their best, but in the Vedic scriptures we find that if one has taken to the devotional service of the Lord in Kṛṣṇa consciousness, he can very easily uproot the deep-rooted desire for fruitive activities. Sāṅkhya philosophy will be broadcast by Kapila Muni for that purpose. His bodily features are also described herein. *Jñāna* does not refer to ordinary research work. *Jñāna* entails receiving knowledge from the scriptures through the spiritual master by disciplic succession. In the modern age there is a tendency to do research by mental speculation and concoction. But the man who speculates forgets that he himself is subject to the four defects of nature: he is sure to commit mistakes, his senses are imperfect, he is sure to fall into illusion, and he is cheating. Unless one has perfect knowledge from disciplic succession, he simply puts forth some theories of his own creation; therefore he is cheating people. *Jñāna* means knowledge received through disciplic succession from the scriptures, and *vijñāna* means practical application of such knowledge. Kapila Muni's Sāṅkhya system of philosophy is based on *jñāna* and *vijñāna*.

## TEXT 18

एष मानवि ते गर्भं प्रविष्टः कैटभार्दनः ।
अविद्यासंशयग्रन्थिं छित्त्वा गां विचरिष्यति ॥१८॥

*eṣa mānavi te garbhaṁ*
*praviṣṭaḥ kaiṭabhārdanaḥ*
*avidyā-saṁśaya-granthiṁ*
*chittvā gāṁ vicariṣyati*

*eṣaḥ*—the same Supreme Personality of Godhead; *mānavi*—O daughter of Manu; *te*—your; *garbham*—womb; *praviṣṭaḥ*—has entered; *kaiṭabha-ardanaḥ*—the killer of the demon Kaiṭabha; *avidyā*—of ignorance; *saṁśaya*—and of doubt; *granthim*—the knot; *chittvā*—cutting off; *gām*—the world; *vicariṣyati*—He will travel over.

## TRANSLATION

**Lord Brahmā then told Devahūti: My dear daughter of Manu, the same Supreme Personality of Godhead who killed the demon Kaiṭabha is now within your womb. He will cut off all the knots of your ignorance and doubt. Then He will travel all over the world.**

## PURPORT

Here the word *avidyā* is very significant. *Avidyā* means forgetfulness of one's identity. Every one of us is a spirit soul, but we have forgotten. We think, "I am this body." This is called *avidyā*. *Saṁśaya-granthi* means "doubtfulness." The knot of doubtfulness is tied when the soul identifies with the material world. That knot is also called *ahaṅkāra*, the junction of matter and spirit. By proper knowledge received from the scriptures in disciplic succession and by proper application of that knowledge, one can free himself from this binding combination of matter and spirit. Brahmā assures Devahūti that her son will enlighten her, and after enlightening her He will travel all over the world, distributing the system of Sāṅkhya philosophy.

The word *saṁśaya* means "doubtful knowledge." Speculative and pseudo yogic knowledge is all doubtful. At the present moment the so-called *yoga* system is prosecuted on the understanding that by agitation of the different stations of the bodily construction one can find that he is God. The mental speculators think similarly, but they are all doubtful. Real knowledge is expounded in *Bhagavad-gītā:* "Just become Kṛṣṇa conscious. Just worship Kṛṣṇa and become a devotee of Kṛṣṇa." That is real knowledge, and anyone who follows that system becomes perfect without a doubt.

## TEXT 19

अयं सिद्धगणाधीशः साङ्ख्याचार्यैः सुसम्मतः ।
लोके कपिल इत्याख्यां गन्ता ते कीर्तिवर्धनः ॥१९॥

*ayaṁ siddha-gaṇādhīśaḥ*
*sāṅkhyācāryaiḥ susammataḥ*
*loke kapila ity ākhyāṁ*
*gantā te kīrti-vardhanaḥ*

*ayam*—this Personality of Godhead; *siddha-gaṇa*—of the perfected sages; *adhīśaḥ*—the head; *sāṅkhya-ācāryaiḥ*—by *ācāryas* expert in Sāṅkhya philosophy; *su-sammataḥ*—approved according to Vedic principles; *loke*—in the world; *kapilaḥ iti*—as Kapila; *ākhyām*—celebrated; *gantā*—He will go about; *te*—your; *kīrti*—fame; *vardhanaḥ*—increasing.

## TRANSLATION

**Your son will be the head of all the perfected souls. He will be approved by the ācāryas expert in disseminating real knowledge, and among the people He will be celebrated by the name Kapila. As the son of Devahūti, He will increase your fame.**

## PURPORT

Sāṅkhya philosophy is the philosophical system enunciated by Kapila, the son of Devahūti. The other Kapila, who is not the son of Devahūti, is an imitation. This is the statement of Brahmā, and because we belong to Brahmā's disciplic succession we should accept his statement that the real Kapila is the son of Devahūti and that real Sāṅkhya philosophy is the system of philosophy which He introduced and which will be accepted by the *ācāryas*, the directors of spiritual discipline. The word *susammata* means "accepted by persons who are counted upon to give their good opinion."

## TEXT 20

मैत्रेय उवाच

तावाश्वास्य जगत्स्रष्टा कुमारैः सहनारदः ।
हंसो हंसेन यानेन त्रिधामपरमं ययौ ॥२०॥

*maitreya uvāca*
*tāv āśvāsya jagat-sraṣṭā*
*kumāraiḥ saha-nāradaḥ*
*haṁso haṁsena yānena*
*tri-dhāma-paramaṁ yayau*

*maitreyaḥ uvāca*—Maitreya said; *tau*—the couple; *āśvāsya*—having reassured; *jagat-sraṣṭā*—the creator of the universe; *kumāraiḥ*—along with the Kumāras; *saha-nāradaḥ*—with Nārada; *haṁsaḥ*—Lord Brahmā; *haṁsena yānena*—by his swan carrier; *tri-dhāma-paramam*—to the highest planetary system; *yayau*—went.

## TRANSLATION

**Śrī Maitreya said: After thus speaking to Kardama Muni and his wife Devahūti, Lord Brahmā, the creator of the universe, who is also known as Haṁsa, went back to the highest of the three planetary systems on his swan carrier with the four Kumāras and Nārada.**

## PURPORT

The words *haṁsena yānena* are very significant here. *Haṁsa-yāna*, the airplane by which Brahmā travels all over outer space, resembles a swan. Brahmā is also known as Haṁsa because he can grasp the essence of everything. His abode is called *tri-dhāma-paramam*. There are three divisions of the universe—the upper planetary system, the middle planetary system and the lower planetary system—but his abode is above even Siddhaloka, the upper planetary system. He returned to his own planet with the four Kumāras and Nārada because they were not going to be married. The other *ṛṣis* who came with him, such as Marīci and Atri, remained there because they were to be married to the daughters of Kardama, but his other sons—Sanat, Sanaka, Sanandana, Sanātana and Nārada—went back with him in his swan-shaped airplane. The four Kumāras and Nārada are *naiṣṭhika-brahmacārīs*. *Naiṣṭhika-brahmacārī* refers to one who never wastes his semen at any time. They were not to attend the marriage ceremony of their other brothers, Marīci and the other sages, and therefore they went back with their father, Haṁsa.

## TEXT 21

गते शतधृतौ क्षत्तः कर्दमस्तेन चोदितः ।
यथोदितं स्वदुहितॄः प्रादाद्विश्वसृजां ततः ॥२१॥

*gate śata-dhṛtau kṣattaḥ*
*kardamas tena coditaḥ*
*yathoditaṁ sva-duhitṝḥ*
*prādād viśva-sṛjāṁ tataḥ*

*gate*—after he departed; *śata-dhṛtau*—Lord Brahmā; *kṣattaḥ*—O Vidura; *kardamaḥ*—Kardama Muni; *tena*—by him; *coditaḥ*—ordered; *yathā-uditam*—as told; *sva-duhitṝḥ*—his own daughters; *prādāt*—handed over; *viśva-sṛjām*—to the creators of the world's population; *tataḥ*—thereafter.

## TRANSLATION

**O Vidura, after the departure of Brahmā, Kardama Muni, having been ordered by Brahmā, handed over his nine daughters, as instructed, to the nine great sages who created the population of the world.**

## TEXTS 22–23

मरीचये कलां प्रादादनसूयामथात्रये ।
श्रद्धामङ्गिरसेऽयच्छत्पुलस्त्याय हविर्भुवम् ॥२२॥

पुलहाय गतिं युक्तां क्रतवे च क्रियां सतीम् ।
ख्यातिं च भृगवेऽयच्छद्वसिष्ठायाप्यरुन्धतीम् ॥२३॥

*marīcaye kalāṁ prādād*
*anasūyām athātraye*
*śraddhām aṅgirase 'yacchat*
*pulastyāya havirbhuvam*

*pulahāya gatiṁ yuktāṁ*
*kratave ca kriyāṁ satīm*
*khyātiṁ ca bhṛgave 'yacchad*
*vasiṣṭhāyāpy arundhatīm*

*marīcaye*—unto Marīci; *kalām*—Kalā; *prādāt*—he handed over; *anasūyām*—Anasūyā; *atha*—then; *atraye*—unto Atri; *śraddhām*—Śraddhā; *aṅgirase*—unto Aṅgirā; *ayacchat*—he gave away; *pulastyāya*—unto Pulastya; *havirbhuvam*—Havirbhū; *pulahāya*—unto Pulaha; *gatim*—Gati; *yuktām*—suitable; *kratave*—unto Kratu; *ca*—and; *kriyām*—Kriyā; *satīm*—virtuous; *khyātim*—Khyāti; *ca*—and; *bhṛgave*—unto Bhṛgu; *ayacchat*—he gave away; *vasiṣṭhāya*—unto the sage Vasiṣṭha; *api*—also; *arundhatīm*—Arundhatī.

## TRANSLATION

**Kardama Muni handed over his daughter Kalā to Marīci, and another daughter, Anasūyā, to Atri. He delivered Śraddhā to Aṅgirā, and Havirbhū to Pulastya. He delivered Gati to Pulaha, the chaste Kriyā to Kratu, Khyāti to Bhṛgu, and Arundhatī to Vasiṣṭha.**

## TEXT 24

अथर्वणेऽददाच्छान्तिं यया यज्ञो वितन्यते ।
विप्रर्षभान् कृतोद्वाहान् सदारान् समलालयत् ॥२४॥

*atharvaṇe 'dadāc chāntiṁ*
*yayā yajño vitanyate*
*viprarṣabhān kṛtodvāhān*
*sadārān samalālayat*

*atharvaṇe*—to Atharvā; *adadāt*—he gave away; *śāntim*—Śānti; *yayā*—by whom; *yajñaḥ*—sacrifice; *vitanyate*—is performed; *vipra-ṛṣabhān*—the foremost *brāhmaṇas; kṛta-udvāhān*—married; *sa-dārān*—with their wives; *samalālayat*—maintained them.

## TRANSLATION

**He delivered Śānti to Atharvā. Because of Śānti, sacrificial ceremonies are well performed. Thus he got the foremost brāhmaṇas married, and he maintained them along with their wives.**

## TEXT 25

ततस्त ऋषयः क्षत्तः कृतदारा निमन्त्र्य तम् ।
प्रातिष्ठन्नन्दिमापन्नाः स्वं स्वमाश्रममण्डलम् ॥२५॥

*tatas ta ṛṣayaḥ kṣattaḥ*
*kṛta-dārā nimantrya tam*
*prātiṣṭhan nandim āpannāḥ*
*svaṁ svam āśrama-maṇḍalam*

*tataḥ*—then; *te*—they; *ṛṣayaḥ*—the sages; *kṣattaḥ*—O Vidura; *kṛta-dārāḥ*—thus married; *nimantrya*—taking leave of; *tam*—Kardama; *prātiṣṭhan*—they departed; *nandim*—joy; *āpannāḥ*—obtained; *svam svam*—each to his own; *āśrama-maṇḍalam*—hermitage.

## TRANSLATION

**Thus married, the sages took leave of Kardama and departed full of joy, each for his own hermitage, O Vidura.**

## TEXT 26

स चावतीर्णं त्रियुगमाज्ञाय विबुधर्षभम् ।
विविक्त उपसङ्गम्य प्रणम्य समभाषत ॥२६॥

*sa cāvatīrṇaṁ tri-yugam*
*ājñāya vibudharṣabham*

*vivikta upasaṅgamya*
*praṇamya samabhāṣata*

*saḥ*—the sage Kardama; *ca*—and; *avatīrṇam*—descended; *tri-yugam*—Viṣṇu; *ājñāya*—having understood; *vibudha-ṛṣabham*—the chief of the demigods; *vivikte*—in a secluded place; *upasaṅgamya*—having approached; *praṇamya*—offering obeisances; *samabhāṣata*—he spoke.

## TRANSLATION

**When Kardama Muni understood that the Supreme Personality of Godhead, the chief of all the demigods, Viṣṇu, had descended, Kardama approached Him in a secluded place, offered obeisances and spoke as follows.**

## PURPORT

Lord Viṣṇu is called *tri-yuga.* He appears in three *yugas*—Satya, Tretā and Dvāpara—but in Kali-yuga He does not appear. From the prayers of Prahlāda Mahārāja, however, we understand that He appears garbed as a devotee in Kali-yuga. Lord Caitanya is that devotee. Kṛṣṇa appeared in the form of a devotee, but although He never disclosed Himself, Rūpa Gosvāmī could understand His identity, for the Lord cannot hide Himself from a pure devotee. Rūpa Gosvāmī detected Him when he offered his first obeisances to Lord Caitanya. He knew that Lord Caitanya was Kṛṣṇa Himself and therefore offered his obeisances with the following words: "I offer my respects to Kṛṣṇa, who has now appeared as Lord Caitanya." This is also confirmed in the prayers of Prahlāda Mahārāja: in Kali-yuga He does not directly appear, but He appears as a devotee. Viṣṇu, therefore, is known as *tri-yuga.* Another explanation of *tri-yuga* is that He has three pairs of divine attributes, namely power and affluence, piety and renown, and wisdom and dispassion. According to Śrīdhara Svāmī, His three pairs of opulences are complete riches and complete strength, complete fame and complete beauty, and complete wisdom and complete renunciation. There are different interpretations of *tri-yuga,* but it is accepted by all learned scholars that *tri-yuga* means Viṣṇu. When Kardama Muni understood that his son, Kapila, was Viṣṇu Himself, he wanted to offer his obeisances. Therefore, when Kapila was alone he offered his respects and expressed his mind as follows.

## TEXT 27

अहो पापच्यमानानां निरये स्वैरमङ्गलैः ।
कालेन भूयसा नूनं प्रसीदन्तीह देवताः ॥२७॥

*aho pāpacyamānānāṁ*
*nirayе svair amaṅgalaiḥ*
*kālena bhūyasā nūnaṁ*
*prasīdantīha devatāḥ*

*aho*—oh; *pāpacyamānānām*—with those being much afflicted; *niraye*—in the hellish material entanglement; *svaiḥ*—their own; *amaṅgalaiḥ*—by misdeeds; *kālena bhūyasā*—after a long time; *nūnam*—indeed; *prasīdanti*—they are pleased; *iha*—in this world; *devatāḥ*—the demigods.

## TRANSLATION

**Kardama Muni said: Oh, after a long time the demigods of this universe have become pleased with the suffering souls who are in material entanglement because of their own misdeeds.**

## PURPORT

This material world is a place for suffering, which is due to the misdeeds of the inhabitants, the conditioned souls themselves. The sufferings are not extraneously imposed upon them; rather, the conditioned souls create their own suffering by their own acts. In the forest, fire takes place automatically. It is not that someone has to go there and set a fire; because of friction among various trees, fire occurs automatically. When there is too much heat from the forest fire of this material world, the demigods, including Brahmā himself, being harassed, approach the Supreme Lord, the Supreme Personality of Godhead, and appeal to Him to alleviate the condition. Then the Supreme Personality of Godhead descends. In other words, when the demigods become distressed by the sufferings of the conditioned souls, they approach the Lord to remedy the suffering, and the Personality of Godhead descends. When the Lord descends, all the demigods become enlivened. Therefore Kardama Muni said, "After many, many years of human suffering, all the demigods are now satisfied because Kapiladeva, the incarnation of Godhead, has appeared."

## TEXT 28

बहुजन्मविपक्वेन सम्यग्योगसमाधिना ।
द्रष्टुं यतन्ते यतयः शून्यागारेषु यत्पदम् ॥२८॥

*bahu-janma-vipakvena*
*samyag-yoga-samādhinā*
*draṣṭuṁ yatante yatayaḥ*
*śūnyāgāreṣu yat-padam*

*bahu*—many; *janma*—after births; *vipakvena*—which is mature; *samyak*—perfect; *yoga-samādhinā*—by trance in *yoga; draṣṭum*—to see; *yatante*—they endeavor; *yatayaḥ*—the *yogīs; śūnya-agāreṣu*—in secluded places; *yat*—whose; *padam*—feet.

## TRANSLATION

**After many births, mature yogīs, by complete trance in yoga, endeavor in secluded places to see the lotus feet of the Supreme Personality of Godhead.**

## PURPORT

Some important things are mentioned here about *yoga.* The word *bahu-janma-vipakvena* means "after many, many births of mature *yoga* practice." And another word, *samyag-yoga-samādhinā*, means "by complete practice of the *yoga* system." Complete practice of *yoga* means *bhakti-yoga;* unless one comes to the point of *bhakti-yoga*, or surrender unto the Supreme Personality of Godhead, one's *yoga* practice is not complete. This same point is corroborated in the *Śrīmad Bhagavad-gītā. Bahūnāṁ janmanām ante:* after many, many births, the *jñānī* who has matured in transcendental knowledge surrenders unto the Supreme Personality of Godhead. Kardama Muni repeats the same statement. After many, many years and many, many births of complete practice of *yoga*, one can see the lotus feet of the Supreme Lord in a secluded place. It is not that after one practices some sitting postures he immediately becomes perfect. One has to perform *yoga* a long time—"many, many births"—to become mature, and a *yogī* has to practice in a secluded place. One cannot practice *yoga* in a city or in a public park and declare that he has become God simply by some exchange of dollars. This is all bogus propaganda. Those who are actually *yogīs* practice in a secluded place, and after many, many births they become successful, provided they surrender unto the Supreme Personality of Godhead. This is the completion of *yoga.*

## TEXT 29

स एव भगवानद्य हेलनं नगणय्य नः ।
गृहेषु जातो ग्राम्याणां यः स्वानां पक्षपोषणः ॥२९॥

*sa eva bhagavān adya*
*helanaṁ na gaṇayya naḥ*
*gṛheṣu jāto grāmyāṇāṁ*
*yaḥ svānāṁ pakṣa-poṣaṇaḥ*

*saḥ eva*—that very same; *bhagavān*—Supreme Personality of Godhead; *adya*—today; *helanam*—negligence; *na*—not; *gaṇayya*—considering high and low; *naḥ*—our; *gṛheṣu*—in the houses; *jātaḥ*—appeared; *grāmyāṇām*—of ordinary householders; *yaḥ*—He who; *svānām*—of His own devotees; *pakṣa-poṣaṇaḥ*—who supports the party.

## TRANSLATION

**Not considering the negligence of ordinary householders like us, that very same Supreme Personality of Godhead appears in our homes just to support His devotees.**

## PURPORT

Devotees are so affectionate toward the Personality of Godhead that although He does not appear before those who practice *yoga* in a secluded place even for many, many births, He agrees to appear in a householder's home where devotees engage in devotional service without material *yoga* practice. In other words, devotional service to the Lord is so easy that even a householder can see the Supreme Personality of Godhead as one of the members of his household, as his son, as Kardama Muni experienced. He was a householder, although a *yogī*, but he had the incarnation of the Supreme Personality of Godhead Kapila Muni as his son.

Devotional service is such a powerful transcendental method that it surpasses all other methods of transcendental realization. The Lord says, therefore, that He lives neither in Vaikuṇṭha nor in the heart of a *yogī*, but He lives where His pure devotees are always chanting and glorifying Him. The Supreme Personality of Godhead is known as *bhakta-vatsala*. He is never described as *jñāni-vatsala* or *yogi-vatsala*. He is always described as *bhakta-vatsala* because He is more inclined toward His devotees than toward other transcendentalists. In *Bhagavad-gītā* it is confirmed that only a devotee can understand Him as He is. *Bhaktyā mām abhijānāti:* "One can understand Me only by devotional service, not otherwise." That understanding alone is real because although *jñānīs*, mental speculators, can realize only the effulgence, or the bodily luster, of the Supreme Personality of Godhead, and *yogīs* can realize only the partial representation of the Supreme Personality of Godhead, a *bhakta* not only realizes Him as He is but also associates with the Personality of Godhead face to face.

## TEXT 30

स्वीयं वाक्यमृतं कर्तुमवतीर्णोऽसि मे गृहे ।
चिकीर्षुर्भगवान् ज्ञानं भक्तानां मानवर्धनः ॥३०॥

*svīyaṁ vākyam ṛtaṁ kartum*
*avatīrṇo 'si me gṛhe*
*cikīrṣur bhagavān jñānaṁ*
*bhaktānāṁ māna-vardhanaḥ*

*svīyam*—Your own; *vākyam*—words; *ṛtam*—true; *kartum*—to make; *avatīrṇaḥ*—descended; *asi*—You are; *me gṛhe*—in my house; *cikīrṣuḥ*—desirous of disseminating; *bhagavān*—the Personality of Godhead; *jñānam*—knowledge; *bhaktānām*—of the devotees; *māna*—the honor; *vardhanaḥ*—who increases.

## TRANSLATION

**Kardama Muni said: You, my dear Lord, who are always increasing the honor of Your devotees, have descended in my home just to fulfill Your word and disseminate the process of real knowledge.**

## PURPORT

When the Lord appeared before Kardama Muni after his mature *yoga* practice, He promised that He would become Kardama's son. He descended as the son of Kardama Muni in order to fulfill that promise. Another purpose of His appearance is *cikīrṣur bhagavān jñānam*, to distribute knowledge. Therefore, He is called *bhaktānāṁ māna-vardhanaḥ*, "He who increases the honor of His devotees." By distributing Sāṅkhya He would increase the honor of the devotees; therefore, Sāṅkhya philosophy is not dry mental speculation. Sāṅkhya philosophy means devotional service. How could the honor of the devotees be increased unless Sāṅkhya were meant for devotional service? Devotees are not interested in speculative knowledge; therefore, the Sāṅkhya enunciated by Kapila Muni is meant to establish one firmly in devotional service. Real knowledge and real liberation is to surrender unto the Supreme Personality of Godhead and engage in devotional service.

## TEXT 31

**तान्येव तेऽभिरूपाणि रूपाणि भगवंस्तव ।**
**यानि यानि च रोचन्ते स्वजनानामरूपिणः ॥३१॥**

*tāny eva te 'bhirūpāṇi*
*rūpāṇi bhagavaṁs tava*
*yāni yāni ca rocante*
*sva-janānām arūpiṇaḥ*

*tāni*—those; *eva*—truly; *te*—Your; *abhirūpāṇi*—suitable; *rūpāṇi*—forms; *bhagavan*—O Lord; *tava*—Your; *yāni yāni*—whichever; *ca*—and; *rocante*—are pleasing; *sva-janānām*—to Your own devotees; *arūpiṇaḥ*—of one with no material form.

## TRANSLATION

**My dear Lord, although You have no material form, You have Your own innumerable forms. They truly are Your transcendental forms, which are pleasing to Your devotees.**

## PURPORT

In the *Brahma-saṁhitā* it is stated that the Lord is one Absolute, but He has *ananta*, or innumerable, forms. *Advaitam acyutam anādim ananta-rūpam.* The Lord is the original form, but still He has multiforms. Those multiforms are manifested by Him transcendentally, according to the tastes of His multidevotees. It is understood that once Hanumān, the great devotee of Lord Rāmacandra, said that he knew that Nārāyaṇa, the husband of Lakṣmī, and Rāma, the husband of Sītā, are one and the same, and that there is no difference between Lakṣmī and Sītā, but as for himself, he liked the form of Lord Rāma. In a similar way, some devotees worship the original form of Kṛṣṇa. When we say "Kṛṣṇa" we refer to all forms of the Lord—not only Kṛṣṇa, but Rāma, Nṛsiṁha, Varāha, Nārāyaṇa, etc. The varieties of transcendental forms exist simultaneously. That is also stated in the *Brahma-saṁhitā: rāmādi-mūrtiṣu . . . nānāvatāram.* He already exists in multiforms, but none of the forms are material. Śrīdhara Svāmī has commented that *arūpiṇaḥ*, "without form," means without material form. The Lord has form, otherwise how can it be stated here, *tāny eva te 'bhirūpāṇi rūpāṇi bhagavaṁs tava:* "You have Your forms, but they are not material. Materially You have no form, but spiritually, transcendentally, You have multiforms"? Māyāvādī philosophers cannot understand these transcendental forms of the Lord, and being disappointed, they say that the Supreme Lord is impersonal. But that is not a fact; whenever there is form there is a person. Many times in many Vedic literatures the Lord is described as *puruṣa*, which means "the original form, the original enjoyer." The conclusion is that the Lord has no material form, and yet, according to the liking of different grades of devotees, He simultaneously exists in multiforms, such as Rāma, Nṛsiṁha, Varāha, Nārāyaṇa and Mukunda. There are many thousands and thousands of forms, but they are all *viṣṇu-tattva*, Kṛṣṇa.

## TEXT 32

त्वां सूरिभिस्तत्त्वबुभुत्सयाद्धा
सदाभिवादार्हणपादपीठम् ।
ऐश्वर्यवैराग्ययशोऽवबोध-
वीर्यश्रिया पूर्तमहं प्रपद्ये ॥३२॥

*tvāṁ sūribhis tattva-bubhutsayāddhā*
*sadābhivādārhaṇa-pāda-pīṭham*
*aiśvarya-vairāgya-yaśo-'vabodha-*
*vīrya-śriyā pūrtam ahaṁ prapadye*

*tvām*—unto You; *sūribhiḥ*—by the great sages; *tattva*—the Absolute Truth; *bubhutsayā*—with a desire to understand; *addhā*—certainly; *sadā*—always; *abhivāda*—of worshipful respects; *arhaṇa*—which are worthy; *pāda*—of Your feet; *pīṭham*—to the seat; *aiśvarya*—opulence; *vairāgya*—renunciation; *yaśaḥ*—fame; *avabodha*—knowledge; *vīrya*—strength; *śriyā*—with beauty; *pūrtam*—who are full; *aham*—I; *prapadye*—surrender.

## TRANSLATION

**My dear Lord, Your lotus feet are the reservoir that always deserves to receive worshipful homage from all great sages eager to understand the Absolute Truth. You are full in opulence, renunciation, transcendental fame, knowledge, strength and beauty, and therefore I surrender myself unto Your lotus feet.**

## PURPORT

Actually, those who are searching after the Absolute Truth must take shelter of the lotus feet of the Supreme Personality of Godhead and worship Him. In *Bhagavad-gītā* Lord Kṛṣṇa advised Arjuna many times to surrender unto Him, especially at the end of the Ninth Chapter—*man-manā bhava mad-bhaktaḥ:* "If you want to be perfect, just always think of Me, become My devotee, worship Me and offer your obeisances to Me. In this way you will understand Me, the Personality of Godhead, and ultimately you will come back to Me, back to Godhead, back home." Why is it so? The Lord is always full in six opulences, as mentioned herein: wealth, renunciation, fame, knowledge, strength and beauty. The word *pūrtam* means "in full." No one can claim that all wealth belongs to him, but Kṛṣṇa can claim it, since He has full wealth. Similarly, He is full in knowledge, renunciation, strength and beauty. He is full in everything, and no one can surpass Him. Another one of Kṛṣṇa's names is *asamaurdhva*, which means that no one is equal to or greater than Him.

## TEXT 33

परं प्रधानं पुरुषं महान्तं
कालं कविं त्रिवृतं लोकपालम् ।
आत्मानुभूत्यानुगतप्रपञ्चं
स्वच्छन्दशक्तिं कपिलं प्रपद्ये ॥३३॥

*paraṁ pradhānaṁ puruṣaṁ mahāntaṁ*
*kālaṁ kaviṁ tri-vṛtaṁ loka-pālam*
*ātmānubhūtyānugata-prapañcaṁ*
*svacchanda-śaktiṁ kapilaṁ prapadye*

*param*—transcendental; *pradhānam*—supreme; *puruṣam*—person; *mahāntam*—who is the origin of the material world; *kālam*—who is time; *kavim*—fully cognizant; *tri-vṛtam*—three modes of material nature; *loka-pālam*—who is the maintainer of all the universes; *ātma*—in Himself; *anubhūtya*—by internal potency; *anugata*—dissolved; *prapañcam*—whose material manifestations; *sva-chanda*—independently; *śaktim*—who is powerful; *kapilam*—to Lord Kapila; *prapadye*—I surrender.

## TRANSLATION

**I surrender unto the Supreme Personality of Godhead, descended in the form of Kapila, who is independently powerful and transcendental, who is the Supreme Person and the Lord of the sum total of matter and the element of time, who is the fully cognizant maintainer of all the universes under the three modes of**

**material nature, and who absorbs the material manifestations after their dissolution.**

## PURPORT

The six opulences—wealth, strength, fame, beauty, knowledge and renunciation—are indicated here by Kardama Muni, who addresses Kapila Muni, his son, as *param.* The word *param* is used in the beginning of *Śrīmad-Bhāgavatam,* in the phrase *paraṁ satyam,* to refer to the *summum bonum,* or the Supreme Personality of Godhead. *Param* is explained further by the next word, *pradhānam,* which means the chief, the origin, the source of everything—*sarva-kāraṇa-kāraṇam*—the cause of all causes. The Supreme Personality of Godhead is not formless; He is *puruṣam,* or the enjoyer, the original person. He is the time element and is all-cognizant. He knows everything—past, present and future—as confirmed in *Bhagavad-gītā.* The Lord says, "I know everything—present, past and future—in every corner of the universe." The material world, which is moving under the spell of the three modes of nature, is also a manifestation of His energy. *Parāsya śaktir vividhaiva śrūyate:* everything that we see is an interaction of His energies (*Śvetāśvatara Up.* 6.8). *Parasya brahmaṇaḥ śaktis tathedam akhilaṁ jagat.* This is the version of the *Viṣṇu Purāṇa.* We can understand that whatever we see is an interaction of the three modes of material nature, but actually it is all an interaction of the Lord's energy. *Loka-pālam:* He is actually the maintainer of all living entities. *Nityo nityānām:* He is the chief of all living entities; He is one, but He maintains many, many living entities. God maintains all other living entities, but no one can maintain God. That is His *svacchanda-śakti;* He is not dependent on others. Someone may call himself independent, but he is still dependent on someone higher. The Personality of Godhead, however, is absolute; there is no one higher than or equal to Him.

Kapila Muni appeared as the son of Kardama Muni, but because Kapila is an incarnation of the Supreme Personality of Godhead, Kardama Muni offered respectful obeisances unto Him with full surrender. Another word in this verse is very important: *ātmānubhūtyānugata-prapañcam.* The Lord descends either as Kapila or Rāma, Nṛsiṁha or Varāha, and whatever forms He assumes in the material world are all manifestations of His own personal internal energy. They are never forms of the material energy. The ordinary living entities who are manifested in this material world have bodies created by the material energy, but when Kṛṣṇa or any one of His expansions or parts of the expansions descends on this material world, although He appears to have a material body, His body is not material. He always has a transcendental body. But fools and rascals, who are called *mūḍhas*, consider Him one of them, and therefore they deride Him. They refuse to accept Kṛṣṇa as the Supreme Personality of Godhead because they cannot understand Him. In *Bhagavad-gītā* Kṛṣṇa says, *avajānanti māṁ mūḍhāḥ:* "Those who are rascals and fools deride Me." When God descends in a form, this does not mean that He assumes His form with the help of the material energy. He manifests His spiritual form as He exists in His spiritual kingdom.

## TEXT 34

आ स्माभिपृच्छेऽद्य पतिं प्रजानां
त्वयावतीर्णर्ण उताप्तकामः ।
परिव्रजत्पदवीमास्थितोऽहं
चरिष्ये त्वां हृदि युञ्जन् विशोकः ॥३४॥

*ā smābhipṛcche 'dya patiṁ prajānāṁ*
*tvayāvatīrṇarṇa utāpta-kāmaḥ*
*parivrajat-padavīm āsthito 'haṁ*
*cariṣye tvāṁ hṛdi yuñjan viśokaḥ*

*ā sma abhipṛcche*—I am inquiring; *adya*—now; *patim*—the Lord; *prajānām*—of all created beings; *tvayā*—by You; *avatīrṇa-ṛṇaḥ*—free from debts; *uta*—and; *āpta*—fulfilled; *kāmaḥ*—desires; *parivrajat*—of an itinerant mendicant; *padavīm*—the path; *āsthitaḥ*—accepting; *aham*—I; *cariṣye*—I shall wander; *tvām*—You; *hṛdi*—in my heart; *yuñjan*—keeping; *viśokaḥ*—free from lamentation.

## TRANSLATION

**Today I have something to ask from You, who are the Lord of all living entities. Since I have now been liberated by You from my**

**debts to my father, and since all my desires are fulfilled, I wish to accept the order of an itinerant mendicant. Renouncing this family life, I wish to wander about, free from lamentation, thinking always of You in my heart.**

## PURPORT

Actually, *sannyāsa*, or renunciation of material household life, necessitates complete absorption in Kṛṣṇa consciousness and immersion in the self. One does not take *sannyāsa*, freedom from family responsibility in the renounced order of life, to make another family or to create an embarrassing transcendental fraud in the name of *sannyāsa*. The *sannyāsī's* business is not to become proprietor of so many things and amass money from the innocent public. A *sannyāsī* is proud that he is always thinking of Kṛṣṇa within himself. Of course, there are two kinds of devotees of the Lord. One is called *goṣṭhy-ānandī*, which means those who are preachers and have many followers for preaching the glories of the Lord and who live among those many, many followers just to organize missionary activities. Other devotees are *ātmānandī*, or self-satisfied, and do not take the risk of preaching work. They remain, therefore, alone with God. In this classification was Kardama Muni. He wanted to be free from all anxieties and remain alone within his heart with the Supreme Personality of Godhead. *Parivrāja* means "an itinerant mendicant." A mendicant *sannyāsī* should not live anywhere for more than three days. He must be always moving because his duty is to move from door to door and enlighten people about Kṛṣṇa consciousness.

## TEXT 35

श्रीभगवानुवाच
मया प्रोक्तं हि लोकस्य प्रमाणं सत्यलौकिके ।
अथाजनि मया तुभ्यं यदवोचमृतं मुने ॥३५॥

*śrī-bhagavān uvāca*
*mayā proktaṁ hi lokasya*
*pramāṇaṁ satya-laukike*
*athājani mayā tubhyaṁ*
*yad avocam ṛtaṁ mune*

*śrī-bhagavān uvāca*—the Supreme Personality of Godhead said; *mayā*—by Me; *proktam*—spoken; *hi*—in fact; *lokasya*—for the people; *pramāṇam*—authority; *satya*—spoken in scripture; *laukike*—and in ordinary speech; *atha*—therefore; *ajani*—there was birth; *mayā*—by Me; *tubhyam*—to you; *yat*—that which; *avocam*—I said; *ṛtam*—true; *mune*—O sage.

## TRANSLATION

**The Personality of Godhead Kapila said: Whatever I speak, whether directly or in the scriptures, is authoritative in all respects for the people of the world. O Muni, because I told you before that I would become your son, I have descended to fulfill this truth.**

## PURPORT

Kardama Muni was to leave his family life to completely engage in the service of the Lord. But since he knew that the Lord Himself, as Kapila, had taken birth in his home as his own son, why was he preparing to leave home to search out self-realization or God realization? God Himself was present in his home—why should he leave home? Such a question may certainly arise. But here it is said that whatever is spoken in the *Vedas* and whatever is practiced in accordance with the injunctions of the *Vedas* is to be accepted as authoritative in society. Vedic authority says that a householder must leave home after his fiftieth year. *Pañcāśordhvaṁ vanaṁ vrajet:* one must leave his family life and enter the forest after the age of fifty. This is an authoritative statement of the *Vedas*, based on the division of social life into four departments of activity—*brahmacarya*, *gṛhastha*, *vānaprastha* and *sannyāsa*.

Kardama Muni practiced *yoga* very rigidly as a *brahmacārī* before his marriage, and he became so powerful and attained so much mystic power that his father, Brahmā, ordered him to marry and beget children as a householder. Kardama did that also; he begot nine good daughters and one son, Kapila Muni, and thus his householder duty was also performed nicely, and now his duty was to leave. Even though he had the Supreme Personality of Godhead as his son, he had to respect the authority of the *Vedas*. This is a very important lesson. Even if one has God in his home as his son, one should still follow the Vedic injunctions. It is stated, *mahājano yena gataḥ sa panthāḥ:* one should traverse the path which is followed by great personalities.

Kardama Muni's example is very instructive, for in spite of having the Supreme Personality of Godhead as his son, he left home just to obey the authority of the Vedic injunction. Kardama Muni states here the main purpose of his leaving home: while traveling all over the world as a mendicant, he would always remember the Supreme Personality of Godhead within his heart and thereby be freed from all the anxieties of material existence. In this age of Kali-yuga *sannyāsa* is prohibited because persons in this age are all *śūdras* and cannot follow the rules and regulations of *sannyāsa* life. It is very commonly found that so-called *sannyāsīs* are addicted to nonsense—even to having private relationships with women. This is the abominable situation in this age. Although they dress themselves as *sannyāsīs*, they still cannot free themselves from the four principles of sinful life, namely illicit sex life, meat-eating, intoxication and gambling. Since they are not freed from these four principles, they are cheating the public by posing as *svāmīs.*

In Kali-yuga the injunction is that no one should accept *sannyāsa.* Of course, those who actually follow the rules and regulations must take *sannyāsa.* Generally, however, people are unable to accept *sannyāsa* life, and therefore Caitanya Mahāprabhu stressed, *kalau nāsty eva nāsty eva nāsty eva gatir anyathā.* In this age there is no other alternative, no other alternative, no other alternative than to chant the holy name of the Lord: Hare Kṛṣṇa, Hare Kṛṣṇa, Kṛṣṇa Kṛṣṇa, Hare Hare. The main purpose of *sannyāsa* life is to be in constant companionship with the Supreme Lord, either by thinking of Him within the heart or hearing of Him through aural reception. In this age, hearing is more important than thinking because one's thinking may be disturbed by mental agitation, but if one concentrates on hearing, he will be forced to associate with the sound vibration of Kṛṣṇa. Kṛṣṇa and the sound vibration "Kṛṣṇa" are nondifferent, so if one loudly vibrates Hare Kṛṣṇa, he will be able to think of Kṛṣṇa immediately. This process of chanting is the best process of self-realization in this age; therefore Lord Caitanya preached it so nicely for the benefit of all humanity.

## TEXT 36

एतन्मे जन्म लोकेऽस्मिन्मुमुक्षूणां दुराशयात् ।
प्रसंख्यानाय तत्त्वानां सम्मतायात्मदर्शने ॥३६॥

*etan me janma loke 'smin*
*mumukṣūṇāṁ durāśayāt*
*prasaṅkhyānāya tattvānāṁ*
*sammatāyātma-darśane*

*etat*—this; *me*—My; *janma*—birth; *loke*—in the world; *asmin*—in this; *mumukṣūṇām*—by those great sages seeking liberation; *durāśayāt*—from unnecessary material desires; *prasaṅkhyānāya*—for explaining; *tattvānām*—of the truths; *sammatāya*—which is highly esteemed; *ātma-darśane*—in self-realization.

## TRANSLATION

**My appearance in this world is especially to explain the philosophy of Sāṅkhya, which is highly esteemed for self-realization by those desiring freedom from the entanglement of unnecessary material desires.**

## PURPORT

Here the word *durāśayāt* is very significant. *Dur* refers to trouble or *duḥkha*, miseries. *Āśayāt* means "from the shelter." We conditioned souls have taken shelter of the material body, which is full of troubles and miseries. Foolish people cannot understand the situation, and this is called ignorance, illusion, or the spell of *māyā*. Human society should very seriously understand that the body itself is the source of all miserable life. Modern civilization is supposed to be making advancement in scientific knowledge, but what is this scientific knowledge? It is based on bodily comforts only, without knowledge that however comfortably one maintains his body, the body is destructible. As stated in *Bhagavad-gītā*, *antavanta ime dehāḥ:* these bodies are destined to be destroyed. *Nityasyoktāḥ śarīriṇaḥ* refers to the living soul, or the living spark, within the body. That soul is eternal, but the body is not eternal. For our activity we must have a body; without a body, without sense organs, there is no activity. But people are not inquiring whether it is possible to have an eternal body. Actually they aspire for an eternal body because even though they engage in sense enjoyment, that sense enjoyment is not eternal. They are therefore in want of something which they can enjoy eternally, but they do not understand how to attain that perfection.

Sāṅkhya philosophy, therefore, as stated herein by Kapiladeva, is *tattvānām.* The Sāṅkhya philosophy system is designed to afford understanding of the real truth. What is that real truth? The real truth is knowledge of how to get out of the material body, which is the source of all trouble. Lord Kapila's incarnation, or descent, is especially meant for this purpose. That is clearly stated here.

## TEXT 37

एष आत्मपथोऽव्यक्तो नष्टः कालेन भूयसा ।
तं प्रवर्तयितुं देहमिमं विद्धि मया भृतम् ॥३७॥

*eṣa ātma-patho 'vyakto*
*naṣṭaḥ kālena bhūyasā*
*taṁ pravartayituṁ deham*
*imaṁ viddhi mayā bhṛtam*

*eṣaḥ*—this; *ātma-pathaḥ*—path of self-realization; *avyaktaḥ*—difficult to be known; *naṣṭaḥ*—lost; *kālena bhūyasā*—in the course of time; *tam*—this; *pravartayitum*—to introduce again; *deham*—body; *imam*—this; *viddhi*—please know; *mayā*—by Me; *bhṛtam*—assumed.

## TRANSLATION

**This path of self-realization, which is difficult to understand, has now been lost in the course of time. Please know that I have assumed this body of Kapila to introduce and explain this philosophy to human society again.**

## PURPORT

It is not true that Sāṅkhya philosophy is a new system of philosophy introduced by Kapila as material philosophers introduce new kinds of mental speculative thought to supersede that of another philosopher. On the material platform, everyone, especially the mental speculator, tries to be more prominent than others. The field of activity of the speculators is the mind; there is no limit to the different ways in which one can agitate the mind. The mind can be unlimitedly agitated, and thus one can put forward an unlimited number of theories. Sāṅkhya philosophy is not like that; it is not mental speculation. It is factual, but at the time of Kapila it was lost.

In due course of time, a particular type of knowledge may be lost or may be covered for the time being; that is the nature of this material world. A similar statement was made by Lord Kṛṣṇa in *Bhagavad-gītā. Sa kāleneha mahatā yogo naṣṭaḥ:* "In course of time the *yoga* system as stated in *Bhagavad-gītā* was lost." It was coming in *paramparā*, in disciplic succession, but due to the passage of time it was lost. The time factor is so pressing that in the course of time everything within this material world is spoiled or lost. The *yoga* system of *Bhagavad-gītā* was lost before the meeting of Kṛṣṇa and Arjuna. Therefore Kṛṣṇa again enunciated the same ancient *yoga* system to Arjuna, who could actually understand *Bhagavad-gītā.* Similarly, Kapila also said that the system of Sāṅkhya philosophy was not exactly being introduced by Him; it was already current, but in course of time it was mysteriously lost, and therefore He appeared to reintroduce it. That is the purpose of the incarnation of Godhead. *Yadā yadā hi dharmasya glānir bhavati bhārata. Dharma* means the real occupation of the living entity. When there is a discrepancy in the eternal occupation of the living entity, the Lord comes and introduces the real occupation of life. Any so-called religious system that is not in the line of devotional service is called *adharma-saṁsthāpana.* When people forget their eternal relationship with God and engage in something other than devotional service, their engagement is called irreligion. How one can get out of the miserable condition of material life is stated in Sāṅkhya philosophy, and the Lord Himself is explaining this sublime system.

## TEXT 38

गच्छ कामं मयापृष्टो मयि संन्यस्तकर्मणा ।
जित्वा सुदुर्जयं मृत्युममृतत्वाय मां भज ॥३८॥

*gaccha kāmaṁ mayāpṛṣṭo*
*mayi sannyasta-karmaṇā*

*jitvā sudurjayaṁ mṛtyum*
*amṛtatvāya māṁ bhaja*

*gaccha*—go; *kāmam*—as you wish; *mayā*—by Me; *āpṛṣṭaḥ*—sanctioned; *mayi*—to Me; *sannyasta*—completely surrendered; *karmaṇā*—with your activities; *jitvā*—having conquered; *sudurjayam*—insurmountable; *mṛtyum*—death; *amṛtatvāya*—for eternal life; *mām*—unto Me; *bhaja*—engage in devotional service.

## TRANSLATION

**Now, being sanctioned by Me, go as you desire, surrendering all your activities to Me. Conquering insurmountable death, worship Me for eternal life.**

## PURPORT

The purpose of Sāṅkhya philosophy is stated herein. If anyone wants real, eternal life, he has to engage himself in devotional service, or Kṛṣṇa consciousness. To become free from birth and death is not an easy task. Birth and death are natural to this material body. *Sudurjayam* means "very, very difficult to overcome." The modern so-called scientists do not have sufficient means to understand the process of victory over birth and death. Therefore, they set aside the question of birth and death; they do not consider it. They simply engage in the problems of the material body, which is transient and sure to end.

Actually, human life is meant for conquering the insurmountable process of birth and death. That can be done as stated here. *Māṁ bhaja:* one must engage in the devotional service of the Lord. In *Bhagavad-gītā* also the Lord says, *man-manā bhava mad-bhaktaḥ:* "Just become My devotee. Just worship Me." But foolish so-called scholars say that it is not Kṛṣṇa whom we must worship and to whom we must surrender; it is something else. Without Kṛṣṇa's mercy, therefore, no one can understand the Sāṅkhya philosophy or any philosophy which is especially meant for liberation. Vedic knowledge confirms that one becomes entangled in this material life because of ignorance and that one can become free from material embarrassment by becoming situated in factual knowledge. Sāṅkhya means that factual knowledge by which one can get out of the material entanglement.

## TEXT 39

मामात्मानं स्वयंज्योतिः सर्वभूतगुहाशयम् ।
आत्मन्येवात्मना वीक्ष्य विशोकोऽभयमृच्छसि ॥३९॥

*mām ātmānaṁ svayaṁ-jyotiḥ*
*sarva-bhūta-guhāśayam*
*ātmany evātmanā vīkṣya*
*viśoko 'bhayam ṛcchasi*

*mām*—Me; *ātmānam*—the Supreme Soul, or Paramātmā; *svayam-jyotiḥ*—self-effulgent; *sarva-bhūta*—of all beings; *guhā*—in the hearts; *āśayam*—dwelling; *ātmani*—in your own heart; *eva*—indeed; *ātmanā*—through your intellect; *vīkṣya*—always seeing, always thinking; *viśokaḥ*—free from lamentation; *abhayam*—fearlessness; *ṛcchasi*—you will achieve.

## TRANSLATION

**In your own heart, through your intellect, you will always see Me, the supreme self-effulgent soul dwelling within the hearts of all living entities. Thus you will achieve the state of eternal life, free from all lamentation and fear.**

## PURPORT

People are very anxious to understand the Absolute Truth in various ways, especially by experiencing the *brahmajyoti*, or Brahman effulgence, by meditation and by mental speculation. But Kapiladeva uses the word *mām* to emphasize that the Personality of Godhead is the ultimate feature of the Absolute Truth. In *Bhagavad-gītā* the Personality of Godhead always says *mām*, "unto Me," but the rascals misinterpret the clear meaning. *Mām* is the Supreme Personality of Godhead. If one can see the Supreme Personality of Godhead as He appears in different incarnations and understand that He has not assumed a material body but is present in His own eternal, spiritual form, then one can understand the nature of the Personality of Godhead. Since the less intelligent cannot understand this point, it is stressed everywhere again and again. Simply by seeing the form of the Lord as He presents Himself by His own internal potency as Kṛṣṇa or Rāma or Kapila, one can directly see the *brahmajyoti*, because the *brahmajyoti* is no more than the effulgence of His bodily luster. Since the sunshine is the luster of the sun planet, by seeing the sun one automatically sees the sunshine; similarly, by seeing the Supreme Personality of Godhead one simultaneously sees and experiences the Paramātmā feature as well as the impersonal Brahman feature of the Supreme.

The *Bhāgavatam* has already enunciated that the Absolute Truth is present in three features—in the beginning as the impersonal Brahman, in the next stage as the Paramātmā in everyone's heart, and, at last, as the ultimate realization of the Absolute Truth, Bhagavān, the Supreme Personality of Godhead. One who sees the Supreme Person can automatically realize the other features, namely the Paramātmā and Brahman features of the Lord. The words used here are *viśoko 'bhayam ṛcchasi*. Simply by seeing the Personality of Godhead one realizes everything, and the result is that one becomes situated on the platform where there is no lamentation and no fear. This can be attained simply by devotional service to the Personality of Godhead.

## TEXT 40

मात्र आध्यात्मिकीं विद्यां शमनीं सर्वकर्मणाम् ।
वितरिष्ये यया चासौ भयं चातितरिष्यति ॥४०॥

*mātra ādhyātmikīṁ vidyāṁ*
*śamanīṁ sarva-karmaṇām*
*vitariṣye yayā cāsau*
*bhayaṁ cātitariṣyati*

*mātre*—to My mother; *ādhyātmikīm*—which opens the door of spiritual life; *vidyām*—knowledge; *śamanīm*—ending; *sarva-karmaṇām*—all fruitive activities; *vitariṣye*—I shall give; *yayā*—by which; *ca*—also; *asau*—she; *bhayam*—fear; *ca*—also; *atitariṣyati*—will overcome.

## TRANSLATION

**I shall also describe this sublime knowledge, which is the door to spiritual life, to My mother, so that she also can attain perfection and self-realization, ending all reactions to fruitive activities. Thus she also will be freed from all material fear.**

## PURPORT

Kardama Muni was anxious about his good wife, Devahūti, while leaving home, and so the worthy son promised that not only would Kardama Muni be freed from the material entanglement, but Devahūti would also be freed by receiving instruction from her son. A very good example is set here: the husband goes away, taking the *sannyāsa* order for self-realization, but his representative, the son, who is equally educated, remains at home to deliver the mother. A *sannyāsī* is not supposed to take his wife with him. At the *vānaprastha* stage of retired life, or the stage midway between householder life and renounced life, one may keep his wife as an assistant without sex relations, but in the *sannyāsa* order of life one cannot keep his wife with him. Otherwise, a person like Kardama Muni could have kept his wife with him, and there would have been no hindrance to his prosecution of self-realization.

Kardama Muni followed the Vedic injunction that no one in *sannyāsa* life can have any kind of relationship with women. But what is the position of a woman who is left by her husband? She is entrusted to the son, and the son promises that he will deliver his mother from entanglement. A woman is not supposed to take *sannyāsa.* So-called spiritual societies concocted in modern times give *sannyāsa* even to women, although there is no sanction in the Vedic literature for a woman's accepting *sannyāsa.* Otherwise, if it were sanctioned, Kardama Muni could have taken his wife and given her *sannyāsa.* The woman must remain at home. She has only three stages of life: dependency on the father in childhood, dependency on the husband in youth and, in old age, dependency on the grown-up son, such as Kapila. In old age the progress of woman depends on the grown-up son. The ideal son, Kapila Muni, is assuring His father of the deliverance of His mother so that His father may go peacefully without anxiety for his good wife.

## TEXT 41

मैत्रेय उवाच
एवं समुदितस्तेन कपिलेन प्रजापतिः ।
दक्षिणीकृत्य तं प्रीतो वनमेव जगाम ह ॥४१॥

*maitreya uvāca*
*evaṁ samuditas tena*
*kapilena prajāpatiḥ*
*dakṣiṇī-kṛtya taṁ prīto*
*vanam eva jagāma ha*

*maitreyaḥ uvāca*—the great sage Maitreya said; *evam*—thus; *samuditaḥ*—addressed; *tena*—by Him; *kapilena*—by Kapila; *prajā-patiḥ*—the progenitor of human society; *dakṣiṇī-kṛtya*—having circumambulated; *tam*—Him; *prītaḥ*—being pacified; *vanam*—to the forest; *eva*—indeed; *jagāma*—he left; *ha*—then.

## TRANSLATION

**Śrī Maitreya said: Thus when Kardama Muni, the progenitor of human society, was spoken to in fullness by his son, Kapila, he circumambulated Him, and with a good, pacified mind he at once left for the forest.**

## PURPORT

Going to the forest is compulsory for everyone. It is not a mental excursion upon which one person goes and another does not. Everyone should go to the forest at least as a *vānaprastha.* Forest-going means to take one-hundred-percent shelter of the Supreme Lord, as explained by Prahlāda Mahārāja in his talks with his father. *Sadā samudvigna-dhiyām (Bhāg.* 7.5.5). People who have accepted a temporary, material body are always full of anxieties. One should not, therefore, be very much affected by this material body, but should try to be freed. The preliminary process to become freed is to go to the forest or give up family relationships and exclusively engage in Kṛṣṇa consciousness. That is the purpose of going to the forest. Otherwise, the forest is only a place of monkeys and wild animals. To go to the forest does not mean to become a monkey or a ferocious animal. It means to accept exclusively the shelter of the Supreme Personality of Godhead and engage oneself in full service. One does not actually have to go to the forest. At the present moment this is not at all advisable for a man who has spent his life all along in big cities. As explained by Prahlāda Mahārāja (*hitvātma-pātaṁ gṛham andha-kūpam*), one should not remain always engaged in the responsibilities of family life because family life without Kṛṣṇa consciousness is just like a blind well. Alone in a field, if one falls into a blind well and no one is there to save him, he may cry for years, and no one will see or hear where the crying is coming from. Death is sure. Similarly, those who are forgetful of their eternal relationship with the Supreme Lord are in the blind well of family life; their position is very ominous. Prahlāda Mahārāja advised that one should give up this well somehow or other and take to Kṛṣṇa consciousness and thus be freed from material entanglement, which is full of anxieties.

## TEXT 42

व्रतं स आस्थितो मौनमात्मैकशरणो मुनिः ।
निःसङ्गो व्यचरत्क्षोणीमनग्निरनिकेतनः ॥४२॥

*vrataṁ sa āsthito maunam*
*ātmaika-śaraṇo muniḥ*
*niḥsaṅgo vyacarat kṣoṇīm*
*anagnir aniketanaḥ*

*vratam*—vow; *saḥ*—he (Kardama); *āsthitaḥ*—accepted; *maunam*—silence; *ātma*—by the Supreme Personality of Godhead; *eka*—exclusively; *śaraṇaḥ*—being sheltered; *muniḥ*—the sage; *niḥsaṅgaḥ*—without association; *vyacarat*—he traveled; *kṣoṇīm*—the earth; *anagniḥ*—without fire; *aniketanaḥ*—without shelter.

## TRANSLATION

**The sage Kardama accepted silence as a vow in order to think of the Supreme Personality of Godhead and take shelter of Him exclusively. Without association, he traveled over the surface of the globe as a sannyāsī, devoid of any relationship with fire or shelter.**

## PURPORT

Here the words *anagnir aniketanaḥ* are very significant. A *sannyāsī* should be completely detached from fire and any residential quarters. A *gṛhastha* has a relationship with fire, either for offering sacrifices or for cooking, but a *sannyāsī* is freed from these two responsibilities. He does not have to cook or offer fire for sacrifice because he is always engaged in Kṛṣṇa consciousness; therefore he has already accomplished all ritualistic performances of religion. *Aniketanaḥ* means "without lodging." He should not have his own house, but should depend completely on the Supreme Lord for his food and lodging. He should travel.

*Mauna* means "silence." Unless one becomes silent, he cannot think completely about the pastimes and activities of the Lord. It is not that because one is a fool and cannot speak nicely he therefore takes the vow of *mauna*. Rather, one becomes silent so that people will not disturb him. It is said by Cāṇakya Paṇḍita that a rascal appears very intelligent as long as he does not speak. But speaking is the test. The so-called silence of a silent impersonalist *svāmī* indicates that he has nothing to say; he simply wants to beg. But the silence adopted by Kardama Muni was not like that. He became silent for relief from nonsensical talk. One is called a *muni* when he remains grave and does not talk nonsense. Mahārāja Ambarīṣa set a very good example; whenever he spoke, he spoke about the pastimes of the Lord. *Mauna* necessitates refraining from nonsensical talking, and engaging the talking facility in the pastimes of the Lord. In that way one can chant and hear about the Lord in order to perfect his life. *Vratam* means that one should take a vow as explained in *Bhagavad-gītā, amānitvam adambhitvam*, without hankering for personal respect and without being proud of one's material position. *Ahiṁsā* means not being violent. There are eighteen processes for attaining knowledge and perfection, and by his vow, Kardama Muni adopted all the principles of self-realization.

## TEXT 43

**मनो ब्रह्मणि युञ्जानो यत्तत्सदसतः परम् ।**
**गुणावभासे विगुण एकभक्त्यानुभाविते ॥४३॥**

*mano brahmaṇi yuñjāno*
*yat tat sad-asataḥ param*

*guṇāvabhāse viguṇa*
*eka-bhaktyānubhāvite*

*manaḥ*—mind; *brahmaṇi*—on the Supreme; *yuñjānaḥ*—fixing; *yat*—which; *tat*—that; *sat-asataḥ*—cause and effect; *param*—beyond; *guṇa-avabhāse*—who manifests the three modes of material nature; *viguṇe*—who is beyond the material modes; *eka-bhaktyā*—by exclusive devotion; *anubhāvite*—who is perceived.

## TRANSLATION

**He fixed his mind upon the Supreme Personality of Godhead, Parabrahman, who is beyond cause and effect, who manifests the three modes of material nature, who is beyond those three modes, and who is perceived only through unfailing devotional service.**

## PURPORT

Whenever there is *bhakti*, there must be three things present—the devotee, the devotion and the Lord. Without these three—*bhakta, bhakti* and Bhagavān—there is no meaning to the word *bhakti*. Kardama Muni fixed his mind on the Supreme Brahman and realized Him through *bhakti*, or devotional service. This indicates that he fixed his mind on the personal feature of the Lord because *bhakti* cannot be executed unless one has realization of the personal feature of the Absolute Truth. *Guṇāvabhāse:* He is beyond the three modes of material nature, but it is due to Him that the three modes of material nature are manifested. In other words, although the material energy is an emanation of the Supreme Lord, He is not affected, as we are, by the modes of material nature. We are conditioned souls, but He is not affected, although the material nature has emanated from Him. He is the supreme living entity and is never affected by *māyā*, but we are subordinate, minute living entities, prone to be affected by the limitations of *māyā*. If he is in constant contact with the Supreme Lord by devotional service, the conditioned living entity also becomes freed from the infection of *māyā*. This is confirmed in *Bhagavad-gītā: sa guṇān samatītyaitān.* A person engaged in Kṛṣṇa consciousness is at once liberated from the influence of the three modes of material nature. In other words, once the conditioned soul engages himself in devotional service, he also becomes liberated like the Lord.

## TEXT 44

निरहंकृतिर्निर्ममश्च निर्द्वन्द्वः समदृक् स्वदृक् ।
प्रत्यक्प्रशान्तधीर्धीरः प्रशान्तोर्मिरिवोदधिः ॥४४॥

*nirahaṅkṛtir nirmamaś ca*
*nirdvandvaḥ sama-dṛk sva-dṛk*
*pratyak-praśānta-dhīr dhīraḥ*
*praśāntormir ivodadhiḥ*

*nirahaṅkṛtiḥ*—without false ego; *nirmamaḥ*—without material affection; *ca*—and; *nirdvandvaḥ*—without duality; *sama-dṛk*—seeing equality; *sva-dṛk*—seeing himself; *pratyak*—turned inward; *praśānta*—perfectly composed; *dhīḥ*—mind; *dhīraḥ*—sober, not disturbed; *praśānta*—calmed; *ūrmiḥ*—whose waves; *iva*—like; *udadhiḥ*—the ocean.

## TRANSLATION

**Thus he gradually became unaffected by the false ego of material identity and became free from material affection. Undisturbed, equal to everyone and without duality, he could indeed see himself also. His mind was turned inward and was perfectly calm, like an ocean unagitated by waves.**

## PURPORT

When one's mind is in full Kṛṣṇa consciousness and one fully engages in rendering devotional service to the Lord, he becomes just like an ocean unagitated by waves. This very example is also cited in *Bhagavad-gītā:* one should become like the ocean. The ocean is filled by many thousands of rivers, and millions of tons of its water evaporates into clouds, yet the ocean is the same unagitated ocean. The laws of nature may work, but if one is fixed in devotional service at the lotus feet of the Lord, he is not agitated, for he is introspective. He does not look outside to material nature, but he looks in to the spiritual nature of his existence; with a sober mind, he simply engages in the service of the Lord. Thus he realizes his own self without false identification with matter and without affection for material possessions. Such a great devotee is never in trouble with others because he sees everyone from the platform of spiritual understanding; he sees himself and others in the right perspective.

## TEXT 45

वासुदेवे भगवति सर्वज्ञे प्रत्यगात्मनि ।
परेण भक्तिभावेन लब्धात्मा मुक्तबन्धनः ॥४५॥

*vāsudeve bhagavati*
*sarva-jñe pratyag-ātmani*
*pareṇa bhakti-bhāvena*
*labdhātmā mukta-bandhanaḥ*

*vāsudeve*—to Vāsudeva; *bhagavati*—the Personality of Godhead; *sarva-jñe*—omniscient; *pratyak-ātmani*—the Supersoul within everyone; *pareṇa*—transcendental; *bhakti-bhāvena*—by devotional service; *labdha-ātmā*—being situated in himself; *mukta-bandhanaḥ*—liberated from material bondage.

## TRANSLATION

**He thus became liberated from conditioned life and became self-situated in transcendental devotional service to the Personality of Godhead, Vāsudeva, the omniscient Supersoul within everyone.**

## PURPORT

When one engages in the transcendental devotional service of the Lord one becomes aware that his constitutional position, as an individual soul, is to be eternally a servitor of the Supreme Lord, Vāsudeva. Self-realization does not mean that because the Supreme Soul and the individual soul are both souls they are equal in every respect. The individual soul is prone to be conditioned, and the Supreme Soul is never conditioned. When the conditioned soul realizes that he is subordinate to the Supreme Soul, his position is called *labdhātmā*, self-realization, or *mukta-bandhana*, freedom from material contamination. Material contamination continues as long as one thinks that he is as good as the Supreme Lord or is equal with Him. This condition is the last snare of *māyā. Māyā* always influences the conditioned soul. Even after much meditation and speculation, if one continues to think himself one with the Supreme Lord, it is to be understood that he is still in the last snares of the spell of *māyā.*

The word *pareṇa* is very significant. *Para* means "transcendental, untinged by material contamination." Full consciousness that one is an eternal servant of the Lord is called *parā bhakti.* If one has any identification with material things and executes devotional service for attainment of some material gain, that is *viddhā bhakti,* contaminated *bhakti.* One can actually become liberated by execution of *parā bhakti.*

Another word mentioned here is *sarva-jñe.* The Supersoul sitting within the heart is all-cognizant. He knows. I may forget my past activities due to the change of body, but because the Supreme Lord as Paramātmā is sitting within me, He knows everything; therefore the result of my past *karma,* or past activities, is awarded to me. I may forget, but He awards me suffering or enjoyment for the misdeeds or good deeds of my past life. One should not think that he is freed from reaction because he has forgotten the actions of his past life. Reactions will take place, and what kind of reactions there will be is judged by the Supersoul, the witness.

## TEXT 46

आत्मानं सर्वभूतेषु भगवन्तमवस्थितम् ।
अपश्यत्सर्वभूतानि भगवत्यपि चात्मनि ॥४६॥

*ātmānaṁ sarva-bhūteṣu*
*bhagavantam avasthitam*
*apaśyat sarva-bhūtāni*
*bhagavaty api cātmani*

*ātmānam*—the Supersoul; *sarva-bhūteṣu*—in all living beings; *bhagavantam*—the Supreme Personality of Godhead; *avasthitam*—situated; *apaśyat*—he saw; *sarva-bhūtāni*—all living beings; *bhagavati*—in the Supreme Personality of Godhead; *api*—moreover; *ca*—and; *ātmani*—on the Supersoul.

## TRANSLATION

**He began to see that the Supreme Personality of Godhead is seated in everyone's heart, and that everyone is existing on Him, because He is the Supersoul of everyone.**

## PURPORT

That everyone is existing on the Supreme Personality of Godhead does not mean that everyone is also Godhead. This is also explained in *Bhagavad-gītā:* everything is resting on Him, the Supreme Lord, but that does not mean that the Supreme Lord is also everywhere. This mysterious position has to be understood by highly advanced devotees. There are three kinds of devotees—the neophyte devotee, the intermediate devotee and the advanced devotee. The neophyte devotee does not understand the techniques of devotional science, but simply offers devotional service to the Deity in the temple; the intermediate devotee understands who God is, who is a devotee, who is a nondevotee and who is innocent, and he deals with such persons differently. But a person who sees that the Lord is sitting as Paramātmā in everyone's heart and that everything is depending or existing on the transcendental energy of the Supreme Lord is in the highest devotional position.

## TEXT 47

इच्छाद्वेषविहीनेन सर्वत्र समचेतसा ।
भगवद्भक्तियुक्तेन प्राप्ता भागवती गतिः ॥४७॥

*icchā-dveṣa-vihīnena*
*sarvatra sama-cetasā*
*bhagavad-bhakti-yuktena*
*prāptā bhāgavatī gatiḥ*

*icchā*—desire; *dveṣa*—and hatred; *vihīnena*—freed from; *sarvatra*—everywhere; *sama*—equal; *cetasā*—with the mind; *bhagavat*—unto the Personality of Godhead; *bhakti-yuktena*—by discharging devotional service; *prāptā*—was attained; *bhāgavatī gatiḥ*—the destination of the devotee (going back home, back to Godhead).

## TRANSLATION

**Freed from all hatred and desire, Kardama Muni, being equal to everyone because of discharging uncontaminated devotional service, ultimately attained the path back to Godhead.**

## PURPORT

As stated in *Bhagavad-gītā*, only by devotional service can one understand the transcendental nature of the Supreme Lord and, after understanding Him perfectly in His transcendental position, enter into the kingdom of God. The process of entering into the kingdom of God is *tri-pāda-bhūti-gati*, or the path back home, back to Godhead, by which one can attain the ultimate goal of life. Kardama Muni, by his perfect devotional knowledge and service, achieved this ultimate goal, which is known as *bhāgavatī gatiḥ.*

*Thus end the Bhaktivedanta purports of the Third Canto, Twenty-fourth Chapter, of the* Śrīmad-Bhāgavatam, *entitled "The Renunciation of Kardama Muni."*

# Appendixes

# The Author

His Divine Grace A. C. Bhaktivedanta Swami Prabhupāda appeared in this world in 1896 in Calcutta, India. He first met his spiritual master, Śrīla Bhaktisiddhānta Sarasvatī Gosvāmī, in Calcutta in 1922. Bhaktisiddhānta Sarasvatī, a prominent religious scholar and the founder of sixty-four Gauḍīya Maṭhas (Vedic institutes), liked this educated young man and convinced him to dedicate his life to teaching Vedic knowledge. Śrīla Prabhupāda became his student, and eleven years later (1933) at Allahabad he became his formally initiated disciple.

At their first meeting, in 1922, Śrīla Bhaktisiddhānta Sarasvatī Ṭhākura requested Śrīla Prabhupāda to broadcast Vedic knowledge through the English language. In the years that followed, Śrīla Prabhupāda wrote a commentary on the *Bhagavad-gītā*, assisted the Gauḍīya Maṭha in its work and, in 1944, without assistance, started an English fortnightly magazine, edited it, typed the manuscripts and checked the galley proofs. He even distributed the individual copies and struggled to maintain the publication. Once begun, the magazine never stopped; it is now being continued by his disciples in the West and is published in nineteen languages.

Recognizing Śrīla Prabhupāda's philosophical learning and devotion, the Gauḍīya Vaiṣṇava Society honored him in 1947 with the title "Bhaktivedanta." In 1950, at the age of fifty-four, Śrīla Prabhupāda retired from married life, adopting the *vānaprastha* (retired) order to devote more time to his studies and writing. Śrīla Prabhupāda traveled to the holy city of Vṛndāvana, where he lived in very humble circumstances in the historic medieval temple of Rādhā-Dāmodara. There he engaged for several years in deep study and writing. He accepted the renounced order of life (*sannyāsa*) in 1959. At Rādhā-Dāmodara, Śrīla Prabhupāda began work on his life's masterpiece: a multivolume translation of and commentary on the eighteen-thousand-verse *Śrīmad-Bhāgavatam* (*Bhāgavata Purāṇa*). He also wrote *Easy Journey to Other Planets.*

After publishing three volumes of the *Bhāgavatam*, Śrīla Prabhupāda came to the United States, in 1965, to fulfill the mission of his spiritual master. Subsequently, His Divine Grace wrote more than sixty volumes of authoritative translations, commentaries and summary studies of the philosophical and religious classics of India.

In 1965, when he first arrived by freighter in New York City, Śrīla Prabhupāda was practically penniless. It was after almost a year of great difficulty that he established the International Society for Krishna Consciousness in July of 1966. Before his passing away on November 14, 1977, he guided the Society and saw it grow to a worldwide confederation of more than one hundred *āśramas*, schools, temples, institutes and farm communities.

In 1968, Śrīla Prabhupāda created New Vrindaban, an experimental Vedic community in the hills of West Virginia. Inspired by the success of New Vrindaban, now a thriving farm community of more than one thousand acres, his students have since founded several similar communities in the United States and abroad.

In 1972, His Divine Grace introduced the Vedic system of primary and secondary education in the West by founding the Gurukula school in Dallas, Texas. Since then, under his supervision, his disciples have established children's schools throughout the United States and the rest of the world. As of 1978, there are ten *gurukula* schools worldwide, with the principal educational center now located in Vṛndāvana, India.

Śrīla Prabhupāda also inspired the construction of several large international cultural centers in India. The center at Śrīdhāma Māyāpur in West Bengal is the site for a planned spiritual city, an ambitious project for which construction will extend over the next decade. In Vṛndāvana, India, is the magnificent Kṛṣṇa-Balarāma Temple and International Guesthouse. There is also a major cultural and educational center in Bombay. Other centers are planned in a dozen other important locations on the Indian subcontinent.

Śrīla Prabhupāda's most significant contribution, however, is his books. Highly respected by the academic community for their authoritativeness, depth and clarity, they are used as standard textbooks in numerous college courses. His writings have been translated into twenty-eight languages. The Bhaktivedanta Book Trust, established in 1972 exclusively to publish the works of His Divine Grace, has thus become the world's largest publisher of books in the field of Indian religion and philosophy.

In just twelve years, in spite of his advanced age, Śrīla Prabhupāda circled the globe fourteen times on lecture tours that took him to six continents. In spite of such a vigorous schedule, Śrīla Prabhupāda continued to write prolifically. His writings constitute a veritable library of Vedic philosophy, religion, literature and culture.

# References

The purports of *Śrīmad-Bhāgavatam* are all confirmed by standard Vedic authorities. The following authentic scriptures are specifically cited in this volume:

*Bhagavad-gītā,* 79, 105, 135, 146, 195, 337

*Brahma-saṁhitā,* 180, 288

*Śrīmad-Bhāgavatam,* 123, 351

*Śvetāśvatara Upaniṣad,* 31, 339

*Vedānta-sūtra,* 79

*Viṣṇu Purāṇa,* 108

# Glossary of Personal Names

## A

**Agni**—the presiding demigod of fire.

**Ambarīṣa Mahārāja**—a great devotee king who perfectly executed all nine devotional practices (hearing, chanting, etc.).

**Arjuna**—one of the five Pāṇḍava brothers; Kṛṣṇa became his chariot driver and spoke to him the *Bhagavad-gītā.*

## B

**Bhaktisiddhānta Sarasvatī Ṭhākura**—the spiritual master of His Divine Grace A. C. Bhaktivedanta Swami Prabhupāda.

**Bhaktivinoda Ṭhākura**—the spiritual master of Śrīla Bhaktisiddhānta Sarasvatī Ṭhākura.

**Bharata**—the son of Mahārāja Duṣyanta who renounced his kingdom and family at an early age. He became very advanced in spiritual practice, but later became attached to a pet deer and had to take two more births before achieving liberation.

**Brahmā**—the first created living being and secondary creator of the material universe.

## C

**Caitanya Mahāprabhu**—the incarnation of the Lord who descended to teach love of God through the *saṅkīrtana* movement.

**Cāṇakya Paṇḍita**—the *brāhmaṇa* advisor of King Candragupta who was responsible for checking Alexander the Great's invasion of India.

## D

**Devahūti**—the mother of the Lord's incarnation Kapila.

**Dhṛtarāṣṭra**—the uncle of the Pāṇḍavas whose attempt to usurp their kingdom for the sake of his own sons resulted in the Kurukṣetra war.

**Dhruva Mahārāja**—a great devotee who at the age of five performed severe austerities and realized the Supreme Personality of Godhead.

**Diti**—the wife of Kaśyapa Muni and mother of the demons Hiraṇyākṣa and Hiraṇyakaśipu.

**Durgā**—the personified material energy and wife of Lord Śiva.

**Durvāsā Muni**—a powerful mystic *yogī,* famous for his fearful curses.

**Duryodhana**—the eldest son of Dhṛtarāṣṭra and chief rival of the Pāṇḍavas.

## G

**Gandhārī**—the faithful wife of King Dhṛtarāṣṭra and mother of one hundred sons.

**Garbhodakaśāyī Viṣṇu**—the expansion of the Lord who enters into each universe.

**Garuḍa**—the great eagle who is the eternal carrier of Lord Viṣṇu.

**Govinda**—a name of the Supreme Personality of Godhead, who gives pleasure to the land, the cows and the senses.

## H

**Hanumān**—the great monkey servitor of Lord Rāmacandra.

**Haryakṣa**—*See:* Hiraṇyākṣa

**Hiraṇyakaśipu**—a demoniac king killed by the Lord's incarnation Nṛsiṁhadeva.

**Hiraṇyākṣa**—the demoniac son of Kaśyapa who was killed by Lord Varāha.

## I

**Indra**—the chief of the administrative demigods and king of the heavenly planets.

## J

**Jaḍa Bharata**—Bharata Mahārāja in his final birth.

**Jaya and Vijaya**—two doorkeepers of Vaikuṇṭha who were cursed on account of offending the four Kumāra Ṛṣis, and who thus both had to take birth three times in the material world as great demons.

## K

**Kālī**—*See:* Durgā

**Kaṁsa**—a demoniac king of the Bhoja dynasty and maternal uncle of Kṛṣṇa.

**Kapila**—the incarnation of the Lord who expounded *sāṅkhya-yoga*, the analysis of matter and spirit, as a means of cultivating devotional service to the Lord.

**Kāraṇodakaśāyī Viṣṇu**—the expansion of the Lord from whom all material universes emanate.

**Kardama Muni**—the father of Lord Kapila.

**Kaśyapa**—a great saintly person who was the father of many demigods, including Lord Vāmanadeva, the Lord's dwarf-*brāhmaṇa* incarnation.

**Keśī**—a demon who attacked the inhabitants of Vṛndāvana in the form of a wild horse, but was killed by Lord Kṛṣṇa.

**Kṛṣṇa**—the Supreme Personality of Godhead appearing in His original, two-armed form.

**Kṣīrodakaśāyī Viṣṇu**—the expansion of the Lord who enters the heart of every created being as the Supersoul.

## L

**Lakṣmī**—the goddess of fortune and eternal consort of the Supreme Personality of Godhead Nārāyaṇa.

## M

**Mahā-Viṣṇu**—*See:* Kāraṇodakaśāyī Viṣṇu

**Maitreya Muni**—the great sage who spoke *Śrīmad-Bhāgavatam* to Vidura.

**Manu**—an original father and law-giver of the human race. There are fourteen Manus appearing in one day of Brahmā, namely (1) Svāyambhuva, (2) Svārociṣa, (3) Uttama, (4) Tāmasa, (5) Raivata, (6) Cākṣuṣa, (7) Vaivasvata, (8) Sāvarṇi, (9) Dakṣa-sāvarṇi, (10) Brahma-sāvarṇi, (11) Dharma-sāvarṇi, (12) Rudra-sāvarṇi, (13) Deva-sāvarṇi and (14) Indra-sāvarṇi.

**Marīci**—one of the seven great sages who were born directly from Lord Brahmā.

**Mukunda**—a name of the Supreme Personality of Godhead, the giver of liberation.

## N

**Nārada Muni**—a pure devotee of the Lord who travels throughout the universes in his eternal body, glorifying devotional service. He is the spiritual master of Vyāsadeva and of many other great devotees.

**Nārāyaṇa**—a name of the Supreme Personality of Godhead, who is the source and goal of all living beings.

**Nityānanda**—the incarnation of Lord Baladeva who is the principal associate of Lord Śrī Caitanya Mahāprabhu.

**Nṛsiṁha**—the incarnation of the Lord as half-man and half-lion who killed the demon Hiraṇyakaśipu.

## P

**Pāṇḍavas**—Yudhiṣṭhira, Bhīma, Arjuna, Nakula and Sahadeva: the five warrior-brothers and intimate friends of Lord Kṛṣṇa, who were given rulership of the world by Him after their victory in the Battle of Kurukṣetra.

**Parīkṣit Mahārāja**—the emperor of the world who heard *Śrīmad-Bhāgavatam* from Śukadeva Gosvāmī and thus attained perfection.

**Patañjali**—the author of the original *yoga* system.

**Prabodhānanda Sarasvatī**—a great Vaiṣṇava poet and devotee of Lord Śrī Caitanya Mahāprabhu.

**Prahlāda Mahārāja**—a devotee persecuted by his demoniac father but protected and saved by the Lord.

## R

**Rādhā**—the eternal consort and spiritual potency of Lord Kṛṣṇa.

**Rahūgaṇa Mahārāja**—the king who received spiritual instruction from Jaḍa Bharata.

**Rāmacandra**—the incarnation of Lord Kṛṣṇa as the perfect king.

**Rāvaṇa**—a demoniac ruler who was killed by Lord Rāmacandra.

**Romaharṣaṇa**—the father of Sūta Gosvāmī. He was originally the speaker at the Naimiṣāraṇya assembly, but was killed by Lord Balarāma on account of his disrespect to the Lord.

**Rukmiṇī**—Lord Kṛṣṇa's principal queen in Dvārakā.

**Rūpa Gosvāmī**—the chief of the six Vaiṣṇava spiritual masters who directly followed Lord Śrī Caitanya Mahāprabhu and systematically presented His teachings.

## S

**Śaṅkarācārya**—the incarnation of Lord Śiva who, ordered by the Supreme Lord, propagated the impersonal Māyāvāda philosophy, which maintains that there is no distinction between the Lord and the living entity.

**Śatarūpā**—the wife of Svāyambhuva Manu and mother of Devahūti.

**Saubhari Muni**—a powerful mystic who became attracted to sex by accidently seeing a pair of mating fish.

**Śaunaka Ṛṣi**— the chief of the sages present at Naimiṣāraṇya when Sūta Gosvāmī spoke *Śrīmad-Bhāgavatam.*

**Sītā**—the eternal consort of Lord Rāmacandra.

**Śiva**—the presiding demigod of the mode of ignorance and the destruction of the material manifestation.

**Śrīdhara Svāmī**—the author of the oldest existing Vaiṣṇava commentaries on *Śrīmad-Bhāgavatam* and *Bhagavad-gītā.*

**Śukrācārya**—the spiritual master of the demons.

**Sūta Gosvāmī**—the sage who recounted the discourses between Parīkṣit and Śukadeva to the sages assembled in the forest of Naimiṣāraṇya.

**Svāyambhuva Manu**—the original father of the human race.

## U

**Uttānapāda**—a son of Svāyambhuva Manu and father of Dhruva Mahārāja.

## V

**Vaivasvata Manu**—*See:* Manu

**Varāha**—the incarnation of the Supreme Personality of Godhead as a boar.

**Varuṇa**—the presiding demigod of the oceans.

**Vasudeva**—the father of Lord Kṛṣṇa.

**Vidura**—a great devotee who heard *Śrīmad-Bhāgavatam* from Maitreya Muni.

**Vijaya and Jaya**—*See:* Jaya and Vijaya

**Viṣṇu**—a name of the Supreme Personality of Godhead, the creator and maintainer of the material universes.

**Viśvanātha Cakravartī Ṭhākura**—a Vaiṣṇava spiritual master and commentator on *Śrīmad-Bhāgavatam* in the disciplic succession from Lord Śrī Caitanya Mahāprabhu.

**Vṛtra**—a great demon killed by Indra. He was actually the devotee Citraketu who had been cursed by mother Durgā to take such a low birth.

**Vyāsadeva**—the original compiler of the *Vedas* and *Purāṇas* and author of the *Vedānta-sūtra* and *Mahābhārata.*

## Y

**Yadus**—the descendants of Yadu, in which dynasty Lord Kṛṣṇa appeared.

**Yayāti**—the king who, because of his lust, was cursed by Śukrācārya to prematurely accept old age.

# General Glossary

## A

**Ācārya**—a spiritual master who teaches by example.
**Artha**—economic development.
**Āśramas**—the four spiritual orders of life: celibate student, householder, retired life and renounced life.
**Aṣṭāṅga-yoga**—the mystic *yoga* system propounded by Patañjali.
**Asuras**—atheistic demons.
**Āyur-veda**—the scriptures which describe the Vedic science of medicine.

## B

**Bhagavad-gītā**—the discourse between the Supreme Lord, Kṛṣṇa, and His devotee Arjuna expounding devotional service as both the principal means and the ultimate end of spiritual perfection.
**Bhagavān**—a name of the Supreme Personality of Godhead, the possessor of all opulences.
**Bhāgavata Purāṇa**—*See: Śrīmad-Bhāgavatam*
**Bhakti-yoga**—linking with the Supreme Lord by devotional service.
**Bhārata-varṣa**—India, named after King Bharata.
**Brahmacārī**—a celibate student under the care of a bona fide spiritual master.
**Brahmacarya**—celibate student life; the first order of Vedic spiritual life.
**Brahmajyoti**—the bodily effulgence of the Supreme Lord, which constitutes the brilliant illumination of the spiritual sky.
**Brahmaloka**—the planet, ruled by Lord Brahmā, which is the highest planet in the material universe.
**Brāhmaṇas**—those wise in the *Vedas* who can guide society; the first Vedic social order.
**Brahma-saṁhitā**—Lord Brahmā's prayers in glorification of the Supreme Lord.

## C

**Cāturmāsya**—the four months of the Indian rainy season (from about the middle of July to the middle of October), during which time special vows for purification are recommended.

**Causal Ocean**—*See:* Kāraṇa Ocean

**Cintāmaṇi**—a mystically potent "touchstone" described in Vedic literatures.

## D

**Dharma**—eternal occupational duty; religious principles.

**Dvāpara-yuga**—the third in the cycle of four ages. It lasts 864,000 years.

**Dvārakā**—the site of Lord Kṛṣṇa's city pastimes as an opulent prince.

## G

**Garbhādhāna-saṁskāra**—the Vedic purificatory ritual for obtaining good progeny; performed by husband and wife before conceiving a child.

**Gauḍīya Vaiṣṇavas**—devotees of Lord Kṛṣṇa coming in the disciplic succession begun by Lord Śrī Caitanya Mahāprabhu.

**Goloka Vṛndāvana**—the highest spiritual planet, Lord Kṛṣṇa's personal abode.

**Gopīs**—Kṛṣṇa's cowherd girl friends, His most confidential servitors.

**Gṛhastha**—regulated householder life; the second order of Vedic spiritual life.

## I

**Ilāvṛta-varṣa**—the original name of the earth, before it became known as Bhārata-varṣa.

## J

**Jīva**—the living entities, atomic parts of the Lord.

**Jñāna**—theoretical knowledge.

**Jñāna-yoga**—the process of approaching the Supreme by the cultivation of knowledge.

**Jñānī**—one who cultivates knowledge by empirical speculation.

## K

**Kali-yuga (Age of Kali)**—the present age, characterized by quarrel; it is last in the cycle of four and began five thousand years ago.

**Kāma**—lust.

**Kāraṇa Ocean**—the corner of the spiritual universe in which Lord Mahā-Viṣṇu lies down to create the entirety of material universes.

**Karma**—fruitive action, for which there is always reaction, good or bad.

**Karma-yoga**—(1) action in devotional service; (2) fruitive actions performed in accordance with Vedic injunctions.

**Kīrtana**—chanting the glories of the Supreme Lord.

**Kṛṣṇaloka**—*See:* Goloka Vṛndāvana

**Kṣatriyas**—warriors and administrators; the second Vedic social order.

**Kuśa**—auspicious grass used in Vedic rituals.

## M

**Mahābhārata**—Vyāsadeva's epic history of the Kurukṣetra war.

**Mahātmā**—a "great soul," who is advanced in realizing love of God.

**Mahat-tattva**—the total material energy in its original, undifferentiated form.

**Mantra**—a sound vibration that can deliver the mind from illusion.

**Manu-saṁhitā**—the original lawbook of human society.

**Manvantaras**—the lifetimes of each of the various Manus (original projenitors of humankind).

**Mathurā**—Lord Kṛṣṇa's abode, surrounding Vṛndāvana, where He took birth and later returned to after performing His childhood pastimes.

**Māyā**—illusion; forgetfulness of one's relationship with Kṛṣṇa.

**Māyāvādīs**—impersonal philosophers who confuse the separate identities of God and the created living beings.

**Mokṣa**—liberation into the spiritual effulgence surrounding the Lord.

## N

**Naimiṣāraṇya**—a sacred forest in central India, considered the exact center of the universe.

## P

**Paramahaṁsa**—the highest stage of the *sannyāsa* order; a topmost devotee of the Lord.

**Paramparā**—the chain of spiritual masters in disciplic succession.

**Pitās**—departed ancestors who have been promoted to honorable positions on one of the higher planets.

**Prasāda**—food spiritualized by being offered to the Lord.

**Purāṇas**—Vedic histories of the universe in relation to the Supreme Lord and His devotees.

## R

**Rajas**—the material mode of passion.

**Rājasūya**—the great sacrifice performed by King Yudhiṣṭhira and attended by Lord Kṛṣṇa.

**Rāmāyaṇa**—the original epic of Lord Rāmacandra, written by Vālmīki Muni.

**Ṛṣis**—sages.

## S

**Sāma Veda**—one of the four original *Vedas*. It consists of musical settings of the sacrificial hymns.

**Sampradāya**—a disciplic succession of spiritual masters.

**Sāṅkhya**—the philosophical analysis of matter and spirit and the controller of both.

**Saṅkīrtana**—public chanting of the names of God, the approved *yoga* process for this age.

**Sannyāsa**—renounced life; the fourth order of Vedic spiritual life.

**Śāstras**—revealed scriptures.

**Satya-yuga**—the first in the cycle of four ages. It lasts 1,728,000 years.

**Smṛti-śāstra**—supplementary explanations of the *Vedas*.

**Sudarśana cakra**—Lord Viṣṇu's disc weapon.

**Śūdras**—common laborers; the fourth of the Vedic social orders.

## T

**Tretā-yuga**—the second in the cycle of four ages. It lasts 1,296,000 years.

## U

**Upaniṣads**—the philosophical section of the *Vedas*, meant for bringing the student closer to understanding the personal nature of the Absolute Truth.

## V

**Vaikuṇṭha**—the spiritual world.

**Vaiṣṇava**—a devotee of Lord Viṣṇu, Kṛṣṇa.

**Vaiśyas**—farmers and merchants; the third Vedic social order.

**Vānaprastha**—one who has retired from family life; the third order of Vedic spiritual life.

**Varṇas**—the four occupational divisions of society: the intellectual class, the administrative class, the mercantile class and the laborer class.

**Varṇāśrama**—the Vedic social system of four social and four spiritual orders. *See also: Āśramas; Varṇas*

**Vedānta-sūtra**—Vyāsadeva's philosophical summary of the conclusions of Vedic knowledge in the form of short aphorisms.

**Vedas**—the original revealed scriptures, first spoken by the Lord Himself.

**Virāṭ-puruṣa**—the "universal form" of the Lord as the totality of all material manifestations.

**Viṣṇu-tattva**—the original Personality of Godhead's primary expansions, each of whom is equally God.

**Vṛndāvana**—Kṛṣṇa's personal abode, where He fully manifests His quality of sweetness.

## Y

**Yajña**—an activity performed to satisfy either Lord Viṣṇu or the demigods.

**Yoga**—various processes of spiritual realization, all ultimately meant for attaining the Supreme.

**Yogamāyā**—the internal, spiritual potency of the Lord.

**Yoga-siddhis**—material perfections achieved by practice of mystic meditation, such as the abilities to become lighter than air or smaller than the atom.

**Yogī**—a transcendentalist who, in one way or another, is striving for union with the Supreme.

**Yugas**—ages in the life of a universe, occurring in a repeated cycle of four.

# Sanskrit Pronunciation Guide

*Vowels*

अ a आ ā इ i ई ī उ u ऊ ū ऋ ṛ ॠ ṝ

ऌ ḷ ए e ऐ ai ओ o औ au

ं ṁ *(anusvāra)* ः ḥ *(visarga)*

*Consonants*

| | | | | | |
|---|---|---|---|---|---|
| Gutturals: | क ka | ख kha | ग ga | घ gha | ङ ṅa |
| Palatals: | च ca | छ cha | ज ja | झ jha | ञ ña |
| Cerebrals: | ट ṭa | ठ ṭha | ड ḍa | ढ ḍha | ण ṇa |
| Dentals: | त ta | थ tha | द da | ध dha | न na |
| Labials: | प pa | फ pha | ब ba | भ bha | म ma |
| Semivowels: | य ya | र ra | ल la | व va | |
| Sibilants: | श śa | ष ṣa | स sa | | |
| Aspirate: | ह ha | ऽ ' *(avagraha)* – the apostrophe | | | |

**The numerals are:** ० -0 १ -1 २ -2 ३ -3 ४ -4 ५ -5 ६ -6 ७ -7 ८ -8 ९ -9

**The vowels above should be pronounced as follows:**

a – like the *a* in org*a*n or the *u* in b*u*t
ā – like the *a* in f*a*r but held twice as long as short *a*
i – like the *i* in p*i*n
ī – like the *i* in p*i*que but held twice as long as short *i*

u – like the *u* in p*u*sh
ū – like the *u* in r*u*le but held twice as long as short *u*
ṛ – like the *ri* in *ri*m
ṝ – like *ree* in *ree*d
ḷ – like *l* followed by *ṛ* (*lṛ*)
e – like the *e* in th*ey*
ai – like the *ai* in *ai*sle
o – like the *o* in g*o*
au – like the *ow* in h*ow*
ṁ (*anusvāra*) – a resonant nasal like the *n* in the French word *bon*
ḥ (*visarga*) – a final *h*-sound: *aḥ* is pronounced like *aha; iḥ* like *ihi*

**The vowels are written as follows after a consonant:**

ा ā ि i ी ī ु u ू ū ृ ṛ ॄ ṝ े e ै ai ो o ौ au

**For example:** क ka का kā कि ki की kī कु ku कू kū
कृ kṛ कॄ kṝ के ke कै kai को ko कौ kau

**The vowel "a" is implied after a consonant with no vowel symbol.**

**The symbol virāma (्) indicates that there is no final vowel:** क्

**The consonants are pronounced as follows:**

k – as in *k*ite
kh – as in Ec*kh*art
g – as in *g*ive
gh – as in di*g-h*ard
ṅ – as in si*ng*
c – as in *ch*air
ch – as in staun*ch-h*eart
j – as in *j*oy
jh – as in he*dgeh*og
ñ – as in ca*ny*on
ṭ – as in *t*ub
ṭh – as in ligh*t-h*eart
ḍ – as in *d*ove
ḍha- as in re*d-h*ot
ṇ – as r*na* (prepare to say the *r* and say *na*)

**Cerebrals are pronounced with tongue to roof of mouth, but the following dentals are pronounced with tongue against teeth:**

t – as in *t*ub but with tongue against teeth
th – as in ligh*t-h*eart but with tongue against teeth

d – as in *d*ove but with tongue against teeth
dh – as in re*d-h*ot but with tongue against teeth
n – as in *n*ut but with tongue between teeth
p – as in *p*ine
ph – as in u*ph*ill (not *f*)
b – as in *b*ird
bh – as in ru*b-h*ard
m – as in *m*other
y – as in *y*es
r – as in *r*un
l – as in *l*ight
v – as in *v*ine
ś (palatal) – as in the *s* in the German word *sprechen*
ṣ (cerebral) – as the *sh* in *sh*ine
s – as in *s*un
h – as in *h*ome

**Generally two or more consonants in conjunction are written together in a special form, as for example:** क्ष kṣa त्र tra

**There is no strong accentuation of syllables in Sanskrit, or pausing between words in a line, only a flowing of short and long (twice as long as the short) syllables. A long syllable is one whose vowel is long (ā, ī, ū, e, ai, o, au), or whose short vowel is followed by more than one consonant (including anusvāra and visarga). Aspirated consonants (such as kha and gha) count as only single consonants.**

# Index of Sanskrit Verses

This index constitutes a complete listing of the first and third lines of each of the Sanskrit poetry verses of this volume of *Śrīmad-Bhāgavatam*, arranged in English alphabetical order. The first column gives the Sanskrit transliteration, and the second and third columns, respectively, list the chapter-verse reference and page number for each verse.

## J



## K



## L



## M

# General Index

Numerals in boldface type indicate references to translations of the verses of *Śrīmad-Bhāgavatam.*


## A

*Abhavāya* defined, 31
*Abhaya* defined, 257
Absolute Truth
impersonalists misunderstand, 176
inquiry into, 166
Lord as, 348, 349
Lord reveals, **337**
Māyāvāda misconception about, 97
via Sāṅkhya philosophy, 345
three features of, 349
*See also:* Kṛṣṇa, Lord; Supreme Lord
*Ācāryas* defined, 326
*See also:* Authority, spiritual; Disciplic succession; Spiritual master; *names of specific ācāryas*
Activity
body needed for, 344
devotional service as goal of, 301
fruitive, devotional service dispels, 323
of God. *See:* Supreme Lord, activities of; Supreme Lord, pastimes of
in Kṛṣṇa consciousness, 94, 175–76, 212
Lord witnesses, 105
material, 2, 151, 160, 161, 246
material vs. spiritual, 204
sinful. *See:* Sinful activities
spiritual, in early morning, 132
*See also: Karma*
*Adhi-māsa* defined, 162
*Adhokṣaja* defined, 73
*Advaitam acyutam anādim ananta-rūpam* quoted, 336
Advancement, spiritual
good wife helps, 156–57, 216
Advancement, spiritual
health & luster as sign of, 193
instruction in, 159, 297
in Kṛṣṇa consciousness, 243
by saintly person's association, 299, **300**
by self-control, 307
of society, 198, 199
via spiritual master, 93, 257
Africa as island, 140
Age, current. *See:* Kali-yuga; Modern Age; Present Age
Age (time of life)
for marriage, 219
for renouncing family life, 342
for son to deliver mother, 350
Ages, the four (*yuga* cycle), 89, 244, 330
*See also:* Dvāpara-yuga; Kali-yuga; Satya-yuga; Tretā-yuga
Agni, **196,** 284
*Ahaṅkāra* defined, 324
*See also:* Ego, false
*Ahiṁsā* defined, 353
Air moving & Kardama traveling, analogy of, **286**
Airplane
in ancient times, 223
of Brahmā, 326, 327
*See also:* Space travel
*Ajña* defined, 30
*Akāma* devotees, 170
*Akṛtātmā* defined, 210
*Akṣaja* defined, 181
Ākūti, 143
*Amānitvam adambhitvam* quoted, 353
Ambarīṣa Mahārāja, 70, 353

Atheists
birth & death bind, 39
in bodily concept, 107
Lord displeased by, 34
*See also:* Demons; Impersonalists; Māyāvādīs
*Ātmā* defined, 210
*See also:* Soul
*Ātmānandī* defined, 341
Atri, 320, 327, **328**
Attachment, material
to bodily relations, 107–8
spiritual knowledge breaks, 308
*See also:* Association; Bodily concept of life; Desires, fruitive; Desires, material
Auspicious substances before & after bathing, 278
Austerity
for *brahmacarya*, 192
four principles of, 137
*See also:* Sacrifices
Australia as island, 140
Author, the (A.C. Bhaktivedanta Swami Prabhupāda), met Bhaktisiddhānta Sarasvatī, 208–9
Authority, spiritual
benefit of approaching, 2
hearing from, 82, 215
knowledge via, 98
sex as approved by, 139, 140
*Vedas* as, 342–43
*See also: Ācāryas;* Devotees, pure devotees; Disciplic succession; Spiritual master
*Avajānanti māṁ mūḍhāḥ*
quoted, 29, 340
*Avatāra* defined, 80
*See also:* Incarnations; Supreme Lord, advent of
*Avidyā* defined, 324
*See also:* Ignorance
*Avidyā pañca-parvaiṣā*
verse quoted, 108
*Avyakta-mārga-vit* defined, 98
*Āyur-veda*, cited on begetting male or female children, 263, 293
Āyur-vedic medicine, *āsavam* as, 276

## B

*Bahūnāṁ janmanām ante*
quoted, 332
Baladeva, Lord, 180
Ball-playing, princesses engaged in, 223
Barhiṣmatī, 235, **236–37**, **239**
Bathing
auspicious substances before & after, 278
ladies' directions for, 277–78
in pilgrimage places, 272
*See also:* Purification
Beauty
facial, 279
of Kardama's castle, **265–70**, 271
material, 121, 123
material vs. spiritual, 119–20
of twilight woman, **118–25**
of woman, 119, 282, 319
Beings. *See:* Living entities
Benediction from God, 257
*See also:* Supreme Lord, mercy of
Bengal, dacoits in, 56
*Bhagavad-gītā*
*See also: Bhagavad-gītā*, cited; *Bhagavad-gītā*, quotations from
demigod worship condemned in, 56
Indian royalty hears, 241
insatiably interesting, 95
Lord spoke, 94
Vaivasvata Manu in, 141
Viśvanātha Cakravartī cited on, 309
*Bhagavad-gītā*, cited
on birth in good family, 241–42
on demigod worshipers, 155
on destinations according to nature's modes, 245
on devotee as calm ocean, 355
on devotees, two types of, 154–55
on devotional service & greatest danger, 162
on devotional service surpassing nature's modes, 183, 245

## D

## E

## G

## J

## M

Male
birth of, 263
discharge of, during sex, 293
female attracted to, 308
*See also:* Father; Husband; Man; Son
*Mām* defined, 348
Man
woman combined with, 320, 321
woman contrasted to, 251
woman's sex desire exceeds, 290
*See also:* Father; Husband; Male; Son
*Man* comes from *Manu*, 238
Man-eaters (Rākṣasas), **109, 110,** 111
*Maṅgala* defined, 171
*Maṅgalārātrika* ceremony, 241
Mankind. *See:* Human beings; Society, human
*Man-manā bhava mad-bhaktaḥ*
quoted, 179, 337, 347
"Man proposes, God disposes," 174
Mansion, aerial
Kardama & Devahūti in, **282–86, 291**
Kardama created, **264–70,** 271
*Mantra*
for "becoming God," 122–23, 212
Hare Kṛṣṇa. *See:* Hare Kṛṣṇa *mantra*
*See also:* Chanting of the Supreme Lord's holy names; Sound, material vs. spiritual
Manu(s)
Brahmā created, **134,** 135
in Brahmā's day, 141
duty & duration of, 89–90
humans descend from, 238
life-span of, 244, **245**
as Lord's representative, 196
*man* comes from, 238
Svāyambhuva. *See:* Svāyambhuva Manu
Vaivasvata, 89, 141
*Manu-saṁhitā,* cited on woman, 233
*Manu-smṛti,* cited on marriage, 221–22
*Maraṇaṁ hy andha-tāmisraṁ*
verse quoted, 108
Marīci, **99, 313,** 320, 327, **328**
Marriage
by astrology, 320–21
different kinds of, 220–22
Marriage
happiness in, 254
intercaste, 174
in Kali-yuga, 157, 222, 321
parents arranged, 320
sex as basis of, 321
unhappiness in, 321
in Vedic culture, 172–74, 218, 221–22, 231, 320–21
Vedic vs. modern, 156
woman's position in, 233
*See also:* Children; Family life; Father; Householders; Husband; Mother; Parents; Sex life; Wife
Mars planet, **10**
Maruts, **72**
Material body. *See:* Body, material
Material desires. *See:* Attachment, material; Desires; Enjoyment, material; Sense gratification; Sex life
Material energy. *See:* Elements, material; Energy, illusory (material); Material world; *Māyā;* Nature, material
Material enjoyment. *See:* Enjoyment, material
Materialism. *See:* Bodily concept of life; Fruitive activity; Materialists; Sense gratification
Materialists
activities of, 151
in illusion, 302
lack love of God, 258–59
Lord punishes, 24
seek sex life, 291
spiritual realization not achieved by, 137
as warmongers, 23, 24, 28
*See also:* Atheists; Demons; Nondevotees; Souls, conditioned
Material life. *See:* Life, material; Material world
Material nature. *See:* Nature, material
Material world
compared to forest fire, 331
demons allured by, 121–22
devotees not meant for, 164–65
fear in, 1–2, 257
goodness in, 314

## N

## O



## P

## R

## S

Supreme Lord
love for
Caitanya distributed, 259
materialists lack, 258–59
as perfection, 257–59
*See also:* Devotional service; Kṛṣṇa consciousness
as Madhusūdana, **310**
maintains everyone, 339
Manu represents, 196
Manu worshiped, **237,** 238
materialists punished by, 24
*māyā* controlled by, 97
Māyāvādī misunderstands, 34, 87, 336
"meditation" for becoming, 122–23, 144, 289
mercy of
activities for achieving, 307
birth-death cycle stopped by, 162
on devotee, 168, 169
love of God as, 257–59
via spiritual master, 257
understanding by, 347
wealth as, 238
modes of nature under, **354**
mortality lesson taught by, 16
as mystic master, 70, 73–74
name(s) of
as Lord Himself, 343
as nondifferent, 180
*See also:* Chanting of the Supreme Lord's holy names; Hare Kṛṣṇa *mantra*
nature controlled by, 37, 101
as *nirvikāra,* 207
offering everything to, 175
offering fruit & flower to, 231
one & different, 177
one & many, 180, 207–8
oneness with, 176–77, 179
opulence as mercy of, 238
opulences of, 330, **337**–38
as original person, 79
as origin of all, 79, 228
as origin of species, 79

Supreme Lord
pastimes of
devotees benefit by, 88
devotee's pastimes related to, 84
devotees relish, **95**
hearing of, 82, 83, 86, 87, **94**
Indian royalty hears, 241
as Lord Himself, 86
talking & thinking of, 353
transcendental, 95
*See also:* Supreme Lord, activities of
as person, 336, **338,** 339
planets floated by, 36–37
pleased by fruit-&-flower offering, 231
pleased by social cooperation, 207
as pleasure reservoir, 153
potency of, inconceivable, 31, 72, 74, 101, 289, 290
praying to, benefit of, 173
as proprietor, 40, 158, 176–77, 207
protection by
active-but-aloof, 207
for *brāhmaṇas* & cows, **205**–6
for demigods, 38
for devotee, 34
for Kṛṣṇa conscious society, 207
for pious people, 195
for surrendered souls, 115–16
as *puruṣa,* 322, 336, 339
quoted
on Brahmā's impure body, **116**
on His fulfilling Kardama's desires, **169, 170**
*See also: Bhagavad-gītā,* quotations from
religion as laws of, **158,** 59
remembrance of, as meditation's goal, 146
as root of everything, 33
as *sac-cid-ānanda-vigraha,* 163
sacrifices for satisfying, 135, 238
as sacrificial enjoyer, **69,** 70, **77,** 78, 175
scientist subordinate to, 106
as seen
as Absolute Truth, 349
by *bhakti-yoga,* 153–54
at death, 75, 76

## W

## Y